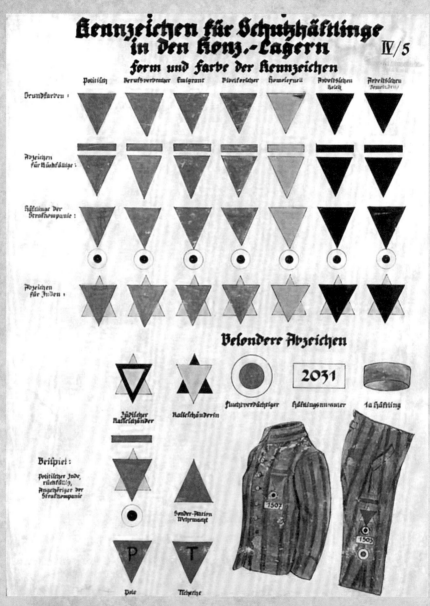

Badges used to identify groups of prisoners in concentration camps, 1936

After the Annex

Bas von Benda-Beckmann

Translated from the Dutch by Plym Peters and Tony Langham

After the Annex

Anne Frank, Auschwitz and Beyond

UNICORN

anne frank house

Published in 2023 by
Unicorn, an imprint of Unicorn Publishing Group LLP
Charleston Studio
Meadow Business Centre
Lewes BN8 5RW
www.unicornpublishing.org

ISBN 978 1 914414 49 7
10 9 8 7 6 5 4 3 2 1

Design by newtonworks.uk
Jacket design by Brigitte Slangen
Printed in Turkey by FineTone Ltd

This publication has been made
possible with financial support from
the Dutch Foundation for Literature.

N ederlands
N letterenfonds
dutch foundation
for literature

FRONTISPIECE PHOTOGRAPHS:

Edith Frank	Anne Frank
Otto Frank	Margot Frank
Peter van Pels	Hermann van Pels
Fritz Pfeffer	Auguste van Pels

Contents

Introduction

CHAPTER ONE
"You asked me if I could tell you anything more"
A search for the people in hiding in the Annex

WHERE ANNE'S DIARY CAME TO AN END   11
EDITH, ANNE, MARGOT AND OTTO FRANK   13
AUGUSTE, HERMANN AND PETER VAN PELS   34
FRITZ PFEFFER   37
GOING INTO HIDING AND ARREST   42
THE SEARCH   48
AN INCOMPLETE PUZZLE   51

CHAPTER TWO
"Mum, did you know that Margot was here?"
Prison and Camp Westerbork

PRISON   63
CAMP WESTERBORK   69
ARRIVAL   79
EVERYDAY LIFE IN THE CRIMINAL BARRACKS   84
MEETING PEOPLE IN WESTERBORK   92
"THAT TERRIBLE JOURNEY": THE TRANSPORT OF 3 SEPTEMBER   100
KNOWLEDGE AND EXPECTATIONS OF MASS MURDER   112

CHAPTER THREE

"Being there was like living in hell"
Auschwitz

AUSCHWITZ AND THE GENOCIDE OF THE EUROPEAN JEWS   123
A DEVELOPING CAMP   136
FUNKTIONSHÄFTLINGE (KAPOS)   141
THE ARRIVAL, SELECTION AND REGISTRATION IN AUSCHWITZ OF THE
PRISONERS FROM THE ANNEX   149
STAMMLAGER: THE MEN IN AUSCHWITZ I   160
HERMANN VAN PELS MURDERED IN THE GAS CHAMBER   162
PARCELS   168
SURVIVING IN AUSCHWITZ   173
DEPARTURE   183

CHAPTER FOUR

"You couldn't raise her spirits because there weren't any"
*Edith, Anne and Margot Frank, and Auguste van Pels in
Auschwitz-Birkenau*

LIFE IN THE CAMP: HUNGER, COLD AND SELECTIONS   193
GUARDS AND VIOLENCE IN THE WOMEN'S CAMP   198
IN THE "DUTCH BARRACKS": EDITH, ANNE AND MARGOT FRANK, AND
AUGUSTE VAN PELS   204
ANOTHER DEPARTURE: ANNE, MARGOT AND AUGUSTE LEAVE   207
"EDITH BECAME ILL": THE DEATH OF EDITH FRANK   210

CHAPTER FIVE

"I don't remember seeing her standing on her feet"
Anne and Margot Frank and Auguste van Pels in Bergen-Belsen

FROM AUSCHWITZ TO BERGEN-BELSEN   217
BERGEN-BELSEN: PRISON CAMP, TRANSIT CAMP AND CONCENTRATION
CAMP   219
MARGOT AND ANNE FRANK AND AUGUSTE VAN PELS IN
BERGEN-BELSEN   229
MEETINGS AT THE FENCE   244
THE DEATHS OF MARGOT AND ANNE FRANK   250

6

CHAPTER SIX

"I remember Gusta van Pels – she was of German origin"
Auguste van Pels in Raguhn

"THANK GOD, A SMALL CAMP"   259
WORKING IN THE AIRCRAFT INDUSTRY   260

CHAPTER SEVEN

"They never came back"
Peter van Pels in Mauthausen and Melk

THE DEATH MARCH FROM AUSCHWITZ TO MAUTHAUSEN   268
A CABINETMAKER WITH AN OVAL FACE   276

CHAPTER EIGHT

"The largest proportion of deaths was amongst the Dutch"
Fritz Pfeffer in Neuengamme

NEUENGAMME   288
FRITZ PFEFFER IN NEUENGAMME   294

CHAPTER NINE

"I don't know where the children are"
Otto's search

BACK HOME   303
EVERY CRUMB   311

Chart and maps   315
Notes   327
Archives   367
Bibliography and other sources   369
Photographs   377
Index   379

Introduction

In many respects, this book is the result of a joint effort. The most important basis and the thread which runs through the work consists of the research carried out by Erika Prins between 2012 and 2016, when she was working as a historical researcher for the Anne Frank House. This research resulted in *Onderzoeksverslag naar het verblijf van de acht onderduikers in de kampen* ("Research report on life in the camps where the eight people in hiding were prisoners") (Amsterdam 2016). In the following years, there were additions to her report by Esther Göbel, who had edited an earlier version of the chapter about Auschwitz, and by Gertjan Broek and Teresien da Silva. In 2019 the research was continued by Bas van Benda-Beckman, who wrote this book on the basis of the 2016 research report and new discoveries.

However, there are other people who also contributed to this project. The authors, researchers and the Anne Frank House would like to thank the various archivists, readers and advisors who helped to make this book possible. In addition to the people working in the different archives and heritage centers, this includes Professor Wichert ten Have, former Director of the NIOD Institute for war, holocaust and genocide studies, who not only expertly supervised and commented on the project, but also insisted in 2019 that it should be published in book form.

Valuable commentary was also added by Daan de Leeuw and Guido Abuys, and by Josje Kraamer and Annette Portegies from Querido, the Dutch publisher, who provided feedback for the manuscript. Of course, there are also all our colleagues at the Anne Frank House who contributed to this book in a variety of ways. In addition to the people mentioned above, these include Karolien Stocking Korzen, who researched the photographs, and Liselot van Heesch, Menno Metselaar, Eugenie Martens and Tom Brink, who read the text and were involved in the publication of the Dutch edition of this book. This English edition was translated by Tony Langham and Plym Peters.

Finally, this book would never have happened without the many witnesses who were interviewed in the context of the oral history project of the Anne Frank House and by other institutions. It is thanks to them that we were able to conduct this search into the experiences in the camps of the group of eight who had been in hiding. Therefore, we would like to express our particular gratitude to all the witnesses who shared their stories.

CHAPTER ONE

"You asked me if I could tell you anything more"

A search for the people in hiding in the Annex

Eyewitnesses are the only people who can speak on behalf of the dead.

Arnon Grunberg (speech on 4 May 2020)

WHERE ANNE'S DIARY CAME TO AN END

On 4 August 1944, the *Sicherheitspolizei* (security police) raided the offices of Opekta at Prinsengracht 263 in Amsterdam. They discovered eight Jewish people who had been hiding in an annex since July 1942. One of them was a 15-year-old girl called Anne Frank. Since her thirteenth birthday, she had been recording the events of her life in detail in her diary, a document that was to become one of the most famous books in the world. Because of the diary, which has been published in more than seventy languages and filmed several times, the story of these eight people who went into hiding became one of the best-known personal histories of the Second World War. Through Anne's eyes, the world learned about those eight people who remained hidden for two years on the Prinsengracht from an intimate description of the experiences of an adolescent growing up.

This book is about those eight people: the Franks – Otto, Edith, Margot and Anne; the Van Pels – Hermann, Auguste and Peter; and Fritz Pfeffer. They were all Jews who had fled

The façade of the office building at Prinsengracht 263 (center), in about 1947.

Nazi Germany during the 1930s to build a new life in the Netherlands. Eight people who went into hiding together in the summer and autumn of 1942 in order to survive the Nazi's persecution of the Jews.

This book picks up the story where Anne's diary comes to an end. It examines, as precisely as possible, what happened to them after they were arrested and transferred to different concentration and extermination camps, where seven of them died.

No matter how famous Anne Frank and her seven fellow victims are, this book needs an introduction to them. To follow the history of their lives in the camps accurately, it is important to take a short look at what preceded their arrests: who they were, the circumstances under which they escaped Nazi Germany, and how they ended up in the Annex in 1942.

EDITH, ANNE, MARGOT AND OTTO FRANK

First of all, there was the Frank family. Father Otto was a businessman who had grown up in a prosperous banking family in Frankfurt am Main. He had a liberal Jewish background and had fought in the German army as an officer during the First World War.[1] In 1925, Otto married Edith Holländer, and their wedding took place in Aachen, Edith's hometown. Like Otto, she had a liberal Jewish background, although she was considerably more religious than her husband and felt a stronger attachment to Jewish traditions. After they were married, Edith and Otto lived in Frankfurt, where they had two daughters: Margot was born in 1926, followed by Anne in 1929.

In Frankfurt, the family were aware of the threat of the growing Nazi movement and, following a period of rising fear and insecurity, they made the decision to finally leave for the Netherlands. After the war, Otto Frank remembered how the menacing atmosphere in Germany in the early 1930s increasingly made him and Edith think about the possibility of emigration:

> I remember SA groups marching by as early as 1932, singing: "When the blood of Jews splashes off my knife." Everyone could see what was happening. I immediately asked my wife: "How can we leave here?" But of course, the question is how can you continue to make a living when you leave and more or less give up everything?[2]

The bridal couple Otto and Edith Frank-Holländer with their wedding guests, 12 May 1925. Otto celebrated his thirty-sixth birthday on the same day.

The impetus for the Frank family to actually leave Germany arrived when Adolf Hitler came into power with his National Socialist German Workers Party (NSDAP) in January 1933. The effects of the new regime immediately became noticeable in their hometown of Frankfurt. As soon as Hitler was appointed Chancellor, the Nazis wanted to show the Jews that there was no room for them anymore. In March of that year, the Nazis announced a national boycott that was enforced throughout the country on 1 April. Following this, antisemitic terror took on increasingly violent forms.

Jewish shops, businesses and doctors were boycotted throughout Germany. With its Jewish community of approximately 31,000 people (roughly 6 per cent of the city's inhabitants), the consequences were enormous in Frankfurt.[3] On 13 March 1933, the *Sturmabteilung* (SA) – the paramilitary

Edith Frank, May 1935.

Otto Frank, May 1936.

Margot and Anne in Aachen, October 1933.

thugs of the National Socialists – stormed the town hall, raised swastika flags and replaced the liberal *Oberbürgermeister* Ludwig Landmann with the National Socialist lawyer Friedrich Krebs. That afternoon, the SA blocked the entrances of the shops and department stores of Jewish owners in different places in the city and intimidated the shoppers and customers. In the following days, the threats increased, and on 1 April 1933, there was a national boycott of Jewish businesses that was

Nazis hanging the swastika flag at the town hall in Frankfurt am Main,
13 March 1933.

often enforced with a great deal of violence and intimidation.
By 21 March, during a large demonstration by the NSDAP,
the new police commissioner in Frankfurt indicated that the
boycott of Jewish business was particularly necessary in his

city: "Frankfurt must become German. You Jews don't have to be afraid. We'll follow the law. We'll obey the law so much that you'll feel quite uncomfortable about it."[4]

It was thinly veiled threats such as these that convinced Otto and Edith Frank that there was no longer any future for them in Germany. Financial problems also played a role in the decision. Otto Frank's family banking business was declining quickly, along with his other business activities. In the spring of 1933, the family finally decided to move to the Netherlands, where Otto Frank wanted to establish a Dutch branch of the Opekta business, helped by his brother-in-law Erich Elias. Opekta dealt in pectin, a gelling agent for making jam.

Advertisements for Opekta.

In mid-August 1933, Otto left for Amsterdam to start his new company and prepare for the arrival of his wife and children, who had been staying with Edith's mother in Aachen for a few months.[5] In December that year the family moved into a large family home on the Merwedeplein in the new Rivieren-buurt district in Amsterdam. Otto Frank initially rented a number of rooms in the Candida premises on the Nieuwezijds

A postcard of the Merwedeplein in Amsterdam dating from the 1930s.
The Frank family lived at number 37.

The Frank family on the Merwedeplein,
May 1941. This is the last known
photograph of the whole family.

Voorburgwal for his company, before relocating to the Singel from 1934. In 1938 he also bought the Pectacon company, a business dealing in spices and conserving agents, from its founder Johannes Kleiman, who continued as one of Otto's closest colleagues. From December 1940 he established both businesses at the Prinsengracht 263, a seventeenth-century building with a front office and an annex, a sufficient number of offices, warehouses and storage room for the two companies. There was also a mill for the spices.

The Frank family built a new life in Amsterdam. The girls went to school, where they quickly settled in and soon managed to master the Dutch language, and Otto and Edith also made many new friends and acquaintances. These were predominantly Jews living in the area who had also fled from Germany, but there were also Dutch neighbors, business connections and colleagues from Otto Frank's company, Opekta-Pectacon. Otto Frank had a particularly close relationship with his colleagues Victor Kugler, Johannes Kleiman, his secretaries Miep Santrouschitz (who subsequently married Jan Gies) and Bep Voskuijl, and Bep's father Johannes. These were the people who were responsible for looking after the group of eight people who went into hiding in the Annex from the summer of 1942 to August 1944. They brought food, new clothes, company and news from the outside world to the isolated life of the Frank family and the others in hiding.

After the Frank family came to the Netherlands in 1933, they continued to closely follow the developments in Germany. They heard the reports from family and friends about the continuing violence raging there and the increasingly aggressive persecution of Jews in their home country, but they also saw what was happening with their own eyes. Up to 1938 – the year

Otto and the helpers, October 1945. From left to right: Miep Gies, Johannes Kleiman, Otto Frank, Victor Kugler and Bep Voskuijl.

Jan Gies, early 1940s.

Johannes Voskuijl, December 1940.

in which anti-Jewish violence increased radically – Otto and Edith regularly visited their family in Germany, with Anne and Margot staying with their grandmother in Aachen every year,

Edith and her brother, Walter, 1920s.

Rosa Holländer, Edith's mother, at the end of the 1930s.

usually around Christmas.[6] In this predominantly Catholic city close to the Dutch border, the NSDAP had a clearly discernible influence on the daily life of the small Jewish community. Edith's mother Rosa and her two brothers, Walter and Julius, who together ran a successful metal recycling company, were regularly confronted with the new regime.[7]

In June 1933, the Gestapo arrested a good friend of Edith's older brother Julius, the lawyer Karl Löwenstein.[8] Löwenstein was the president of the board of the synagogue on which Julius Holländer also had a seat. Together with his brother, and without any provocation, Löwenstein was taken into *Schutzhaft* (preventive custody) for several weeks.[9] Walter and Julius Holländer's metal recycling company also ran into increasingly serious financial problems as a result of the anti-Jewish measures that had been introduced.[10] It also became increasingly difficult for Walter, Julius and their mother Rosa Holländer-Stern to visit the synagogue for the Sabbath service in the Neue Synagoge in Aachen, which they regularly attended each week, with SA officers often stood outside the entrance in order to

The synagogue of Aachen was set on fire and destroyed, 10 November 1938.

prevent people from entering. Additionally, Jews were increasingly expelled from public life.

After the massive eruption of anti-Jewish violence on 9 and 10 November 1938, Anne and Margot's annual visits to Aachen came to an end. That night came to be known as the *Kristallnacht* or the *Reichskristallnacht*. The origins of this term are not completely clear. As far as we know, it was first used in 1939 by a Nazi official and was meant to be a cynical reference to the broken glass of all the shop windows that had been smashed. Although it never became an official term of propaganda in Nazi Germany, its use remained controversial, particularly in the German literature, which has recently opted instead for terms such as the "November Pogrom" or the "Night of the Pogrom". (This is partly because any reference to broken glass does not do justice to the large-scale violence that took place on that night.)[11]

A shop with a smashed window in Berlin, 10 November 1938.

24

In a nationally coordinated campaign of terror, groups of National Socialists set fire to synagogues and destroyed Jewish shops throughout the German Reich, which by now also included Austria. They kicked in the doors of Jewish homes and abused the people living there, trashing their possessions. About 30,000 Jewish men were arrested and temporarily incarcerated in the concentration camps of Buchenwald, Sachsenhausen and Dachau, camps which had been set up by the Nazis in 1933 to imprison their political opponents.

Walter and Julius Holländer were arrested in November 1938. Julius was soon released because he had been wounded during the First World War and had a special status as a veteran, but Walter was imprisoned in the Sachsenhausen concentration camp for three weeks and was only released when he was admitted to a Dutch refugee camp with Otto Frank's help. Whilst there, he waited for his application for a visa to the United States to be processed, and both brothers eventually managed to escape to the United States via the Netherlands. Rosa Holländer-Stern, Anne's grandmother, also left Aachen and moved in with the Frank family on the Merwedeplein. The campaign of terror during the night of 9–10 November 1938 was the writing on the wall: a clear sign that Jews no longer had any legal rights in Nazi Germany.[12]

A year and a half later, on 10 May 1940, it became clear that it was no longer safe in the Netherlands either. The German army had forced the Netherlands to surrender in only five days. From the late summer of 1940, the occupying regime introduced increasingly far-reaching antisemitic measures under the leadership of the Reich Commissioner, Arthur Seyss-Inquart, an Austrian lawyer and Nazi politician. It was one of the first things Anne described in her diary, which she had started in June 1942:

Dr. Arthur Seyss-Inquart. Seyss-Inquart was an Austrian official, appointed by Hitler as Reich Commissioner in the Netherlands.

Now that the Germans are in charge here, things are getting really bad for us. First, there was the distribution of food and everything had to be bought with coupons, and in the two years that they've been here, there've been all sorts of Jewish laws. […] Jews have to wear a Star of David; Jews have to hand over their bicycles, Jews are not allowed on the trams; Jews are not allowed in cars, not even in a private car; Jews can only do their shopping between 3 and 5 o'clock, except in Jewish shops which have to state that they are Jewish premises; Jews can only go to a Jewish hairdresser, Jews are not allowed outside from 8 in the evening to 6 o'clock in the morning, Jews are not allowed to go to theatres, cinemas and other places of entertainment; Jews are not allowed to go to a swimming pool or a tennis court, hockey pitch or other sports venues; Jews are not allowed to row or take part in any other sports; Jews can no longer sit in their gardens after 8 o'clock in the evening or visit their friends; Jews may not go to the houses of Christians; Jews must go to Jewish schools and so on. That's how our lives were and we couldn't do this and we couldn't do that. Jacque [one of Anne's friends] always said to me: "I don't dare do anything anymore because I'm afraid that it won't be allowed."[13]

Top left: These signs appeared in the streets from September 1941.
Top right: "Forbidden for Jews". The beach in Zandvoort, spring 1941.
Below: Open-air swimming pool in Krimpen aan de Lek with the sign "Forbidden for Jews".]

A notice stating "Forbidden for Jews" at the City cinema in Amsterdam, 2 January 1941.

On 3 May 1942, Jews over the age of six were obliged to wear a Star of David that was clearly visible on their clothes.

In this way, the German occupation completely overturned the lives of the Frank family that they had taken so much effort to build up. In addition to the measures listed by Anne, there were other consequences. First, the financial appropriation: the Opekta and Pectacon companies had to be "Aryanized", and it was only with a clever financial arrangement that Otto Frank managed to have his companies taken over by employees who were also friends, namely Johannes Kleiman, Victor Kugler and Jan Gies, the husband of his secretary Miep. In this way, he succeeded in preventing a manager appointed by the Germans from taking over the company.

Meanwhile, Otto Frank made two further attempts to emigrate. By 1937 the Frank family had been making serious plans to establish a company in England. When this failed, Otto Frank submitted an application to emigrate to the United States, probably in 1938 or 1939.[14] During the bombing of Rotterdam on 14 May 1940, the American consulate there was hit and the records of applications for visas to the United States were completely destroyed. When the consulate reopened a few weeks later, everyone who had applied and was on the waiting list had to hand in their receipts, so that a new waiting list could be created. Although none of Otto Frank's documentation showing that he submitted this proof has survived, his file does show that his application for a visa continued after 1940. Emigrating to the United States had now become extremely difficult, but with the help of his American friend Nathan Straus and Edith's two brothers, who had left for Boston in the United States in 1938, he tried again. On 14 April 1941 he wrote to his friend Nathan Straus in New York: "I can only hope we can emigrate and as far as I can see, the USA is the only country we can go to."[15]

On 28 May 1941, Nathan Straus and his wife contacted the Migration Department of the National Refugee Service (NRS) and it started a new application, File A-23007, in the name of Otto Frank, the following day. Together with the Holländer brothers and the Boston Committee for Refugees, which had also been contacted, Straus and his wife wrote a letter of recommendation and provided a guarantee to support the application for a visa for Otto Frank and his family.[16]

All hope of emigrating to the United States came to a definite end by the summer of 1941: in June, the American consulates

BOSTON COMMITTEE FOR REFUGEES

COOPERATING WITH NATIONAL REFUGEE SERVICE, INC.

24 PROVINCE STREET, BOSTON, MASS.

TELEPHONE, CAPITOL 8425

November
17th
1 9 4 1

Miss Augusta Mayerson, Acting Director
Migration Department
National Refugee Service
165 West 46th Street
New York, N. Y.

RE: FRANK, Otto and Edith
Amsterdam, Holland
Case # A-23007

Dear Miss Mayerson:

Mr. Julius Hollander was in to see us today with reference to your letter of November 12, 1941. He wished us to send you this supplementary information which we believe will have great bearing on the arrangements which are to be undertaken by the Strauss'.

Mr. Hollander pointed out that there are five persons involved in this immigration problem, rather than the original four. Apparently Mrs. Rosa Hollander, the mother of Mrs. Frank, 74 years of age, and who has been living with the Franks since April 1939, was never mentioned in the arrangements for the immigration of the entire family group.

Mr. Hollander also wanted us to point out to you that instead of two minor children of 10 years of age being involved, actually the ages of Margot and Anne Frank are, respectively, 15 and 12.

Inasmuch as the aforementioned facts will necessitate a change in the financial plans by the Strauss', Mr. Hollander wants us to call these things to your attention.

In order to meet this changed situation, Mr. Hollander authorized us to say that he and his brother will pay $2,500.00 for the immigration of the entire family group. This information we know changes the contents of our letter of October 21, 1941.

Mr. Hollander, or his brother Walter, are quite anxious to talk over the entire Frank situation with you. Both men are employed at unusual hours during the week, and it appears that the only time available for a conference with you would be on a Saturday morning. Could you, by chance, inform us in a day or so whether Mr. Walter or Mr. Julius Hollander can see you at your office Saturday, November 22, 1941, at a convenient hour?

Please accept our thanks for your willingness to cooperate with this family group, and count on our continued cooperation in their behalf.

Sincerely yours,

Maurice Krinsky

MK:BC

SERVING BOSTON AND GREATER NEW ENGLAND AREAS   Executive Secretary

Letter from the Boston Committee for Refugees dated 17 November 1941 about the Frank family's attempts to emigrate.

30

had closed and all the pending applications for emigration now had to be resubmitted to the Jewish Council. Once again, Otto Frank appealed to Straus and his brothers-in-law for help, this time with an application for a visa for Cuba, for which he also needed a transit visa for the neutral country of Spain. Because of the complicated procedure, the great financial risk and the small chance of success, Otto Frank asked for a Cuban visa only for himself, just to see whether it would be possible to obtain one. Over the course of October and November 1941, it became clear that despite all his efforts, his attempts to emigrate would not be successful because no further visas were being granted for travel. From 7 December 1941, the United States was at war with Germany, and four days later the application procedure for Otto Frank's Cuban visa finally came to an end. According to a brief note in his immigration file from 19 December 1941, "Application for Cuban visas for Otto Frank has been cancelled. […] In view of present international situation."[17]

Meanwhile, the persecution of the Jews was increasing in the Netherlands, although now it was no longer limited to appropriation and theft, but changed to genocide. The first group of Jews were summonsed on 5 July 1942 to register for "work expansion under police supervision". Margot Frank was one of the people in this first group.[18] This was the moment they had feared the most. Although no one knew exactly what was meant by "work expansion", the phrase terrified the Franks, and the day after they received the call to register, they went into hiding in the Annex of the offices on the Prinsengracht.

In the previous months, Otto Frank had made careful preparations for this operation. He approached his colleagues, Victor Kugler, Johannes Kleiman, Bep Voskuijl and Miep Gies, and asked them whether they would help him if it became

Zentralstelle für jüdische
Auswanderung Amsterdam
Adema v. Scheltemaplein 1
Telefoon 97001

Heinrich Schussheim
Amsterdam
Parnassusweg 26 hs.
12.2.1910

OPROEPING!

U wordt hiermede bevolen aan den onder politie toezicht staande werkverruiming in Duitschland deel te nemen en heeft U zich dientengevolge op

15 JULI 1942 ____ om **1·50** ____ uur

aan het Centraal Station, Amsterdam, te bevinden.

Als bagage mag medegenomen worden:

1 koffer of rugzak
1 paar werklaarzen
2 paar sokken
2 onderbroeken
2 hemden
1 werkpak
2 wollen dekens
2 stel beddengoed (overtrek met laken)
1 eetnap
1 drinkbeker
1 lepel en
1 pullover

en eveneens marschproviand voor 3 dagen en de voor die tijd geldige distributiekaarten.

Niet medegenomen mogen worden:

Waardepapieren, deviezen, spaarbankboekjes enz., waardevoorwerpen allerlei soort (goud, zilver, platina) - met uitzondering van de trouwringen - levend huisraad.

Wanneer U aan deze oproeping geen gevolg geeft, wordt U met maatregelen van de Sicherheitspolizei gestraft.
Dit schrijven geldt als reisvergunning en geeft U tegelijkertijd het recht de genoemde trein kosteloos te benutten.

In opdracht
get. Wörlein
SS-Hauptsturmführer

V

K 372

4922

The "summons" received by several Jews in June 1942. It stated exactly what you could take, such as work clothes and food for three days.

necessary to go into hiding.[19] He also made significant modifications to the building. He had an extra staircase built from the landing in front of the private office on the first floor to the corridor leading to the entrance of the Annex. In August 1942, this entrance was concealed behind a rotating bookcase. It was not clear whether the new staircase was built deliberately for the purpose of going into hiding or for more mundane business reasons, but it did prove to be of great importance. Initially, there was a staircase to the second floor that could only be reached by a separate outside door. However, with the new staircase, there was to be a direct connection between the offices on the first floor and the entrance to the Annex on the second floor. The helpers could get into the Annex using this new staircase without being seen by the staff in the warehouse and without having to walk outside the office entrance to the other front door. During the same period, the kitchen that had initially been on the landing by the bookcase was moved to the

The stairs for the helpers from the office floor to the space with the bookcase, 1954.

Annex. As for the staircase, it is uncertain whether moving the kitchen was a deliberate preparatory step for going into hiding, but it did prove to be an important change which made the whole arrangement possible.[20]

In the weeks leading up to the move to Prinsengracht, Otto and Edith took clothes and supplies to the premises as unobtrusively as possible, and Johannes Kleiman and his brother took bedding, blankets and towels.[21]

AUGUSTE, HERMANN AND PETER VAN PELS

In addition to their own family, Otto and Edith also involved the family of the other Jewish colleague at Opekta-Pectacon in the plan. Hermann van Pels joined the Franks in the Annex, together with his wife Auguste and his son Peter. On 8 July 1942, Anne described what her parents had told her about the plans for going into hiding, just before their sudden departure:

> Mother and father told me a lot. We were going to father's office and above it a floor had been cleared for us. Van Pels would come as well, so there would be seven of us and the Van Pels cat was also coming, so that would be a distraction. We arrived at the office without a problem and went straight upstairs where there was a toilet and a small bathroom, with a new washbasin next to a small room with two single beds, the room for Margot and me. There were three built-in wardrobes and it bordered on a room for mother and father where there were also two single beds and two small tables, as well as a smoking table, a bookcase and a cupboard containing 150 tins of vegetables and all sorts of other foodstuffs. Then there was a small corridor and another two doors, one to the

corridor to go down to dad's office and one back to our bathroom. There was a very steep staircase upstairs with a large kitchen and living room for the Van Pels and a small room for Peter with an attic and loft above it.[22]

Hermann van Pels had a Dutch father and therefore had Dutch nationality, but had grown up in Germany and had lived there all his life. He worked for his father's company in Osnabrück, which dealt in herbs and spices for the meat processing industry. In 1925 he married Auguste Röttgen.

Auguste came from a village called Buer, situated near Recklinghausen and Gelsenkirchen, and moved to Essen with her parents and two older sisters when she was six years old. Her family had a company in the center of the city that

Auguste and Hermann van Pels, July 1941.

Peter van Pels, 1942.

made clothes.[23] Although Anne Frank described Auguste as a rather small-minded and intellectually limited woman, she was actually better educated than Anne's own mother. Like Edith, Auguste had been to a girls' school, but then went on to study macro-economics at the University of Cologne for one semester.[24]

After they married, Auguste and Hermann lived in Osnabrück, where their son Peter was born in 1926.[25] In contrast with the Franks, the Van Pels family did not leave Germany immediately after Hitler came into power, but tried hard to continue their lives there as best they could. That was not easy. Between 1933 and their departure in the summer of 1937, it became increasingly unsafe for the small group of approximately 400 Jews in Osnabrück. They had to cope with a very aggressive boycott of Jewish businesses, extremely hostile

Class photograph of the Israelitische Elementarschule in Osnabrück. Peter van Pels is shown second from the left in the third row in the class of his teacher Abraham Trapp, 1934.

attacks in the local press and constant eruptions of violence. Although the Van Pels family were not physically attacked or personally arrested as far as is known, the threat was enormous. Peter attended the small Jewish school in Osnabrück and saw the number of pupils steadily declining during the 1930s. There was constant intimidation by the *Hitlerjugend* (Hitler Youth) and fighting on the street. One of Peter's school friends remembers that fights with boys from the *Hitlerjugend* were frequent.[26]

In 1937, Hermann and Auguste felt they could no longer stay in Osnabrück, and because Hermann had Dutch nationality, it was fairly easy for them to move to Amsterdam.[27] In the Netherlands, Hermann van Pels first established his own company with his brother-in-law, but he soon left, and in 1939 entered the employment of Opekta, Otto Frank's business dealing in spices. He moved into the Annex with his family a week after the Franks and lived on the floor above them, together with Auguste and Peter.

FRITZ PFEFFER

The last person to join the group in hiding in the Annex was Fritz Pfeffer, a dentist. On 21 September 1942, when Anne Frank had already been in hiding for six weeks, she wrote in her diary: "They're talking about Mr. Pfeffer coming here as well, so that we can help him too."[28] It is worth noting that Pfeffer was still hesitating about going into hiding. When he actually did – probably on 17 November – he asked Miep Gies, who had proposed the idea to him, to put it off for a week because he wanted to continue working and was waiting for the salary due to him from the dentist in whose practice he had been working illegally. However, on behalf of the others, Miep Gies put

Fritz Pfeffer with his son Werner, in about 1937. Werner was successfully sent to Great Britain on a *Kindertransport* (children's transport). He survived the war and moved to the United States, where he changed his name to Peter Pepper.

Charlotte Kaletta, 1930s.

pressure on him to decide quickly – any further delays could have put the whole operation in danger.[29]

Fritz Pfeffer had got to know Otto Frank in 1940 through his landlord in Amsterdam, a former acquaintance of Otto's from Frankfurt.[30] Pfeffer had only been living in the Netherlands for a short while, waiting the longest out of the whole group to flee Germany. He had grown up in Giessen and studied medicine and dentistry in Würzburg and Berlin. From 1913 he worked as a dentist in Berlin, where he gained his doctorate in 1920, interrupting his career only to serve in the German army, where, like Otto Frank, he eventually attained the rank of an officer.[31]
His first marriage was to Vera Bynthiner, with whom he had a son, Werner. The marriage broke down and ended in divorce in 1933. Soon afterwards, Fritz had a relationship with Charlotte Kaletta, who was not Jewish. Although they never officially married, Fritz and Charlotte considered themselves to be a married couple, and Fritz would introduce Charlotte to everyone as "Mrs. Pfeffer". Nevertheless, the Nuremberg race laws of 1935 meant that they were not allowed to marry. Even when they went to live in the Netherlands from 1938, a multilateral treaty prevented them from getting married there.[32]

Initially, Fritz Pfeffer tried to continue working as a dentist in Berlin, despite the increasing exclusion and discrimination against Jews. It was only after the terror of the *Kristallnacht* (9–10 November) that he decided to escape. During that night and the following days, about 12,000 Jewish men were arrested in Berlin and taken to Sachsenhausen and Buchenwald.[33] Fritz, however, managed to avoid being arrested. Although he did not leave any personal records behind, and it is not known whether he was personally harassed or mistreated, it's clear that he must have experienced the terror of that night at very close quarters.

Synagogue in the Passauer Strasse in Berlin, near
Fritz Pfeffer's house, in the 1930s.

There had been a synagogue of the Religionsverein Westen on
the Passauer Strasse, only 200 meters from his home, since
1905, but it was completely destroyed by a mob during *Kristall-nacht*.[34] A little further from Pfeffer's home, on the other side
of the Kurfürstendamm, Joseph Goebbels personally ordered
stormtroopers from the SA to burn down the famous liberal
synagogue on the Fasanenstrasse on the same night.[35]

For Fritz Pfeffer, his son Werner and his fiancée Charlotte,
this outburst of violence served as a warning to leave the
country as soon as possible. With the help of his non-Jewish

An English policeman talks to five Jewish girls
from Nazi Germany. They arrived by boat in
Harwich, England, 12 December 1938.

housekeeper, Else Messmer-Hoeft, Pfeffer first arranged
for Werner to escape to England. Werner traveled with the
so-called *Kindertransport*, an initiative of British religious and
government organizations that sought to take in German Jewish
children in England. He traveled by boat from Bremerhaven
to Harwich and was eventually taken to Minehead, a coastal
town in southwest England.[36] Fritz Pfeffer himself traveled to
the Netherlands at the beginning of December 1938, once again
helped by his housekeeper and Charlotte Kaletta, who arrived
in the Netherlands a few weeks later.[37]

It isn't possible to ascertain the effect these events – the flight of his son, and then his own sudden departure with his beloved Charlotte – had on Fritz Pfeffer on the basis of the sources. However, Charlotte did say something about the response to their stories in the Netherlands when she talked to Ernst Schnabel, the German journalist who would go on to write a biography of Anne Frank, and who interviewed about forty witnesses for it in the 1950s. The response was characterized above all by incredulity: "The Dutch just couldn't imagine that the Germans were like that. They simply didn't believe the stories the German migrants told. Even the Dutch Jews didn't believe those stories."[38] In Amsterdam, Charlotte and Fritz lived together until, with a heavy heart, he joined the others in hiding in the Annex in November 1942. From that point on, he was separated from her and could only hear about her occasionally through Miep Gies, who was given parcels of foodstuffs for him.

GOING INTO HIDING AND ARREST

The group of eight in hiding lived in the Annex for about two years, in constant fear of being discovered. During that time, Anne recorded their daily life with great perceptiveness of the group's interpersonal relationships and with enormous stylistic skill. Her diary provides an intimate insight into the thoughts and emotions of an adolescent girl struggling with herself and with the constant tensions and constraints of life in the Annex. She shows how the two families and Fritz Pfeffer were oppressed by the isolation of living in hiding, and how this sometimes led to tensions in their relationships. She describes the fear, the irritation and the quarrels, but also the sense of solidarity and resilience of the seven people with whom she had to share the

The back of the house on Prinsengracht 263. The group in hiding lived on the second and third floor. The top window is the attic of the Annex.

cramped quarters. A youthful romance blossomed between Anne Frank and Peter van Pels for a short time, though this subsequently cooled off for Anne. She and Fritz Pfeffer were both frustrated at having to share a very small room and regularly fought about using the small writing table.

On 16 March 1944, Anne wrote in her diary:

Now I know why I'm so much more restless than Peter. He has his own room where he works, dreams, thinks and sleeps. I'm being pushed from one corner to another. I'm never alone in my shared room and I long for that so much. That's why I escape to the attic. There, with you, I can be myself for a little while. But I don't want to make a fuss about my desires; on the contrary, I want to be brave! So fortunately they don't notice any of my inner feelings downstairs, except for the fact that I'm becoming cooler and more contemptuous towards Mother by the day, I have fewer cuddles with Father and I don't say much to Margot anymore, but remain a closed book. More than anything else I must maintain my outward appearance of certainty and no one can know that there's still a war raging inside me, a war between my desires and my reason. Up to now the latter has been victorious, but won't the former be the strongest in the end? Sometimes I'm afraid and often I long for this to happen.[39]

These are the sorts of intimate self-reflections that make her diary so intriguing. Through it we can follow Anne's struggle with her own identity, her lack of privacy, her longing for freedom and her constant fear of discovery. "It oppresses me more than I can say that we can never go outside, and I'm so afraid that we'll be discovered and shot. Obviously, that's not

The bookcase concealing the door into the Annex, 1954.

a very nice prospect," she wrote at the beginning of December 1942.[40]

Almost two years later, on 4 August 1944, this prospect became a reality. The *Sicherheitspolizei* turned up at the premises of Prinsengracht 263 between half past ten and eleven o'clock in the morning. Miep Gies was working on the first floor when the door suddenly opened. The officers walked into the office of Victor Kugler, who by that time had become the director. They questioned him and took him along to search the building. During this inspection, they entered the area with the rotating bookcase that blocked the entrance to the Annex. They discovered the secret entrance and surprised the group in hiding.

Otto Frank later remembered that at the time of the arrest he was on the top floor of the Annex, where he was helping Peter with his schoolwork in his room. As he was pointing out a mistake in his dictation, he heard someone running up the stairs: "Suddenly someone came running up the stairs, a door opened and a man stood in front of us holding a gun in his hand. Everyone had been gathered together downstairs. My wife,

The Austrian office *SS-Hauptscharführer* Karl Joseph Silberbauer. He was in charge on 4 August 1944 when the eight people in hiding and the helpers Kleiman and Kugler were arrested.]

the children and the Van Pels family were standing there with their hands up."[41] Shortly afterwards, Fritz Pfeffer was brought into the room. The Austrian officer *SS-Hauptscharführer* Karl Joseph Silberbauer, who was in charge, took their valuables and shook out and emptied Otto's briefcase, in which Anne also kept the pages of her diary. These papers fell onto the wooden floor and were later discovered by Miep Gies and Bep Voskuijl. All those who had been in hiding, as well as the two helpers, Victor Kugler and Johannes Kleiman, were arrested. They were all taken to the building of the *Zentralstelle für jüdische Auswanderung* in Amsterdam on the Adama van Scheltemaplein, where they were locked up in a single large cell, to be interrogated one by one, later on.[42]

The arrest was an important moment in the story of Anne Frank and the seven others who had been in hiding with her.

The *Zentralstelle für jüdische Auswanderung* at Adama van Scheltemaplein 1 in Amsterdam.

How Silberbauer had discovered them, whether they were betrayed, and if so by whom, are questions that still give rise to a lot of speculation. For example, the biographies of Anne Frank by Carol Ann Lee and Melissa Müller produce different theories about who might have betrayed them, while the Dutch Institute for War Documentation (NIOD Institute for War, Holocaust and Genocide Studies) also published a report in which the various scenarios were considered.[43] In 2016, Gertjan Broek published a research report on behalf of the Anne Frank House in which a new scenario was set out. The arrest might not have been the result of betrayal, but could have resulted from a police enquiry that was actually focusing on the distribution of counterfeit rationing coupons, and this theory continues to be a subject of research and speculation today.[44] In January 2022, The Betrayal of Anne Frank – a cold case investigation by Canadian author Rosemary Sullivan was published. Herein she records the results of an investigation into the arrest of the people in hiding at 263 Prinsengracht by an international coldcase team led by retired special agent and FBI detective Vince Pankoke. The team claimed, based on an anonymous accusation and some circumstantial evidence, that it could prove the betrayal of the Frank family by Jewish attorney Arnold van den Bergh, a former member of the Jewish Council, with 'an 85% certainty'. In order to protect his own family, Arnold van den Bergh, allegedly passed on lists with addresses of hiding places, amongst which the address of the Annex, supposedly in his possession to the occupying forces.

The book and the claims made therein were mainly critically received and, shortly after publication, its theory convincingly refuted by several historians. The theory not only lacks tangible evidence against van den Bergh, there is also no proof that supports the assumption that the Jewish Council compiled lists with addresses of hiding places, let alone that the address of 263 Prinsengracht would have been on them. In addition, the researchers incorrectly assume that the attorney was still living at his home address when the police raided the Annex, while in reality he himself was in hiding elsewhere.

The Coldcase investigation sparked a fierce controversy over the investigators' methods and ethical considerations, as well as the manner in which the media initially unquestioningly adopted the conclusion. Particularly in the Netherlands the book was strongly scrutinized resulting in its withdrawal from the shops in March 2022 by the Dutch publisher. The discussion, here only briefly touched upon, clearly shows that the arrest on 4 August 1944 still remains, after all these years, a subject of research and speculation.[45]

THE SEARCH

The arrest of the group in hiding was also an important turning point from another point of view. On that day, 4 August 1944, the lively and extremely personal story told in Anne's diary came to an end, and the long, very sparsely documented trip began that took her and the others through German-occupied Europe. From that moment, their lives are shrouded in uncertainty: eight people in a sea of millions of deportees and victims of the Holocaust.[46] What we do know about their fate is based on scraps of information and the testimony of surviving witnesses.

The first person to collect these scraps was Otto Frank himself, the only one to survive and return from the camps. After the war, he tried to find out as much as possible about the fate of his wife and his two daughters. In addition, because of the subsequent fame of Anne Frank, several other witnesses have stepped forward over the course of time. For example, Hanneli Goslar and Nanette Blitz, who had been in Anne's class at school, talked about meeting her in the camp in Bergen-Belsen. The sisters Rebecca ("Lientje") and Janny Brilleslijper, and Annelore and Ellen Daniel, have also provided important witness statements about Anne and Margot's last moments.[47] Most of these witness statements and the record of Otto's search were recorded by authors such as Ernst Schnabel, Melissa Müller and Carol Ann Lee in their biographies of Anne and Otto Frank, and by the documentary filmmaker Willy Lindwer, who produced the groundbreaking film *The Last Seven Months of Anne Frank* (1988).[48]

These earlier chroniclers of Anne Frank's life story collected testimonies and reported the stories of the most important witnesses of the last months of Edith, Anne and Margot Frank. However, what is missing is a systematic and comprehensive historical study of the experiences and events in the lives of Anne Frank and her seven fellow victims in the camps. This book, which is based on the research report written by Erika Prins in 2016 for the Anne Frank House, aims to provide a more detailed reconstruction of what happened to the group of eight after they had been arrested than what has been provided in earlier documentaries and books.[49] By collecting together all the available archive materials – however fragmented they may be – supplemented with witness statements and "indirect evidence", an attempt has been made to describe the experiences of the group in the camps as closely as possible. What happened when they were deported? How and when were they separated? How and when did they end up in the different camps, and under what circumstances? What did they experience there and how did seven of them die?

In addition, this book would like to show how the story of the main characters can be understood in the broader historical context of genocide and persecution by the Nazi regime. As Nikolaus Wachsmann emphasized in his comprehensive work on the concentration camp system, *KL: A History of the Nazi Concentration Camps*, the camps are often considered by the public to be synonymous with mass murder using gas. In reality, the camps had several overlapping purposes and functions: they were used to instill terror, as prisons, for the production of weapons, and as a reservoir for slave labor and to carry out medical experiments on humans. In addition, the concentration camp system and the conditions in the different camps were constantly developing. When a prisoner arrived in a particular place, it could make a big difference.[50] As such, it's important to examine the individual cases of Otto, Edith, Margot and Anne Frank, Hermann, Auguste and Peter van Pels, and Fritz Pfeffer and to interpret them against the background of the deportations, the characters of the different camps where they were sent and the prevailing circumstances there.

This search fulfills two functions. First, it is about reconstructing the eight individual life stories as accurately as possible. Secondly, the search offers the possibility of reflecting on a number of important developments in the persecution and systematic murder of European Jews. The fate of the group of eight was part of the extermination, slave labor (often resulting in death), and large-scale evacuation and clearing transports which can only be properly understood if we have the most accurate possible picture of the general circumstances in the camps at the time that these eight people arrived there.[51] What was the prevailing regimen at the camp at the moment they arrived? Who was in charge? And what were the most important developments in the organization and the living conditions resulting in starvation, sickness and murder?

Many questions about conditions in the concentration camps can be answered on the basis of existing historical publications.[52] However, these history books say little about the individual fates of the group of eight. For this purpose, use was made of administrative information such as transport lists and registers, as well as personal sources such as contemporary personal documents, and postwar reports and interviews. There was a search in the archives of the NIOD, the Dutch Red Cross (NRK), the Arolsen Archives (International Center on Nazi Persecution, formerly the International Tracing Service), and the collections of various memorial centers for information about the time spent in the camps, and the experiences and the circumstances related to the death or survival of these eight people.[53]

There are various gaps and limitations in these archive materials. In the first place, most of the camp records were destroyed. When Germany had almost lost the war, an order came from Berlin to destroy the administrative records in the various camps. To a great extent, these attempts to erase the traces were successful.[54] For this reason, the original German camp and prison records from the time of the occupation have survived in only a very fragmentary way in most cases, and were sometimes destroyed completely. However, organizations such as the Red Cross and the Arolsen Archives made all sorts of attempts after the war to reconstruct the information about deportations and camp organization as well as possible.

As regards the eight members of the group, we have some transport lists, the Jewish Council card index (also used and supplemented for the postwar tracing of missing persons) and cards in the archives of the population administration in Westerbork. We also have the registration of Auguste van Pels in Raguhn, the book of the dead of Neuengamme containing the name of Fritz Pfeffer, the registration of Peter van Pels in the camp in Mauthausen, and the book of the dead with his name and the list of the dead, both drawn up shortly after the camp was liberated. Finally, Otto Frank took a *Raucherkarte* with him from Auschwitz. This was a card with which "prisoner B914" (Otto Frank) could get tobacco in the prison canteen.[55]

However, while administrative sources can tell us a lot about where and when things happened, they provide little insight into experiences. For this we are dependent on witnesses and personal documents such as letters, notes, memoirs and interviews.[56] Arnon Grunberg, who compiled and introduced a book of literary testimonies about Auschwitz in 2020, and gave the memorial lecture on 4 May of the same year, formulated the importance of commemoration as follows, and also states one of the objectives of this book: "Commemoration is […] a way of speaking on behalf of the dead, and it is only possible to speak on behalf of the dead by giving eyewitnesses the chance to bear witness."[57]

To gain an insight into what the group of eight saw and experienced in the camps, we are therefore dependent on eyewitnesses. Again, there are gaps and limitations. Seven of the eight did not survive the camps, and there were no personal documents left behind after they left the Annex. The testimony of other people who have direct stories to tell about the experiences of the group after their arrest and during their time in the camps have only survived to a limited extent. Furthermore, there are hardly any sources from this period itself.[58] However, there are various brochures and personal documents which appeared just after the war. One of the most important of these is the booklet *Aan de gaskamer ontsnapt!* ("Escaping the Gas Chambers!") that Rosa de Winter-Levy published about her experiences in Auschwitz in August 1945. De Winter-Levy was on the same train from Westerbork to Auschwitz as the group of eight, befriended Edith Frank and her daughters in Auschwitz, and wrote about them in detail in this booklet.[59]

The booklet *Aan de gaskamer ontsnapt!* by Rosa de Winter-Levy was published in 1945, shortly after the end of the war. It mentions the death of Edith Frank in Auschwitz.

Rosa de Winter-Levy with Otto and Fritzi Frank,
Switzerland, 1950.

The most direct postwar testimonies come from Otto Frank
himself, the only one of the eight who returned from the camp.
He recorded his experiences up to his return in Amsterdam on 3
June 1945, in short sentences in a small red notebook which he
managed to obtain just after the liberation. During his journey
back, he also wrote a number of letters to his family in Basel and
London.[60]

After this, he did not talk in public directly about the events and his own experiences from the moment of the arrest in 1944 up to his liberation from Auschwitz. The later statements and interviews with Otto Frank, as well as his correspondence, nevertheless contain many interesting details. For example, Otto Frank wrote a short text entitled "Bitte schreiben Sie" ("Please

A bag made of camp clothes in which Otto Frank kept his possessions, including the red notebook, during his journey back to the Netherlands.

Otto Frank's notebook, which he was given shortly after the liberation of Auschwitz.

Het Achterhuis was published on 25 June 1947. Helmut Salden designed the cover, featuring the sun disappearing behind black clouds.

Write") in the 1960s, in which he wrote eleven pages of answers to questions sent to him from readers of *The Secret Annex*.[61]

Yet Otto Frank's role goes beyond that of being the most important witness: he was also the person who attempted to find out about the fates of the others who had been in hiding with him, chiefly his wife and children. He not only recorded his own memories but also went in search of other witnesses who could tell him something about his family. Immediately on his return to Amsterdam, he did everything he could to find out what had happened to his two daughters. In this way, he came into contact with various witnesses who could tell him about the deaths of Margot and Anne in Bergen-Belsen.[62]

When Otto Frank heard from Hanneli Goslar that Nanette Blitz had seen Anne and Margot in Bergen-Belsen, he wrote her a short letter asking whether she could tell him more about

Hanneli Goslar with her sister Gabi, 1941.

his daughters. On 31 October 1945, whilst she was staying in the Provincial Hospital in Santpoort, Nanette wrote him a short account of what she knew. She also told him what she had heard from Margot Drach-Rosenthal, who was in the same hospital.

> You asked me whether I could tell you any more about Anne and Margot. Perhaps you remember Margot Drach-Rosenthal from Westerbork, who spent quite a bit of time with Anne? She's in the bed next to me and told me this: they went to Birkenau together with your wife and children and stayed there together until November. Then Margot and Anne went to Bergen-Belsen, where they arrived on 3 November. I met them there. (Another girl who's in this hospital too was in the bunk above them.) I wasn't in their barracks but I often visited them. Meanwhile, Margot (known as Monika) Rosenthal arrived in Bergen-Belsen in January and told them that she had spoken to your wife in Birkenau, which really cheered them up because they'd had very little hope when the selection took place because it had separated them from your wife. In January Margot and Anne went to the Schonungsblock, where I saw them. Then there was a big move and I didn't speak to them again, though I know from the girl here that someone spoke to them in February.[63]

This businesslike letter tries to describe the course of events during the period following the separation of Otto from his wife and children as accurately as possible. As an early source, the letter contains valuable information about the chronology, but at the same time it says very little about the experiences which the Frank sisters had in the camp, apart from the comment that they "cheered up" when they heard news about their mother.

As discussed above, Otto Frank's search for witnesses who had information about his wife and daughters was continued later and in more detail by journalists and documentary film-makers. The interviews they conducted are also an important source for this book, as is the Anne Frank House's extensive collection of interviews with witnesses. It started by taking witness statements in the 1990s and carrying out a large oral history project in 2005 in which almost a hundred family members and acquaintances of the Frank family and the others who were in hiding with them were interviewed. These also include several people who were in the concentration camps with them.[64]

These interviews and witness statements provide a wealth of information, but they are not without problems. People's memories are both fallible and subjective. Memory is a process of selection, ordering and recalling a chaotic series of events to produce a coherent story.[65] The traumatic character of the experiences of these witnesses in the camps also meant that painful memories – including memories that they were ashamed of or about which there are taboos – could be suppressed and removed in order to be less painful.[66]

However, as Primo Levi, an Italian Jew and one of the most important witnesses of the Holocaust, emphasizes, there is another fundamental problem: because the survivors are such a small and non-representative minority, they can never provide a representative picture of the experiences of those who died of hunger, disease and misery, or those who were murdered in the gas chambers. At the same time, and despite these limitations, the witness statements of the survivors are also our only way into the experiences of those who died.[67]

The fact that the story told in Anne Frank's diary has become so famous that it affects postwar witness statements in different ways is of a completely separate order. Witnesses' own memories may be influenced by the many different books written and films made about Anne Frank later on.[68] With regard to a number of statements about meeting the Frank family in the camp, it is difficult to establish the accuracy of the memories at the level of details, dates and chronology. It is therefore necessary to take into account the limitations of individual memories. Wherever possible, these have been compared against other sources.

However, it is also important to reflect on the specific dynamics which apply to witnesses who are interviewed if they are not the main subject of the interview themselves. Furthermore, a small number of the interviewees express mixed feelings about the fact that it is not their own experiences that they are first asked about, but those of Anne Frank. Sometimes they feel uncomfortable about the fact that they can't remember much about Anne and her family. At other times, they reveal their irritation about the fact that Anne Frank's story has become so famous, and is repeated so often, while there are millions of other stories which do not attract any attention. For example, Bloeme Emden, who knew Anne and Margot at the Jewish Lyceum and then met them both again in Westerbork and Auschwitz, expressed her reservations about the "excessive" attention that has always been paid to Anne Frank which, in her opinion, sometimes resulted in a "personality cult": "In itself it's very interesting to get to know the feelings of a Jewish child who went into hiding [...]. But there are so many of these sorts of testimonies [...] and we all have more or less the same history." During her interview, Emden reminded the interviewer of the discrepancy between what she was being

Bloeme Emden, in about 1942.

asked and what she was able to tell her: "You never stop asking about the Frank family and unfortunately I can't tell you very much about that."[69]

This tension often emerges in interviews. Nevertheless, even those who reveal their mixed feelings all endorse the symbolic and moral significance of the diary and Anne Frank's life story. Most of the witnesses also emphasize that they consider Anne Frank and her diary to be a good way of educating younger generations about the Holocaust. Freda Wineman-Silberberg, who often visited schools as a victim of the Holocaust to talk about the persecution of the Jews, formulated this as follows:

I found in the work that we do as survivors, going to the schools, the fact that these children have read Anne Frank's diary, helps us a lot. [...] Every story is unique, but it gives us a chance to tell our story. [...] So, it's important for us if they have read Anne Frank. And if they have digested the story, you know, if they have learned something from it. Then when we come in, they also listen to our story, you know. That's a different story, but it's a story about <u>our</u> Holocaust.[70]

It is important to consider both the limitations of human memory and the specific dynamics related to the memories of Anne Frank, but it does not detract from the historical and moral value of the testimonies. They are essential sources, providing an insight into experiences and events, both for this specific book and for the written history of the Holocaust.

In his essay *The Ethics of Memory*, the philosopher Avishai Margalit states that witnesses of genocidal violence not only have a historical function but also a moral one. In his opinion, the moral witness is someone who not only observed the suffering and crimes, but was also directly affected themselves. The moral witness plays a crucial role in exposing the terror inflicted on him or her by speaking from personal experience: "The moral witness plays a special role in uncovering the evil he or she encounters. Evil regimes try hard to cover up the enormity of their crimes, and the moral witness tries to expose it."[71] It is only from the perspective of individual experience and memory that it's possible to do justice to the moral dimension of what happened in the camps. In this way, the testimonies provide a picture of how the witnesses see themselves and how they struggle with the traumatic memories of hunger, pain, mistreatment and the fear of death.[72] It is only through these individual and subjective statements that we can form a picture of the actual experiences that the group of eight from the Annex suffered.

As such, for this book we not only looked for specific information about these eight people, but also for testimonies that could give an insight into the experiences of people who were in the same place at the same time. Some of the witnesses did not have any direct memories of Anne and the others, but mention important details of the circumstances and the way in which they experienced them.[73] This book therefore opted to recount the words of those who were as close as possible to the eight people from the Annex. These included survivors who had ended up in the camps in the German Empire from Wes terbork in the Netherlands, just as they had – people who had been in the same part of the camp at the same time, and can therefore tell us more about what happened there.

This book is an incomplete jigsaw puzzle with pieces of different shapes and sizes. It is partly based on earlier research and well-known sources, but also on new discoveries in different archives. This makes it possible to gain a better insight into the fate and experiences of Anne Frank and the others after they were arrested in August 1944. First of all, it describes their shared route from the prison in Amsterdam to the transit camp in Westerbork and on to Auschwitz-Birkenau, where the men and women were separated. Then it describes the experiences of the eight individuals through the various camps of Bergen-Belsen, Mauthausen, Neuengamme and Raguhn. Finally, it follows Otto Frank, the only survivor, during his trip back to Amsterdam: the moment that the search for his loved ones began.

CHAPTER TWO

"Mum, did you know that Margot was here?"

Prison and Camp Westerbork

PRISON

The arrest of the group in hiding in the Annex on 4 August 1944 took place at a time when most Jews had already been deported from the Netherlands. The planned deportations started on 5 July 1942, when a group of Jews aged between the ages of fifteen and forty years received a summons to register for "work expansion" in Germany.[1] As indicated earlier, Margot Frank was one of them, and her summons was the immediate reason for the Frank family to go into hiding earlier than they had planned.[2]

Between July and December 1942, the *Zentralstelle für jüdische Auswanderung* and department IVb4 of the *Sicherheitspolizei und Sicherheitsdienst* (Sipo-SD) transported almost 47,000 Jews to the Westerbork *Durchgangslager* (transit camp) with the help of the Dutch police. From 15 July 1942, large deportations regularly left from this transit camp to the extermination camp in Auschwitz.[3] After a terrible journey of two or three days in freight wagons, most prisoners were immediately sent to the gas chambers when they arrived. The remaining prisoners stayed in Auschwitz or were transported to other camps or subcamps.[4] These prisoners provided enormous potential as a cheap slave labor force. They had to work in the camp, factories, mines or industries that directly or indirectly served the German war industry.[5] The living conditions of the prisoners were extremely grim, and the chance of survival was small.[6]

During a large number of raids and razzias in 1943, the German and Dutch police departments rounded up approximately 42,000 more Jews. In that year, deportations also left Westerbork for the extermination camp in Sobibor.[7] On 29 September 1943, the Reich Commissioner Arthur Seyss-Inquart proudly declared that the city of Amsterdam was "Judenfrie": approximately 80,000 Jewish inhabitants in the capital had been taken to concentration camps by then. It was only Jews in mixed marriages and their children that were still present in the city.[8] In the following months, Camp Westerbork filled up with large number of "criminal cases" – Jewish prisoners who had been arrested for the infringement of anti-Jewish legislation, particularly people who had gone into hiding and had been arrested. Between July 1942 and September 1944, with the help of the Dutch police, the Sipo-SD arrested almost 12,000 Jewish people

A group of arrested Jews, Amsterdam, 20 June 1943.

One of the last razzias in Amsterdam took place on 20 June 1943. This photograph was taken near the Merwedeplein, where the Frank family lived.

in hiding.[9] When the Sipo-SD arrested the group in hiding in the Annex on 4 August 1944, the period of the big razzias had ended.[10] The last extensive deportations from Amsterdam to Westerbork had already taken place by 7 July 1944.[11]

After their arrest on 4 August 1944, after a short interrogation, the eight people who had been in hiding and the helpers Johannes Kleiman and Victor Kugler were taken to the office of the *Zentralstelle für jüdische Auswanderung* in Amsterdam at Adama van Scheltemaplein 1. Once there, Otto Frank was questioned briefly by the leader of the arresting team, the Austrian officer *SS-Hauptscharführer* Karl Joseph Silberbauer.[12] The interrogation was calm; Silberbauer did not use any violence and only asked a few questions. Otto did not know anything about other people who had gone into hiding and so he was left alone.[13]

The next day, 5 August, they were all taken to the *Huis van Bewaring* (detention center) on the Weteringschans in

Detention center on the Weteringschans, after the war.

Amsterdam. From that moment, all eight were imprisoned as criminals in the inescapable process of deportation. Johannes Kleiman and Victor Kugler were imprisoned in the Havenstraat detention center in Amsterdam and were subjected to a different process through the German prison system, which is not considered here.

In the detention center, the men and women were separated and accommodated in two separate large cells. According to the description given by Jacob Swart, another prisoner who was taken to the detention center on the Weteringschans after his arrest on 26 May 1944, the cell was:

[…] a large bare room with three rough wooden tables and a few benches in the middle, ten beds on the left and another ten beds (iron cots with a sack of straw) on the gallery. There was a list of rules and a mirror on the wall, and all the walls had holes or "eyes" through which you would be watched every now and again.[14]

As soon as the cells were full, with approximately forty men and forty women, the prisoners were transported to Westerbork.[15] Jacob Swart remembers that the cell was virtually empty at the time that he was locked up because a train had just left for Westerbork on the morning of 26 May. He described how seven or eight new prisoners arrived every day, usually Jewish people who had been in hiding and had been arrested. In the end, there were so many that there were not enough beds, and newcomers had to sleep on the ground on sacks filled with straw. Once a day, the prisoners were able to get a breath of fresh air in the courtyard for quarter of an hour (men and women separately). Swart wrote that the food wasn't too bad: in the mornings and

Jacob Swart.

evenings he was given four plain slices of bread, a drink that was supposed to be coffee, and at lunchtime there was a "bite of hot food". He also described how some people put their ear against the cell door to hear their wives' voices when they threw away the water for washing at the fountain in the corridor or were allowed to refresh their drinking water.[16] The female prisoners were in the adjoining cell. Ronnie Goldstein-van Cleef stayed there for a few days before she went to Westerbork on 1 July 1944. She said there was secret contact with the men being held there whereby the women prisoners asked whether they could be allowed to darn their husbands' socks and hid notes in them.[17]

On Tuesday 8 August 1944, the eight people from the Annex had been in the (by now) overcrowded cells of the detention center on the Weteringschans for three days when they were taken to Westerbork, together with approximately eighty other prisoners. First, the prisoners left for the Central Station by tram under police guard.[18] What we know about the subsequent train journey is limited to a number of administrative details and witness statements, including that of Otto Frank himself. The often-quoted statement by Janny Brandes-Brilleslijper, in which she said that she'd met the Frank family – "an extremely worried-looking father, a nervous mother and two sporting looking girls with rucksacks" – at the Central Station in Amsterdam is probably based on a mistake.[19] Otto Frank briefly described the train journey in "Bitte schreiben Sie" and in an interview with Ernst Schnabel.[20] They took a normal train to Westerbork with carriages that were guarded and locked on both sides.[21] The weather was beautiful that day: the sun shone, a gentle wind blew from the northwest, and it was about 19 degrees.[22] Otto Frank wrote that during the train ride he was particularly worried about Victor Kugler and Johannes Kleiman, as they had also been arrested. Apart from that, the mood was relatively positive: "We were together again and we'd been given some food for the journey. We knew where we were going, but it was still as though we were going on another trip together, and actually we were quite cheerful […], at least when I compare this trip with the next one."[23] The train ride from Amsterdam to Westerbork took between five and six hours.[24] The route went from Amsterdam Central Station via Hilversum, Amersfoort, Zwolle and Meppel to Hooghalen; after that, the train went on to Westerbork on a branch line.[25]

CAMP WESTERBORK

From October 1939, Westerbork served as a camp for German Jewish refugees who had come to the Netherlands, particularly after the *Kristallnacht*. At the end of March 1940 there were 350 people there. Following the capitulation in May 1940, the management of the camp remained in Dutch hands for the time being, but the regime became stricter under the supervision of the new director, Jacques Schol. Although there was no fence around the camp, it was prohibited for refugees to leave without permission, and there were severe punishments for infringing the camp rules. On 1 July 1942, the camp was officially transferred to the German authorities. Westerbork was then officially known as *Polizeiliches Judendurchgangslager* under the authority of the *Befehlshaber der Sicherheitspolizei und Sicherheitsdienst* and the *Reichssicherheitshauptamt*. From that date. the camp was part of the extensive system of German concentration camps and served as an important transit point for the systematic murder of the Dutch Jews.[26]

Camp Westerbork was fenced with barbed wire and there were seven watchtowers with SS guards, manned from 1943 by the security police. In the summer of 1944, the Amsterdam police force took over responsibility for guarding the entire camp.[27]

Westerbork became a transit camp for the deportations to the concentration and extermination camp at Auschwitz, the extermination camp at Sobibor, and the concentration camps in Bergen-Belsen and Theresienstadt. The transports that arrived and left completely dominated the daily life in the camp. The time that prisoners spent in Westerbork varied enormously – from only a few hours to days or weeks or months, sometimes even years.[28] However, prisoners like the group who had been hiding in the Annex, who were considered criminal cases, usually had to go on the next transport.

Almost all of the people who traveled with the Frank family on the transport of 8 August 1944 were considered to be criminal cases.[29] They were directly transferred to the subcamp specially organized for the criminal prisoners, where there were three so-called "criminal" barracks, separated from the rest of the camp by a double fence of barbed wire, the area euphemistically known as the "free camp".[30] There was a passageway through the barbed wire fence that was guarded day and night. The criminal barracks were intended primarily for prisoners who had committed an offence against camp discipline. During the course of 1943, large numbers of Jews were locked up there because they had violated the anti-Jewish measures outside the camp and had therefore been arrested and taken to Westerbork; they might be Jews who had been arrested because they were not wearing a Star of David or who had moved house without permission. After the Netherlands was declared "free of Jews" in the summer of 1943, the majority of the "S" cases (as the criminal prisoners were known in the camp jargon) were

The main road through Camp Westerbork. The railway line was next to this road and the trains left from the so-called "Rampe" for the concentration and extermination camps in the east.

The camp commandant,
SS-Obersturmführer Albert Konrad
Gemmeker.

people such as the Frank and Van Pels families, who had been arrested while they were in hiding. In an unknown number of cases, non-Jews who had helped Jews to go into hiding were also imprisoned in the criminal barracks in Westerbork.[31]

The camp commandant, *SS-Obersturmführer* Albert Konrad Gemmeker, was in charge of Westerbork from 13 October 1942. Gemmeker was a keen bureaucrat and ran the camp very efficiently, using the existing internal camp organization, which was an extension of what had been initially established by the German Jewish refugees.[32] Although he didn't hesitate to use violence against the prisoners when he felt it was necessary, he preferred not to get his hands dirty himself.[33] Instead, Gemmeker applied a divide and rule strategy by making the internal camp administration responsible for organizing the deportations. It was only when he considered it necessary that he personally took identity cards from the filing system, or determined who or which group should be transported. The rest of the time it was up to the internal camp administration to determine who was essential in the camp and could therefore stay. This resulted in a complicated system of nepotism, so that the SS played only a very limited role in the internal camp organization in Westerbork.[34]

In March 1944, Gemmeker commissioned a film about the camp in which he wanted to show how well and efficiently it was run.[35] This film was obviously propaganda, but it provides an interesting picture of the operation of the camp five months before the group of eight arrived. However, it remains a limited view, because images of everyday life in the barracks and the operation of the camp administration and the hospital in Westerbork are missing. Nevertheless, the film shows the school, relaxation and entertainment, people working on the land, weaving on looms, in the smithy, doing carpentry and recycling batteries, as well as the departure of a train with prisoners to Auschwitz in the section on "Arrivals and Departures". One of Gemmeker's other special interests featured in the film was the industrial area of the camp, where work was carried out for the German war industry. He was keen to show how his camp contributed to the increased production and significantly expanded this "industry" in the summer of 1944.[36]

It was mainly the criminal prisoners, such as the group of eight from the Annex, who worked there under guard, recycling silver foil and batteries and taking parts of aircraft apart.[37] On 3 August 1944, just before they arrived, Gemmeker refined the regimen. With *Lagerbefehl* (camp order) 86, he imposed stricter discipline and demanded that the production for the war industry should be multiplied four- or fivefold.[38] He stated that this was for articles that contributed to the war effort, and that sabotage would therefore become a military crime. On 10

August 1944, two days after the arrival of the Frank family and the others, Gemmeker prohibited any contact inside or outside the camp with immediate effect (*Lagerbefehl* 87). Prisoners in the criminal barracks and the prisoners in the "free" part of the camp could therefore no longer visit or talk to each other.[39] The *Joodse Ordedienst* (Jewish order service; OD) also had to strictly supervise this while prisoners were working.[40]

It is striking that there were very few German SS officers in Westerbork, with at most fifteen officers making up the SS staff.[41] As mentioned, it was initially the Dutch police who were responsible for guarding the camp,[42] but from 1943 the police were only charged with guarding prisoners outside the camp and the enforcement of everyday law and order; guarding the passageway between the free camp and the criminal barracks became the responsibility of the OD. These Jewish prisoners, identifiable

Transport from Westerbork, probably autumn 1942. The two men wearing overalls are probably members of the *Joodse Ordedienst*.

Lagerkommandantur
Lager Westerbork.

Lager Westerbork, den 10.August 1944.

Lagerbefehl Nr.87.

1.)Betrifft Sperrstunde.

Ab 11.August 1944 wird die Sperrstunde auf 22,00 Uhr verlegt. Dem-
zufolge ist das Licht in den Barakken um 22.45 Uhr zu löschen.
Lagerinsassen,die vom Nachtdienst
kommen oder zum Nachtdienst gehen
oder von der Spätschicht kommen,ha-
ben das Licht so schnell wie möglich,
längstens aber nach 20 Minuten zu löschen.

1.)Betreft: Spertijd.

Met ingang van 11 Augustus 1944
wordt de spertijd op 22 uur vast-
gesteld.Derhalve moet het licht
in de barakken om 22.45 uur uit-
geschakeld worden.Kampingezetenen,
die van hun nachtdienst thuiskomen of zich naar hun nachtdienst
begeven of van de avondploeg
thuiskomen,dienen het licht zoo
snel mogelijk, echter uiterlijk
na 20 minuten,uit te draaien.

2.)Betrifft Häftlinge.

Ab sofort wird für Häftlinge jeglicher Postverkehr verboten.Ausserdem
werden Besuche von Häftlingen im Krankenhaus und Besuche von Häftlingen
durch Lagerinsassen in den Strafbaracken ab sofort verboten. Die Lagerinsassen haben sich jeden Verkehrs mit Häftlingen mit Ausnahme von dienst-
lichen Anlässen zu enthalten. Lagerinsassen, die Häftlingen Postverkehr
ermöglichen oder in anderer Form Verbindung mit Häftlingen aufnehmen,
werden unverzüglich als Häftlinge in die Strafbaracke eingewiesen. Unter
dieses Verbot fällt auch das Abgeben von Lebensmitteln oder Gebrauchsge-
genständen auf unmittelbarem oder mittelbarem Wege. Dem OD ist es aus-
drücklich verboten, Lebensmittel, Gegenstände oder Post für Häftlinge
entgegenzunehmen.
Selbstverständlich fallen unter die vorstehenden Verbote auch die in
Bar.51 einsitzenden Häftlinge oder Lagerinsassen.Jeder Versuch, sich
mit Insassen der Strafbaracken oder der Bar.51 in Verbindung zu setzen,
wird als Beihilfe zur Flucht bei Insassen dieser Baracken angesehen und
je nach Lage des Falles mit der oben angedrohten oder einer schwereren
Strafe belegt.
Da es unvermeidlich ist, dass während der Arbeitszeit Häftlinge mit Lagerinsassen zusammenarbeiten, haben die Dienst- und Gruppenleiter beson-
ders auf die Einhaltung dieser Anordnungen zu achten und, wenn sie selbst
eine Bestrafung vermeiden wollen, rücksichtslos Uebertretungen dieser
Verbote zu melden.

2.)Betreft: Strafgevallen.

Met onmiddellijke inwerkingtreding wordt ieder postverkeer voor strafgevallen verboden. Bovendien is het bezoek van strafgevallen in het ziekenhuis en het bezoek van kampingezetenen aan strafgevallen in de strafbarakken van nu af aan verboden. De kampingezetenen dienen zich van ieder
verkeer met de strafgevallen - tenzij uit hoofde van hun dienst - te ont-
houden.Kampingezetenen,die postverkeer voor de strafgevallen mogelijk
maken of op andere wijze zich met strafgevallen in verbinding stellen,
worden onverwijld zelf als strafgevallen naar de strafbarak overgebracht.
Onder dit verbod valt eveneens het afgeven van levensmiddelen of gebruiks-
voorwerpen langs directen of indirecten weg. Het is den O.D.uitdrukkelijk
verboden, levensmiddelen,voorwerpen of post voor strafgevallen in ont-
vangst te nemen.
Het spreekt vanzelf, dat onder de bovenstaande verbodsbepalingen ook
die strafgevallen of kampingezetenen vallen, die zich in barak 51 bevin-
den.Iedere poging,om zich met bewoners van de strafbarakken of van barak 51 in verbinding te stellen wordt als medeplichtigheid aan ontvluch-
ting der bewoners van deze barakken beschouwd en naar gelang van de
ernst van het geval gestraft met de boven bedreigde of met een zwaardere
straf.
Daar het niet te vermijden is, dat gedurende de arbeidstijd strafgevallen en kampingezetenen tezamen werken, moeten de dienst- en groepenlei-
ders speciaal op de handhaving van deze bepalingen letten en - willen
zij zelf niet bestraft worden - zonder consideratie overtredingen van
deze verbodsbepalingen melden.

Der Lagerkommandant,

Grimweth,

ɲ-Obersturmführer.

Lagerbefehl 87.

by their green overalls, had to guard the criminal barracks, escort prisoners to and from their work, receive prisoners who had just arrived, and process everyone through the extensive registration procedure. The Dutch police were also involved in the razzias in Amsterdam and had to help to empty the Jewish psychiatric hospital, Het Apeldoornsche Bosch in Apeldoorn, at the end of January 1943.[43] The members of the OD were at least provisionally exempt from deportation, and in exchange they vigorously joined in with the punishment of the other prisoners, as well as loading the deportation trains to the camps in the East.

The Jewish Austrian Arthur Pisk was the head of the OD and in charge of the internal security until the liberation of Westerbork on 12 April 1945. Pisk and his OD had a fearsome reputation amongst the prisoners. Philip Mechanicus, who kept a diary in Westerbork between 28 May 1943 and 28 February 1944, described Pisk as a "pirate" and "the head of the Jewish Gestapo".[44] In a note made on 12 February 1944 he expressed his indignation about the way in which the OD treated the prisoners, and in his opinion, they were only interested in looking after themselves.

> You're powerless against the members of the OD. They're the officially recognized guards who maintain order, though they often have no understanding of what order is and only act when there's "something to organize" or to mess around with girls. They're hated for their brutality and because they always get away with it. A few days ago one of them broke the nose of a young man who wanted to go into the canteen and put his foot in the door, and he's still walking round with his nose in the air, free and unpunished: "Look at me. Aren't I the hero?"[45]

Arthur Pisk.

The members of the OD were also hated and feared by many of the prisoners because of their role in the deportations. On the evening before the transport, the OD read out the names of those who were on the transport list, and then took the

Jewish prisoners in Westerbork just before being deported.

A train with prisoners ready to leave Camp Westerbork.

prisoners and their luggage to the trains and shut the doors of the wagons.[46]

The use of the OD was part of a broader strategy that the Nazis used to make victims of persecution complicit with the system of concentration camps. So-called *Funktionshäftlinge* (prisoner functionaries), otherwise known as kapos, were appointed in all the concentration camps and made responsible for carrying out particular tasks in the camp organization.[47] Although the extent to which they were involved in the violence and genocidal process in camps such as Auschwitz and Bergen-Belsen was on a different scale (as will be shown in later chapters), the OD was in a comparable position of moral ambiguity.[48] By leaving the supervision and internal security virtually entirely to the OD, and because members of the Jewish Council passed on the names for the transport lists to Auschwitz, it strengthened a system in which the victims of the persecution of the Jews collaborated with the mistreatment and deportation

78

of others and themselves. In his books on the guards at Wester-bork, the historian Frank van Riet shows how members of the OD were often hated and despised by the prisoners, but that certain prisoners looked more favorably on them. Some even believe that Pisk sabotaged the orders of the camp authorities on occasion. Van Riet also refers to the pressure put on the members of the OD, with Gemmeker making them liable for internal order and severely punishing those he felt were respon-sible for escapes and disruption.[49]

In addition, Van Riet noted that although Pisk and a number of other members of the OD managed to stay in Westerbork until it was liberated, they nevertheless had no security them-selves right up to the time of the last deportations. When most of the exemptions were withdrawn in Westerbork in 1944, 164 members of the OD were transported and only fifteen of them survived. Thirty-two members of the OD remained behind in the camp and managed to survive as a result.[50]

ARRIVAL

When the group of eight from the Annex arrived in Wester-bork, they first had to be registered. This was a process which could take hours for large transports, but for the relatively small group that included Anne and the others, the registration was probably very quick.[51] The registration of the newcomers on the large deportations in 1942 and 1943 always took place in barracks number 9, which was also used for theatrical and concert performances. From 1944, when the groups of newcomers became smaller and smaller, the registrations were generally carried out in the administration barracks number 34, where the newcomers were also checked for lice. This was probably also the case when the transport with which the group

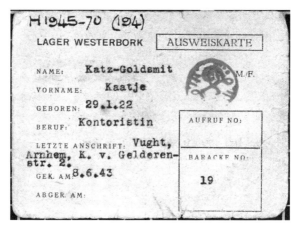

Camp pass of Kaatje Katz-Goldsmit from 1943.

from the Annex arrived in Westerbork.[52] All the prisoners were first ordered to form themselves into long lines and told to wait in the large courtyard. Members of the Jewish OD then took them to the various sections of the registration process.

All their luggage was removed. First, a list of arrivals was drawn up (*Eingangsliste*) and any identity documents and distribution documents had to be handed in. The prisoners were then registered in the *Zentralkartei* (central administration) where they were given a *Lagerpass* (camp pass).[53]

The *Zentralkartei* was the most important administrative instrument in the camp for sending the transports, and the main reason for the existence of the camp during the German occupation. Only the camp commandant and the *Zentralstelle für jüdische Auswanderung* had access to this system.[54] All the personal details were shown on the cards of the *Zentralkartei*, including their history in the camp, requests that had been submitted, exemptions, admittance to the camp hospital, work, moving barracks, barracks numbers, etc. A delay for deportation was indicated with a cross on the top right of the card and the reason for the delay was shown on the back of the card. Criminal cases had their card marked with a red "H" for *Häftling* (prisoner). The transport lists were drawn up on the basis of these cards just before the train departed; cards of prisoners who were not given a delay (so-called *Congesperden*) were removed. The *Zentralkartei* was arranged alphabetically so that the members of a family were close together in the administration. In this way, they were also included on the transport list and that is why the group of eight from the Annex were grouped together.[55]

One important part of the registration procedure was the registration office, the *Antragstelle*, which was run by the German lawyer, Hans Ottenstein. Ottenstein was one of the group of Jews who were already in Westerbork before the Germans took over the running of the camp. He had been put in charge in January 1942 because of this legal background, which meant he had one of the most influential positions in the camp. His office not only organized the registration of the newcomers in the camp, but also dealt with the applications for provisional exemptions from deportation to the camps in the east. Prisoners who fulfilled certain conditions (for example, because they had a partially non-Jewish background, had been christened or were in a mixed marriage, had emigration papers for Palestine, or because of their "essential" presence in Camp Westerbork) were given an exemption from deportation on Ottenstein's recommendation.[56]

A note was made on the cards in Ottenstein's office about whether there were grounds which justified the postponement of deportation, otherwise known as a *Sperre*. Prisoners could also submit an *Antrag* (request) to this office in order to

The camp pass of prisoner Werner Sterzenbach. This card also shows Sterzenbach's *Sperre*. He is *"zurückgestellt"* (exempted) from deportation because he has the status of Alter.

lose their criminal case status (for example, someone might be able to demonstrate that he had been baptized a Christian, was half-Jewish or had special papers).[57] As the criminal cases generally had to go on the next deportation, obtaining a *Sperre* could be vitally important. As long as a request was being dealt with, that person would not be transported and was deemed *gesperrt*, or *zurückgestellt bis auf weiteres* (a provisional postponement until further notice).[58]

The registration process of the group from the Annex ended with a medical examination. All the men and women had to get undressed and were checked for contagious diseases and head lice. After this, they were allocated a place in one of the barracks. They all ended up in criminal barracks 67.[59] They had to hand in their shoes and clothes, which were stored in a jute sack showing their name. They were given blue overalls with a red piece of material on the shoulder, a white armband showing

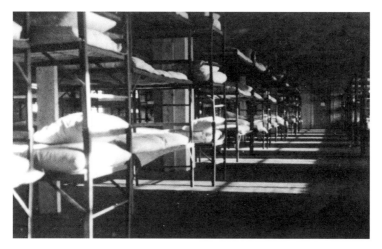

Barrack interior, Concentration Camp Westerbork.

Prisoner working in the smithy in Camp
Westerbork.

an "S" for *strafgeval* (Dutch: criminal case), a Star of David and clogs. In addition, the men were given a red and blue cap. These clothes identified them clearly as criminal cases, meaning they were taken to the criminal barracks by the OD and allocated a place to sleep.

The next morning, the men were shaved bald in the washing area of the barracks.[60] This also happened to Otto Frank, Herman and Peter van Pels, and Fritz Pfeffer. From that moment onwards, they wore a cap.[61] Auguste van Pels, Edith, Margot and Anne Frank kept their hair like the other girls and women. It was only the women who had lice – as shown during the medical examination at the end of the registration process – who were shaved bald and were given a "petroleum cap", and the available declarations do not indicate that this was the case for Auguste, Edith or the two girls.[62]

EVERYDAY LIFE IN THE CRIMINAL BARRACKS

What was life like for Anne Frank and her seven fellow victims in the criminal barracks? By September 1944, the group from the Annex were sharing an overcrowded barracks with 400–500 people. Barracks 67 was divided into half between men and women. Everyone had to register with the leader of the barracks or room each morning and evening. After a day of work, the men, women and families could spend time together. The kitchen was located in the middle of the barracks. Food would be handed out there, and prisoners would then go through the kitchen and turn either left or right to the male or female parts of the barracks. At ten in the evening, everyone had to be back in their own area, the door between the two parts of the barracks was locked, and lights went out at a quarter past ten.[63]

At the end of the barracks where they slept, there was a washing area with rectangular sinks with taps and a single toilet, which could only be used at night. Outside the barracks were small red toilet facilities (referred to as "egg racks" by the prisoners), separated for men and women, which could only be used during the day. Smoking was forbidden, but people smoked secretly in the toilet houses outside. The prisoners slept in triple bunk beds with straw mattresses, but sometimes there were none available. There were lots of complaints about fleas in the mattresses and the bedding. The prisoners ate at the tables in the middle of the barracks, but it was so crowded that people sometimes had to eat standing up.[64] The group of eight from the Annex had been given time to pack their things by Silberbauer;[65] however, many prisoners who had been arrested in a hurry had not been able to take anything with them and lacked basic things like underclothes, blankets or toilet articles.[66]

In her book about the prison experiences of Jews in Camp Westerbork, the historian Eva Moraal concludes that everyday life there and the prisoners' experience of it differed enormously. To an important extent, the experience of daily life in Westerbork depended on the position of the prisoner in the camp. The status and privileges that prisoners had were also determined by different factors. First of all, there was a great difference between the newcomers – largely Dutch Jews – and the German Jewish refugees in the camp who were already in Westerbork before the first deportations in 1942.[67]

The latter group, which also included the above-mentioned Ottenstein and Pisk, often quickly managed to acquire important jobs, which gave them access to privileges such as better sleeping quarters, food and, most importantly, a good *Sperre* that protected them from being deported to the east. Moraal showed that a prisoner's place in the camp hierarchy had an enormous influence on the way in which he or she experienced imprisonment and the related fear and insecurity.

The criminal cases, including the group of eight from the Annex, were at the bottom of the ladder. Apart from a few exceptions, criminal cases had no chance of a *Sperre*. Because they were generally the first in line for deportation, this group of prisoners had little time in the camp to build up a life there and acquire a better position. There were a few exceptions. For example, Philip Mechanicus and Edgar Weinberg were both criminal cases, but because of their social position and talents – Mechanicus was a well-known journalist and Weinberg had a great deal of technical knowledge – they managed to acquire a good job with a *Sperre*.[68]

Author and journalist Philip Mechanicus, 1930.

Edgar Weinberg in Westerbork. A still from the film commissioned by Camp Commandant Gemmeker in the spring of 1944 and filmed by the prisoner Rudolf Breslauer.

It is not known whether Otto Frank also attempted to lose his "S" (as a move away from the criminal barracks was known in the camp jargon) by submitting an application.[69] He could certainly have tried to do so by appealing to his status as a veteran of the First World War. After the end of the Second World War, when he talked about his arrest at the Prinsengracht building, he referred several times to how *Hauptscharführer* Karl Joseph Silberbauer's attitude changed when he heard that Otto had served as an officer in the German army during the First World War. Silberbauer had told him at the time that on these grounds he would be eligible to go to Theresienstadt, a camp where the chances of survival were significantly higher. However, during the time that Otto Frank spent in Westerbork, only veterans with the *Verwundetenabzeichen* (proof that they had been wounded on the front) were still eligible to go to Theresienstadt. As the cards of the *Zentralkartei* and the *Antragstelle* have not survived, it is no longer possible to check whether Otto Frank made any attempts to organize something for himself and his family.

This cannot be ascertained for Fritz Pfeffer either, who had fought on the German side during the First World War and had been an officer. However, in his case, it is also quite possible. There are examples of other criminal prisoners who managed to lose that status just before the deportation on 3 September 1944, and ended up in the "free" camp as a result, or were sent to Theresienstadt on 4 September.[70] But as a result of the stricter rules of the camp regime at the start of August 1944, the possibilities for the Frank family and the others to postpone deportation were extremely limited.

Daily life in Camp Westerbork was determined to a great extent by work. Everyone in Westerbork between the ages of fifteen and sixty-five years old had to work six days a week for ten hours a day.[71] In addition, the criminal cases also had to do punishment exercises from six until eight on Sunday mornings (for the men) or compulsory gymnastics (for the women).[72]

Eva Moraal noted that this heavy work was a particularly abrupt reversal for adolescents like Anne, Margot and Peter compared with the lives they had got used to before Westerbork, either at school or while they were in hiding.[73] This applied in particular for children like Anne, who came from the middle classes and had not grown up with heavy physical work. Edith, Margot and Anne Frank's work involved recycling old batteries. Work "in the batteries" (as it was known) was certainly very heavy, filthy and unhealthy.[74] Although the prisoners who had to do this work were given an extra ration of milk every day, many of them tried to change to a better job. Janny Brilleslijper,

Prisoners taking batteries apart in Westerbork.

who did the same work and was in regular contact with Edith Frank and her daughters, described it like this: "You had to open up the batteries with a chisel and a hammer and then throw the tar into one basket and the carbon stick that you removed into another basket. You had to knock the metal hat off with a metal screwdriver and that went into the third basket."[75] After work, they were all pitch black and went to the showers to clean themselves, supervised by the OD. However, most people had no soap with which to wash themselves.

In order to get a better job you generally needed contacts or a good relationship with someone in the OD. Rachel Frankfoorder, who was thirty years old at the time and had been arrested on a train with a false identity document, was lucky to be assigned to the "internal service" in Westerbork. This was a much sought-after job requiring her to clean the toilets, scrub

Rachel Frankfoorder at the beginning of the war.

the floors, and to hand out the clogs and overalls to the new prisoners when a transport arrived. She remembers meeting the Frank family in the criminal barracks and that Otto Frank asked her to arrange a job in the cleaning team for Anne. Although Anne made a good impression on her, she did not have many opportunities to help her:

> Otto Frank came to me with Anne and asked if Anne could help me. Anne was very friendly and also asked if she could help me. She said: "I can do anything, I can be really useful". She was truly delightful, a little older than in the photograph we know of her, cheerful and lively. Unfortunately I had no say in the matter and sent her to the leaders of the barracks. Obviously I couldn't do anything more about this.[76]

As a result, Anne continued to work in the battery department, like her sister and mother. It is not clear what work the others from the Annex had to do. In an interview, Rose de Liema-van Gelder, whose husband Sal later became a good friend of Otto Frank in Auschwitz, suggests that Otto Frank and Peter and Hermann van Pels were also assigned to the battery team.

> We were in a huge room as big as this one, and it was full of batteries and baskets at the top and that's where we had to work in the daytime. We sat up there [...] and by chance the whole Frank family, Otto, his wife, the children, the Van Pels family, Peter and all of them, and my husband and I were all sitting up there. But for me, the mother and the girls and Mrs. Van Pels were just other ordinary prisoners. I mean, I never particularly spoke about things which they went through together.[77]

Rose and Sal de Liema at their wedding, 20
December 1942. They pinned a corsage on their
clothes to hide the Star of David.

No other facts have been discovered to confirm this, and Otto
Frank's own statements do not make it clear whether the men
and women did the same work at Westerbork.

Otto Frank said that everyone had to work but that they were
free in the evenings.[78] As such, we can only know about the
daily routine in Westerbork in a general sense. The prisoners
in the criminal barracks were woken up at half past five in the
morning. After washing, getting dressed, fetching their food
and having breakfast, they had to line up in blocks of three by
three next to the barracks at quarter to seven. They were then
taken through the gate to the industry barracks in the "free"

camp, supervised by the OD. They worked there from seven until midday. Then they returned to the barracks to eat (usually mashed potatoes with red cabbage or turnips), again supervised by the OD, and were taken back to work again from two until seven in the evening.[79] Prisoners were allowed to talk while they worked, but the OD also kept a strict eye on them to make sure there was no contact with prisoners from the other parts of the camp. Prisoners needed permission to go to the toilet.[80] After work and after the showers (for those who worked on the batteries), there was bread to eat in the criminal barracks.[81]

MEETING PEOPLE IN WESTERBORK

Otto Frank remembers that everyday life in Westerbork was made easier, particularly for the children, because they were able to make contact with other people.[82] The Frank family ran into all sorts of acquaintances in Westerbork, including people from their own area and classmates of the children. Bram Asscher, who was in the same class as Margot Frank at the Jewish Lyceum, wrote to his mother from Westerbork on 25 August 1944: "Mum, did you know that Margot was here, that friend of Trees? You must remember her. She's here with her parents and her sister in the S, it's a really pity!"[83] Bram was in Westerbork together with his brother Jeannot. They both survived the camps and regularly wrote letters to their mother and stepfather. Their mother, Stephanie Fischer, remarried a non-Jewish man after the death of her first husband (Bram's father) and therefore had a *Sperre* as a result of that marriage. Her sons, however, did not get one. In the letter, Bram thanks his mother for the fine toothbrush and other things.

Bram himself was in the "free" part of the camp, and was allowed to write one letter or two postcards once a fortnight

Bram Asscher and Trees Lek, shortly after the war.

and to receive parcels. The group of eight from the Annex did not have these privileges because they were criminal cases, and without contacts inside or outside the camp they were unable to do anything to change their situation. Because of the stricter

The letter that Bram Asscher wrote to his mother on 25 August 1944.

measures introduced from the beginning of August, they were not able to inform anyone about their situation, and were thus unable to have items like food parcels sent. (Prisoners regularly received parcels in order to supplement the menu, which was always the same.) Nor could the Annex group get anyone to change their status as criminal cases. The correspondence doesn't reveal whether Bram ever saw or even spoke to Margot himself, as she was in a separate part of the camp.

Another pupil from Margot's school, Bloeme Emden, who arrived in the camp as a criminal case in August 1944 just after the Frank family, also remembers that she recognized them as soon as she arrived. They were standing by the fence looking at the other new arrivals coming into the camp:

> The people standing at the gate were looking to see who had arrived included the Frank family with the two children who we recognized immediately, as they did me. We said hello to each other, and were rather sad that we were meeting in this situation. Then you were taken away. You couldn't do anything about it. I did come across them regularly because we'd been in the same class. We'd been at the same school. You […] became a number.[84]

There is another witness statement by Vera Cohn about the Frank family in Westerbork. Cohn worked at the camp's registration office. In an interview with the journalist Harold Berman in 1956, she remembered that when she saw Otto Frank, she was struck by his calm demeanor as well as that of his family.

> Mr. Frank was a handsome man, courteous and dignified. He stood before me with his head up and answered my routine questions calmly […]. None of the family looked

desperate at all […]. They stood around my table quietly and controlled. No matter how bitter and frightened he felt, Mr. Frank refused to surrender his dignity and his wife and daughters followed his example.[85]

This is referred to in Carol Ann Lee's biographies of Anne and Otto to give an impression of the mood and attitude of the Frank family in Westerbork, but there are problems in several respects. Cohn did not know the family before she registered them, and remembered the encounter in great detail a long time later. Although it's certainly possible that this really was the impression the Frank family gave when she registered them, we also have to take into account the possibility that she confused different people and added the almost stereotypical characterization of a family who retained their "human dignity" despite all the "feelings of bitterness and fear" later on. After all, the question remains whether Cohn could really remember the Frank family, whom she didn't know and never met again, amongst the many thousands of people that passed by her desk.

Other statements by witnesses about the Frank family vary a great deal. Ronnie van Cleef remembered many years later that the Frank family seemed lost and bewildered in the chaotic conditions of the criminal barracks. They kept themselves to themselves, and Anne Frank clung onto her father's arm.[86]

In contrast, there are the statements made by Vera Cohn and Rosa de Winter-Levy to the German journalist Ernst Schnabel, who systematically collected testimonies about Anne Frank for the first time in the 1950s, as mentioned above. De Winter-Levy had been arrested together with her husband and her daughter Judik at the place where they had been in hiding near Arnhem, and they were then taken to Westerbork just before the group of eight arrived from the Annex. De Winter-Levy only became a close friend of Edith Frank in Auschwitz, but remembers that she had already noticed the family in Westerbork. She saw Anne as a potential friend for her own daughter Judik and therefore kept a close eye on them. She told Schnabel about the impression the family made on her. De Winter-Levy said that Edith Frank had walked round Westerbork "quietly and looked almost paralyzed". Margot was also very quiet, but Edith seemed almost mute: "She didn't say anything while she was working and in the evening she was always doing the washing. The water was dirty and there was no soap but she still had to keep on washing all the time. Anne's father was also quiet, but it was a more encouraging quietness [...]."[87] De Winter-Levy particularly emphasized the contrast with Anne, who she remembers walking round Westerbork "happy and free", making many contacts with other people, as well as spending a lot of time with Peter van Pels:

> I saw Anne Frank and Peter van Daan [Peter van Pels] every day in Westerbork. They were always together and often said to my husband: "Just look at those two beautiful young people…". Anne was beautiful in Westerbork, so radiant it even had an impact on Peter. At first, she was very pale, but her gentle and expressive face was so attractive that Judik did not dare to contact her at first. Perhaps I shouldn't really say that Anne's eyes shone. But they did shine, you know? And she was so free in all her movements and how she looked that I often wondered whether she was really happy here. She was happy in Westerbork even though that's almost impossible to understand because it was very difficult in the camp.[88]

It's striking how much this interpretation differs from that of many of the other witnesses. The image suggested of Anne and Peter as "radiant" and probably in love raises the question of whether this is in fact an interpretation which she projected onto her memories retrospectively, as was probably the case with the above-mentioned Vera Cohn. The account given by De Winter-Levy is different from that of Cohn because it was established that she had built up a close relationship with Edith Frank and her daughters, and had written about the Frank family in her account of Auschwitz long before Anne Frank's story became well known after the publication of *The Annex*.[89]

After the war, Otto Frank himself did not speak much about Westerbork, but did remember that arriving in the camp had been a relief for his daughter in some ways. "We all had to work in the camp, but in the evenings we were free and we could be together. For the children particularly, it was a sort of relief to no longer be locked up and to be able to talk to other people".[90] Young people in Westerbork could walk between the barracks in the evening to meet each other and chat. It was summer when they first arrived and the weather was fine, and even in the criminal barracks, where prisoners had no access to the concerts and the entertainment that were organized in the other part of the camp, they tried to amuse themselves to some extent. In an interview in 1970, Otto Frank recalled that one evening a young Jewish woman sang Yiddish songs.[91] Rose de Lima-Van Gelder also remembered that she sang songs in the criminal barracks, together with the Van Pels and Frank families.[92] Others who were in the criminal barracks at the same time also emphasized the importance of music. For example, Frieda Brommet (better known by her married name, Frieda Menco) remembered that she took part in a cabaret in the criminal barracks. She said how

Frieda Brommet, in about 1940.

this entertainment contributed to temporarily reducing the fear of deportation amongst the younger prisoners: "I don't know whether […] my father had any thoughts about this. I think that when he saw me leaping around in Westerbork with all those boys, joining in a sort of cabaret, not hungry anymore […]. I think he probably thought: 'Well, let her be. […] We're lucky it's still possible.'"[93]

The well-known violinist Benny Behr, who was in the criminal barracks with the Frank family from 1 August 1944, also remembers that he played the violin for the prisoners there. In an interview with Willy Lindwer, he explained: "Of course I played some cheerful school songs for the children, but the older people sometimes wanted to hear some classical music. Amongst other things, I played some pieces by Kreisler and that's how I tried to entertain people". He also emphasized that the music served to reduce the constant fear of deportation:

Westerbork could best be characterized by a "sense of defeatism", but also by "hopeful expectation". You could

Benny Behr plays the violin for the children in Westerbork.

see this on the faces of the people who were on the list to be transported. And you could see it on the faces of the people who had been exempted from transport, sometimes temporarily. They might be smiling, while others would be closer to tears. We were all terribly afraid, especially of the transports which left on Tuesday evening.[94]

Apart from this, the picture of the time that the group of eight from the Annex spent in Westerbork is unclear. There are hardly any witness statements about the Van Pels family or Fritz Pfeffer. Even the witnesses who had memories of the Frank family have little to say about the others. This lack of memories is related to the relatively short time that the group were in Westerbork, and more generally with the fact that in the criminal barracks the "camp community" developed much less strongly than in the other part of Westerbork.[95]

The prisoners, particularly the criminal cases, constantly had to consider the fact that they would be transported to the east at some point. Jules Schelvis – who was not himself a criminal case and had already been taken from Westerbork to Sobibor in 1943 – called this "the fear of the unknown".[96] How afraid were the group from the Annex of their possible deportation? It is difficult to say. Rose de Liema-van Gelder remembers a discussion in which everyone was talking over each other, and Otto Frank particularly expressed an optimism about what was happening in the war. According to De Liema, he was counting on the fact that the liberation would come soon:

> Well, Otto Frank would usually say: "Oh, it'll be over soon, it can't take much longer." But I would say: "How can we remain here?" We just hoped that it would all be over soon. But we never said anything like: "Now they're sending us to a different camp, or this or that, or not at all". Suddenly, someone would turn up and say, "You'll be on the transport tomorrow, get all your things ready", and you'd have to pack your cases. But we never spoke about the danger of death in Westerbork.[97]

However, Otto Frank would later write that although he had not wanted to lose courage, he certainly was extremely frightened of deportation:

> The older people were very afraid of being deported to the infamous extermination camps [...]. Unfortunately, this happened on 3 September. During that terrible transport – three days in locked cattle trucks – I was

100

with my family for the last time. We all tried to be as brave as possible and not to give up. After arriving in Auschwitz-Birkenau I was separated from my family.[98]

Whether Otto Frank was already aware of the extermination camps, or whether it was formulated in this way with hindsight, is a question which will be dealt with in more detail below. But like the others, he would have been afraid of what would happen to him and his family in the camps.

This was to be the last big deportation transport from Westerbork to Auschwitz. At that point, there were about 4,000 prisoners in Westerbork, at least 1,000 of whom were held in the overcrowded criminal barracks.[99] The previous transport to Auschwitz had taken place on 19 May 1944, and the criminal barracks had gradually filled up during those three months.[100] The prisoners hoped and expected that there would be no further transports and that it would not be long until they were liberated.[101]

At the beginning of September, Gemmeker received orders from Berlin to send the majority of the prisoners in the camp to either Auschwitz, Theresienstadt or Bergen-Belsen.[102] During this period, large numbers of prisoners were sent to Auschwitz from every direction, to be sent on to other camps for slave labor.[103] This was the last transport from the Netherlands to Auschwitz. Virtually all the prisoners from the criminal barracks went on it and afterwards the barracks was closed down.[104] Therefore, the group of eight from the Annex had to join the next transport. After staying in Westerbork for twenty-six days, they went on the transport of 3 September 1944.

That transport was probably a hastily improvised reaction to the rapid advance of the Allied army. The day before, British and

American troops had entered Belgium on several fronts, and this raised the expectation that the Netherlands would soon be liberated. On Tuesday 5 September, which was described in the

Transport list of 3 September 1944 with the names of the Frank family.

history books as "Mad Tuesday", rumors that the Allied forces were on their way led to a spontaneous festive spirit breaking out amongst the population everywhere in the Netherlands;

Transport list of 3 September 1944 with the names of the Van Pels family and Fritz Pfeffer.

103

German occupying forces and Dutch collaborators started to panic, and many decided to flee. Although there is no hard evidence that the transport of 3 September was the direct consequence of this mood of panic, it was striking that this was the only transport from Westerbork to leave on a Sunday, whereas all the other transports had left on a Tuesday (especially since Sunday was a day when in principle there should have been no work). It is therefore a clear indication that the authorities were in a hurry to clear the camp and that the transport took place earlier than planned for that reason.[105]

The transport list of 3 September 1944 contained the names of 1,019 people.[106] It comprised different categories of prisoners: 149 "normal" prisoners, 675 *Häftlinge* (criminal cases) and 195 *Schutzhäftlinge* (protective custody prisoners).[107] The last group consisted of mixed marriages or half-Jewish people who were suspected of a crime. The *Schutzhaft* regulation enabled the German police to detain suspects indefinitely without a judicial decision, including those who were suspected of being in the Resistance or had an "anti-German" attitude. It also allowed them to deport "half-Jews and mixed marriages" to one of the camps without any sort of trial. Despite their different status, the *Schutzhäftlinge* in Westerbork were held in the criminal barracks together with the punishment cases, but they were probably taken to Auschwitz in a different wagon.[108]

The evening before the transport, someone from the OD read out the list of names in the criminal barracks. Everyone had to respond when his or her name was called. Hans Goudsmit, who was also there at that time, wrote to his wife in a letter that he smuggled out: "Saturday evening, 10 o'clock, 2/9, my dearly beloved darlings. At last I have a minute to let you know that my train will leave tomorrow to the unknown."[109] The list of

Johan (Hans) Goudsmit, in about 1920.

names was long and reading it out took quite a while. Henriëtte Sachs, who was also on this list, said in an interview that she spent the whole night of 2–3 September awake after hearing her name, waiting for the transport together with the others. She remembered that she and a few of the others were "sitting together feeling down without saying a word", while others were responding emotionally to the news that they were to be taken to the east: "Some were in complete panic, some just let it go over their heads and yes, some just sat and cried."[110]

Early on Sunday morning, the criminal cases were given the jute bag containing their clothes and were told to hand in their overalls and clogs. They walked in long lines from the criminal barracks to the train, which was ready to depart. The other prisoners in the camp had to stay in their barracks. About 70–75 prisoners were put in each wagon. Each wagon contained a barrel of water and a toilet barrel, as shown in the Westerbork film.[111]

The train consisted of sixteen wagons for the prisoners and five wagons for the sick.[112] At the front and the back there were

The sign on the train which traveled back and forth from Westerbork to Auschwitz. It also said that no wagons may remain behind in Auschwitz and that the whole train must return to Westerbork.

generally ordinary passenger carriages for the German guards, as shown in the Westerbork film.[113] As for all the trains leaving from Westerbork, the Bremer *Polizeibataillon* 105, which was part of the *Ordnungspolizei* (Order Police), was in charge of the transport and of guarding the prisoners. A leader and a group of fifteen heavily armed men guarded the train;[114] Jewish prisoners were also appointed to be responsible for certain tasks.

The transport list of 3 September 1944 mentions that there was a *Wagenleiter* (wagon leader) and *Sanitäter* (nurse) for every wagon. The *Zugführer* (train leader) and his deputy were in wagon 3.[115] The wagon leader had to pass on the exact number of prisoners with the accompanying wagon number to the train leader, who then had to pass it on to the guards. There were two doctors for the five wagons for the sick.[116] According to the witness statement of Janny Hamburger-Bolle (later Moffie-Bolle)[117] to the NRK, nurses were appointed for the wagons for the sick. They wore a Red Cross armband and had a small case with bandages.[118]

Although the deportations from Westerbork were significantly remembered for the image of the cattle wagons, approximately 60 per cent of them took place in passenger carriages. The first two transports from Westerbork were carried out in freight wagons, but up to March 1943, most of the Jewish prisoners were taken to the camps in the eastern parts of the German Empire in ordinary trains. These were usually third-class carriages which were often in poor condition. From mid-1943, the occupying forces prohibited the use of passenger carriages for deportations to Auschwitz and Sobibor, and the prisoners were once again transported in cattle wagons and freight wagons, with an average of fifty to sixty people per wagon.[119]

Once it had been accurately determined how many people there were in the wagons, the members of the OD closed and barred them. The train left at about eleven in the morning,[120] traveling via Zwolle and Oldenzaal to the German border.[121] Once at the border, the Dutch locomotive was uncoupled from its engine driver and stoker and replaced by a locomotive of the Deutsche Reichsbahn, which was standing ready.[122] From there, the transport made a big detour to Bremen, Hamburg and then further to the east towards Berlin, Breslau and Katowice, before eventually reaching Auschwitz.[123] Rachel Frankfoorder, a survivor of the camp, related how a man of Polish origin followed the route through the barred window and recognized Katowice, where he had once lived.[124]

The journey took between thirty-six and forty-four hours.[125] The people on board tried to pass the time to distract themselves. Some were lost in their own thoughts or would try and console their loved ones; others tried to protect themselves against the aggressive behavior of another prisoner in the

A detail from Lenie de Jong-van Naarden's identity card.

overcrowded wagons.[126] There were no windows, only a barred grille or hole for ventilation, and you could see the rails through the gaps between the planks. The prisoners stood, sat and slept in close contact. The toilet barrel stood uncovered in a corner and the stench was unbearable. Henriëtte van Bekkum-Sachs, a survivor of the camps, said that the lack of privacy meant that you constantly had to change your boundaries.[127] Lenie de Jong-van Naarden, who was in the same wagon as the Frank family, remembers that the bucket soon overflowed, but that a few young men managed to empty it through a gap between the doors.[128] Another barrel contained their drinking water. According to the eyewitnesses, this was not filled up and the prisoners were very thirsty.[129]

Sometimes the prisoners were given food for the three-day journey, and in some cases they were even able to take some of their own food.[130] According to Rosa de Winter-Levy, the doors opened somewhere in Germany, and they were given some bread and jam.[131] Many witnesses said that the train often stopped. According to some, the doors remained barred throughout the journey;[132] others remember German soldiers or guards who opened the doors when the train stopped and took all their valuables such as money, jewelry and fountain pens.[133]

Some people escaped, and a few people even managed to escape from the train in which Anne and her family traveled.[134] At least seven of these escaped while they were still in Dutch territory. Three of the prisoners had smuggled tools from the sawmill at Westerbork in their socks; immediately after they left, they started to bore a hole in the back door of the wagon until there was enough room to use the saw and make a larger hole. They then jumped from the moving train through the hole and managed to go into hiding.[135] After the train arrived in Auschwitz-Birkenau, the wagon leader, Salomon Tas, a police officer who was in a mixed marriage, had to justify this escape. According to Rica Rozenthal, who had arrived with the same deportation train, he was "beaten very severely".[136] Tas would survive Auschwitz. Another witness said that the prisoners were less inclined to escape because of the appointment of a wagon leader. In his wagon, the wagon leader had even spoken to them: "I just happen to be the Waggonführer, so don't try to escape because it'll cost me my life."[137]

As well as the train leader and wagon leader, doctors were appointed for every transport.[138] For the 3 September 1944 journey, these were Samuel Kropveld and Abraham Jacobson. There are no testimonies from these particular doctors, but statements by doctors on other deportation trains can give us an idea of the work they had to do.[139] For example, the Amsterdam doctor Joel van der Kous was the train doctor for the deportation of 14 September 1943. When the train arrived, he was asked by the SS officer carrying out the selection about any illnesses there might have been in Westerbork.[140] Another Jewish doctor who was deported to Auschwitz in 1943 declared after the war that he had "been called to another wagon a few times where people had become ill. I was appointed to be the train doctor with three other colleagues and wore an armband to signify this; but obviously the whole thing was totally meaningless."[141] Leo Maurits Muller, the leader of a wagon for the sick to Birkenau, never saw any of the people he traveled with again.[142]

The seriously ill were put in separate wagons with Jewish medical supervision. Janny Hamburger-Bolle, a Jewish trainee nurse who had been appointed in Westerbork to look after the sick, was told by a colleague that she shouldn't bother as the sick would certainly be gassed when they arrived in Auschwitz, together with those who looked after them: "It was the first time I'd heard about people being gassed. I was shocked. 'Gassed', it sounded so unreal, but it really scared me." She decided to jump out of the wagon to which she had been allocated, took off her Red Cross armband and joined her husband Max Hamburger

Janny Bolle, a trainee nurse in the Nederlands Israëlitisch Ziekenhuis (NIZ), in 1942.

in another wagon. During the trip, she distributed the contents of her medical kit amongst her fellow travelers. (After the trains had set off, there were no further checks to see that people were in the correct wagons.)[143]

It's hardly possible to describe the desperate mood in the crowded wagons.[144] Lenie de Jong-van Naarden has the following memories of the transport from Westerbork to Auschwitz:

> That was the only time that I cried, when our number was called out and our names, and that we had to get ready to be transported. We'd already heard this. Where would we be going? No one knew exactly. But you had to get ready for this to be the end of your life. By chance, we found ourselves together with the Frank family in the cattle truck. There were about seventy people in the carriage with a pail to do your business in. That was terrible. It was a dark wagon and someone had hung up a tin with a candle in it from the ceiling so that there was some light […]. It's so difficult to put into words what was happening in the wagon that was moving at a huge speed […]. People had turned into animals, crowded together. They couldn't get up and they couldn't sit down either.[145]

De Jong-van Naarden also remembers a detail about the Frank family. In one interview, she describes how Edith Frank had smuggled her work overalls onto the transport and set to work removing the red shoulder pad that had identified her as a criminal case in Westerbork, imagining that a distinction might also be made in Auschwitz between criminal cases and "ordinary prisoners". That was how she wanted to make sure that she would not be identified as a criminal case.[146]

The testimonies of this transport from Westerbork to Auschwitz also shed light on the expectations the Jewish prisoners from Westerbork had about Auschwitz and the other camps in the east. Many of the Jews who were in Westerbork didn't know exactly where they were going, let alone what was awaiting them.[147] All they did know was that it would be terrible. The remark quoted above by Otto Frank, in which he indicates that when he was in Westerbork he was afraid of the "extermination camps", suggests that he already knew at that point what was happening in occupied Poland.[148] Janny Brilleslijper and Sonja Wagenaar-van Dam – the latter being one of the people who managed to escape from the deportation train of 3 September 1944 – stated in interviews that they had a fairly realistic idea of camps such as Auschwitz.[149] According to Janny Brilleslijper, "We knew that Auschwitz was a *Vernichtungslager* [extermination camp]. So we knew what to expect".[150] In an interview with Sonja Wagenaar-van Dam, she remembered: "We knew that we were all going to Auschwitz, that much we knew. They

Sonja Wagenaar-van Dam in about 1940.

told us that we were going to a work camp, but they were extermination camps." She couldn't believe that she would really be sent to a work camp because there had been no news at all from those who had been deported earlier.[151]

The question whether Otto Frank and the women quoted above actually knew this in 1944 or whether they unconsciously remembered it retrospectively is difficult to answer. Moreover, it touches on a broader historical debate about the knowledge, rumor and suspicions of the mass murder of Jews. In a study published in 2012 titled *Wij weten niets van hun lot. Gewone Nederlanders en de Holocaust* ("We know nothing about their fate: Ordinary Dutch people and the Holocaust"), the historian Bart van der Boom states, on the basis of a study of witness diaries, that while both Jewish and non-Jewish Dutch people had admittedly heard many rumors about what was happening in the camps, there was a lack of specific "knowledge". The expectations differed from person to person, and although many Jews imagined they would not survive the camps, very few people had a specific idea about what was actually happening there, namely mechanized mass murder.[152]

Van der Boom's book was initially well received, but it was also fiercely criticized not long after its publication.[153] Historians such as Jaap Cohen, Remco Ensel, Evelien Gans and Guus Meershoek argued that Van der Boom's definition of "knowledge" about the Holocaust was too limited to make his point. His critics emphasize that information about the Holocaust was widespread in the illegal press, on British radio and through other channels. For example, Meershoek states that leading members of the Resistance such as Koos Vorrink and Henk van Randwijk referred to "mass murder" at an early stage, and that this term is often found in people's diaries.[154]

113

The question of what people knew about the mass murder in the camps proves to be difficult to answer and depends on the definition of "knowledge" and "know" that is used. For example, the literature about the dissemination of this knowledge shows that detailed information about the first stage of the genocide – the mass executions by *Einsatzgruppen* in Eastern Europe – had been spread both in Germany and outside by countless letters from German soldiers on the front.[155] However, the Nazi regime adopted a much stricter policy of secrecy with regards to the extermination camps. That policy did not prevent all sorts of stories and descriptions from being leaked. For example, by the end of the war the Allies were receiving increasingly detailed reports of what was happening from prisoners who had escaped, and British and American newspapers also regularly reported on the camps. But the policy of German secrecy did mean that this information was largely spread by imprecise rumors. And so the knowledge of the extermination camps and the methods used there remained fragmented. This left room for doubt and uncertainty, and the repression of information that simply seemed to be unimaginable.[156]

At the moment that they were arrested, the group of eight from the Annex also appear to have assumed that Jews might be murdered after they were deported.[157] This is shown in the first instance in Anne Frank's diary, when she wrote on 3 February 1944 that they all considered it to be a "fact" that "millions and millions" of people were being murdered and gassed in Poland and Russia.[158] In the rewritten version of her diary, retrospectively dated 9 October 1942, but actually written after 20 May 1944, she states: "If it's so bad in Holland, what will life be like in the faraway barbaric regions where they are being sent? We assume that most people will be murdered. The English radio talks about people being gassed; perhaps that's the quickest way to die."[159]

These somber and, as it turned out, fairly realistic expectations could in any case be partly explained by their personal experiences. As discussed briefly in Chapter 1, the group had experienced the terror of the Nazi regime at close quarters as Jews who had fled Germany in the 1930s. In November 1938, Edith Frank's older brother Julius had been locked up in the Sachsenhausen camp, though he was released a few weeks later on the condition that he would emigrate as quickly as possible. The father of Hermann van Pels had also been arrested in Osnabrück, where he lived in November 1938.[160] As described above, Fritz Pfeffer had personally experienced the November pogrom in Berlin, and had seen how the synagogue in his own street had been destroyed and how thousands of other people in the city had been arrested.[161]

In addition, the big razzias in February and June 1941 played an important role in their growing realization that most Jews would not survive being deported. The first razzias took place on 22 and 23 February 1941, following some fights between Dutch Nazis and Jewish boys. When a patrolman of the *Grünepolizei* was sprayed with ammonia during one of these riots in the Koco ice cream parlor on the Van Woustraat, run by two German Jewish refugees, the German occupying forces responded by arresting 427 Jewish men on and around the Waterlooplein. Most of the men in this group were sent to the camp in Mauthausen and only two of them survived the war. This razzia directly gave rise to the February strike which started on 25 and 26 February 1941 on the initiative of the Amsterdam division of the Dutch Communist Party. Workers, shop assistants and civil servants stopped work in Amsterdam (and shortly afterwards

Logo of the Koco ice cream parlor, 1939. The site later became the center of the razzias in Amsterdam and the February strike.

in Haarlem, Utrecht, the Zaan region, Velsen and Hilversum) to protest against the increasing anti-Jewish terror. The German occupying forces were completely surprised by this sudden protest and responded with force. About 200 people who were striking were arrested in Amsterdam and mistreated, especially the civil servants who had gone on strike, as well as a number of arbitrarily arrested communists and Jews. Another hundred people who had gone on strike were also arrested up to the beginning of April.[162]

A second large razzia occurred on 11 June 1941, this time in Amsterdam South, in response to a bombing carried out by a Dutch Resistance group. To avoid a repetition of the February strike, the chief of the Amsterdam *Sicherheitspolizei*, Willy Lages, decided not to organize a large-scale street razzia but to have a large group of Jewish men arrested by the Dutch police at home, with the support of the German *Ordnungspolizei*. These were mainly former inhabitants of the Jewish Working Village at Nieuwesluis in the Wieringermeer polder, who had been forced to move to Amsterdam in March. A number of Jewish men were also arrested that evening on the Merwedeplein, watched by the shocked residents of the district, including the Frank family. When it became clear that many of the men who had been selected were not at home, scores of Jewish boys

116

On 22 and 23 February 1941, 427 Jewish men were arrested at random near the Waterlooplein in Amsterdam.

were then arrested in the street, in cafés and at sports clubs. Altogether, more than 300 young men were arrested in Amsterdam South that evening. Most of them ended up in Mauthausen via the camp in Schoorl.[163]

This time the Amsterdam population reacted differently and there were no large-scale protests. Many people had been surprised by the severity of the way in which the February strike had been dealt with and were very scared. Their fears became even greater during the new razzia on 11 June. Rian Verhoeven, who wrote a book about the Merwedeplein, described "a shadow" falling over the district. The whole square was affected by the fear and uncertainty about the fate of the boys in the

117

Razzias on the Jonas Daniël Meijerplein in Amsterdam,
22–23 February 1941.

district who had been taken away. In addition, after only a few days, a large number of death notices arrived for the families that had been left behind – often indicating that someone had been "shot dead trying to flee" – which indicated that the Jewish men who had been arrested were being murdered in the camp in Mauthausen on a large scale.[164]

The Frank family was greatly affected by this razzia that had taken place in their own neighborhood. All sorts of neighbors and acquaintances had been arrested, including Karl Lewkowitz, the son of one of Otto Frank's good friends.[165] Otto Frank later described how much this razzia had affected him: "It included some of my friends, young people who were being taken away. We heard about their deaths after eight days. So you definitely knew that these people were being murdered."[166]

The Röttgen family in about 1940. The girl on the right is probably Auguste, and the girl standing to the right of her mother is Lotte.

119

Fritz Pfeffer and the Van Pels family must also have experienced the consequences of the razzia at close quarters. Auguste van Pels's family in particular were keenly aware of the Nazi's intentions, with Auguste's youngest sister Lotte lost to the Nazi genocide before Auguste had even gone into hiding.

Lotte had been one of a group of more than 900 Jews in the Düsseldorf and Wuppertal region who had been deported to the city of Minsk in Belarus on 10 November 1941. She had lived in Düsseldorf with her husband Max Gutmann. On the morning of their deportation, they had to register at the Düsseldorf-Dehrendorf freight station before boarding a long freight train for Essen and Wuppertal, where the train picked up more Jews before continuing on to Minsk.[167]

This transport marked a crucial transition in the persecution of the Jews by the Nazis. As discussed in more detail in Chapter 3, historians suspect that Hitler's and Himmler's decision to murder all the European Jews in a systematic way was made in October 1941. In the months before this, the German offensive on the Eastern Front had acquired the character of a war of extermination. While the *Einsatzgruppen* murdered Jewish men, women and children on a massive scale behind the lines of the Eastern Front in Russia and the Baltic states, top SS officers became convinced that the increasingly empty ghettos in cities such as Riga and Minsk were suitable places to take Jews from the German Empire, so that they could then be murdered there. In the winter of 1941–2, the Nazis deported thousands of Jews from Germany, Austria and the Protectorate of Bohemia and Moravia to Minsk. Many of them were shot dead immediately after they arrived and only ten of them survived the war.[168]

One surviving report of this transport, drawn up by *Hauptmann der schutzpolizei* Wilhelm Meurin, gives an impression of the terrible conditions of the transport with which Lotte and Max were taken to Minsk. With icy cynicism, Meurin reported that the extreme temperatures of minus 18 degrees and the lack of drinking water had seriously weakened the men and women who were deported:

> At that time the Jews were very weak because the train had not moved for quite a while and was not heated. From the moment we entered Russian territory there was no further possibility to take any water on board. The water there has to be boiled first and it was not possible to have water boiled for almost 1,000 people. I did not want diarrhea or typhoid fever to break out during the journey.[169]

Once they arrived in Minsk, Meurin reported that a third of the deported men and women could hardly walk, but the Latvian police assisting them, who had "recent experiences of Russian Jews" and "showed an appropriate attitude which clearly speeded up things", chased everyone into the ghetto.[170] It is not known whether Lotte or Max Gutmann were murdered immediately after arriving, died as a result of the extremely bad conditions, or were killed in the ghetto during one of the mass executions, when tens of thousands of Jews from Minsk were once again shot dead in February and March 1942.[171]

Neither is it known exactly what Auguste knew about the fate of her sister and brother-in-law in 1942. It is quite possible that in some way she had heard that Max and Lotte had been arrested and transported in Düsseldorf; she certainly had to consider the possibility that they had not survived, but there are no sources to confirm this. The question of what conclusions she might have drawn once she arrived in Westerbork herself can only be guessed at. But the personal experiences of the Nazi regime of the eight who had been in hiding in the Annex will certainly have had a strong influence on their expectations of the camps. On the basis of the available sources, it is not possible to determine that they really "knew" what awaited them in occupied Poland, but it is clear that they were full of foreboding. Like the other Jews in Westerbork, they probably swung back and forth between hope and despair and were faced with great fear, doubt and uncertainty at the moment they were deported to Auschwitz.[172]

CHAPTER THREE

"Being there was like living in hell"

Auschwitz

AUSCHWITZ AND THE GENOCIDE OF THE EUROPEAN JEWS

The train arrived in Auschwitz-Birkenau on the night of 5–6 September 1944, after the prisoners had been crowded together in the wagons for three days and two nights.[1] This transport was one of the three from the Netherlands which arrived on the *Rampe* – a platform in the middle of the Auschwitz-Birkenau camp.[2] Because of the central role of Auschwitz in the mass murder of the European Jews, and because all eight people from the Annex were there for a while, we shall examine this camp in great detail.[3] To describe their experiences in the camp accurately, it is important to consider the development and organization of the camp system that is often referred to as "Auschwitz", but which actually comprised several camps a few miles apart. Furthermore, in order to gain an accurate picture of the circumstances in which they arrived, it is important to examine a number of developments in history of the Holocaust.

From the summer of 1942, when the Frank family went into hiding, the persecution of the Jews was increasingly characterized by mass murder and genocide, or in the terminology used by the Nazis, *die Endlösung* (the final solution). The Nazis started *die Endlösung* in the spring of 1942 with the systematic and large-scale deportation of Jews from Germany and

From left to right: Richard Baer, Josef Mengele and Rudolf Höss, 1944.

from the occupied territories to extermination camps. Over time, Auschwitz grew to become the largest German concentration and extermination camp complex. In November 1943, the Auschwitz complex was so extensive that it was organizationally divided into three camps: Auschwitz I (the base camp, or *Stammlager*), Auschwitz II (Auschwitz-Birkenau) and Auschwitz III. The latter consisted of the Monowitz work camp at the site of IG Farben, and more than forty smaller camps and subcamps that belonged to other industrial companies, and most of which were in a radius of 10 kilometers from Auschwitz.[4] During the course of the war, in addition to acting as an extermination camp, Auschwitz I and II increasingly functioned as a collection point for prisoners who were subsequently sent to the subcamps of Auschwitz III as slave labor.[5]

Like most of the other concentration camps, the whole of the Auschwitz complex fell directly under the SS, first under the *Inspektion der Konzentrationslager*, and from March 1942 under the *Wirtschafts-Verwaltungshauptamt* (WVHA), the SS organization which was responsible for the management and exploitation of concentration camps under the command of *SS-Obergruppenführer* Oswald Pohl. The SS staff – including the commandant, officers, doctors and guards – were responsible for these elements. Violence, executions, abuse, brutality, corruption and self-enrichment were rife. Auschwitz has now become synonymous with the Nazi genocide of the Jews in Europe.[6]

When the group from the Annex arrived, *SS-Sturmbannführer* Richard Baer was the camp commandant. He had replaced the site's first commandant, *SS-Hauptsturmführer* Rudolf Höss, in July 1944, under whose command Auschwitz had developed to become one of the centers of the mass murder of European Jews. Höss left Auschwitz in November 1943 to work for the WVHA in Berlin as the head of Amtsgruppe D1, but returned in May 1944 to run Operation Höss: the mass murder of 430,000 Hungarian Jews.[7]

The complete absence of any moral boundaries in this camp is illustrated by the use of prisoners of the Auschwitz complex in medical experiments. In Auschwitz-Birkenau, the camp doctor, Josef Mengele, ran a research program financed by the German scientific organization *Deutsche Forschungsgemeinschaft*, using human guinea pigs such as monozygotic twins and people with dwarfism. He made use of a number of different medical experts amongst the prisoners to assist him in this. They often performed extremely cruel experiments in which prisoners were given poisonous injections or were deliberately infected with contagious fatal diseases in order to analyze the course of the disease. Mengele's most notorious research involved twins, wherein they would be sewn together, have their eyes injected with liquids, and be subjected to all sorts of other horrific experiments.

However, Mengele was not the only doctor who carried out experiments on people in Auschwitz. Johann Paul Kremer, who had originally gone to Auschwitz for the medical treatment of SS officers, experimented on starving prisoners who were first interviewed about their health and then murdered with a fatal injection and analyzed. Carl Clauberg, who also started his research in Auschwitz-Birkenau, had access to women in block 10 of the *Stammlager* Auschwitz and sterilized them with experimental medicines.[8]

Auschwitz I was established in a former Polish military barracks near the town of Oświęcim (known as "Auschwitz" in German). The cynical text "Arbeit macht frei" ("work means freedom") on the large gateway gave the impression that it was a work camp.[9] The *Reichsführer-SS* Heinrich Himmler had looked for suitable sites in all the border areas to establish concentration camps for political opponents. On 27 April 1940, he decided that a concentration camp should be established in Auschwitz, initially to incarcerate political prisoners from Upper Silesia in southern Poland.[10] Himmler ordered the above-mentioned *SS-Hauptsturmführer* Rudolf Höss to implement this as the camp commandant. The first transport of Polish prisoners arrived on 14 June 1940. This was followed by large groups, almost all of whom were used for the rebuilding of the camp, adding an extra floor to the existing barracks.[11]

At first, it was mainly Polish prisoners of war and political prisoners from Germany who were sent to the camp. After the German attack on the Soviet Union on 22 June 1941, they were joined by tens of thousands of Russian prisoners of

126

The gates of Auschwitz I, with the text "Arbeit macht frei".
Photograph taken after the war.

war. Just as in other concentration camps, Auschwitz made
use of a system in which prisoners were distinguished from
each other by different types of triangles sewn onto the camp
clothes: political prisoners, who were mainly Poles, wore a red
triangle; *Berufsverbrecher* (habitual offenders) wore a green
triangle; *Asoziale*, a category which applied for various groups

of prisoners (for example, unemployed people who had been arrested, prostitutes, Sinti and Roma) wore a black triangle; Jehovah's Witnesses were given a purple triangle; and homosexuals wore a pink triangle. Jews, who became the large majority in Auschwitz later on in the war, were initially given an upside-down red triangle and yellow triangle which together formed a Star of David. Later, a rectangular yellow line was added to this. After 1944, Jewish prisoners from transit camps were no longer given triangles.[12]

The attack on the Soviet Union marked an important turning point in the genocide of the Jews and other minorities. Operation Barbarossa was run as a total war of extermination. The army was supported in this by both *Einsatzgruppen* of the SS and special police battalions who had to eliminate the enemies of the Third Reich behind the front lines.[13] In the instructions they were given, Bolshevism and Judaism were presented as two fundamentally interlinked entities, legitimizing this first stage in the Jewish genocide. The SS and the police were ordered to execute Russian Jews with jobs "in the party or for the state" and to promote pogroms. By the end of 1941, half a million Jewish men, women and children, as well as non-Jewish Soviet citizens, had been murdered in these mass executions.[14]

The first experiments with the extremely toxic prussic acid gas Zyklon B were carried out in Auschwitz I in August 1941. Large groups of Russian prisoners of war were murdered with this for the first time on about 5 September 1941.[15] (There is some disagreement amongst historians about whether the gassing of the Russian prisoners of war in 1941 should be seen as a dress rehearsal for the genocide of European Jews.)

The historian Franciszek Piper considers that the gassing of Russian prisoners of war shows that Himmler already saw

Auschwitz playing a central role in his plan to exterminate the European Jews.[16] However, historians such as Christopher Browning, Mark Mazower, Yitzhak Arad and Nikolaus Wachsmann convincingly demonstrate that the Holocaust was not a premeditated plan. They argue that the use of Zyklon B in 1941 was still on too small a scale and that its use was far from systematic. The first systematic gassing in Auschwitz started between the end of March and the beginning of April 1942, and Auschwitz-Birkenau only became the center of the Holocaust from 1943.

Wachsmann emphasizes that when the decision about these murderous campaigns was taken in the course of 1941, the Nazi regime had not yet decided to promote the immediate mass murder of the European Jews to an official policy. The activities were related to the attempts of the SS to restart the so-called program of euthanasia in the concentration camps, referred to as Aktion 14f13.[17] This resulted in experiments with different methods of murder. Nevertheless, according to Wachsmann, these camps were not established and equipped to murder large numbers of Jews until 1942.[18]

Mazower sees the turning point as taking place in about October 1941, when the policy to force Jews to emigrate was definitively abolished and replaced by a policy of mass murder. Yitzhak Arad refers to three important moments: the decision to exterminate the Jewish population of the Soviet Union taken at the beginning of August 1941, followed by the decision to kill the approximately 2.3 million Polish Jews in October, and by a third decision taken in mid-December to exterminate the Jewish population of the whole of Europe.[19]

These differences of opinion arise from different interpretations of the way in which the systematic mass murder developed. While historians like Franciszek Piper consider that the genocide was the result of a premeditated master plan, historians like Nikolaus Wachsmann, Yitzhak Arad and Christopher Browning emphasize that the systematic murder of the European Jews was actually the result of a lengthy process in which improvisation and local initiatives played an important role. Most historians agree that the anti-Jewish policy assumed a previously unknown radical character as a result of the invasion of the Soviet Union. In general, it is assumed that the definitive decision to murder the European Jews on a massive scale was taken in the second half of 1941.[20] During the Wannsee conference on 20 January 1942, a number of representatives of the most important ministries, government institutions and Nazi organizations met together on the initiative of Reinhard Heydrich in order to plan the implementation and distribution of tasks with regard to the deportations. However, the main aim was already clear at that point: the European Jews would be herded together to the occupied east and be murdered, either directly or by "Vernichtung durch Arbeit" ("annihilation by work").[21]

In the autumn of 1941, the plans for the mass murder of the more than 2 million Jews in the Generaal Gouvernement (the occupied part of Poland) were elaborated in more detail. A number of extermination camps were established, first in Chelmno, and then under the code name Aktion Reinhard, as well as in Belzec, Sobibor, and Treblinka.[22] Technical experts who had cooperated previously on the T4 secret program of euthanasia were secretly sent to the Generaal Gouvernement to establish a system of gas chambers.[23] At least 1.7 million Jews were murdered in these "Reinhard camps". Only a few Jews were kept alive to help with the process of extermination.

- 6 -

L a n d	Zahl
A. Altreich	131.800
Ostmark	43.700
Ostgebiete	420.000
Generalgouvernement	2.284.000
Bialystok	400.000
Protektorat Böhmen und Mähren	74.200
Estland - judenfrei -	
Lettland	3.500
Litauen	34.000
Belgien	43.000
Dänemark	5.600
Frankreich / Besetztes Gebiet	165.000
Unbesetztes Gebiet	700.000
Griechenland	69.600
Niederlande	160.800
Norwegen	1.300
B. Bulgarien	48.000
England	330.000
Finnland	2.300
Irland	4.000
Italien einschl. Sardinien	58.000
Albanien	200
Kroatien	40.000
Portugal	3.000
Rumänien einschl. Bessarabien	342.000
Schweden	8.000
Schweiz	18.000
Serbien	10.000
Slowakei	88.000
Spanien	6.000
Türkei (europ. Teil)	55.500
Ungarn	742.800
UdSSR	5.000.000
Ukraine 2.994.684	
Weißrußland aus- schl. Bialystok 446.484	
Zusammen: über	11.000.000

K210405   372029

Inventory of Jews in Europe, as drawn up during the Wannsee conference, January 1942.

Reinhard Heydrich in about 1942.

Aktion Reinhard came to an end in November 1943 and the extermination camps were dismantled.[24]

Six days after the Wannsee conference, Himmler informed the concentration camp inspector Richard Glücks about the agreements that had been made and his decision to send large numbers of Jews to concentration camps. Two concentration camps were designated for this: Auschwitz and Majdanek, a camp near the city of Lublin in eastern Poland.[25]

Auschwitz-Birkenau, also known as Auschwitz II, was located approximately 3 kilometers northwest of the *Stammlager* Auschwitz I, near the village of Brzezinka (Birkenau). The construction of a gigantic camp started there in the autumn of 1941, initially with the aim of interning tens of thousands of Russian prisoners. Auschwitz-Birkenau was built by Russian prisoners of war and forced labor,[26] and hardly anyone survived the heavy work and the inhuman conditions under which the work was carried out. After the first group of Russian prisoners of war had virtually all died as a result of starvation and exhaustion, the Nazis moved tens of thousands of Jews to Birkenau as slave labor to carry on with the work. The decision to murder the European Jews gave rise to modifications to the infrastructure and aim of the camp: under the management of Höss, the main aim of the camp now became the extermination of Jews and the selection of slave labor.

When the Jewish transports arrived from the beginning of July 1942, selections were carried out. In the words of *Untersturmführer* Heinrich Kinna, an SS officer who reported on the selections in Auschwitz in December 1942, it was "necessary to remove imbeciles, idiots, the deformed and the sick as quickly as possible by means of liquidation [...] to relieve the camp."[27] His words reflect the dehumanization of the Jewish prisoners in the minds of the SS. In Birkenau, SS doctors selected the Jews who were able to work; the rest went to the gas chamber. In the first instance, these were the sick, the elderly, pregnant women and women with small children.[28] Himmler not only saw the Jewish prisoners as a "problem" that had to be resolved with mass murder, but also as potential slaves for German industry. He insisted that the majority of the deported Jews should be young and able to work. However, the transports could also include a small number of Jews, about 10 per cent of whom were not able to work. It was quite clear what their fate would be.[29] In about September 1942, most of them were murdered. Of all the deported Jews on these transports – a total of 11,172 people – only twenty-five men and two women survived the war.[30]

Karl Bischoff, the leader of the *Zentralbauleitung der Waffen-SS und Polizei Auschwitz*, ordered the construction of a large crematorium in the autumn of 1941. The leaders of the camp anticipated that because of the extreme conditions, the large numbers of Jews who would now be coming to Birkenau as prisoners would not survive.[31] The management of Auschwitz-Birkenau was first carried out by Fritz Harjenstein, who was succeeded in May 1944 by Josef Kramer.[32] The construction of gas chambers on two empty farms began in the spring of 1942. These were to be used to murder Jews as soon as they arrived.

A start had probably already been made in May 1942 in Birkenau to select the weak prisoners who were unable to work.[33] The first gas chamber in Birkenau, Bunker I, also known as "the little red house" by the SS because of its unrendered red bricks, probably started operating in the middle or end of that same month.[34] Bunker II (the "small white house") was probably ready for use at the end of June or beginning of July. After Bunker I and II, the construction of crematoria and gas chambers II–V followed between March and June 1943.[35]

Auschwitz-Birkenau was still developing by May 1942, but now that it had been set up as an extermination camp, it largely took over the murderous practices of Auschwitz I. In the autumn of 1942, the gassing of prisoners ceased in the camp crematorium in Auschwitz I because the SS moved the large-scale gassing to Birkenau. They considered it a solution to the practical problems of mass murder, as it was easier to kill the selected prisoners in Birkenau itself rather than send them to the main camp and have them gassed there. Apart from the fact that it was more efficient, and because the crematorium in Auschwitz I was not equipped to deal with so many bodies, the murders that took place in the gas chambers of Birkenau – some of which were underground – were less noticeable than those in the gas chambers of Auschwitz I, which were above ground and in which the screaming of the prisoners who were being murdered caused a great deal of disturbance amongst the other prisoners.[36]

A separate women's camp was also organized in Birkenau from the beginning of August 1942. The enormous complex consisted of parts BI and BII (at a later stage part BIII was established, though it was never finished). Each of these was subdivided into smaller camp sections, with BIa and BIb incorporating the women's camp. Eventually, women were also accommodated in parts BIIa (the quarantine barracks) and BIIb (the part for families who had come from Theresienstadt), and the women's camp in part BIIc.[37] The need to establish a special section for women in Auschwitz was the result of the Nazi policy to intensify the slave labor carried out by Jewish prisoners. A section for women had already been organized in Auschwitz in the spring of 1942 and was separated from the men's section by a wall. The large numbers of women who were sent to Auschwitz during the second half of the war were accommodated in blocks 1 to 10 of the *Stammlager*. About half of all the women prisoners in Auschwitz worked for the camp itself. As the women were used for activities in the camp like agriculture and animal husbandry, large groups of men could be used elsewhere, and would often work on the expansion of the camp and in the German arms industry.[38]

In mid-August 1942 it was decided to send a large number of the women prisoners in Birkenau to sector B1a, which had just been finished.[39] They were accommodated in thirty barracks – fifteen made of stone and fifteen of wood (originally intended for horses). Another five wooden barracks were added in 1943 between the line of stone barracks and the place where the latrines and sanitary barracks were located.[40] From the end of the summer of 1942, Birkenau played an increasingly prominent role in the organized murder. While the "Reinhard camps" – Belzec, Sobibor and Treblinka – were shut down in the course of 1943 and the deportations to Majdanek also came to a halt, the four large crematoria and gas chambers that had already been added to the existing gas chambers in Bunkers I and II were finished in Birkenau. With six gas chambers, Auschwitz-Birkenau now became the center of the mass murder of the European Jews.[41]

A DEVELOPING CAMP

The significance of the Auschwitz complex for the planned mass murder of the European Jews gradually increased from the beginning of 1942. More than a million Jews were killed

Prisoners in Auschwitz-Birkenau shortly after its liberation in January 1945.

Heinrich Himmler on an inspection visit in Auschwitz-Monowitz, 18 July 1942.

there between March 1942 and November 1944.[42] The first group of Jews to be the victims of the new gas chambers in Birkenau in May 1942 came from Silesia. During the course of that month, Jews arrived from different cities in Upper Silesia who were considered unable to work.[43] On 17 and 18 July 1942, Heinrich Himmler visited the Auschwitz complex for an inspection. He observed Dutch Jews who had been taken in the first transport of 15 July 1942 being gassed in the almost completed Auschwitz-Birkenau.[44]

A new phase started in 1943. While the number of transports of Jews to Auschwitz increased enormously in 1943, the number of prisoners in the camp itself was decimated. This was because of the extreme conditions in the camp, the violence and the systematic murders. However, in the course of that year, the

SS were put under pressure to improve the conditions due to the increasing value of slave labor for the war industry.[45] For example, a number of improvements were introduced in the medical treatment of the sick, more trained doctors were sent to the sick bays and additional infirmaries were built. Both the medical equipment and the supply of medicines increased, and for some patients the provision of food improved with food parcels, which only non-Jewish prisoners could receive.

Although these matters sometimes benefited individual prisoners, the general situation hardly improved at all. For instance, many improvements in the field of hygiene were undone because of the growing over-population that was a direct result of the demand for more slave labor. In addition, the infirmaries continued to be faced with systematic shortages, neglect and mistreatment.[46] Furthermore, any improvements took a long time to implement. For example, a start was made on adding washing and sanitary areas in a number of barracks at Birkenau in 1944, though they were still not finished when the camp was liberated.[47]

In the spring of 1943, Himmler ended Aktion 14f13, the SS program of euthanasia which was aimed at the mass murder of prisoners who were unable to work. The camp commandants were ordered to exempt all prisoners from selection who could no longer work, with the exception of prisoners with a psycho-logical disorder. From August 1943, only Jewish prisoners were included in the selections[48] and the general death rate tempor-arily dropped. In general, the prisoners had a slightly higher chance of survival in the autumn of 1943. However, this did not apply to the Jews, who were the largest group of prisoners in Auschwitz and Majdanek at that time. The registered Jewish prisoners still rarely survived for longer than a few months because the attitude of the SS had not changed. The fact that Jews died on a massive scale as a result of the extreme working conditions remained a consciously calculated element in the policy of persecution which, as indicated earlier, was not only aimed at genocide itself, but was also based on considerations of productivity.[49]

Himmler was proud of the work carried out by KZ (concentration camp) prisoners, but the slave labor in the camps was much less productive than he claimed. Many prisoners were not put to work at all because they were sick or because there was no work. According to the figures of the SS for the spring of 1944, more than a quarter of the prisoners in Auschwitz were too weak or too sick to do anything, and the majority of the prisoners who were able to work were much less strong than ordinary laborers. Furthermore, at the beginning of 1944, the *Reichsministerium für Ernährung und Landwirtschaft* once again reduced the food rations for KZ prisoners.[50]

On 18 September 1942, the principle of "annihilation" was extended to some non-Jewish groups in the concentration camp, including the Sinti and Roma, and Russian and Ukrainian prisoners.[51] At the end of 1943, large groups of Roma were deported to Auschwitz-Birkenau and accommodated in a special *Zigeunerlager* in sector BIIe. The situation in this camp was also extremely bad. When there was an outbreak of typhus, the gypsy camp was placed under quarantine and the sick were taken to the gas chambers. Groups of non-registered Roma were also murdered immediately after arrival when it became apparent that typhus was raging amongst them. In the summer of 1943, Himmler had already decided on the liquidation of the gypsy camp, but this happened only on 2 August 1944 when all the remaining prisoners were murdered.[52] Of the 245 Sinti and Roma who had been transported from Westerbork to Auschwitz-Birkenau on 19 May 1944, only thirty survived. [53]

The extermination in the Auschwitz complex was at its height in the spring of 1944. The trains continued to arrive, especially from France, the Netherlands, Slovakia, Greece, Italy and Hungary. In the summer of 1944, the murder machine in Birkenau reached its peak. At the same time, the SS forced more prisoners than ever before to work for the war industry.[54]

Shortly after the mass murder of Hungarian Jews between May and July 1944, the character and function of the Auschwitz complex changed again. Auschwitz became a place where large transports of prisoners of different nationalities were gathered together before being sent on to camps in Germany for forced labor.[55] In this way, thousands of Polish and Hungarian women were sent from Auschwitz to Bergen-Belsen in mid-August 1944, to be moved on after a few days or weeks to external subcamps where they had to work (for example, in airplane factories).[56]

In 1944, the majority of these prisoners were transported from the main camps of Auschwitz I and II to one of the many smaller subcamps, such as Gleiwitz and Bismarckhütte, where there was a constant need for new laborers.[57] The main camps now served as enormous transit centers. When the Red Army advanced from the east in the summer of 1944 and approached the camps in occupied Poland, more and more prisoners were deported to the camps in Germany as slave labor.[58] At the same time, the Nazis' attempts to eradicate traces of the mass murder in Auschwitz began.[59] From the beginning of November 1944, no more prisoners were gassed in Birkenau. The gas chambers and crematoria were dismantled and blown up. When the Red Army advanced even closer, the large evacuation transports started from Auschwitz in January 1945. Around 58,000 men and women – including Peter van Pels – were forced to go on these so-called death marches because the Germans wanted to keep them as slave labor for the war industry. The prisoners who survived ended up in factories and industrial complexes in Germany.[60] The leaders of the camp disappeared while the SS guards accompanied the death marches to other camps.[61] A small group of prisoners remained behind in the infirmaries, including Otto Frank – the only survivor of the group who had gone into hiding in the Annex.

FUNKTIONSHÄFTLINGE (KAPOS)

As in Westerbork and many other camps, the SS were responsible for guarding Auschwitz, but prisoners were also used to maintain internal order. As indicated earlier, the concentration camp organization was based on sharp distinctions and great inequality between the prisoners. This resulted in a tight-knit hierarchy in which prisoners, the so-called *Funktionshäftlinge*, were put in charge at several levels. For example, the *SS-Lagerführer* was supported by a prisoner whose job was *Lagerälteste*. At another level, the *SS-Blockführer* was helped by a prisoner, the *Blockälteste*, a job that could be done by both men and women. Janny Brilleslijper describes the *Blockälteste* as "the authority, the mayor of a block, who was responsible for the fair distribution of things and this fair distribution meant: 'Me first, then me and you, and you a little bit, and you a little bit, and then the rest of the block.'"[62]

Together with the other *Funktionshäftlinge*, the *Block-ältesten* were a small elite in the camp because their privileged position involved a degree of luxury and comfort compared with the situation of ordinary prisoners, wherein the majority of the prisoners died or barely managed to survive. This elite "sometimes appeared to live in a different world", as Nikolaus Wachsmann wrote in his comprehensive work *KL: A History of the Nazi Concentration Camps*.[63] They had access to goods, power and privileges, and were even given the opportunity to engage in sport and to relax under strictly regulated conditions. These so-called kapos were still subordinate to the camp SS, yet a privileged position such as theirs in the camp could mean the difference between life and death.

It was a hierarchical system in which the camp SS looked for prisoners they considered would be the most likely to obey orders, carry them out or impose them on the other prisoners. By making a small group of prisoners accessories to oppressing the rest, and by encouraging differences between the prisoners, the SS hoped to reduce the pressure on their own personnel and at the same time completely suppress any resistance amongst the prisoners. Initially, the SS gave priority to German prisoners. This corresponded with the ideological world view of the National Socialists that considered Germans to be superior to the other nations, but there were also practical reasons, such as that orders and instructions could be passed on in their own language more easily. Although many survivors emphasized that the SS preferred to choose professional criminals for the *Funktionshäftlinge*, Nikolaus Wachsmann suggested that in practice this was seldom the case. In many camps, the SS actually preferred to opt for political prisoners; furthermore, the majority of the prisoners identified as *Berufsverbrecher* (habitual offender) by the Nazis had actually not been arrested for organized crime, but far more often for minor offences. Jews came at the bottom of the hierarchy in the camp and were rarely given leadership jobs at first. Nevertheless, in parts of the camp where there were only Jews, the SS increasingly often opted for Jewish *Funktionshäftlinge*.[64]

As indicated above, another name for the *Funktionshäftlinge* was *kapo*, sometimes written as "capo", presumably a reference to the French word *caporal* (corporal) or the Italian word *capo* (chief, boss).[65] Apart from the prisoners who were in charge of barracks, sections and rooms, this also referred to the prisoners who were used as assistant guards to support the SS.[66] In his story "The Capo", based on his own experiences of the camp in Bergen-Belsen, which will be discussed in more detail below, Abel Herzberg described how prisoners were turned into accomplices of the genocide. Because it is such a striking and universal description of the job of the kapo, we include it here:

> The Kapo is the prisoner who is appointed as a frontline worker, a guard and someone to drive on his fellow prisoners. Sometimes he can also be a spy, but a specific order for this was often superfluous. This is the good kapo who knows what is required of him automatically.

Abel Herzberg as a young man in about 1913.

In general, he must pass on the pressure that the Nazi wishes to put on his victim. He is rewarded with better sleeping accommodation, sufficient food, the right to appropriate the clothes of survivors as a priority, or to steal them in another way, as long as it's not too obvious. The technical term for this is organization. In addition, he has the invaluable luck to be able to beat others as hard as he likes and as often as he wants without being afraid of being beaten himself. He may issue commands and actually has to do so. Any opposition is *niedergeshmettert* (smashed). In this way he is bought, and it also ensures that there is a privileged class amongst the army of prisoners so that individual opposition can be nipped in the bud and cannot even appear at all. The Germans knew that there is something in many people that is prepared to accept this privilege and even acknowledges it, despite all the hatred. In any case this suited their system, that consequently involved the consistent exploitation of the prisoners and the slave in mankind.[67]

Sometimes kapos were in charge of large work *kommandos*, but more often they led smaller *kommando* units.[68]

The Dutch Jewish doctor and psychiatrist Eddy de Wind examined in detail the huge inequalities that existed in the camp in his postwar report of his imprisonment, titled *Last Stop Auschwitz*. In 1942, shortly after completing his medical degree, De Wind voluntarily applied to work as a doctor in the hospital as the Westerbork camp, after his mother was taken there. Although he had been promised that he and his mother would be allowed to stay in Westerbork, he was sent to Auschwitz in mid-September 1943 and eventually started

Eddy de Wind in the 1930s.

working in the infirmary there. In his report, he describes the hierarchy in the camp as a system in which everyone reacted against what they were given to endure from the top:

> It was like this with the Nazis everywhere. The SS officers screamed at everyone, also at the Blockältesten, the Blockältesten screamed and beat people, including the Poles, and they in turn chose the weakest to scream at [...]. Just like a billiard ball that stops when it hits another ball, the men calmed down when they screamed at and hit the prisoners.[69]

Some of the prominent figures in the camp were prisoners who worked in the infirmary. In Last Stop Auschwitz, De Wind describes noticing prisoners arriving, and how the prisoners who had managed to acquire a position as an assistant doctor – a prominent position in the camp – were easy to identify.

> By the door there were men in white suits. They looked well. On the back of their jacket there was a red line as

well as on the seams of their trousers. These were certainly the doctors. They barely looked at the newcomers, but Hans[70] saw that their lack of interest was for a different reason than in all those thousands of prisoners outside. Amongst prisoners doing slave labor it was their exhaustion and deep sense of hopelessness which made any psychological effort impossible. In these people who looked well, there was a sort of arrogance. After all, they were the prominent figures in the camp.[71]

Approximately 2,200 prisoners who were forced to be part of the *Sonderkommando* in Auschwitz had a special position. The *Sonderkommando* consisted of strong male prisoners, mainly Jews, who had been selected by the camp leaders to help gas their fellow prisoners. They lived together in a separate part of the camp and had to help to force Jewish prisoners into the gas chambers; afterwards, they had to drag the bodies outside. Other members of the *Sonderkommando* removed all the valuable articles from the bodies. Gold teeth were extracted and collected to be melted down into gold bars, and the hair of the murdered prisoners was cut to be recycled for the textile industry. They then had to bury the bodies or, after the crematoria were established, drag them there to be burnt.[72]

In "exchange" for their services, they were given extra food and other privileges, and sometimes developed personal relationships with the SS guards through their close cooperation. Because of their close participation in the genocide, many other prisoners viewed them with contempt and disgust. However, after the war, various historians and survivors emphasized that life in the *Sonderkommando* was largely a "choiceless choice" – that is, a choice that wasn't really a choice.[73] No one did the job voluntarily, and if you refused you were immediately shot. In general, the members of the *Sonderkommando* were also murdered after a few months, and only a few managed to survive.

The way in which the members experienced their position differed from person to person. While most did not see any option other than to make sure that the gassing process went as smoothly as possible, and that they did not give the SS any excuse to punish them, there were a few occasions when this group resisted. For example, one member of the *Sonderkommando*, the Greek Alberto Errera, managed to record the murder of a group of Jews from Lodz with a camera in August 1944. Hidden in the gas chamber of Crematorium V in Birkenau, he recorded how a large number of bodies were burned outside. The roll of film was smuggled out of the camp, after which the Polish Resistance illegally distributed the photographs in an edited form. The originals were discovered only after the war.[74]

On 7 October 1944, a group of members of the *Sonder-kommando* resisted during a selection to be transferred to another camp because they expected to be murdered by the Germans once they arrived. They attacked the SS officers with hammers, stones, axes and iron rods and then set fire to the crematorium. However, this brief resistance ended in failure. Because of the lack of time, they were insufficiently prepared and the men who resisted were not supported by resistance in the rest of the camp. Most of them initially managed to escape, but the majority were arrested by the SS in the following weeks during large-scale reprisals and then murdered. Nevertheless, this clearly shows that the image of Jewish prisoners as passive victims is not always correct, and that some prisoners still managed to find the strength to resist the genocide even under the extreme conditions in Auschwitz.[75] Some members of the *Sonderkommando* who survived were also amongst the most important witnesses of the mass murder at Auschwitz, and because of their proximity of the murders, they were able to provide detailed descriptions of the Nazi genocide which are lacking in other accounts by witnesses.[76]

One of the photographs that was secretly taken from the gas chambers in August 1944 by the prisoner Alberto Errera, a member of the *Sonderkommando* in Auschwitz.

The group from the Annex arrived in Auschwitz at an important
moment of transition, specifically when it changed from being
a camp primarily focusing on mass murder to one in which
the use of slave labor was becoming more important.[77] The
transport from Westerbork on Sunday 3 September 1944 with
the Frank family, the Van Pels family and Fritz Pfeffer arrived
on the platform at Auschwitz-Birkenau on the night of Tuesday
5 September.[78] A number of survivors who had been taken to
Auschwitz on the same train still have strong memories of the
moment of arrival. Lenie de Jong-Van Naarden remembers:

After arriving in Auschwitz-Birkenau, the men and women were
separated on the platform.

At a certain point the train started to slow down and then stopped. I really can't remember whether it was morning or evening when we arrived. The doors were pulled open and immediately there was a tremendous shouting and screaming through the loudspeakers. There were many uniformed police officers and soldiers on the platform. Everyone fell out of the cattle wagons together, the dead, the sick, children. The screaming through the loudspeakers was telling us that we had to leave our luggage behind and that we should line up with our hand luggage, women on one side, men on the other side, and walk forward. It's totally undignified to describe how they were waiting for us with whips and dogs: it would have been best to fall down dead, but if you didn't do that you just had to move on.[79]

It was dark, the floodlights were bright, there was screaming, and dogs were barking.[80] Everything had to be done very quickly. The prisoners had to leave their luggage behind, but some managed to keep hold of some of their smaller possessions. The bodies of prisoners who had died during the transport remained behind and were taken to the crematorium to be burnt there.[81] The men were separated from the women by SS guards with dogs and sticks and were put into large blocks of five by five, with the SS officers in charge. It all happened so quickly that there was hardly any time to say goodbye. That's where Otto Frank saw his family for the last time.[82]

After being separated, there was a selection, made by one of the camp doctors, between those who were able to work and those who were not. Children and older people who were not considered able to work were separated from those who could work and murdered immediately. Although the criteria had not been determined precisely and varied at different times, children of fifteen years and younger and adults above the age of fifty were generally selected for the gas chambers. Mothers with children under the age of fifteen were also sent directly to the gas chambers regardless of their age, as were pregnant women.[83] Therefore, three of the eight prisoners who had come from the Annex were immediately in great danger when they arrived in Auschwitz. Anne Frank was fifteen years old when she arrived; Otto Frank and Fritz Pfeffer were both fifty-five. Margot Frank (aged eighteen) and Peter van Pels (aged seventeen) would probably have survived the selection – as would Edith Frank (aged forty-four), Auguste van Pels (aged forty-three) and Hermann van Pels (aged forty-six) – even if the criteria had been stricter.

The selection of prisoners on the platform of Auschwitz-Birkenau.

Most of the survivors who arrived on the same transport from Westerbork remember this selection as being chaotic. It was only later that they heard from prisoners who had been there for a while that some of the new arrivals were selected to be murdered immediately. Ronnie van Cleef remembers the selection as an unreal event:

> Then there was a selection which we didn't understand at all, fortunately, in fact. Mengele stood there and pointed – he didn't say anything, he just pointed. We were on the right, younger people and in his view the healthiest people. The others, the elderly and the children were sent to the left. We didn't understand what was happening. I thought, we'll see them again in a while.[84]

The survivors of this transport all identified Josef Mengele as the *SS-Lagerarzt* (camp doctor) who carried out the selection.[85] However, the question arises whether it really was Mengele who was on duty that evening. The Austrian former prisoner and

Ronnie van Cleef in about 1940.

historian Hermann Langbein refers to the process of memory displacement that occurs in many witness testimonies with regard to Mengele and other iconic war criminals. Because of the widespread attention that Mengele received as part of the public's image of Auschwitz, he became much better known than his colleagues. The result is that survivors projected their experiences with other doctors and guards onto Mengele, although sometimes this could not possibly be correct: "More than once I heard survivors say that Mengele did this or that to them, even though Mengele had not yet arrived in Auschwitz at the time."[86]

Mengele certainly was working in Auschwitz on 4 September 1944, but this doesn't detract from the fact that the same process of projection could also have arisen here. Some witnesses also said that they "assumed" that it must have been Mengele; Rachel Frankfoorder, for example, remarked, "I don't know, he didn't introduce himself". Although it's quite possible that Mengele was on duty that day, there's no official source available to confirm this. In *The Nazi Doctors*, the historian Robert Jay

SS-Standortarzt Eduard Wirths.

Lifton reveals that there were several *Lagerärzt* working in Auschwitz, and they carried out the selection alternately in pairs. The head of the selections was not Mengele, but *Standort-arzt* Eduard Wirths, who was in charge from 1943, under the direct supervision of the camp commandant. Wirths was the head of staff of a number of camp doctors who alternated for "platform duty", and he also made sure that he regularly carried out the selections himself, a task which he considered to be so important that he gave priority to this work over his other responsibilities.[87]

The selection was carried out in haste and on the basis of the fleeting impressions received by the camp doctor on duty. In consultation with Himmler and the camp commandants, Wirths usually decided in advance approximately how many people should pass the selection and what proportion should be murdered immediately.[88] In Auschwitz, between 10 and 30 per cent of the prisoners were normally selected for slave labor (i.e. on average 20 per cent).[89] However, a much higher proportion of the deportees on the transport of 3 September 1944, the train on which Anne and her family came from Westerbork to Auschwitz, passed the selection upon arrival.[90] There were 1,019 people on the transport list and 672 passed the selection (i.e. more than 65 per cent).[91] All eight prisoners from the Annex passed the selection, even Otto Frank and Fritz Pfeffer, who didn't really comply with the selection criteria as they were fifty-five years old. As there are several examples of men over the age of fifty who survived the selection from this transport, it is likely that the selection criteria were being applied less strictly by then, in view of the need for slave labor for the war industry.[92]

From this transport, 347 men, women and children were immediately murdered in the gas chambers. They had to walk there themselves, but there was a truck waiting for the invalids.[93] Mothers with children who could not yet walk also went to the gas chambers in the trucks. Ronnie van Cleef remembers:

> After we passed Mengele we arrived at a large field with army trucks. There we were put into two lines. The line on the left was taken directly to the gas chambers in army trucks. It all happened really quickly. One moment Suze and Aunt Bloeme were still standing next to me, I took hold of the child's hand. And a minute later [...] my aunt was gone! My niece was gone![94]

One of the survivors of the transport remembers that there was an announcement that you could also take the truck if you were tired or sick. So a number of people walked to the truck that served as a "bus".[95]

From that moment, the men and women were separated for good. The 400 men and 249 women walked in separated blocks of five by five, approximately 1.5 kilometers from the platform to the *Zentralsauna* (central sauna). This was a brick building where the new arrivals were registered, their heads were shaved and disinfected, and they were tattooed with their camp number.[96] According to one Dutch prisoner, "The Sauna played an extremely important role in the camp, everything happened in this complex."[97] The prisoners waited in the open area just in front of this building for the rest of the night, until the humiliating ritual of the registration process started.[98]

Registration went as follows: first, the prisoners had to stand in a line in alphabetical order. A prisoner from the *Aufnahme-kommando* (administration) then wrote down the names on a list (*Eingangsliste*) and numbered them. All the newcomers were given a note with their number. Then they went into the

Zentralsauna building, where they had to get undressed and hand over their last possessions. Prisoners who tried to hang onto anything were beaten by the guards. Ronnie van Cleef remembers that she was having her period when she arrived and therefore refused to get undressed completely. A guard beat her on the head and violently pulled down her pants: "I thought this was the end. I found it terribly difficult and I saw that he was doing it to others as well. You just can't think of the words – we were completely devastated."[99]

The prisoners then had to walk to the next area completely naked, where there were prisoners of the *Aufnahmekommando* (admissions command) sitting at tables. For every newly arrived prisoner, they completed a preprinted form registering the personal details, physical characteristics and condition, and the number they had just been given. Ronnie van Cleef describes how this number was then tattooed on the lower left arm: "Female Polish prisoners then came to tattoo the number onto your arm. Some would do it very neatly but others didn't take care, they made a mess of it; and then a new number was tattooed on top resulting in inflammation and a swollen arm."[100]

All the body hair was shaved, and the pubic area and underarms were treated with a disinfectant. Some women remember that the hair on their head was first cut short and that they were shaved bald only at a later stage.[101] Then the prisoners entered an area with showers with alternating unpleasant hot and icy cold water and sometimes steam to disinfect them. For many people, the shower was the first opportunity in days to quench their thirst.[102]

Ronnie van Cleef describes how a guard then came in to spray the prisoners with a hose:

156

Suddenly a German came in, an SS officer with a wooden leg, I'll never forget it. He had a stick under his knee. The guy was crazy, he picked up a big hose and started to spray us and he enjoyed it enormously. He sprayed us so much that we didn't know which way to turn. We called out to him to go away, because you wondered what would happen next: the man was clearly enjoying himself. At last he stopped, we were completely exhausted and there was nothing to dry ourselves with. There were some curtains and we used them to dry ourselves as best we could.[103]

There were no towels or soap. Other prisoners described that they had to dry themselves in the air, in the draughty building or outside. Ronnie remembers that the group of prisoners had to walk outside naked, where their clothes were thrown at them. Prior to 1943, prisoners were given striped uniforms to wear, but these were subsequently replaced by used clothing because there were no uniforms left. The women were given arbitrary clothes to wear, but most witnesses agree these did not include underclothes.[104] Sometimes, red lines were painted onto the back of the clothes.[105] Leny Boeken-Velleman, one of the survivors of the transport of 3 September, remembers that her clothes were painted with red paint: "I was given a sort of black sack which looked like a dress, with a large white square sewn onto the back. A large red patch was painted in that white square. Imagine if you wanted to escape, you would be recognized very quickly and there was a clear target on your back."[106]

In addition, the women were given wooden clogs or worn shoes. These came from the so-called *Kanada* depots, the warehouses where the luggage of newly arrived prisoners was

Leny Boeken-Velleman in the
early 1940s.

stored and sorted by members of a special group of *kapos*, who
were soon known to the prisoners as the *Kanadakommando*, a
cynical reference to the relatively rich country of Canada.[107]

It is not clear whether the men were given prison uniforms;
witness statements don't say anything about this.[108] The camp
survivor Sal de Liema remembers that he had striped clothes,
a jacket and trousers in Auschwitz I.[109] Male prisoners in
Auschwitz usually wore wooden shoes or sandals.[110] After the
registration procedure, the prisoners were sent to the barracks
and that was the start of a period of quarantine.

Auschwitz was the only camp where prisoners were
tattooed with their prisoner numbers to identify them, and we
only know the number of Otto Frank, which was B9174; the
numbers given to Fritz Pfeffer and Hermann and Peter van Pels
were between B9276 and B9294.[111] In principle, the number was
also worn on their clothes: on the left of the chest, and for men
along the outer seam of the right trouser leg.[112] However, this

Jewish prisoners sort through the possessions of the newly arrived Jews in the so-called *Kanada* depot.

principle does not appear to have been adopted consistently; later witness statements and the few photographs which have survived from the last months of 1944 show that the practice was inconsistent. Because there was a lack of formal camp uniforms, many prisoners wore a random selection of clothes based on what they could find. Eva Geiringer, who was to be Otto Frank's stepdaughter, remained in Auschwitz-Birkenau from May 1944 until the liberation. She remembers that she did not wear a number on her clothes and that she was regularly given other clothes after a selection or when prisoners had been to one of the frequent disinfections.[113]

Once prisoners had been registered in the camp, there was generally a period of quarantine, which took place in specially designated parts of the camps and barracks. It was only after this period of quarantine that the prisoners were assigned to labor *kommandos* or sent on to other camps.[114] In principle, the quarantine was meant to prevent the spread of contagious diseases, but the prisoners experienced it mainly as a way of being subjected to the camp regime.[115] The quarantine had a destructive effect on their morale. Some prisoners became completely apathetic, others took their own lives (one method was by throwing themselves against the electric fence). Many died very quickly as a result of the combined torture of senseless labor and little food. The quarantine barracks were often overcrowded and also served to separate the weak from the strong, and during the quarantine period there were regular selections for the gas chambers. The period could last from a few days to eight weeks.[116]

From the time that they arrived, the prisoners were completely overwhelmed by all the shouting and cruelty. In the beginning, they often didn't understand any of the kapos' commands, which were usually shouted in Polish or Yiddish.[117] They had to stand for the roll call for hours, the food was poor, and they were completely at the mercy of the arbitrary moods of the *Blockführer* and *Blockältesten*. Then they were assigned to different labor *kommandos* and moved to other barracks. Depending on the *kommando*, the conditions could vary. In the next section, we try to describe the impact of all this on the eight prisoners from the Annex as accurately as possible.

STAMMLAGER: THE MEN IN AUSCHWITZ I

All the men on the transport of 3 September 1944 who survived the selection when they arrived in Birkenau walked to Auschwitz I after the registration procedure.[118] Once there, they ended up in quarantine block 8. Eddy de Wind, the young doctor who had been in Auschwitz since September 1943, and after a while had been given a job looking after the sick, describes it as "a filthy and shabby quarantine block".[119] The prisoners slept in three-tiered bunk beds, often with two or more people to a bed. The quarantine block was overcrowded. Only the *Blockältesten* and other privileged prisoners had their own small space with a table, chair and bed.

Everyone had to work during the quarantine. Most worked on the *Straßenbau* (building roads) or in the *Kiesgrub* (gravel pit), where they had to load gravel onto carts and take it to reinforce the roads.[120] It was very heavy work that lasted all day, and many people were wounded or injured. The kapos and guards also beat the prisoners when they thought they weren't working quickly enough. After the war, Otto Frank said that he had been assigned to a *kommando* that had to move gravel. In a declaration drawn up for Joseph Spronz, his fellow prisoner in the camp, Otto Frank briefly summarized his own experiences: "As I was in a gravel kommando for a time myself, I know a lot about the heavy labor involved and the mistreatment that often took place there."[121] The businesslike tone of his statement, which also characterizes many of his other statements, gives little insight into what he actually experienced there. However, for further information about the quarantine period of the men from the Annex, there are testimonies provided by other witnesses. Eddy de Wind describes how he was assigned to building roads shortly after he arrived in Auschwitz; he had to pull a gravel cart with steel wire from the pit to the camp together with fifteen other prisoners: "He also pulled it himself and was a wheel in a machine with fifteen cogs – if he didn't pull hard enough for minute, he would be kicked immediately by the Pole walking behind him."[122] The other prisoners hardened the roads with this gravel.

The quarantine period of the men on the transport of 3 September ended with two selections at the beginning of October 1944, when another group of male prisoners who were no longer deemed to be capable of heavy labor were murdered in the gas chambers. These selections also resulted in the death of Hermann van Pels. The first selection took place amongst the prisoners who had been given permission not to work because of sickness or an injury – *Blockschonung* – followed shortly afterwards by a second selection of Jewish men who were sick in the infirmary.[123] Fritz Simon, a fellow prisoner from the transport of 3 September, remembers how these selections were carried out:

> During my time there were two selections. In the first selection all the people who had Blockschonung were selected, which meant that they had been exempted from work for a few days because of some injury. The people selected in this way ended up a special block and were sent away after two days, obviously to be gassed in Birkenau. Those two days were dreadful for them because they knew exactly what awaited them. Here the mixed marriages were eventually removed after they had been in mortal fear. The second selection took place in a comparable way, only this time the infirmary was emptied first.[124]

The selection of the sick in the infirmary of block 9 was described by Eddy de Wind, who had been given a job caring for the sick as a doctor.[125] He describes how he met the well-known Amsterdam professor of economics Herman Frijda in the infirmary. Like the eight prisoners from the Annex, Frijda had arrived in Auschwitz on the transport of 3 September

Herman Frijda was Professor
of Economics at the Municipal
University of Amsterdam, 1921

1944 and had been put to work in the gravel pit. His witness
statement is particularly interesting, not only because Frijda was
an acquaintance of Otto Frank and the father of Margot's school
friend Jetteke Frijda,[126] but also because Frijda must have died
as a result of the hard work under more or less the same circumstances as Hermann van Pels. Eddy de Wind remembers Frijda:
"The old man had arrived with the last Dutch transport […]. In
Auschwitz he was assigned to the Straßenbau kommando. He
only managed to drag the carts for a few weeks and that's how
he ended up in the infirmary."[127]

De Wind then describes how he had to note the number of all
the people that he imagined might stay in the infirmary longer

than two weeks, and that the SS then took over the administration in order to decide on the selection. As he imagined that these very sick people would be gassed, he discussed with his French colleague whether it would be possible to save Frijda, who was very popular with the doctors according to De Wind, because of his "friendly and modest attitude". This did not prove to be possible: "We couldn't say that he was healthy. He would have been discharged from the infirmary straight away and he could hardly walk 100 meters. The next day the trucks arrived on the pretext that these selected men would be put to work in the Birkenau weaving workshop, but they were taken to the gas chamber." The information from the Red Cross and various witnesses indicates that Herman Frijda was gassed on 3 October 1944.[128]

The men who had been identified as being unable to work at the end of the quarantine period in the second selection were also gassed on 3 October. It is almost certain that Hermann van Pels was part of this group. In the postwar investigation into his fate, it was first assumed that he was gassed immediately after arriving in Auschwitz-Birkenau.[129] Later, the NRK used a method of collective reconstruction to determine that the date of his death was 15 March 1945. It was assumed that Hermann van Pels was one of the group of prisoners who had reached the Stutthof concentration camp after the quarantine up to 1 October 1944. This means that his death must have taken place between 1 October 1944 and 9 May 1945, the day on which Stutthof was liberated.[130] Several of the people missing from the transport list of 3 September 1944 were given the date of 15 March 1945 as their date of death. However, Hermann van Pels was not on the transport list for Stutthof for 26 October 1944, which probably means that he didn't survive the selection of 3 October.[131]

There are only a few brief witness statements about the fate of Hermann van Pels. In one statement, his fellow prisoner Fritz Simon says that he didn't see "Hermann van Pels from Amsterdam Z, Amstellaan 34" after the two selections at the end of the quarantine.[132] Otto Frank repeatedly stated that Van Pels was gassed after he had been selected on 5 October 1944 while in the *Blockschonung* or during *Stubendienst*.[133] He had injured his hand during the heavy work in the *Straßenbau* and had been given dispensation from work for a few days at his own request. Otto Frank believed that the selection was fatal for him. In the *Kalendarium* of the events in the whole of the Auschwitz camp, Danuta Czech gives 2 October 1944 as the date for a selection of 101 men during the quarantine,[134] and we know that other prisoners who arrived with the transport of 3 September 1944 died the following day, on 3 October 1944.[135] It is more or less certain that they were killed in one of the gas

Hermann van Pels's registration card, taken from the records of the Jewish Council.

chambers of Auschwitz-Birkenau, together with Hermann van Pels. He was forty-six years old at the time.

No one can say exactly what happened when Hermann van Pels, Herman Frijda and the other men from the quarantine were gassed, but the description by the Slovakian Jew Filip Müller, who had arrived in Auschwitz-Birkenau in April 1942, gives an impression. Müller was assigned to the *Sonderkommando* and managed to survive until the camp was liberated by the Russians. In his memoir, he gives a heartfelt description of an otherwise undated event when a large number of prisoners were gassed, which, as a member of the *Sonderkommando*, he experienced at close quarters. He gives an impression of the circumstances in which Hermann van Pels was murdered:

> After a while I heard piercing screams from the gas chamber, banging on the door as well as groaning. The people began to cough, and their coughing became worse every minute. This showed that the gas was certainly working. The first increasingly loud noise that you couldn't help but hear, quietened from minute to minute and soon turned into a large-scale muffled gurgling that was sometimes drowned out by more coughing. The deadly gas had penetrated the prisoners' lungs and soon paralyzed the respiratory system [...]. When the gas chamber was opened, in order to free the entrance, we were first ordered to remove the bodies which had fallen out and which were lying behind the doors. We did this by putting a loop of a leather belt around one of the wrists of the dead and then pulling on it to drag them to the lift and transport them upstairs to the crematorium. When some room had been cleared behind the door the

Filip Müller after the war.

bodies were rinsed off with hoses. This neutralized the crystals of gas which were still present, but also cleaned the bodies [...]. Even though they were still warm and had not yet become rigid, it was very difficult for the people carrying the bodies to pull them apart. Many had their mouths wide open and most had a trace of dried white saliva on their lips. Some had turned blue, and many faces were so deformed as a result of being beaten that they had become almost unrecognizable. Undoubtedly the subterranean labyrinth that the gas chamber had turned into also resulted in people running around in panic in the dark, bumping into each other, falling over each other and trampling each other, resulting in this entangled heap of bodies.[136]

Otto Frank, Fritz Pfeffer and Peter van Pels were probably unaware of these details, but undoubtedly soon heard that Hermann had been selected for the gas chamber. After the war, Otto Frank told Ernst Schnabel that Peter saw his father being marched to the gas chamber with a group of men.[137] A similar statement can be read in an interview with Otto Frank dating from 1979 in the German Newspaper *Welt am Sonntag*, which states that Otto and Peter saw Hermann van Pels in the group of men who had been selected.[138] Rather ironically, the mass murder of 3 October was to be the last time that large numbers of people were gassed in Auschwitz. Four days later, on 7 October, there was a rebellion by the members of the *Sonder-kommando* and one of the crematoria was put out of use. The above-mentioned rebellion was soon quashed, but in view of the advancing Russian army, the SS stopped gassing prisoners in the camp around the end of October and beginning of November 1944. In an attempt to hide the evidence of the size of the mass extermination, the camp authorities started to demolish the gas chambers and crematoria in November.[139]

PARCELS

The men who did survive the selection remained in Auschwitz I after the period of quarantine and were assigned to different labor *kommandos*. Apart from the above-mentioned *Straßenbau*, they were also assigned to digging sand (*Sandgrube*), were sent to the *Schlachthofkommando* (abattoir), or had to peel potatoes in the *Kartoffelschälkommando* (potato peeling *kommando*).[140] Others were assigned to private businesses who used slave labor from Auschwitz, such as the Petersen Kommando, a canal-building business, and the *Hoch- und Tiefbau Aktiengesellschaft* (HUTA) in Katowice, where prisoners had to work in the concrete works. Auschwitz and the other camps provided an enormous amount of slave labor for the Nazis, which benefitted the German economy.

We don't know to which *kommando* Fritz Pfeffer was assigned, as nothing has been discovered about his time in

Auschwitz from the witness statements of survivors. We do know, however, that he was registered in the same group as Hermann and Peter van Pels.[141] Like the others, he remained in quarantine up to approximately 1 October 1944. Selections recommenced in Auschwitz (amongst other sites) from that date, with the gassing of prisoners and deportations to Stutthof.[142] Pfeffer does not appear on the transport list from Auschwitz to Stutthof, and it remains unclear exactly when he was deported from Auschwitz,[143] although it's presumed that this did not happen on 1 October. According to the survivor Aron Gross, a deportation transport left Auschwitz on or about 11 November 1944 to the *Außenlager* Braunschweig (Lower Büssing-NAG) via Neuengamme.[144] Apparently, thirty Jewish doctors and dentists got out at Neuengamme. For this transport, only the card of the doctor Isaac Chatt was discovered in the card index; no date is indicated, only the camp number: 64976. As Fritz Pfeffer's camp number was known to be 64971, and we do know the date on which some other prisoners with slightly higher and slightly lower camp numbers arrived (10 and 18 November), we can deduce that Pfeffer must have arrived in Neuengamme on one of these dates.[145]

We know a little bit more about the experiences of Peter van Pels in Auschwitz, which is mainly because of Otto Frank's witness statements, as will be described in detail below. Peter had a great deal of contact with Otto until their departure in January 1945. He was in quarantine block 8 with the other men from the transport of 3 September 1944. Max Stoppelman, an acquaintance of Otto Frank, made the only other witness statement about Peter in Auschwitz.[146] After his period in quarantine, Peter van Pels went to block 2, where Stoppelman now had the job of *Stubenältester* (leader of the barracks). By this point, Peter had been separated from Otto, who was assigned to a different barracks.[147] Stoppelman, who survived the war, remembers that Peter spoke to him in French, clearly assuming he was French: "He introduced himself in French and I answered him: 'You speak French like a Dutchman', after which he introduced himself as Peter and I introduced myself as Stoppelman." Although they'd never seen each other in Amsterdam, it soon became clear that Peter knew Stoppelman's mother, that she was Jan and Miep Gies' Jewish landlady, and they'd helped her to find an address to go into hiding: "The first thing he told me was that he had heard from Jan and Miep that everything was still alright for my mother. I told him to stay near me as much as possible and that I'd try to get him through." This immediately created a link, and although Stoppelman didn't remember whether they talked to each other much about what Peter had gone through in Amsterdam, he took him under his wing as the *Stubenältester* up to the evacuation of Auschwitz. After that, they lost touch.[148]

Peter van Pels was registered as a metalworker on the transport list of 3 September 1944. Many of the prisoners assumed that when they were deported to a work camp with a profession or a trade they would be considered for skilled labor and would be able to save their lives in this way.[149] Because having a profession increased the chance of a better life, all sorts of professions were made up, such as plasterer, carpenter or bank clerk. During the work selections, prisoners often mentioned a profession to increase their chances of survival, and it's likely that Peter initially had himself registered as a metalworker for that reason.

It's not known whether he was actually assigned to be a metalworker in Auschwitz at first. However, we do know that after a while he managed to get a good job with the postal service, possibly with the help of Stoppelman, who had the necessary influence as the *Stubenältester*. Later, his card in the camp administration for Mauthausen indicates that he was a *Tischler* (cabinetmaker).[150] In an interview after the war, Otto Frank said: "Peter was lucky to get a job at the post office at the camp; it was meant for the SS officers and non-Jewish prisoners who received post and parcels."[151] It's difficult to underestimate the significance of this for his freedom of movement and status. This is revealed by the memories of the prisoner Max Rodrigues Garcia, a Jewish boy from Amsterdam who had arrived in Auschwitz and whose experiences are similar to what we know about Peter van Pels.

After a period in the hospital, Rodrigues Garcia was sent to work at the *Paketstelle*, the postal service where the parcels for prisoners arrived. Jews were not permitted to receive parcels, but many political and other non-Jewish prisoners were. The men who worked for the *Paketstelle* were responsible for opening up the parcels for prisoners who had died and to select

Max Rodrigues Garcia, 1946.

171

the contents. It was not very difficult to appropriate quite a lot of the contents. Rodrigues Garcia describes how he started at the bottom of the hierarchy as a shoe polisher and soon made his way up to the *Prominentenblock*. There were prisoners there with a good position and power who were given a separate room, and they were able to arrange all kinds of things. The regime at the *Paketstelle* was less rigid: the prisoners didn't have to go to the roll call, and they had more freedom of movement. In his book, Rodrigues Garcia explains the advantages of this job:

> The packages for those who had died – those endless packages for the endless dead – were ours to dispose of, a circumstance that put anyone assigned to this Kommando in a position of power and wealth. […] Every day we worked at sorting the contents of the parcels of the dead, cakes went in one bin, salamis and margarine over there, schmaltz (chicken fat, or goose fat, usually from the Poles) and other perishables in jars were placed here. Cookies had yet another compartment. Many of the vegetables were taken to the kitchen once a day, some to be thrown into the daily soup for the camp. The more delectable items were always kept aside for the use of the Kommando workers, who, in turn, supplied the Nazi camp administrators as desired. My co-workers, I observed, walked frequently back and forth from the Paketstelle to their Block. It soon dawned on me that they were helping themselves to a cut of the spoils, and they did so openly, as if this practice were not only accepted but expected. […] My body filled out rapidly. I felt well, fit, and strong. The scars of my pneumonia and abscessed

appendicitis were healed and behind me. I was now well dressed by day, warm at night, I even had cigarettes.[152]

Rodrigues Garcia became stronger and was well fed. On the eve of the evacuation transports in January 1945, he and his comrades made sure they had warm clothes and collected supplies for the guards to take on flat carts.[153]

Although we don't know whether Peter van Pels also made it to the *Prominentenblock*, Rodrigues Garcia provided a good description of the circumstances which ensured that Peter was in relatively good shape in January 1945, and was also able to visit and look after Otto Frank, who was sick.[154] Even the workers of the *Paketstelle*, who were at the bottom of the hierarchy, had access to warm clothes and food and had relatively greater freedom of movement, as shown by Rodrigues Garcia's testimony.[155]

SURVIVING IN AUSCHWITZ

As we will see later, Peter's job also had important consequences for Otto Frank. Otto was the only one who survived the camps, and therefore more traces of his camp experiences have survived. In the notebook, which Otto wrote immediately after the liberation, he mentioned many of the fellow prisoners he met during those months.[156] He spent time with, amongst others, Philip Felix de Jong (the husband of Lenie de Jong-van Naarden), Hans Goudsmit, Hans Bruck, Nico Pimentel and Hans Citroen in *Stube* (room) 8a of quarantine block 8.[157] This *Stube* was on the first floor of one of the former military barracks of Auschwitz I.[158] Otto spent a lot of time with Hermann and Peter van Pels in Auschwitz I, as well as with Fritz Pfeffer.[159] Sal de Liema was also in that block with him.[160]

173

Everyday life consisted mainly of hard work. During the quarantine period, Otto Frank first worked in the *Kiesgrube Kommando*, a gravel mine, where one of his fellow workers was the Hungarian Joseph Spronz. In support of a postwar application for invalidity benefit for Spronz, Otto Frank mentioned the heavy work in the gravel pit and the accompanying mistreatment he knew from his own experience.[161] Afterwards, he was sent to the *Straßenbau*.[162] Whether this happened directly after the period of quarantine is not clear. Other prisoners from block 8 who were put to work in the *Straßenbau* immediately after being dismissed from quarantine were sent to block 2. It is possible that Otto Frank was also accommodated in that block, but there are no sources to confirm this.[163] Every day, the prisoners marched to their work outside the camp in the open air, guarded by SS officers. In the mornings and after returning from work, they had to go to the roll call and be counted.

Joseph Spronz and Otto Frank, 1975/76.

174

When work stopped in the *Straßenbau* because of frost, Otto Frank says he was given better work in the *Kartoffelschälkommando*.[164] He moved to barracks 5 around this time. Spronz, who also worked there for some time, described the work they had to do there: the potatoes were brought in in large boxes before being washed. Only the large ones were peeled and the rest went into the mill with their peel together with the turnips, beetroot and fodder beet. This was the basis for the "soup", the standard meal in Auschwitz and the other camps. The peelers were able to eat some of it secretly and in this way managed to get some extra vitamins. It's also important that the work was carried out inside, sitting down. Prisoners preferred to work inside because it protected them from the rain and the cold and was generally less arduous than working outside.[165]

There was a *Prämienschein* for this work, a sort of coupon worth one mark that could be exchanged in the canteen for a *Raucherkarte* (tobacco coupon). One of these coupons for the *Häftlingskantine* of Auschwitz I is in the collection of the Anne Frank House, used by prisoner B9174 (Otto Frank) of block 5a.[166] (Block 5a was the first floor of block 5.) As far as we know, this is the only original document of Otto Frank from the time that he was a prisoner in Auschwitz.[167] It is not known, however, whether Otto Frank used these sorts of cards to obtain cigarettes. Mahorka cigarettes, poor-quality Russian cigarettes, were an important method of payment or exchange in Auschwitz.[168] These extra rewards for *Häftlinge* were sometimes available, although it was very difficult for Jewish prisoners to get their hands on them. However, there was an extensive underground trade in Auschwitz in which the kapos, other *Funktionshäftlinge* and prisoners who had been assigned to a good *kommando* (such as Peter) played a leading role.[169]

175

Prämienschein for 1 Reichsmark.

Otto Frank's *Raucherkarte* from Auschwitz.

Although Otto Frank was often interviewed after the war, he rarely spoke in detail about daily life in the camp. Nevertheless, there are many eyewitness statements which give a good insight into camp life. One example is the role which faith played for Otto Frank. We know that, unlike his wife Edith, he rarely attended the synagogue before he went into hiding and wasn't very interested in religion, but also that his involvement in the liberal Jewish community increased significantly after 1945. Anne's school friend Hanneli Goslar, who herself had an

176

orthodox background, recalls that Otto Frank told her that he tried to keep up the Jewish rituals in Auschwitz:

> The Frank family often came to celebrate the Sabbath with us on a Friday. After the war, Otto told me that in Auschwitz they wanted to recite the Kiddush [the blessing given at the start of the Sabbath before the main meal] together with other Jewish prisoners, but no one knew it by heart. However, Otto Frank had heard the Kiddush so often at our house that he was the only one who could conduct the ceremony in Hebrew.[170]

Another important witness statement was made by Sal de Liema, who was interviewed in 1995, when he was eighty, by the documentarian Jon Blair about his time in Auschwitz and his relationship with Otto Frank. De Liema summarized the period which he spent in Auschwitz with Otto Frank as "life was hell", and describes the dreadful circumstances in detail, the violent guards and the widespread scarcities in the camp.[171] Prisoners even fought for bits paper to wipe their bottoms: "I'll tell you this: the camp at Auschwitz was possibly the cleanest place on earth. There wasn't a single piece of paper on the ground because if there was any paper anywhere we fought for it just to wipe ourselves, because we had nothing else to do it with."[172]

De Liema also describes how he became a friend of Otto Frank and started to call him Papa Frank after a while. The two men first met about a week after Otto Frank and De Liema had arrived in Auschwitz from Westerbork on the same train of 3 September 1944. Initially, they only talked about the horrors of the camp, such as the burning of the bodies and the lack of food, but Sal and Otto quickly decided to stop talking about those things.

[T]he close relationship with Otto Frank happened after at least a week being here, really, and all people are talking about was of course the crematoria, no food, no clothes […]. But talking about it didn't help. It actually hurt a lot. And then Mr. Frank found me, and I found Mr. Frank and we said: "We have to stop this, because we are killing our brain here, to talk about, all the time about food and clothes. […] We cannot do anything [about] what will happen to our body, and we knew our body was going down every day, but let's try to save our brain."[173]

To suppress the enormous psychological pressure and constant fear, Otto and Sal talked about art and culture:

Let's say: do you remember the melody from […] the 9th symphony of Beethoven and then we start singing to each other. Just to get away from this fear, just to get our brain thinking about other things. We talked about Van Gogh, Rembrandt […] did you ever go to the Rijksmuseum? […] And it really helped I think.[174]

It's clear how important it was to "keep up your spirits" from other eyewitness statements about Auschwitz. Virtually all the survivors describe how a large number of prisoners gave up the struggle to survive and just moved around the camp lethargically without any interest. The Italian Jew Primo Levi, who was in Auschwitz-Monowitz, describes them as emaciated men, "their heads hanging and shoulders bent with no sign of any thought in their eyes or face."[175]

In Auschwitz and some of the other camps, such a prisoner was known as a *Muselmann*. In German, this means "Muslim", and is probably a reference to the similarity with prisoners

178

Primo Levi, 1950s.

who could no longer stand up as a result of exhaustion and the Muslim position of prayer.[176] According to the historian Nikolaus Wachsmann, "These *Muselmänner* were zombies. They were exhausted, apathetic and starving and they'd lost everything. Their bodies consisted only of bones and dry skin covered in sores and crusts. They could hardly speak and looked into the void with hollow, empty eyes." Because they were barely able to work or follow orders, the *Muselmänner* were the first to be chosen for the gas chambers in the selections. Other prisoners generally kept away from them for fear of being associated with them and also being selected for the gas chamber.[177]

After the war, the *Muselmann* was to become one of the most important symbols of the terror of the camps, and for the prisoners it was the ultimate image of fear. With their discussions about art and museums, Sal de Liema and Otto Frank tried to prevent themselves from giving up on the struggle to survive and to become *Muselmänner* as well. Sal de Liema's testimony shows how difficult this was.

Apart from being hungry, in danger of falling sick or freezing, the prisoners were constantly faced with violence, humiliation and mistreatment by the guards. There were also quarrels amongst the prisoners themselves. Again, Otto Frank's own testimony about this is quite brief and we depend on other witnesses for information. For example, after the war, Miep Gies remembered that Otto asked her to accompany him to a shoe shop in the Leidsestraat. He said that he had got to know the owner in Auschwitz and had punched this man in the face during an argument: "When Frank walked into the shop the man recognized him immediately and walked towards him. There was a moment of hesitation and then they embraced each other." When Miep Gies asked Otto afterwards what had happened, he explained that in the camp "moods [...] sometimes became very heated about small and trivial matters."[178]

However, it was above all the guards and kapos who were a constant threat. The description provided by Sal de Liema clearly shows their arbitrary and extreme violence. Life in Auschwitz was a constant struggle to survive. He remembers that when they accompanied the prisoners to their daily work, the kapos were explicitly given the message that of the 250 men who went, only 240 had to return at the end of the day, and that they were therefore permitted to kill ten of them, and this always happened. Once he was walking back with a man who was shot in the back by a guard out of nowhere.[179]

De Liema also remembers that one freezing day he was chased naked into a building with hot showers along with a group of other prisoners, including Otto Frank. Two guards with whips chased the prisoners into the room full of scalding steam. It was so hot and crowded that De Liema fainted and could only just be kept standing by his friends:

[T]he water was so hot, it was unbelievable. In the first let's say 10–15 seconds, it didn't bother us much because we were all frozen. [...] But after maybe 10 seconds you wanted to get out because it was so hot. But there were two German soldiers with whips, and they were acting like in a circus. [...] [A]pparently what happened to me is I blacked out. They told me this later on, I didn't know. It was only for a couple of minutes, but they felt it was a danger, a great danger to me, because if they found somebody on the floor, they'd simply throw him in the fire.[180]

Afterwards, the prisoners had to run back to their barracks in the cold, still naked. Then they had to stand in the cold for the roll call for hours, sometimes even without any clothes. De Liema remembers the sadism of the guards and the remark that one of the guards made to him during a roll call:

I was standing in the snow, naked, after we came back from our work. When we were standing for the roll call [...] a German soldier came and he had his fur coat on, and he looked at me and he said: "Kalt, huh? It is cold." I didn't even answer. I just looked at him. And he said: "You know, you won't survive this, you know that, don't you? But in case you do survive," he said, "I'll take care of it that it's not gonna happen – nobody will believe you, what we did to you people. Nobody."[181]

Another time, De Liema, Otto and other prisoners were ordered to play leapfrog in their underpants; during this, the prisoners kept falling over and were whipped by the guards to get them up again.[182]

Otto Frank experienced several similar situations. He told Ernst Schnabel that he had been beaten so badly when he was peeling potatoes that his resistance broke down completely. The next day, a Sunday, he no longer had the strength to get up.[183] Some fellow prisoners were encouraging him and called a Dutch doctor who had been one of the *Zugärzte* (train doctors) on the transport of 3 September 1944. In a television documentary for the German channel Südwestfunk, Otto finished this story:

> I felt very down one day in Auschwitz and couldn't go on anymore. I'd been badly beaten and this had really affected me, also as regards my morale. It was a Sunday morning and I said: "I can't get up any more". And then my friends – who were all Dutch of course: actually I was a German amongst the Dutch, but they had completely accepted me – they said: "You can't do that, you've got to get up or you'll be lost." Then they went to a Dutch doctor who worked together with the German doctor and this Dutch doctor visited me in my barracks. He said: "Get up and come to the infirmary tomorrow morning early. I'll talk to the German doctor and make sure that you're admitted". And that's what happened and that's what saved me.[184]

This Dutch doctor was called Samuel Kropveld, and together with the other doctor (a man named Fischer, who was not German but in fact Czech), he made sure that Otto was admitted to hospital the next day. On 4 March 1948, Kropveld said:

> [...] In this way I met the father of Anne Franck [sic] who was lying in an attic, extremely dirty and covered

182

Samuel Kropveld.

in lice. He said, "Doctor, please help me" and I went to my Jewish Czech colleague Fischer to ask him for advice. Fischer was a neurologist and was prepared to admit Franck for psychological observation. Franck was admitted and put in a corner where he remained until the Russians liberated him. He still holds it against me that I saved his life.[185]

The last sentence: "He still holds it against me that I saved his life" is in stark contrast with Otto Frank's statements that he had been "saved" with the help of his friends and by being admitted to hospital, and that it was a "miracle" that he was lucky enough to survive Auschwitz.[186]

DEPARTURE

Otto Frank was admitted to the infirmary in Auschwitz somewhere between the beginning of November and 21 November 1944.[187] He went into sickbay 19.[188] Despite the lack of medicines and medical treatment, it was less dangerous to be sent to the hospital during this period than it had been before.

Previously, the sick had been murdered in the gas chambers, but from the beginning of November 1944, no one was gassed in Auschwitz. Life was relatively easier for Otto in the infirmary because he didn't have to work and could sit inside, while it was minus 20 degrees outside. He did everything he could to stay there.[189] His contact with Sal de Liema, who was now also sick and had serious diarrhea, was lost at that point. De Liema remembers that the Dutch doctor Elie Cohen, who was worried about him, strongly dissuaded him from visiting Otto Frank in the infirmary because he might infect him. As a result, they didn't see each other again until after the war.[190]

Meanwhile, Otto Frank made friends with the above-mentioned Hungarian Jew Joseph Spronz in the infirmary.[191] Spronz told him about the cardiac problems he had developed during the hard work in the quarry, and showed him the injuries to his eye and nose after a kapo had punched him in the face.[192] Just after his liberation, Otto wrote to his cousin Milly Stanfield that he remembered two fellow prisoners in the infirmary, neither of whom survived, playing the violin and the cello at Christmas.[193]

However, Otto Frank had by far the most support from Peter van Pels. Because of his job at the *Paketstelle*, Peter was quite fit and had a position which enabled him to help his friends. During the period that Otto was in the infirmary, Peter visited him nearly every day. As Otto remembered later, "Peter helped me like a son. Every day he brought me extra food. He could never stay long. We never talked about serious matters and he never spoke about Anne. I didn't have the impression that he was growing up to be an adult yet."[194] This reflects the mixture of gratitude and criticism with which Otto generally spoke about Peter after the war. But he also spoke a great deal about

Peter's position in the camp. Because of his job at the *Paket-stelle*, he was clearly able to move around quite freely and could also easily get his hands on extra food, which he shared with Otto. He helped Otto to survive in this way until the camp was evacuated.[195]

In the middle of January 1945, Otto and Peter said goodbye to each other. After the big deportations which had taken place from the autumn of 1944, there were still approximately 67,000 prisoners left in the Auschwitz complex at the beginning of 1945, and as the Russian army advanced, the SS started to prepare for the complete evacuation of the camp.[196] These plans involved marching to the west on foot then taking trains to camps in Germany. The evacuation of Auschwitz, with the exception of the infirmaries, started when the Red Army was on the point of taking Kraków, about 60 kilometers away, in the middle of January 1945.[197]

The prisoners heard about the evacuation a few days beforehand.[198] Once again, this followed a selection: only prisoners who were considered suitable for work and were able to walk dozens of miles every day were sent on the marches. Even so, many of the weak and sick also applied to go because they were afraid they would otherwise be murdered.[199] As the Russian offensive took place a week earlier than expected, there was chaos and the prisoners were not guarded as strictly. Consequently, some were able to take extra clothes and food with them from a store that had been looted.[200]

Those who were eligible for evacuation had to go to the roll call, with all the barracks lining up in turn. The route passed by the kitchens, where they were given food rations for the journey. A total of 56,000 people set out on these death marches for the various camps in Germany between 17 or 18 January and 21 January 1945.[201] It was freezing and there was a thick layer of snow; the prisoners' clothes were completely unsuitable for the bitter weather conditions.

Peter van Pels was part of the group of prisoners who were taken to the Mauthausen concentration camp in Austria. According to Otto Frank, he was optimistic about his chances and wanted to join the evacuation transport together with the people with whom he worked.[202] In the late 1970s, Otto Frank told the American journalist Arthur Unger that Peter van Pels visited him in the infirmary just before Auschwitz was evacuated:

> The Germans had to leave Auschwitz and they evacuated all the prisoners. Luckily, I was in the hospital. In the so-called hospital. It was not treatment. It was really you weren't beaten and you had not to be outside. It was twenty below zero. And I did everything to stay in. And Peter came to me and said: we leave. And Peter was well fed and Peter had a good position. He was young. Peter said: "All the people I am working with go, and I'll go, I'll make it." I said: "Peter, hide yourself. You can hide yourself here in the hospital upstairs or somewhere." He did not want to and so he perished.[203]

In his postwar descriptions, Otto Frank characterized Peter's decision not to hide as a fatal mistake and even as a naïve decision: "Peter was a very good boy, really a good-hearted boy. But he wasn't very intelligent," he added later.[204]

Samuel Kropveld confirms that it was a realistic option to hide in the infirmary. But his statement also shows that the prisoners had good reasons not to take this risk. Kropveld, who joined the "healthy" prisoners like Peter and ended up in

Mauthausen and Melk, said in the account of his experiences at the camp that he had seriously considered staying behind:

> When the camp was evacuated, I first considered whether I would try and remain behind. I had a plan and discussed it with the Chief […] but he told me that those who remained behind were the sick and would certainly not be allowed to live. It would not be difficult to hide […] but when I thought that everything might go wrong and the whole lot would be blown up, I decided to join the evacuation transport.[205]

It's probable that Peter had heard similar rumors and, in view of his relatively good condition, he assumed that his chances of survival would increase if he went along with the rest of the prisoners.

Otto Frank remained behind in the infirmary with the other sick prisoners. Just after his liberation, he made a note of a number of important facts in his notebook. On 16 January, he wrote: "SS geht fort" ("SS are off"). After the evacuation of Auschwitz, which actually took place between 17 and 21 January 1945, the infirmary where Otto Frank was staying remained untouched. He stayed behind in Auschwitz with about 8,000 other prisoners. Nobody knew whether they would be liberated or would still be executed.[206] When the last SS officers had left with the prisoners, the prisoners who'd remained behind moved carefully through the camp looking for something to eat and drink. Otto remembered this later:

> Well, after the Germans had left, we were alone. People from the hospital and quite a number. And we had to see there were so much food, there were cellars of food for

the SS, but there was no water because everything was frozen and broken. And there were lakes in the neighborhood. So we went with things to break the ice and we made water from the lakes.[207]

Joseph Spronz remembers how the prisoners who remained organized themselves to bring as much water as possible to the kitchen: "Every patient who could walk was busy bringing water to the kitchen. We only drank boiled water and because of the supplies in the warehouse it was possible to get black coffee at all times."[208]

As indicated above, Otto was convinced that he survived the Holocaust because of his firm decision to stay in the infirmary at any cost when others were getting ready to evacuate the camp.[209] Other former prisoners, like Eddy de Wind, shared that conviction. In the end, because they stayed in the infirmary, they avoided the death marches and survived.[210]

However, what appears to be a considered choice between leaving or attempting to stay in many of the statements was actually a complete gamble. In reality, the prisoners had no idea what awaited them, and insofar as they had any choice anyway, they could only base this on vague rumors and their own intuition. The Dutch doctor Elie Cohen wrote that he and several others had never considered that they might have to walk. They were aware of the existence of "transports on foot" because a number of Dutch prisoners had come to Auschwitz on foot from Lublin. However, despite this knowledge, they couldn't believe that the Germans would manage to take thousands of people "ins Reich" in a short time. That evening, when the men were ready to go and Eddy de Wind went to say goodbye to his fellow prisoners, he said to Elie Cohen: "I don't know who's doing the right thing, you or me, but I don't believe that I would survive the transport and therefore I'm taking the risk to stay here. After the war it'll be clear who was right."[211] It became clear later that there certainly were plans to kill all those who had remained behind.[212] On 26 January, when Otto Frank was busy hacking a hole in a frozen pond to get water together with a few other prisoners, a group of SS officers suddenly appeared and made all the prisoners step forward to be executed.[213] In a letter to his mother dated 8 June 1945, Otto Frank described how he barely escaped death at the end of January: "On the 26th we were taken outside by the SS to be murdered, but the SS were called away before this happened – it was a miracle."[214] Otto Frank's notebook also contains a short mention of this event: "26.I Apell."[215] This incident was also described by Justus Philips, Joseph Spronz and Eddy de Wind.[216] In *Last Stop Auschwitz*, De Wind describes how he had heard from a fellow prisoner that they had only just escaped death:

> At three o'clock in the afternoon, a team of SS officers appeared, those dogs of the extermination kommando, dressed in black and armed to the teeth. They came into the blocks and chased everyone outside with the butts of their rifles. Poor old Slobinsky still has injuries to his head as a result. Even the most seriously ill people were taken outside. They were supported by the *Pfleger* and the other sick prisoners who could still move. Then they told us that we had to go inside again. They would get cars to take us to the train and when they called us, we'd have to go out immediately. Then they went to Birkenau and played the same game there. Many prisoners there

couldn't get out of their beds. With about 1,000 sick people from Birkenau, they started to march in the direction of Auschwitz. When they were a few hundred meters outside the camp a car drove by and called out. The SS men jumped into the car, and after that no one saw them again.[217]

The prisoners had escaped death because the advance of the Red Army was threatening to block the German retreat and the SS officers were suddenly in a big hurry.

The next day, 27 January 1945, Auschwitz was a liberated by the Red Army. After heavy aerial dogfights and vehement attempts by the Wehrmacht to stop the Russian soldiers at the Sola River, the 60th army of the First Ukrainian Front reached the gates of Auschwitz, where they found 8,000 extremely weak

Russian soldiers talk to a group of children shortly after the liberation of Auschwitz, January 1945.

prisoners who had remained behind. "Ruski", Otto Frank later wrote next to this date in his notebook.[218] Later, he remembered very little of the arrival of the Russian soldiers. He was now too weak to get up and only later recalled their "snow white" camouflage jackets and his enormous relief at being liberated at last. At that moment, it didn't matter to him at all that the soldiers were from the Soviet Union that he mistrusted so much: "They were good people, we didn't care whether they were communists or not. We weren't interested in politics, we were interested in the liberation."[219]

The Russian cameraman Aleksandr Vorontsov, who was part of a Red Army film crew and was responsible for documenting what had happened in the camp, later wrote about what he had found:

> The women wept, and – this cannot be concealed – the men wept as well. You could say that there were pyramids on the grounds of the camp. Some were made up of accumulated clothing, others of pots, and others still of human jaws. I believe that not even the commanders of our army had any idea of the dimensions of the crime committed in this largest of camps. The memory has stayed with me my whole life long. All of this was the most moving and most terrible thing that I saw and filmed during the war. Time has no sway over these recollections. It has not squeezed all the horrible things I saw and filmed out of my mind.[220]

Otto Frank had been imprisoned in Auschwitz for twenty weeks and four days. At the time of his liberation, he weighed only 52 kilograms.[221] On 2 February 1945, he moved to the infirmary in block 18, where he was cared for by the Polish Red Cross doctor

Józef Bellert, who was taking care of the prisoners. Although there were virtually no medicines or medical equipment in the camp, Bellert and the other doctors tried to look after the prisoners as best they could.[222] After a while, Otto Frank partially recovered. It was the beginning of a long period of recovery and repatriation, and the start of a search for information about his wife and daughters and the others with whom he had been in hiding.[223]

CHAPTER FOUR

"You couldn't raise her spirits because there weren't any"

Edith, Anne and Margot Frank, and Auguste van Pels in Auschwitz-Birkenau

LIFE IN THE CAMP: HUNGER, COLD AND SELECTIONS

Like the men, the women on the transport of 3 September 1944 were in quarantine in Auschwitz-Birkenau for a while after the registration. It is difficult to determine exactly what Auguste van Pels, Edith Frank and her daughters experienced in Birkenau or when they stayed at different places in the camp, especially as there were constant internal moves during the last months of 1944.[1] Anita Mayer-Ross, who was imprisoned in Auschwitz-Birkenau during the same period, stated that she was forced to move no fewer than six times in the women's camp in Birkenau before she was sent to the external camp at Libau on 26 October 1944.[2]

A few documents that have survived from the camp administration give some insight into the quarantine in Birkenau. For example, food supplies appear to have improved slightly in September 1944. On 10 September 1944, a *Lagerarzt* made a written request for the 1,122 women who were in the quarantine section of the camp BIIa at that time to be given extra sausage and bread twice a week so that they could gain some strength.[3] He also requested 1,000 bars of soap for the women who were in barracks 5 and 6.[4] It's not known whether these requests were met, but they do clarify some organizational aspects.

Bloeme Emden, who was imprisoned in the camp at the same time as the Frank family, remembers the "detailed process" that the new arrivals had to go through after the men were separated from the women:

> You were forced to walk a long way. At the end there was a man who said: this way or that. One of the people I'd met said: "My niece and the child who was just here, where have they gone?" One of the guys in the striped suits who beat us turned out to be Dutch. He was also a prisoner but we didn't know that […] and he told her: "Oh, they're dead already". Then […] I was at the corner, I'd just turned eighteen and we arrived in a place where our hair was shaved, every hair on our head, and a number was tattooed onto your arm. Then we had to undress and all those clothes were thrown onto a heap with the shoes, and then we went into the shower. […] Well, when you came out of the shower it was impossible to find your clothes so you had to just take anything from the heap and look for a pair of shoes. Then you were sent on again, not walking but chased to the barracks where we would live. Three floors providing space for ten women, so there were thirty women in every unit. When there wasn't enough room, more people were added. You become swamped by total despair […] there was a group of friends from the prison who were in bed together. In the end we were a group of thirteen women. I was the youngest and the two oldest were twenty years older than I was. Five of them died in Auschwitz.[5]

Edith, Margot, Anne and Auguste ended up in the quarantine barracks 29, together with other women who were on the transport of 3 September 1944.[6] This is where the quarantine period started for them and continued for about eight weeks until the selections for Libau, Kratzau and Bergen-Belsen started at the end of October 1944.[7] The quarantine barracks where Edith, Margot and Anne were accommodated for the first weeks in Birkenau had been built in 1941 by Russian prisoners of war. They had no foundations; the floor was an earthen floor with a thin layer of cement or loose stones.[8] The barracks were 36 by 11 meters and were divided by stone walls into sixty niches of 2 by 2 meters, with three-tiered platforms made of planks to sleep on.[9] There was a layer of straw and a horsehair blanket on the planks.

Survivors emphasize the lack of space in the barracks. There was nowhere to sit, and sometimes ten to twelve women had to take turns to sleep in a single berth.[10] An anonymous girl who was interviewed by the Red Cross shortly after the liberation described the quarantine barracks: "Inside there were two cages, one above the other – the first of them was very dark. For every cage we were given two sacks of straw and five thin blankets. The intention was that five people should sleep in one cage, but there were too many people, so we ended up with ten of us sleeping in one cage."[11]

This picture was confirmed by Frieda Brommer and Ronnie van Cleef, who arrived in barracks 29 together with Edith, Anne and Margot. They slept next to each other and remembered that Anne, Margot and Edith were immediately above them in the overcrowded cage. Frieda described it as follows:

You were lying there with eight of you next to each other and one at the foot of the cage. And you would be side by side like spoons. If one person turned over, everyone had to turn over. And it was worse for the person at the foot of the cage because they had everyone's feet pointing at them. The Frank women, Edith, Margot and Anne, slept above us.

At that point, Ronnie and Frieda were not yet in contact with the Franks. "You hardly spoke to anyone", said Frieda Brommer in an interview with the Anne Frank House. It was only later when they were in the *Krätzeblock* together – the infirmary where prisoners with *Krätze* (scabies) were accommodated – that they started to talk to each other more."[12]

Witness statements show that the group of Dutch prisoners largely stayed together after the quarantine period.[13] Ronnie van Cleef called it the "Dutch barracks". However, Rosa de Winter-Levy, who also ended up in barracks 29, emphasized that there were not just Dutch women but also about 500 French, Hungarian and Polish women already there when the approximately 200 Dutch women joined them.[14]

The women soon became acquainted with the hard camp regime. Some witnesses declared that for the first few days of the quarantine they were not given anything to eat or drink.[15] Then there was the work – this was not only extremely heavy, but also completely pointless.[16] They had to dig up turfs of grass all day long and throw them onto a heap, or drag sand and stones around without any purpose. Lenie de Jong-van Naarden remembers that she always had to work in Auschwitz: "We were always heaving stones from one place to another and then a different team would have to take them back again."[17] They carried the stones in the lap of their dress or, if they were being punished, with their arms stretched out.[18] The women who had *Stubendienst* were better off and stayed in the barracks during the day to clean them or to get food. But as in Wester-bork, these sought-after jobs could only be acquired with luck and good contacts.[19]

Edith, Margot, Anne and Auguste survived the quarantine period. Like most of the women, they had to do heavy work. Rosa de Winter-Levy describes how the women had to toil with bricks and heavy grass turfs. The women were assembled for roll call twice a day, which was torture.[20] The morning roll call started at four and the evening roll call often lasted until late at night. Many of the women collapsed during these endless routines. Special groups of prisoners then had to remove the lifeless bodies from between the lines of other women.

The Jewish women lived in constant fear of selections. In Birkenau, these mainly took place during the roll calls and when they returned from work, but selections were also carried out in the infirmary and in the showers.[21] One Dutch survivor remembers that selections were held every month, but sometimes also every other week or even every other day.[22]

When she was asked about their feelings, Bloeme Emden said: "We were often subject to very dark moods and fears. But you get used to being terrified. I called it being resigned. You could become indifferent."[23]

Food consisted of "coffee water", watery soup of potatoes or rotten vegetables, bread, and sometimes a piece of sausage, cheese or margarine. As Jews were not allowed to receive any food parcels, they were the first to die from diseases resulting from hunger. Just as in the other camp routines, the distribution of food was accompanied by intimidation and beatings. Women prisoners who were appointed as female kapos by the camp leaders (mainly *Blockältesten* and *Stubenältesten*) often kept the prisoners' food for themselves.[24]

From time to time the women had to go to the *Zentralsauna* to be deloused. Their clothes and blankets would be disinfected, and they were given arbitrary clothes back.[25] One of the women of the transport of 3 September 1944 lost the woolen dress that she'd swapped for two portions of bread and three portions of margarine during one of the disinfections in the *Zentralsauna*.[26] Bloeme Emden confirmed in an interview that there was a "busy trade in bread for clothes".[27]

GUARDS AND VIOLENCE IN THE WOMEN'S CAMP

In Auschwitz-Birkenau, the female prisoners regularly came into contact with male guards, but in the daily life of the camp it was mainly women who were responsible for guarding them. Relatively little attention has been devoted to these women in the historical accounts. Admittedly, the postwar trials of notorious camp guards such as Ilse Koch and Irma Grese were widely covered, but it was only relatively recently that there was a thorough analysis of their role in the concentration camp system. Researchers such as Elissa Mailänder, Kathrin Kompisch and Wendy Lower have revealed that women played a much more important role in National Socialist violence than is often assumed.[28] Their research has largely eroded the stereotypical image of the passive and subordinate role of women in the Third Reich. Furthermore, they showed that while women admittedly never had the same career opportunities as men, they certainly had plenty of scope for their own initiatives and independent action.[29] In camps like Ravensbrück and Auschwitz, women had career opportunities that even gave them access to leading positions.[30]

This applied in particular for the large women's camp in Auschwitz-Birkenau. The Austrian *Oberaufseherin* Maria

Maria Mandel, 1945.

Mandel was the head of the guards at the women's camp in Birkenau. She had gained experience in the concentration camps of Lichtenburg and Ravensbrück and arrived in Auschwitz-Birkenau in October 1942, where she succeeded Johanna Langefeld, who had been criticized as being too soft by the camp commandant Rudolf Höss.[31] Attempts made by Höss to take over the running of the women's camp were not appreciated by Heinrich Himmler, however, who considered that a "women's camp should be run by a woman".[32]

Using the experience she had gained in other camps, Mandel introduced the hard and merciless approach that corresponded with the views of the camp commandant Rudolf Höss. However, he was not really impressed by her organizational skills and established a parallel structure of authority from August 1943, in which a male *Schutzhaftlagerführer*, Franz Hössler, was made responsible for the daily routine in the women's camp, along with the *Aufseherinnen* (female guards).[33]

Despite the power games with Höss, Mandel's position remained largely autonomous at Auschwitz. Höss gave her free rein to carry out the selections and punishments, and officially she was in charge of the women's camp as the chief SS guard. Mandel was notorious for her cruelty and was known among prisoners as "The Beast". She was in charge of approximately 170 female *Aufseherinnen*, who were in turn assisted by the kapos and *Blockältesten*.[34] However, as only a small number of the female guards were brought to trial and the prisoners often didn't know their names, it's difficult to gain a clear picture of the women who guarded Anne, Margot and Edith in Auschwitz.

Apart from Mandel, we only know about a few other notorious female guards. For instance, Elisabeth Volkenrath helped with the selections for the gas chambers in Auschwitz-Birkenau and she was also responsible for the distribution of bread.[35] Irma Grese was another notorious female guard, known as "The Blonde Angel of Death". She was known in particular for her cruelty to prisoners and for helping Mengele, the camp doctor.

It is clear that the female prisoners in Auschwitz-Birkenau were confronted with constant humiliation and violence. Rosa de Winter-Levy describes how the women had to get undressed and were shaved when they arrived, shamelessly watched by the male guards:

> After giving our names, we had to take off all our clothes in front of the SS. Completely naked, we were lined up and shaved bald by Polish women who had been appointed for this. The SS commandants constantly walked amongst us with a big bulldog; we were shaking with fear, exhaustion and shame. We were the butt of their jokes for hours. One of these animals, I don't want to call them anything else, ripped the clothes off the girl next to me. I gave her a sign that she should stand behind

200

me. In this way she could shelter from the predatory eyes of the SS vandals.[36]

The female guards and *Funktionshäftlinge* were also often violent, just like the men. Rosa de Winter-Levy remembers that the deputy *Blockälteste* chased the prisoners out of bed on their first morning in Birkenau, beating them on the way to the morning roll call, where the prisoners had to stand for hours to be "counted". The following day, Rosa saw that another prisoner, who didn't yet know the precise rules of the camp, was walking over a road that ran through the camp which was forbidden for use by the prisoners. Suddenly, a female camp guard stood in front of her holding a whip and screaming at her in German. When the Dutch woman, who couldn't understand her, didn't respond immediately, the guard became furious: "She ordered her to kneel down, whipped her mercilessly and kicked her so much that she remained lying down covered in blood. Later, we had to carry her to the infirmary, where she died of her injuries".[37]

Rosa was also beaten herself. After being in the camp for a while, the women were deloused again in the shower block, and after standing naked almost all day, they were given clothes again. Rosa and her daughter, who both had a fever and diarrhea, could hardly cover themselves with these clothes, with Rosa having to make do with a torn dress. In addition, they were also given a collective punishment by the guards because a number of women had tried to get out of the delousing activity. Everyone had to kneel down and hold a brick aloft. Rosa couldn't manage and asked the male *Blockführer* for a shirt:

> I was kneeling at the front in my torn dress and he could see my naked belly. I asked him for a shirt. He hit me with

the whip and mocked me, saying: "Shit, bare belly, you can drop dead." Then he stood in front of us pointing a revolver at us, saying: "I feel like shooting someone". We had to stand there until late into the night. It was terrible.[38]

Lenie de Jong-Van Naarden and Bloeme Emden, who spent a lot of time together in Auschwitz and belonged to a group of Dutch women, remembered the violence in the camp as well as the exhausting roll calls, the hunger, cold and poor hygiene. According to Emden, they were "constantly beaten". She herself was beaten extremely violently once by one of the female guards, probably a kapo: "She hit me so hard that my eardrum burst. I was left with an infected ear for many years."[39]

Although she doesn't remember seeing Anne and Margot being beaten, this sort of violence was common practice. For example, Bloeme said that her friend Anita was beaten once and became so angry that she almost attacked the SS officer who had mistreated her with the spade she was holding: "That would certainly have cost her her life. It was only because Lenie grabbed her arm and held her back that her life was saved. It was like that – conditions you can't even imagine." Lenie de Jong-van Naarden remembered that her group generally managed to avoid mistreatment by staying together and protecting each other from problems as much as possible, though she did get hit on the head just after she arrived because she started laughing as they were being shaved bald:

I had very long hair and it was held up with all sorts of pins and the girl sitting next to me, Annie,[40] was the same and we both got the giggles because we were so nervous. And then I was hit very hard and that was the first time that I was beaten, because I was laughing.[41]

Although she also emphasized that she "didn't notice the violence" that much because of the protection provided by her group, her interview reveals that the danger of severe punishment was constantly present: "You absolutely had to walk on the left when you were supposed to walk on the left and certainly shouldn't walk on the right. Sometimes people were simply shot dead, even right at the beginning. They would do something slightly wrong [...]."[42]

The prisoners were constantly confronted with death. In her report, Rosa de Winter-Levy noted that women who tried to escape were hanged on a gallows at the camp in order to make the other prisoners more fearful: "It was a terrible sight. We had to walk past it and look at it". The witness statements by women who were in Birkenau at the same time as Auguste, Edith, Anne and Margot show that the arrival of a large group of Hungarian children who were murdered in the gas chambers immediately on arrival made a particularly ineradicable impression. Rosa de Winter-Levy remembers that after working all day, she returned to Birkenau and saw a "whole transport of little Hungarian children": "It was shocking, they had to get undressed and stay standing naked in the rain until they were taken inside. Those poor children thought they were going to be taken to a bathhouse but they were gassed and burnt."[43] It was only then that she realized that bodies were being burnt in the crematoria on a massive scale.

De Winter-Levy told Ernst Schnabel that Anne had seen the Hungarian children as well: "[Anne] was also crying when we marched past the Hungarian children who had been standing waiting in front of the gas chamber naked for half a day because it was not yet their turn. Anne touched me and said: 'Just look at their eyes!'"[44] Lenie de Jong-van Naarden also witnessed the arrival of the Hungarian children: "When you saw so many children walking hand-in-hand it was a really, really terrible thing, seeing them go into the gas chamber".[45]

IN THE "DUTCH BARRACKS": EDITH, ANNE AND MARGOT FRANK, AND AUGUSTE VAN PELS

Edith, Anne, Margot and Auguste had to try to survive in this world of hunger, disease, brutality, violence and death. We can get an idea of what they experienced from the statements of various witnesses. Like the other women, life in the camp for Edith Frank and her two daughters started with the registration and being tattooed on their lower left arms; their numbers were between A25109 and A25116.[46] Following this, they were placed in quarantine in block 29 of the women's camp.[47]

A number of women were still regularly in contact with Edith, Anne and Margot. I. Salomon stated in a report to the Red Cross that she was in block 29, where she had to sleep on wooden planks with straw. In her report, she mentions that Mrs. Frank and her daughters slept above her.[48] Others also have memories of Edith, Margot and Anne Frank in that block.[49] Bloeme Emden and Lenie de Jong-van Naarden formed a close group in Birkenau, together with about ten other Dutch women. They were also in contact with Anne, Margot and Edith, although the Franks were not really part of the group of Dutch women. According to Bloeme, Anne Margot and Edith were an "inseparable trio".[50]

Other witnesses describe how Anne and Margot ended up in the *Krätzeblock*, which was the block for people who had scabies. Soon after they arrived, there was an epidemic of scarlet fever, and Ronnie van Cleef, followed shortly afterwards by Frieda Brommer, had to go to the infirmary. After a few weeks, they were moved to the *Krätzeblock*, where they ran into

Margot and Anne Frank. Lenie remembers that it was actually Margot who had to be admitted and that Anne wanted to stay with her sister and therefore went with her.[51]

These wooden barracks, where the patients lay in bunk beds, two to a bunk, were surrounded by a tall, wide stone wall. The sick, who were largely left to their fate, were dependent on their fellow prisoners. Mirjam Blitz emphasizes the isolated position of the *Krätzeblock*:

> The Krätzeblock was disgusting, so dirty, and so filthy that it made me feel sick when I was smuggled in. There were often Dutch women there and as it was isolated from everything and you needed moral support from outside, I sometimes went in with a few girls.[52]

Now that her daughters were in the scabies barracks, Edith had to think of a way to help them. Together with the mother of Frieda Brommer, and with the help of Lenie de Jong-van Naarden, Edith dug a hole underneath the barracks to be able to pass food to her children.[53] Frieda remembers how they got some extra food through the hole:

> During the period that Ronnie and I were there together, my mother and Mrs. Frank, Edith, were a sort of couple, because they stole things together and […] they dug a hole. Those barracks were […] they were made of wood and were built on sand, so you could dig a hole underneath and that is what my mother did. She dug a hole and one day my mother came and she could speak through the hole and she called "Frieda Frieda!" […] and she said: "Mrs. Frank and I are the only ones who are in the camp now. We've hidden ourselves because the group has gone

on a transport. But we wanted to stay with you and we stole some bread and I'm passing it to you now through the hole and you must share it, the four of you. The four of us meant Margot and Anne […] I couldn't go to the hole because I was too sick – I had typhus then as well. Then Ronnie went and took it and she shared it amongst the four of us.[54]

Lenie de Jong-van Naarden also described the desperate condition of Edith, Margot and Anne when they were in Auschwitz. Above all, Edith's sorrow about her sick and hungry children for whom she could do nothing was a strong memory: "When you see that […] words […] have no point at all. […] I couldn't raise her spirits because there weren't any left."[55]

Ronnie van Cleef stated that, in a sense, she felt "safe" in the *Krätzeblock* because a selection had taken place just before she and Frieda Brommer arrived there. It's not clear whether Margot and Anne were in that selection, because it's not possible to date their time in the *Krätzeblock* with any certainty. When Ronnie van Cleef and Frieda Brommer arrived there, they saw Anne and Margot lying in a bed together. After she got better, Ronnie van Cleef was put back in the "Dutch barracks".[56] This was just before the departure of the female prisoners to Libau and Kratzau on the transport of 26 October 1944.[57] It is therefore unclear how long Anne and Margot had to stay in the scabies block; Frieda knew only that of all four girls, she was the one who remained in the barracks longest: "You see, at a certain point Ronnie and perhaps also Anne and Margot, had to go. But I was so sick that I had to stay; I was the only one."[58]

Another witness of the fate of Edith, Anne and Margot was Rosa de Winter-Levy. She remembers that Anne empathized with her fellow prisoners and often cried about the things she saw: "It was she who was looking at what was happening around her up to the very end. We hardly saw it at all any more […]. But Anne couldn't protect herself from it, up to the end […]. She cried. And you can't imagine how quickly most of us stopped crying."[59]

There are hardly any witness statements about the fourth member of the group who came to Auschwitz-Birkenau from the Annex – Auguste van Pels. What we know about her fate can only be deduced from the few administrative data that have survived. Auguste van Pels's prisoner number in Auschwitz must have been between A25195 and A25203. The women of the transport of 3 September 1944 ended up in block 29 and mainly stayed together up to the selections for Kratzau, Libau and Bergen-Belsen. Auguste van Pels was mentioned only by Anita Meyer-Roos as being present in that block.[60] Rosa de Winter-Levy later said that she didn't see Auguste van Pels again after her arrival, neither in the camp nor in block 29.[61] The prisoner numbers on the list of Bergen-Belsen show that Auguste van Pels was deported from Auschwitz to Bergen-Belsen on the same transport as Anne and Margot Frank.[62]

ANOTHER DEPARTURE: ANNE, MARGOT AND AUGUSTE LEAVE

On 26 October 1944 there was a selection of approximately 100 women. Later, it was shown that fifty of them went to Libau (Silesia) and fifty to Kratzau (Czech Republic) to work in the war industry.[63] They included Ronnie van Cleef, Bloeme Emden and Rosa de Liema-van Gelder. Virtually all the women on the transport of 3 September 1944 who were still alive were deported to Libau and Kratzau. Judik, the daughter of Rosa de

Winter-Levy, also had to go to Kratzau,[64] but Rosa herself was not selected and had to watch her daughter being deported. It's not known whether Edith, Margot and Anne Frank were included in this selection of 26 October 1944. It is possible that they were not selected because of their poor health, or perhaps Anne and Margot were still in the *Krätzeblock*, which was left out of the selection.[65] Although Bloeme Emden thinks that they were still in the *Krätzeblock*, Frieda Brommer remembers that Anne and Margot were dismissed from the infirmary together with Ronnie van Cleef just before the selection.

Four days later, on 30 October 1944, there was another selection of the remaining women after the evening roll call. This took place outside the building of the *Zentralsauna*. There were already hundreds of other women waiting there who had arrived a day earlier with a transport from Theresienstadt. The women had to wait naked for hours to be assessed by the camp doctor. Those who were sick but potentially considered suitable for work were selected to be transported to Bergen-Belsen.[66] In this selection, the distinction that had initially been made for the transport from Westerbork between different categories of prisoners had become irrelevant. Rachel Frankfoorder and the Brilleslijper sisters, despite their status of *Schutzhäftlinge*,

Janny Brilleslijper with her husband, Bob Brandes.

Lientje Brilleslijper, before the war.

therefore had to join the others and work under the same conditions. A number of them were later also put to work in *subkommandos* of the camps at Buchenwald and Flossenbürg.[67]

In her book *Aan de gaskamer ontsnapt!*, Rosa de Winter-Levy wrote that Anne and Margot were included in this selection of 30 October 1944 and that their mother Edith Frank stayed behind on her own.[68] This shared grief over their children brought Rosa and Edith even closer: "We consoled each other and became friends".[69] When Rosa de Winter-Levy wrote about her camp experiences in 1945, Anne Frank's diary had not yet been discovered and she did not yet call "Edith's daughters" by their names. In a later interview with Ernst Schnabel, she went into more detail about her memories of the selection of Anne and Margot:

Another *Blocksperre*, but this time we had to wait naked at the roll call and it took a very long time. Then we had to walk into the barracks one by one. Inside there were floodlights and the doctor was there, and we had to walk into the light. However, this time we saw that he chose many people who were not very sick or old, and then we knew that they would have to go and the old and the sick would be gassed. There was a woman in front of us who was sixty, but she said that she was forty and she was allowed to go to Belsen. Then it was my turn and I also said I was ten years younger and told the doctor: "I'm 29 and I have never had diarrhea." But he gestured with his thumb and sent me to stand with the old and the sick. Then it was Mrs. Frank's turn and she also ended up with us straight away. Then it was the turn of the two girls: Anne and Margot. Anne stood with her face under the floodlights and touched Margot so Margot stood straight up in the light, and they stood there for a minute. Naked and bald. Anne looked at us with her bright face and she stood up straight and then they went. It was no longer possible to see what was happening behind the floodlights and Mrs. Frank screamed: "The children! Oh God!"[70]

The more than one thousand women who had been selected were shut into the barracks until the transport departed the next day, on 1 November 1944.[71]

"EDITH BECAME ILL": THE DEATH OF EDITH FRANK

Rosa de Winter-Levy describes how she and Edith barely managed to escape being gassed. The two selections for Kratzau and Bergen-Belsen, one just after the other, when first Rosa's daughter Judik and then Anne and Margot were separated from their mothers, were intended to separate the prisoners who were still able to work from those who were too weak. The women who had not been selected, like Rosa de Winter-Levy and Edith Frank, were locked in a barracks in the BIIb (the *B-Lager*) and were transferred to BIIa (the *A-Lager*) two days later. This was the area where the infirmaries were situated, and it was clear that they would soon be murdered: "We, the fifty of us who remained behind, knew what would happen to us. We'd probably be killed. The mood was terrible, women crying and weeping, dreadful! I felt as though I'd been turned to stone".[72]

However, an SS officer who came to fetch the group said that a number of prisoners would be taken to Germany for some light work, which raised Rosa's hopes somewhat. That afternoon they were given "good soup with meat in it", and two days later they left camp BIIb together with a few hundred women, expecting that they would be taken to another work camp by train as well. However, after walking for a few kilometers it became clear that there was no train waiting for them. They arrived at the *Zentralsauna*, where hundreds of women from Theresienstadt were already waiting. They also saw the male prisoners there who had to wait naked outside in the freezing cold: "The next morning most of them were lying on the ground half or completely frozen to death. They were thrown onto the wagons by the SS bandits and taken to the crematoria (of which there were several) to be burnt."[73]

In the building of the *Zentralsauna*, the women once again had to take off their clothes and there was another selection. Again, Edith and Rosa failed the selection: "Then suddenly I was in front of the SS officer. He looked at me with a penetrating gaze under the bright light and tapped me on my head, so

I was rejected again. A whole procession of women passed on. Now I was one of the rejected. 'Am I really so thin?' is what I kept thinking."[74]

The selected group of women now had to stand to one side and were guarded by the SS officers while their numbers were written down. At that point, two of the women in the group with Edith and Rosa could no longer bear the stress. They jumped out of the window of the building of the *Zentralsauna* and threw themselves against the electric fence. That night, Rosa and Edith and the other selected women were taken to the scabies barracks:

> There's no light, so in the dark we had to find somewhere to sleep. Edith and I held onto each other and crawled under a blanket somewhere with another woman. We were cold and absolutely exhausted. There were mice and rats scurrying over us, the women were crying and screaming. It was quite unbearable. There was no possibility of sleep. We were all thinking the same thing: tomorrow would be our last day.[75]

But there was one last reprieve. The next morning, the *Blockäl teste* came into the barracks "hurriedly and nervously" and called out some numbers, including those of Rosa and Edith: "Quick, get out, go to Block 42, you have to go for roll call there. We didn't know what that meant." However, it soon became clear when they saw that a truck had stopped in front of the block that they had just left ten minutes before departure: "[And] it was an enormous shock, the women who had remained behind were put onto the truck and driven to the crematorium, so 150 of us women were temporarily saved. We probably owe that to the Blockälteste."[76]

The three other Dutch women who had been chosen for the gas chamber at the same selection – Sientje de Zwarte, Dina Malka Wajnsztok and Klara Kneiberg – escaped the gas chamber in a similar way. Sientje and Klara belonged to Edith and Rosa's group that ended up in the *Schonungsblock* at the very last moment. Dina Malka Wajnsztok was taken away to be gassed, but as they marched towards the gas chamber, she threw herself into a deep pit at an unguarded moment and waited for it to get dark. When it was totally dark, she walked into a barracks, where she was silently accepted.[77]

Edith Frank and Rosa de Winter-Levy had already become close friends because of their shared experiences, and constantly stayed together. Rosa describes how they both tried to survive in the *Schonungsblock*, which was increasingly difficult due to the lack of drinking water, the poor hygiene and the vermin: "Weeks went by, I felt terrible and still had diarrhea. We now have enough bread, but we can hardly eat, we're thirsty and there's no water. We wash in the morning in the snow. The vermin, especially the lice in our clothes, are a terrible torment."

Rosa de Winter-Levy's detailed descriptions show what Edith Frank must have experienced and seen during the last weeks of her life – days full of despair and constant humiliations by the guards. For example, Rosa describes how she picked up a bucket one day and took it to the washing area to fetch drinking water. When she got there, she saw a Polish woman eating a piece of bread with margarine and meat:

> I was staring at her with my mouth open and felt my eyes grow big. Suddenly the woman turned around and screamed: "*Was willst Du, Schmuckstück?*" ["What do you want, jewel?"] I stuttered: "Getting water." She screamed

at me: "There is no water", pushed me to the ground, and then she threw the bucket at me. I went outside crying. Edith was waiting for me. "What is it?" I sobbed: "I saw some bread with meat! You can just imagine what that means."[78]

People who were too ill to go on were constantly dying all around them. Rosa describes one sick young woman who was so feverish that she missed the bucket when she went to do her business and was then beaten to death by a camp guard. It didn't take long for Edith to become so ill that she had to be admitted to the infirmary:

> Edith's sick, she has a high temperature. I wanted her to go to the hospital, but the fear of being gassed was very great because Doctor Mengele came to the infirmary every week to pick out the women he considered to be too thin to go on living. Despite everything, I took Edith there. She had a temperature of 41° and was immediately admitted to the Revier [infirmary]. I'm becoming weaker as well, though I keep on going.[79]

Meanwhile, Rosa moved to another part of the camp, where she again went through a number of selections and was again identified as being *Arbeitsunfähig* (unsuitable for work). In the meantime, her diarrhea got worse and worse: "I feel dizzy and I can hardly stand up straight anymore. I can only get into my bed with difficulty." On 1 December, Rosa ended up in the infirmary with a temperature of 40 degrees and was then transferred to block 18 – the barracks for patients with diarrhea. A Polish prisoner who was working as a doctor diagnosed her: "totally weakened, frozen feet, diarrhea". In the barracks, Rosa met a Dutch woman, and they became friends. She assisted her during the worst moments of her illness. Other than that, it was "complete horror everywhere", as she describes in her book: "Many of the women and young girls died around us, they usually died very calmly, completely exhausted."

While she did her very best to get stronger, and tried to stay in the *Durchfallblock* so that she wouldn't have to go back to the icy work camp, Edith Frank's condition was deteriorating: "One morning, some new patients were brought in. I suddenly recognized Edith, she'd been brought from another department. There was hardly anything left of her. A few days later she died, completely exhausted."[80]

Rosa de Winter-Levy barely survived Auschwitz. She met Otto Frank in Katowice on 22 March 1945, where they were both waiting to be repatriated to the Netherlands. She was the first to tell him that Edith had died on 6 January 1945, ten days before her forty-fifth birthday. Otto wrote a short note in his

Edith Frank's registration card from the Jewish Council's card index.

Betje Jakobs in about 1940.

notebook, saying that Edith had died of hunger and exhaustion on that day. Rosa also told him that his daughters had been deported from Auschwitz to another camp.[81] Another woman from the camp, Betje Jakobs, was also there when Edith died. On 2 August 1945, she made a statement to the employees of the NRK that she "had seen her die close to me: Mrs. Frank from Amsterdam, where her husband had the Opekta company."[82]

CHAPTER FIVE

"I don't remember seeing her standing on her feet"

Anne and Margot Frank and Auguste van Pels in Bergen-Belsen

FROM AUSCHWITZ TO BERGEN-BELSEN

In the early morning of 1 November 1944, approximately 1,000 women left in a long train from the platform of Auschwitz-Birkenau. There were seventy women crowded together in every freight wagon.[1] Most of them came from Hungary and Poland, but there were also French, Belgian and Dutch women, including Anne and Margot Frank and Auguste van Pels. They had been given some bread, a piece of sausage or cheese, and a small piece of margarine for the journey.[2] Some witnesses also mentioned a pan or bucket of water, doors that opened once, and water that was refreshed.[3] The women didn't know their destination.[4] For some, leaving Auschwitz was a relief and they hoped for a better place. Janny Brilleslijper said: "We didn't think it could be any worse, nowhere could be worse than Auschwitz."[5] For first time since they'd been deported, Margot and Anne Frank were without their mother Edith, who had to stay behind in Auschwitz-Birkenau.[6]

Rosa de Winter-Levy's witness statement shows that the selected prisoners assumed that the older and weaker women who had remained behind would all be gassed. The sisters could not know that Edith Frank had avoided this, as had Rosa de

Winter-Levy. In Bergen-Belsen, they were with Auguste van Pels and it's likely that they were also with her during the deportation.

The journey in the freight wagons took three days and two nights,[7] during which the train often stood still for hours as the Allies carried out their bombing raids. The general impression is that the women in the wagons were entirely left alone: "They simply had to use the bucket in the carriage and there was a terrible stench, they could hardly sleep and there was a lot of crying, shouting and quarrels."[8] Rachel Frankfoorder, who was on the same transport, remembered that they had been given "a hunk of bread, a piece of margarine and a piece of goat's cheese."[9] When they arrived at the platform in Bergen on Wednesday 3 November 1944, the doors opened and the women virtually fell out of the train onto the platform.[10] The dead remained behind in the wagons. The women were hungry and thirsty, they were poorly dressed, it was cold, and the temperature was about 7 degrees.[11] They had to line up in blocks of five by five. Then, guarded by soldiers with guns and dogs, they walked to the camp in Bergen-Belsen, about 7 kilometers away. The walk went through a wood and through fields. Despite the cold, hunger and thirst, some of the women were surprised by their beautiful surroundings.[12] Now that they knew that their destination was Bergen-Belsen, some of them also started to raise their hopes because Bergen-Belsen was known as a "good camp", a *Vorzugslager* (a camp with better conditions and circumstances) and *Erholungslager* (convalescence camp).[13] Rachel Frankfoorder remembers: "Bergen-Belsen looked very beautiful. The nature was wonderful, certainly after all the gray of Auschwitz."[14] However, like the other women from Auschwitz, Rachael Frankfoorder soon realized that the "most dreadful period" was still to come.[15]

218

Bergen-Belsen had a special place in the German system of concentration camps. First, it was not a work camp or an extermination camp. There were no gas chambers like Auschwitz and
other SS camps, and it fell under the authority of the WVHA.
In her study of Bergen-Belsen, the historian Alexandra-Eileen
Wenck distinguishes a number of successive functions of this
camp during the course of the war. It served as a prison camp,
and an "exchange camp", and after a while it became an assembly
and transit camp for slave labor. It was a place where the Nazis
took Jews so that they would die there as a result of the overcrowded conditions, inadequate facilities, hunger and disease.[16]

Bergen-Belsen was originally the location of a large exercise
area for armed troops of the Wehrmacht, and a complex of
military barracks near the villages of Bergen and Belsen on the
Lüneburger Heide. There were approximately thirty barracks
on the site built by and for construction workers in the second
half of the 1930s. These barracks were used by the Wehrmacht
in June 1940 for approximately six hundred French and
Belgian prisoners of war. Throughout the war, part of the camp
continued to serve as a prisoner of war camp, whilst part also
continued to be used by the Wehrmacht. In June 1941, the camp
was extended with a large, open area where more than 21,000
Russian prisoners of war were accommodated in July 1941.[17]
The prisoners of war in this *Russenlager* lived in appalling conditions, in the open air and in holes in the ground. The death
rate in the camp was extremely high. Within a year, approximately 14,000 Russian prisoners of war lost their lives as a result
of hunger, cold and infectious diseases such as dysentery and
typhus.[18]

In April 1943, the SS took over a large part of the camp for the prisoners of war from the Wehrmacht to establish the *Aufenthaltslager* Bergen-Belsen, a camp where Jewish prisoners were assembled to be exchanged for Germans interned abroad, German prisoners of war, currency or goods. It was run by *SS-Obersturmbannführer* Adolf Haas, who had previously run the concentration camp at Niederhagen-Wewelsburg. When Haas was in charge, Bergen-Belsen was expanded with barracks, sanitary facilities and a crematorium built by a construction *kommando* of approximately 500 prisoners who had come from Buchenwald, Natzweiler and other camps. Most of them died during its construction.

The first Jewish prisoners arrived in Bergen-Belsen from July 1943.[19] The exchange camp consisted of different sections separated by high barbed wire fences to prevent any contact between the various prisoners.[20] Of all the prisoners from all over Europe who were going to be exchanged, only a relatively small group of approximately 2,500 prisoners were actually exchanged in the end. About 200 Dutch Jews in this so-called *Sternlager* were exchanged.[21]

The *Sternlager* was part of the *Austauschlager*, and consisted of about eighteen barracks. The name *Sternlager* (meaning "bearing a star" in German) was a reference to the camp regime that allowed prisoners to wear their own clothes as long as the Star of David had been sewn on. There were many Jewish prisoners who had come from the Netherlands, and had mainly arrived from Westerbork from eight different deportation transports between January and September 1944.[22]

Families could stay together in the *Sternlager* – although the men and women were in separate barracks, as in Westerbork, contact was possible during the daytime. The prisoners could

The *Sternlager* of Bergen-Belsen, after the liberation.

also occasionally receive post or parcels. Adults from the age of sixteen usually had to work in the shoe *kommando* (recycling the leather of old shoes)[23] or the *Kartoffelschälkommando*. Others were in a work group that had to dig up tree roots or carry out other heavy work on the site. The food situation was bad throughout the camp, but initially slightly better than in other camps. Occasionally, food parcels were delivered by the Red Cross. As Bergen-Belsen operated as an exchange camp, the conditions were initially better there than in the other concentration camps. Many prisoners had arrived on ordinary trains from Westerbork with their luggage, and were sometimes allowed to keep some of their personal belongings. Some managed to keep a diary.[24] The diaries of Abel Herzberg and Renata Laqueur that have survived show how the exchanges kept people's hopes up, but also led to despair.[25] Most of the Dutch witness statements about Bergen-Belsen come from survivors of the camp, but after the summer of 1944, the conditions also deteriorated there.

With the reversal of German fortunes in the war, Bergen-Belsen changed character from the spring of 1944.[26] Jewish prisoners were taken to Germany in large numbers to be used as slave labor in the German war industry, with many of them directed to Bergen-Belsen.[27] From the spring of 1944, part of the camp was also used to admit sick patients from various other concentration camps. Thousands of weak men from other camps arrived in the newly organized prison camp for men in March 1944, which was cynically referred to as a convalescence camp. After "recovering", the prisoners were supposed to be used as a workforce. However, the medical treatment was completely inadequate, and the death rate was high.[28]

In the summer of 1944 it also became a *Durchgangslager* for thousands of women who had been transported to German external camps from the occupied parts of Eastern Europe. In early August 1944, a camp was organized in the southwestern corner with approximately eighteen large tents that were meant for the reception of large deportations due to arrive from mid-August 1944. These were Polish and Hungarian women, mainly from Auschwitz-Birkenau, who were later sent on to work in other camps. The arrival of even more transports took place when barracks were built in September in the yard used for the roll calls.[29]

From mid-August to the beginning of November 1944 about 8,000 women were sent from Auschwitz to Bergen-Belsen, and 3,000 of them arrived in the first days of November.[30] The female prisoners stayed there for a few weeks, a few days or a few hours before being transported to German companies or *subkommandos* of other camps engaged in production for

German industry. The women slept in tents on lice-ridden and dirty straw. There was no light and often no water. The latrine was a dangerous hole in the ground with only a bar with which to hold on.[31] The tent camp was next to the shooting ranges of the Wehrmacht, and prisoners could hear shooting all the time. The people in the camp further on could see the tent camp being built, as well as the transports arriving.[32] Renata Laqueur, who had been a prisoner in the *Sternlager* from March 1943, wrote in her diary on Monday 28 August 1944:

> Last week 1,000 women arrived from Auschwitz. The road was completely blocked and we weren't allowed to see the transport arriving, but we saw them anyway. They were partly shaved bald with bare feet and wearing a sort of uniform dress of different colored cotton. They say that they're Jews, "*Flintenweiber*" [female Russian prisoners, partisans], political prisoners, Poles and so on. Nobody knows.[33]

The women who came with the transport from Auschwitz-Birkenau to Bergen-Belsen on 1 November, including Anne and Margot, were initially accommodated in the tents of the *Durchgangslager*. Shortly after their arrival on 7 November, a storm destroyed much of the tent camp. Consequently, the women were accommodated in a barracks next to the *Sternlager*.[34] As the Russian army advanced, Bergen-Belsen became increasingly overcrowded.

As time passed, the conditions deteriorated in Bergen-Belsen. Under camp commandant Josef Kramer, who had been transferred from Auschwitz to Bergen-Belsen on 2 December 1944 in order to replace Haas (who had been accused of corruption), the strict regime became even stricter. At that time, Kramer was

British allied troops arrest Josef Kramer, the commandant of Bergen-Belsen, on 15 April 1945.

thirty-nine years old and already had a long record of service in the SS camps. From 1934, before he arrived in Auschwitz in 1942, he had worked in six different concentration camps.[35] Kramer brought several male and female guards with him to Bergen-Belsen from Auschwitz, and the mistreatment in the camp increased as a result. The prisoners were assembled for roll calls twice a day to be counted; these were terrible ordeals and could last for hours. If somebody fainted and the numbers were therefore no longer correct, the counting started again.[36]

All the survivors of this period in Bergen-Belsen emphasize how bitterly cold it was in the camp. There were snowfalls throughout the month of January 1945 and the temperatures fell well below freezing.[37] Other factors meant that conditions continued to deteriorate. As Bergen-Belsen became more overpopulated, the prisoners slept two to a bed, even in the

Sternlager, where the situation had been relatively good for a while.[38] The rations also became smaller and smaller. Suze Polak said that they consisted of an eighth of a loaf of bread and half a liter of watery soup a day. In the end, they were only given a piece of bread once every three days.[39] Contagious diseases such as typhus broke out. As the SS increasingly retreated, the prisoners were left to the kapos and the guards. Thousands of people died in those last weeks from disease, hypothermia, hunger and exhaustion.[40] One notorious guard who is often mentioned in survivors' witness statements was the "Blonde Angel of Death", Irma Grese. She made prisoners stand or kneel for hours, holding rocks in their hands. She also beat them mercilessly,[41] not just in the women's camp where Margot, Anne

Irma Grese and Josef Kramer, April 1945.

and Auguste van Pels were, but also in the *Sternlager*, where prisoners had to appear for roll call every day.

Freda Silberberg, who was in the women's camp together with Anne and Margot, has terrible memories of a roll call on New Year's Eve 1944 that lasted all night. She emphasized that the pointless counting of the prisoners was actually aimed at exhausting them and making sure that as many of them as possible died as a result.

> In Bergen-Belsen, the whole camp had to appear for roll call on New Year's Eve, 1944–45, all night. It was in the freezing cold, and it actually snowed. You just had to stay standing there. They even took people out of the hospital, the *Revier*. They all had to go to the roll call as well. So you can imagine how many people died that night in the icy cold. That's what they did in Bergen-Belsen. That's how they tried to get rid of us. I don't know how we survived and how I survived. Can you imagine it? All night![42]

The guards also brutalized the prisoners in Bergen-Belsen in other barbaric ways, and the system was aimed at completely dehumanizing them. Freda Silberberg remembers:

> The guards [...] were cold, cold! They beat us up. They wanted to get us inside and when we went outside, they'd beat us senseless. They were all the same – barbaric, cruel people. I don't know where they got them from. They'd been told that we were *Untermenschen*, that we had no right to live and that they could therefore do with us what they liked. They didn't treat us like human beings; we were only things to destroy. That's what it was. You were no longer a person and you no longer existed as a person.[43]

Abel Herzberg, who had been in the *Sternlager* of Bergen-Belsen since January 1943, attempted to examine the cruelty of the male and female guards in more detail in his postwar essays. "It's very important to know what sort of a person he was, that Joseph Kramer, or the Scharführer Heinz and Fritz and Rau and Lübbe or the Sturmführer X or N."[44]

Herzberg did not look for explanations in intrinsic evil or ideological convictions, but rather in "perfectly ordinary" human behavior and the nihilism arising from it. "Scharführer X is [...] nothing. He's empty. He's seen as being idealistic, but he isn't. [...] Convictions are attributed to him but he has none. Attempts have been made to at least discover patriotism or national enthusiasm in him, but there's no trace of this."[45] According to Herzberg, this "perfectly ordinary man" was neither evil nor good, but was driven by the trivial need for a good life, by fear and by a bad conscience. Herzberg thought that the guards were not so much lacking a conscience, but were people who tried to suppress their lack of conviction and bad conscience with "false certainties" that had to be reinforced with action and cruelty.

> And that's why the first drop of blood is followed by one cruel act after another, always greater, always more vehement. It has been said that Scharführer X must have been lacking a conscience. If only that had been true, he would not have become so cruel. It all arose from nothing. At the very basis of it all there was no conviction, but a lack of conviction that resulted in a constantly growing uncertainty that always had to be covered by a constantly growing sense of uncertainty. The infection had started [...] and in this way Sturmführer N or

Scharführer X, who was potty trained so late as a child and was so anxious as a little boy, so mediocre at school and so "perfectly ordinary" as a man, inevitably became a mass murderer before he knew what was happening.[46]

Herzberg also analyzed the female guards at Bergen-Belsen. In his story "De Griet", he does this by describing a female guard who he named "the blonde Irmy". Herzberg had often seen this woman in action. She "shouldn't be confused with Irma Grese" and never had to appear before a court. Her capricious character surprised him; Herzberg describes how this "blonde Irmy" was touched when a baby was born in the women's camp, and promised the mother that she'd save the child "when you're all gassed or shot."[47] She often had almost friendly chats with the prisoners "about bits of fabric and material, buttons and bows, about children, and about things that are only mentioned in very vague terms, or that you think of when you're actually talking about something else." But from one moment to the next she could again become extremely cruel and behave viciously.

When the blonde Irmy had chatted enough, she would stop: "*So, jetzt geh' ich mal ein bisschen prügeln im Frauenlager*" ["Now I'm going to have some fun in the women's camp"]. She said it and she did it. Next to our camp there was a tent camp for Polish women and women who had been deported from Polish concentration camps. There were also Dutch women there who would shout things through the barbed wire fence at us so that we knew that the inferno there was even worse than our own. Irmy went down there and when she came back up and appeared in our barracks, she'd complain bitterly that her arm hurt so much from all the beatings she'd given.[48]

228

Herzberg referred to the women's camp, where Auguste van Pels and Margot and Anne Frank arrived from Auschwitz on 3 November 1944, as the "deeper inferno". A long line of prisoners passed the shooting ranges of the Wehrmacht together with the approximately 1,000 other women of the transport, and arrived in the southwestern corner of the camp, immediately next to the open space with the tents.[49] The constant noise of shooting was terrifying. Anita Lasker remembers that she saw a sign that read "Zu dem Schießstand" ("To the shooting range") and was afraid she would be shot.[50] When they arrived in the camp, the women were counted and registered. Every camp had its own registration system, so in Bergen-Belsen the prisoners were given new prisoner numbers. No registration data from Bergen-Belsen has survived, but from the transport lists of other camps which were not lost, the NRK has calculated that the prisoners of this transport were given numbers between 7270 and 7360.[51] From that reconstruction, we can also assume that Auguste van Pels was given the number 7306. Rachel Frankfoorder, who arrived at Bergen-Belsen on the same transport as Anne and Margot Frank, and also ended up in the same barracks as them, was given number 7356.[52]

When they arrived in the tent camp, the prisoners were all given a horsehair blanket and a little pan.[53] It was raining and very cold. The women waited for hours with only blankets for protection. Janny Brilleslijper remembers that she saw Anne and Margot again for the first time since Westerbork, wrapped up in two blankets. Shortly afterwards, she found two other sisters she knew from Westerbork, Annelore and Ellen Daniel:

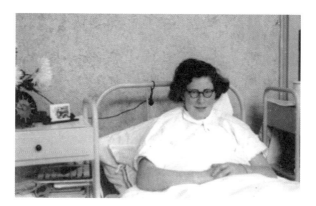

Annelore Daniel during her recouperation in the
sanatorium in Santpoort, 1945–8.

Perhaps it's a sister complex that made the Frank girls
and the Daniel sisters so striking. Sisters or mothers and
sisters tried to stay together. The feeling of togetherness,
at that moment you think, oh, and there are those two
children. We had an almost maternal feeling for them
because they were ten years younger than we were.[54]

Almost all the women were sick, and their condition had deteriorated as a result of the stress and exhaustion of the journey.
When darkness fell, they were given a sort of soup. Then they
were sent into the tents in groups of 400–500. It was chaotic:
the women pushed and pulled to find a place in the leaking
tents, but there was hardly any room. Everyone was lying on
top of each other on the dirty straw. Many of the women had
dysentery, and at night it was almost impossible to find the exit
of the tent to go to the latrine through this mass of people. The
next morning, they had to get up for roll call at six.

A violent storm came on the fourth night after Anne, Margot
and Auguste's arrival on 7 November 1944, and the overcrowded

tents collapsed. We don't know how Anne and Margot experienced this incident, but there are several witness statements that give an impression of what happened that night. For example, Renata Laqueur wrote in her diary: "Last week there was a violent autumn storm in the night and a few tents blew down in the pouring rain. The women remained lying there unprotected in the cold, with hardly any clothes or covers."[55] On 7 November 1944, Ruth Wiener, who had been staying in the *Sternlager* with her mother and sisters since January 1944, wrote in a diary that she had brought from home: "Storm. Tents blown over."[56]

Abel Herzberg, who also published the diary he kept during his imprisonment in Bergen-Belsen, wrote in detail about the arrival of the large group of women from Auschwitz and the dreadful night of the storm of 8 November 1944. Because of their arrival, he also began to realize what had happened in that camp in occupied Poland, and that it was even worse than the horrors of the *Austauschlager* in Bergen-Belsen. Even then, Herzberg found it difficult to believe the stories about selections and gassing:

As far as we know, all these women have come from Auschwitz and have been separated from their husbands. Their children have also been taken away from them. There are the most appalling stories. Apparently the children and all those who were not fit for work were gassed. It's not possible to believe such horrors. In any case there are only women here and they can all be used as a labor force [...]. Everything has been taken away from them, literally everything. They don't own anything except for the rags that they wear. They live here in tents

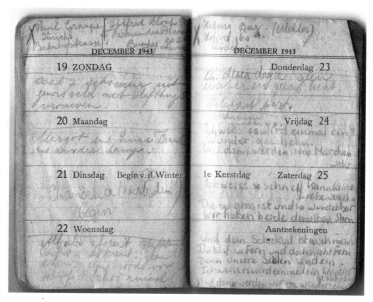

In her diary, Ruth Wiener noted all sorts of things between 1943 and 1945. On 20 December, she noted: "Margot and Anne Frank are in the other camp." (The diary was for 1943, but she also used it for entries in 1944 and 1945.)

Ruth Wiener (left) with her sisters, 1930s.

and sleep on straw on the ground. The November storms have started with rain, hail, snow and penetrating cold. A storm tore up the tents yesterday afternoon so that the women had to stand in the pouring rain and in this atrocious weather without any protection. The barracks where the shoe team is located has now been reserved for them, as well as a large kitchen tent. However, the bottom of that tent has flooded and there's 10cm of water there. It is quite impossible to imagine the effect that this terrible weather has.[57]

After the destructive storm, people were moved about in the camp. One group of women from the *Sternlager* was moved to new barracks, and the women from the tent camp were sent to the barracks of the former *Sternlager*.[58] Anne and Margot ended up in the so-called *Kleinefrauenlager* (small women's camp), which was on the site of the former *Sternlager*. As more transports arrived, the boundary of this women's camp was expanded further and further, reducing the size of the *Sternlager*. On 20 December 1944, Ruth Wiener noted in her diary: "Anne and Margot Frank are in the other camp!"[59] This is the only contemporary document that proves the presence of Anne and Margot Frank in Bergen-Belsen. Ruth Wiener knew them from the liberal Jewish community and the Jewish Lyceum in Amsterdam. She didn't speak to them in Bergen-Belsen, she just saw them. She said that a transport always led to rumors: "Who was on it? Any Dutch people?" Then she always went to have a look. It was forbidden to meet at the fence, but it regularly happened.[60]

Anne, Margot and Auguste van Pels found themselves in an overcrowded barracks inside the *Kleinefrauenlager*. Rachel

Frankfoorder remembers that she saw Anne and Margot, who she'd met in Westerbork, in Bergen-Belsen, this time without their father and mother.

> Their parents weren't there. You didn't ask about that, because you actually knew […] because of your own experience with parents, brothers, etc., well, you had a suspicion, no more. The Frank girls were almost unrecognizable because their hair had been cut off, they were much balder than we were, I don't know why that was. And they were very cold, like we all were. It was winter and you had no clothes. So all the factors for becoming ill were there. They were in an especially bad state.[61]

Annelore and Ellen Daniel, who had also come from Auschwitz-Birkenau on the transport of 1 November 1944, were also there. Ellen Daniel remembers how she and her sister Annelore ended up in a barracks together with a group of other Dutch women. Under the bitter conditions, they tried to find ways to ignore the hunger, cold and lethargy:

> We were in a very large barracks with a number of other Dutch women and we had nothing to do. We sat on our beds all day long or we walked around backwards and forwards but we had hardly any clothes. [I]t was cold and you didn't have a handkerchief, you just used the lining of your coat to blow your nose. […] I don't even know exactly how we slept anymore. My sister and I were in one bed and another pair of sisters in another bed and I'm not sure, there was someone else I knew well, who I got to know there because we slept next to each other and we had an extra blanket. We went to get that extra

Part of the Bergen-Belsen concentration camp shortly after the liberation of April 1945.

blanket. It meant you had some thread and [...] someone had a knife and we made knitting needles from a plank of the bed and I knitted some socks in this way. So there I was in my bed at Bergen-Belsen, knitting socks.[62]

From the spring of 1944, Bergen-Belsen increasingly became a camp where the Nazis sent sick prisoners to die. At the beginning of 1945, the conditions deteriorated even further due to the enormous increase in deportations from other camps. Nikolaus Wachsmann wrote that "never before in the history of concentration camps had there been so many prisoners in one camp dying from starvation, hunger and exhaustion as in Bergen-Belsen in March 1945." Of the 45,500 prisoners who were there that month, more than 18,000 died.[63]

Concentration Camp Bergen-Belsen, after liberation.

Almost all those who survived emphasize that the prisoners in Bergen-Belsen were completely left to themselves. According to Annalore Daniel:

> There was no regularity […] and you [lived like] a sort of slave. When you "had to go", you went outside. We had very little food and I started to get dysentery. I had a terrible sore on my arm and that's how you went downhill. Then you would have to appear at roll call or you would be in the barracks or sometimes we'd be together or with friends. But it was a very monotonous life.[64]

Cato Polak, who, like Annalore Daniel, was in the women's camp of Bergen-Belsen at the same time as Anne and Margot, confirms the total lack of organization.[65] She says that the prisoners didn't work but just hung around; it was cold, and some days there was no food at all.

Ellen Daniel says that many prisoners in Bergen-Belsen gave up the will to go on because of the atrocious combination of boredom, hunger, chaos, sickness and cold. This was more or less what was described in the chapter about Auschwitz, where the male version became known by the term *Muselmann*.[66] Ellen Daniel herself, together with her sister Annelore, tried to prevent sliding down into this state at any cost by finding ways to remain active, and by looking for extra food and ways to protect themselves from the cold:

> With hindsight you can see that the people who didn't survive was because of sort of resignation. I wouldn't say that I am a fighter by nature, certainly not. But at some level you do need the will to live. Of course, we were lucky that there were two of us so if one of didn't do

something, the other would. I sat there knitting and my sister would try and get her hands on a piece of turnip somewhere.[67]

Anne and Margot Frank were very weak by now, and Ellen Daniel saw that their strength to continue fighting was slowly ebbing away. In an interview dating from 1995, she reflected with some bitterness on the contrast between the public image of Anne Frank and her own memory of the completely weak and desperate girl she had seen in Bergen-Belsen: "Well, that famous Anne Frank was also in our barracks. She was in a different part and lay in bed with her sister. The only thing that I remember about her was that she cried all day long. She didn't want anything and couldn't do anything, but you're not allowed to say that about Anne Frank."[68]

Ellen's younger sister Annelore remembers that Margot and Anne Frank were always inseparable, and always with Auguste van Pels. (Initially, Annelore thought that Auguste was the girls' mother.) Apart from the fact that Auguste and the Frank sisters were always together, she remembers in particular their apathetic and desperate condition. According to the Daniel sisters, the three of them barely responded to the other prisoners by that point: "We didn't have any contact with her. Because [...] she was always with Mrs. van Pels, they were their own unit and never spoke to anyone."[69]

The witness statement of Rachel Frankfoorder, and the sisters Janny and Lientje Brilleslijper, shed a slightly different light on events. Rachel remembers that the girls became visibly weaker in Bergen-Belsen, but didn't give up the struggle: "They still went to the fence of the so-called free camp every day, hoping to get something. They went with great determination.

238

I think that they were almost certain they would meet someone they knew". This assumption turned out to be right, as will be discussed below, because Anne had discovered that her school friend Hanneli Goslar was in the *Sternlager*.[70]

The Brilleslijper sisters also had contact with Anne and Margot. They had managed to get work in the infirmary, which was a very sought-after job in Bergen-Belsen. When an *SS-Aufseherin* came to the barracks and asked whether there were any nurses amongst the prisoners, Janny and Lientje applied, even though their experience consisted of no more than a short first aid course.[71] With this job, they tried to support their friends and acquaintances as much as possible, and these included Anne and Margot Frank. The Brilleslijper sisters remember Anne and Margot Frank as being less passive than in the description given by the Daniel sisters.[72] In 1951, Lientje Brilleslijper remembered:

> We saw each other a great deal from November 1944 to March 1945. Of course, Anne and Margot would also sometimes quarrel just like any other sisters. One day Anne came to us very excited and whispered: "In the small block there's some sweet soup. We'll organize something." Margot was angry Anne had shared this secret. But that's what Anne was like: she was kind, very spontaneous, impulsive, oversensitive and open-hearted. She always said what she thought.[73]

Janny Brilleslijper remembers that during the days after the chaotic storm in the tent camp, she started looking for people she knew. Finally, she saw Anne and Margot again in one of the barracks. Her statement differs from Annelore Daniel's, who emphasizes that the Frank sisters and Auguste van Pels kept themselves to themselves in Bergen-Belsen and that they hardly talked to the other prisoners. In contrast, Janny Brilleslijper said that she and Lientje took the Frank sisters under their wing and formed a close group with some other Dutch prisoners, including Auguste van Pels and the Daniel sisters, and that they all did things together and looked out for each other.

In December, they even organized a joint "party" on their bunk bed, celebrating Hanukkah, St Nicholas, Christmas and the New Year, all at the same time. Everyone "saved up" some bread for this and provided a little contribution: "That evening we sat on the top bunks in the stone barracks and all sang together".[74] Janny's sister Lientje also remembers that moment: "This 'party' helped us forget the indescribable horror of our situation for a few moments. We were Anne, Margot, the Daniel sisters and my sister and I."[75]

Janny Brilleslijper remembers that the Dutch prisoners were attacked a day later by a drunk guard, an *SS-Rottenführer* who was known as "Red Müller". This is one of the few testimonies in which a direct confrontation between the Frank sisters and the SS guards is mentioned:

Totally drunk, he tried to pull us off our top bunks. He stood at the sides of the beds and tried to pull us and shake us off, using his whip. We fought tooth and nail to stop him, pressed ourselves against the beds and he couldn't get hold of us. So we could still defend ourselves when it was necessary! The Frank girls and the Daniel girls and Sonja Lopes Cardoso were with us; we sat on our haunches on our top bunk with the sloping roof above us. The experience made a deep impression, it's one you can never forget.[76]

This incident is told in a slightly different way in her sister's memoirs, but is not mentioned at all in the testimonies given by the Daniel sisters.[77] This also applies for one of Janny's other memories, namely that Anne and Margot had helped the Brilleslijper sisters to look after a group of smaller Dutch children who had been taken from the *Sternlager* to the women's camp at a later date. According to Janny, Margot and Anne visited these children a number of times to sing songs and to share "a bit of culture" with them.[78]

Shortly afterwards, the contact between Janny and Lientje Brilleslijper and the Frank sisters dwindled. As "nurses", they were busy looking after the sick, which they did mainly from their own block and where they were regularly visited by people they knew. "The Frank girls, those two big-headed know-alls, didn't come very regularly. When we wanted to look them up, we couldn't find them in the total chaos of Bergen-Belsen because the block kept on being moved. It was chaos and no one knew where anyone was." Meanwhile, Janny had discovered that Anne and Margot were seriously ill.[79] Rachel Frankfoorder, who was also in the same barracks, remembers that the Frank sisters had an uncomfortable place: right next to the door, which kept on opening and letting in the cold: "You constantly heard them shouting: 'Shut the door! Shut the door!' And that sound became a bit weaker every day."[80]

Nanette Blitz, who'd been in Anne Frank's class at the Jewish Lyceum, came to the same conclusion when she met Anne in Bergen-Belsen. She was on the "Palestine list" with her parents and her brother, and was in the *Sternlager* for a possible exchange with German prisoners of war and to travel on to Palestine. Nanette's father's death on 14 November 1944 meant that the family lost that status. Her mother and brother

Nanette Blitz at the Jewish Lyceum, December 1941.

were deported somewhere else; Nanette herself arrived in the *Kleinefrauenlager* on 5 December 1944 and soon ran into Anne.[81] After the war, Otto Frank went looking for anyone who could tell him anything about his daughters. On 31 October 1945, Nanette wrote to him that she'd visited Anne and Margot in January in an infirmary, and had heard more about them in February. Later, she said that Anne was already very ill and had clear signs of typhoid fever. She was walking round "naked" and as thin as a rake, with just a blanket around her. Margot, meanwhile, was "too ill to stand".[82]

In January, Margot Rosenthal was sent from Auschwitz to Bergen-Belsen. She already knew Anne and Margot Frank from Westerbork, and was able to tell them that their mother Edith had not been gassed after the selection for Bergen-Belsen.[83] Just before Margot must have died, Margot Rosenthal met Anne one last time.[84] Sophie Huisman also remembers that she saw Anne during a big roll call. Afterwards, she could only remember Anne's face and that she had been very weak.[85]

242

eure vrouw in Birkenau had
gesproken, wat hem erg opfleur-
de, omdat zij weinig hoop bij
de selectie hadden gehad. De
selectie hadden hen van een
vrouw gesplitst. In Januari
gingen Margot en Anne naar
het Sekoningsblock, waar ik
nog bij hun was. Toen kwam
er een grote verhuizing,
waarna ik hun niet meer
gesproken heb, alsook weet
echter, dat Voreisje hier, dat iemand
hun in Februari nog gesproken
heeft.
        Ik herinner mij U
nog een beetje. Wat bezoek
betreft zijn deze alleen op
de aangewezen uren en deze
zijn zondag. Maandag. Donder-
dag van 3-4.
        In de hoop U hiermee van
dienst te zijn geweest ein-
dig ik met de hartelijke
groeten

                Nanny Blitz

Letter (last page) from Nanette Blitz to Otto Frank, 31 October 1945.

Various diaries reveal that despite the barbed wire fences between the different parts of the camp, there was a surprising amount of communication between the newcomers and the prisoners in the *Sternlager*. The constant exchange of news amongst the prisoners was ironically known to them as the "JPA" (Jewish Press Association).[86] Ruth Wiener noted that the transports from Poland brought together family and acquaintances of people in the *Sternlager*.[87] Renata Laqueur also discovered many people she knew in the tent camp, which is how she got to know something about the "mysteries" of the notorious camp of Auschwitz: "I saw the numbers tattooed on people's arms in Auschwitz, heard about *Vernichtung* [extermination] by gassing, and about life in the camps there. None of us knew anything about that."[88]

The possibility of communication also meant that old acquaintances could find each other in the camp, even if people were in different areas. At dusk, the prisoners in the women's camp sometimes went to the fence that separated them from the *Sternlager* to meet friends, and sometimes to be given various things.[89] This fence consisted of two layers of wire fence and barbed wire, with straw or reeds between them. The prisoners on either side couldn't see each other through this but they could hear each other, so it was possible to make contact. About the *Sternlager*, Cato Polak said: "Fie [Sophie Huisman] had friends there who gave us some much needed clothes. They were actually allowed to keep their own clothes and walked around in them with a star sewn on."[90]

It was too dangerous during the day to make contact at the fence, and you could never miss the roll calls. When the Frank sisters were in the women's camp at Bergen-Belsen, it became dark at about five in the afternoon. Rachel Frankfoorder said that Anne and Margot regularly went to the fence that separated the women's camp from the *Sternlager*.[91] Hanneli Goslar, a neighbor and friend of Anne's in Amsterdam since nursery school, had been in the *Sternlager* since January 1944 with her father, grandmother and sister.[92] In either January or at the beginning of February 1945, somebody came to fetch her because someone on the other side of the fence had seen her friend Anne in the camp.[93]

> I was going crazy because I thought that Anne Frank was in Switzerland and was eating chocolate with her grandmother. How could she be here? So I had no other choice than to go to the barbed wire fence in the evening, as much as I could. And I started shouting across it [...]. And then I went to the barbed wire and called out: "Hello, hello!" The woman who answered me was the mother of Peter, Mrs. van Pels. And she'd been in hiding with Anne – but of course I didn't know that then. But we knew each other. We lived in the same road, the Zuider Amstellaan, and they were friends of the Franks and we were friends of theirs. We weren't friends with the Van Pels family, but we knew each other. She knew that I was a friend of Anne and the first thing she said was: "Oh, of course you want to talk to Anne". I said: "Yes, of course". We talked for half a minute, it was too dangerous, and then she only added [...]: "I can't bring Margot, she can't walk up to the barbed wire any more, but I'll bring Anne." And I stood there and waited, and then after about five minutes I heard a very weak voice and it was Anne. First, we both started to cry and then I said: "How did you come here?

I was hoping you were with your grandmother in Switzerland." And Anne said: "We never tried to get there, we hid in Dad's office and we were betrayed."[94]

The next evening, Hanneli Goslar came back with some food from a Red Cross parcel. In an interview with the Anne Frank House, Hanneli Goslar, now called Hannah Pick-Goslar, made the following statement:

> So I heard Anne on the other side. And I came with something, as much as a small football and everyone had given me something – a sock or a glove or a few dried prunes from a parcel or that Swedish *knäckebrod* that you can keep for a long time. And I said to Anne: "Anne, *Vorsicht* [be careful], I'll throw it over the barbed wire." And then I heard that Anne was crying and shouting and was angry. What happened? No, I couldn't see her, and the barbed wire was high and the night was dark, and I just had to throw at what I could hear. But there were hundreds of other hungry women and another woman had picked up the parcel, ran away with it, and didn't give her anything. Well, first I had to calm Anne down and then I promised: "We'll do it again". And we were able to do it again. I met her three times and then she caught the parcel, I'm sure of it. I have a friend here in the country who was in the camp with her and she remembers that Anne had received a parcel. And that was the last time that I met her. I never saw her, only spoke to her three times. But then my father died and I didn't go for a few days. And when I went again to look for Anne, everything was gone.[95]

People were constantly being moved inside the camp on a large scale. For example, from 20 January 1945, a large number of prisoners were moved from the *Kleinefrauenlager* to the barracks of the former prisoner-of-war camp on the other side of the *Lagerstraße* – the *Große Frauenlager*.[96] There were also regular selections, after which the prisoners were sent to an infirmary.[97] Perhaps Anne and Margot were moved and that's the reason that Hanneli Goslar did not see them anymore, but there are no sources to confirm that.[98]

On the basis of a number of other data, we can conclude that the first meeting between Anne and Hanneli Goslar, when the parcel was stolen, probably took place between 23 January and 7 February. It must have been before 7 February because Auguste van Pels left for Raguhn on that day.[99] We also know from a list that survived that Hanneli Goslar's grandmother received a package from the Swiss Red Cross on 23 January 1945.[100]

Hanneli Goslar's story is confirmed by various witnesses who were in the *Sternlager* with her.[101] Irene Hasenberg remembers that she was present at one of the meetings, that Hanneli threw a bundle to Anne over the fence on that occasion, and that it was grabbed by another prisoner:

I can only remember women from Auschwitz, and Hanneli had found out that Anne Frank was in that camp right next to us but separated with barbed wire and you were not allowed to communicate with anyone. So she heard about it, and she asked to have a message taken to Anne Frank to meet at the fence that evening. It could only [happen] in the evening because if the guard posts would see that there was interaction they would shoot. So we did it after dark and Anne came. This was Hanneli

247

who saw her alone. She was very thin, and she didn't have any clothes.[102] She was cold and just had a blanket wrapped around her, so she asked Hanneli if she could find some clothes for her. And that is the point where Hanneli told me about it and we went together with some clothes to throw over the fence the next night. And we did, and we met Anne and threw over the bundle but she didn't see it in the dark […] and someone else came and took the bundle and ran off with it. And that was the day before my family and I left Bergen-Belsen for the exchange. […] It was many years later that Hanneli told me that she did manage to throw another bundle the next night and Anne did receive it.[103]

Martha van Collem, who was in the *Sternlager* with her mother and sister, had also been present at these meetings once or twice. The Van Collem family knew the Franks from the liberal Jewish community in Amsterdam. When Hanneli told Martha

Martha van Collem, 1943.

in Bergen-Belsen that she had heard that Anne Frank was also there, Martha found it difficult to believe her:

> Anne, that was quite a story. I'm not quite sure whether we received a postcard from the family or someone else, but I remember that my father said to my mother at a certain point [...]: "They've gone, they've fled, they've gone." [...] So when I was in Bergen-Belsen and Hanneli asked me whether I would like to come with her to the fence where she was going to meet Anne, I said: "What do you mean, girl? Anne and her family escaped. We got a postcard to say they were in Belgium." She said "Yes [...] that's right, but they didn't escape, they were in the Netherlands." I said: "I never heard about that", and then she said, "Well come with me and she'll tell you all about it." And she did tell me all about it.[104]

Finally, there's another, more difficult to verify testimony from a prisoner in the *Sternlager* about another parcel that Anne Frank allegedly received. This is a statement from a woman referred to as "Mrs. L." by Ernst Schnabel – it was probably Eva Lek-van Leuwen – who remembers that she had recognized Anne in Bergen-Belsen. She describes how she was able to see her through the fence – something that's not very probable in view of the other descriptions of it – and that when she recognized her, she wanted to give her a parcel of food and clothes.

> Yes, I saw Anne in Belsen. She had come with a transport from Auschwitz, and first they were taken to tents because there was no room in the barracks anymore. But when the weather turned and the autumn came to the Heide, those tents were ripped up and blown over by

a storm one night. Then they were all divided amongst the different blocks, and Margot and Anne ended up in the block right next to us. And I saw Anne behind the barbed wire fence on the other side of the street. On that side, the conditions were even worse than they were for us, because we were able to receive a package from time to time. And I called out "Don't walk away, Anne, wait!" And I ran to the barracks and quickly picked up what I could find and walked back to the fence, but it was a long way off and we were so weak. And while we were still talking about how we could throw the bundle over the fence, Mr Bril walked by.[105] [...] He was very big and I said: "I've got an old dress here, and soap and a piece of bread. Please, Mr. Bril, would you throw it over the fence? There's a child over there!" Mr Bril hesitated and didn't know whether he would risk it because the guards could see us. But he made the effort when he saw the child [...] and he took the bundle of things and threw it to the other side in a big arc.[106]

THE DEATH OF MARGOT AND ANNE FRANK

We do not know exactly when Anne and Margot died. After the war, Otto Frank heard about the death of his daughters in Bergen-Belsen for the first time from the Brilleslijper sisters in July 1945. They told him that they'd known the girls well in Bergen-Belsen, and knew that Anne and Margot were sick because of their role as "nurses". They hadn't been present at their deaths, but told him approximately when Anne and Margot died.[107] Lientje Brilleslijper said that she had known Anne and Margot in the camp, and that the sisters had died at the end of

February/beginning of March.[108] When Otto Frank needed a death certificate for his daughters for the Amsterdam register of births, deaths and marriages, he asked the Brilleslijper sisters to confirm it.[109] On 11 November 1945, Lientje Brilleslijper declared in writing: "I hereby declare that Margot and Anne Frank died in the Schonungsblock number 19 in Bergen-Belsen Häftlingenlager at about the end of February or beginning of March 1945. I was a prisoner myself in the same camp in Block number 1 and I was a friend of the above-mentioned girls."[110]

In 1954, Otto Frank needed an official declaration of his children's death to draw up an inheritance declaration.[111] After the war, the NRK was given the legal task of determining the place and date of the deaths of missing persons. In order to determine this for Anne and Margot, Lientje Brilleslijper made an official declaration on 22 January 1951 in which she remembered that Anne and Margot Frank had died in Bergen-Belsen in "about March 1945".[112]

The Commission for the Registration of Deaths of Missing Persons of the Ministry of Justice would officially date unknown dates of death as the last day of the month if they could link a person's fate to an incident or a witness statement. Therefore, when Lientje Brilleslijper indicated that Anne and Margot died in "about March 1945", the NRK concluded that they had died in Bergen-Belsen "no earlier than on 1.3.45 and at the latest on 31.3.45". As such, in accordance with the standard method, the date of their deaths was determined as 31 March 1945.[113] On 29 October 1954, after the legal period of three months had lapsed, the date of death was issued in the Official Gazette and was officially registered at the registry office.[114]

Like thousands of other prisoners, Anne and Margot had been infected with the rickets bacteria, or epidemic typhus, a

At Otto Frank's request, the Brilleslijper sisters confirmed that Anne and Margot had died in Bergen-Belsen. Rebekka "Lientje" Rebling-Brilleslijper's declaration, 11 November 1945.

Amsterdam 13 Jan 46.

Hiermede verklaar ik dat Anne Frank. en Margo Frank. bij mij in het kamp Bergen Belsen zijn overleden waar ik als verpleegster in bl.1a werkzaam was

M Brandes Brilleslijn
Amstel 101 Amsterdam (C)

Janny Brandes-Brilleslijper's declaration, January 1946.

disease that is passed on by infected lice in clothes and bedding. This disease caused a huge number of deaths amongst prisoners in Bergen-Belsen and many other camps.[115] Although Anne and Margot had been vaccinated against ordinary typhoid fever for their visa application for the United States, they were not protected against the variant transmitted by lice.[116]

The disease of typhus has a clear pattern. Following an incubation period of approximately one week, the first symptoms appear: serious headaches, shaking, fever and muscular pain. This can be followed, after approximately five days, by hallucinations, meningitis and the symptoms of a coma. Once this stage has been reached, virtually all patients die within two weeks.[117] The case fatality rate (that is, the percentage of infected people who died of it) can be up to 50 per cent.

On the basis of what we know about the pattern of this disease and the available witness statements, it is therefore possible to make a more exact estimate of Anne and Margot's probable date of death. To get an idea of the last weeks that Anne and Margot were still alive, we depend on the few witness statements of fellow prisoners. For example, Rachel Frankfoorder and Nanette Blitz saw that Anne and Margot were very ill in January 1945. In an interview with Willy Lindwer, Rachel Frankfoorder recalls, "You could really see them dying, both of them". She described how the typical symptoms of typhus advanced more and more clearly in the two girls. They were "in a sort of apathetic state, combined with better periods, until they were so sick that there was no longer any hope."[118] A short time later, she no longer saw Anne and Margot, and assumed that they had died. Nanette Blitz also remembers this period:

I saw that Margot could no longer stand up. She just lay there. I embraced Anne, but I can't remember Margot standing up. She'd become very, very weak. Then everything shrank, the brain, the stomach, everything [...] and I didn't really talk to her at all anymore. She was already half gone and as weak as anyone can be [...]. But Anne, I did talk to her several times. And I believe that every time that she came, Margot was lying there in the barracks and was not really with it anymore.[119]

She also said that she had seen Anne and Margot alive:

When I found Anne and Margot in camp 8, that was the original camp 8 – it was a women's camp at the time – they were both like skeletons. And I know about Anne that she was wrapped up in a blanket. I can't remember Margot, whether or not she was wrapped up in a blanket, but she was also very weak, completely used up in a way. And perhaps she was also wrapped up in a blanket. It was impossible to wear clothes because they were full of lice. And then I saw them a few times more. I don't know how many times, but I did see them a few times. That was in February 1945, but I must have seen them even in March, because I know that I saw them shortly before I went into the infirmary – which was called the *Schonungsblock* – and that was just before Bergen-Belsen was liberated. So I could say that I saw them both just before they died. And Margot died first. I think that she fell out of her bunk. She fell and Anne died the following day.[120]

In her memoirs, published posthumously in 1995, Lientje Brilleslijper also remembers that the sisters had died in March, one just after the other.

> The end came in March 1945. Margot, the older and more controlled sister died [...] of complete exhaustion and typhus. Anne sadly said: "Now I don't have to come back any more either." She gave up the struggle after Margot died, the struggle against accepting the dreadful fate, and as soon as her will was broken it couldn't be long before the end came. A few days later Anne went to sleep forever, calm and quiet.[121]

There are indications that Anne and Margot probably died earlier than 31 March 1945, the date chosen by the Red Cross, possibly even before the end of February or beginning of March, as indicated by Lientje Brilleslijper and Nanette Blitz. The meetings with Hanneli Goslar and Martha van Collem at the fence took place within a period of a few days after the Goslar family had received a parcel. Hanneli Goslar's grand-mother received her parcel from the Red Cross on about 23 January 1945. This means that the meeting at the fence was at the beginning of February at the latest. Anne and Margot were still alive then, but Margot was very ill. Annelore Daniel, Rachel Frankfoorder and Sophie Huisman were selected for the transport to the women's camp in Raguhn on 7 February 1945, as was Auguste van Pels.[122]

Therefore, their statement that Anne and Margot were very sick and had typhus dated from before this time. Rachel Frankfoorder even said that Anne and Margot had died earlier because she suddenly stopped seeing them in the barracks and concluded that they'd died. At that time, bodies were lying all over the camp and she thought that she might have stepped over them when she left the barracks. It could also be that she didn't see them anymore because they were in an infirmary. Janny Brilleslijper, who worked in the camp as a nurse, had clearly recognized the symptoms of typhus in Anne and Margot and said that the sisters were in an infirmary.[123] In any case, Anne and Margot were certainly very ill in the first week of February.

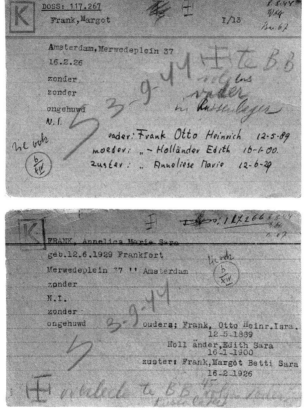

Registration cards for Margot Frank (top) and Anne Frank (bottom), taken from the records of the Jewish Council.

On the basis of these data and a knowledge of the progression of typhus, when virtually all patients die two or three weeks after the appearance of the first symptoms of the disease, it's possible to arrive at a new and more exact estimate of the date of Anne and Margot Frank's death. When Margot was no longer able to stand up at the first meeting between Anne Frank and Hanneli Goslar that had been arranged a few days before 7 February 1945 by Auguste van Pels (which is also confirmed by the statements of Nanette Blitz), and was therefore presumably at the stage when the first serious symptoms of muscular pain appear, the odds that she could have survived until the middle of February 1945 are small. Margot probably didn't reach her nineteenth birthday on 16 February. The same applies for Anne, who was also at an advanced stage of typhus according to the witnesses who saw her just before her death, and who died only a few days after Margot. Therefore they died more than a month earlier than has always been assumed.

"I remember Gusta van Pels – she was of German origin"

Auguste van Pels in Raguhn

"THANK GOD, A SMALL CAMP"

Just before the death of the Frank sisters, Auguste van Pels was again sent on a transport. Bergen-Belsen still operated as a *Durchgangslager*, and selections were carried out quite regularly when groups of women were sent to work camps in other parts of the German Empire.[1] At some point in the first week of February, 500 women of different nationalities were selected on the orders of the camp commandant, and in the presence of several supervisors in civilian clothes, to be sent to the SS-Kommando Heerbrandtwerke AG in Raguhn, which fell under the administration of the Buchenwald concentration camp.[2] As far as we can ascertain, Auguste van Pels was selected together with twenty-eight other Dutch women who had all been taken to Bergen-Belsen from Auschwitz on the transport of 1 November 1944. Eight of them had also been on the transport from Westerbork to Auschwitz on 3 September 1944.[3]

Anne and Margot Frank were not selected for Raguhn in February because they were too ill, although Auguste was also very weak at that time. In retrospect, Annelore Daniel was surprised that Auguste had not stayed behind in Bergen-Belsen because she remembered how frail she was.[4] Cato Polak remembers how the selected women had been assembled in separate barracks, and they all had to sleep on the ground together: "You had to get out of the barracks ten times a night. It was really difficult in the dark to find your way back again. We were all incredibly thin and even if you touched each other for just a second, it really hurt and the screaming was dreadful."[5]

The 500 women who were selected had to walk back to the *Rampe* about 4.5 kilometers away, where the freight wagons were ready to take them to Raguhn. On the way, they saw new transports of prisoners walking to Bergen-Belsen in the opposite direction.[6]

The prisoners arrived in Raguhn three days later, on 10 February 1945.[7] For most witnesses, this was yet another deportation, and they barely described the details of this transport in their statements.[8] However, Freda Silberberg remembers that Germans living in the villages near the camp cursed and spat at the women when they had to walk from the Bergen-Belsen camp to the train station:

> Well, we had to walk to the train station. And the people were not exactly nice to us, they spit on us. The Germans, yeah. Because you walked sometimes through the village you know. And, yes, we were put again in the train and this time we weren't sorry to leave Bergen-Belsen, because we thought it was getting worse. And we arrived in Raguhn, we said: "Thank God, it's a small camp," you know. "Thank God it's a small camp."[9]

WORKING IN THE AIRCRAFT INDUSTRY

Raguhn certainly was much smaller than Bergen-Belsen. It was on the western edge of the town of Raguhn in Saxony-Anhalt near Halle an der Saale, where one of the last subcamps of the Buchenwald concentration camp had been established in February 1945.[10] The main Buchenwald camp had been built in 1937, and was one of the first and largest concentration camps on German territory. Between 1938 and 1945 there were about 24,000 people imprisoned there, a varied group of prisoners of war, political prisoners, Jehovah's Witnesses, Roma, Sinti and Jews. Like many other concentration camps, Buchenwald also had numerous widespread subsidiary departments which were known as subcamps (or *subkommandos*).

The SS-Kommando Heerbrandtwerke AG in Raguhn was run by *SS-Hauptscharführer* Herbert Dieckmann and *SS-Obersturm-führer* Hermann Grossmann. About forty-five male and female guards worked there. The camp started operating on 7 February 1945 as a work camp for a group of women from Bergen-Belsen who were accommodated close by, in the little town of Raguhn. Although the Raguhn subcamp was under the administration of Buchenwald, it was about 170 kilometers away to the northeast.

Hermann Grossman.

With two exceptions, the women prisoners were Jewish, but they had various geographical backgrounds. They came from France, Belgium, Poland, Italy, Hungary and Germany, as well as the Netherlands, and some were even from America and Turkey. Before their arrival in Raguhn, most of them had spent some time in Bergen-Belsen, like Auguste van Pels; another group had arrived in Raguhn via Theresienstadt and Auschwitz. There were between 500 and 700 women in the subcamp who had to work in a factory for aircraft parts, Junkers Flugzeug- und Motorenwerke AG, which was established 15 kilometers further north in Dessau. Junkers was originally a private company which had fallen into the hands of the German Ministry of Aviation in 1936. It was important for the German war industry because various different types of aircraft and airplane engines were built there.

After arriving in Raguhn, the women were registered once again. As the Raguhn *subkommando* was part of the Buchen- wald concentration camp, they were included in that camp's administration and were given "Buchenwald numbers". The women were numbered alphabetically by surname, with numbers ranging from 67001 to 67505.[11] Auguste van Pels was given number 67357.[12]

The women wore striped prisoners' clothes so that they were easily identifiable. This was important both in the Junkers factory where non-prisoners worked, and during their daily walk through the town of Raguhn to the factory, guarded by kapos and SS guards.[13] In the factory, they had to put together airplane parts under the supervision of the foremen. Ellen Daniel remembers that during the work she occasionally talked to them. The women carried out a variety of tasks in the factory.[14] For example, Cato Polak was at a lathe and Freda Silberberg had to solder or weld, whereas Annelore Daniel had to "tap something off plates". (She probably meant the perforated metal plates that were manufactured in the factory.) Her older sister Ellen remembers that she had to work on a large drill.[15]

The teams alternated between day and night shifts every week, and the work was heavy and inefficient. Because of the chaos of the final stage of the war, there was a constant shortage of materials, so there wasn't enough work for all the women from the camp. According to the historian Irmgard Sidel, the women were organized in alternating teams: one half would have to go to the factory while the other half stayed behind in the camp.[16]

The women in Raguhn didn't sleep in standard barracks, but in a number of former workshops and sanitary areas.[17] The prisoners saw this as an improvement on what they had experienced in Bergen-Belsen. Rachel Frankfoorder, who came to Raguhn together with Auguste van Pels, remembers the relatively good conditions in the camp, but also emphasized the importance of a job that provided extra food:

> It was a lot better than in any other camp. We were given clean barracks, there was somewhere to have a wash and we were given a blanket. But was this yet another trick, or was it really as good as it seemed? It was exactly as good as it seemed as long as you could peel potatoes, as long as you worked and ate the good potato soup, and it was not forbidden to eat a potato now and again so we became quite fit there.[18]

Whether this also applied for the other prisoners is not clear. Rachel Frankfoorder had to peel potatoes in a cellar together with eight Polish women and could occasionally take a potato with her for the others.[19] For those who didn't have access to extra food, the conditions were worse. In contrast with Rachel Frankfoorder, Ellen Daniel remembers that the circumstances in Raguhn "were just as bad as anywhere else and the food was no better either."[20]

Freda Silberberg also remembers how a sadistic guard tried to make their hunger worse. When he saw Freda and another prisoner almost fainting from hunger during the work in the machine factory, he promised to bring some extra food with him the next day and then appeared with a few potato peelings:

> But when I was in Raguhn, when we worked in that factory, and we were twelve hours without food. Can you imagine standing on a machine, after all what we already had gone through? I don't know how we stood, making pieces of machinery on a machine, that was working fast. […] There was a fat German, he said: "Tomorrow I will bring you something". So Jeanine and I, we're already dying for the next day to see what he was going to bring us. He brought us some potato peel! And he, he put it in the drawer, you know. And we knew if you would eat that you would have even worse diarrhea. That's how generous he was. Can you imagine how he treated us?[21]

The prisoners were hungry, and approximately 10 per cent of the women were too sick to work. Many had already arrived sick from Bergen-Belsen in clothes covered with lice and suffering from dysentery. After a while, typhus also broke out in Raguhn. Women died in the camp from a variety of diseases, including pneumonia, heart failure, encephalitis and intestinal diseases. The prisoners also regularly had to hide in cellars because of the Allied bombardment.[22]

We know very little about Auguste van Pels's experiences in the eight weeks that she spent in Raguhn. We don't know how often she had to work in the factory, what she did there or whether she got something extra to eat from time to time, like Rachel Frankfoorder, nor do we know when she became ill. The Dutch women who ended up with her in Raguhn only have vague memories of her. All we really know is that she was one of the approximately sixty women who didn't survive the very last transport of the female prisoners in Raguhn.

At the beginning of April 1945, American troops advanced towards the Buchenwald camp and the SS decided to evacuate the Raguhn subcamp. On 9 April 1945, the guards once again loaded the women from Raguhn onto freight wagons, this time heading for Theresienstadt.[23] Ellen Daniel remembers: "From mid-April you heard the shooting coming closer and closer, and we were put into a train once again, but we were lucky. They were closed cattle trucks. We traveled round in these trucks for weeks and then we ended up in Theresienstadt."[24]

It was a chaotic journey, during which they met many other transports. Everyone seemed to be fleeing. The train often stood still for long periods, and at those moments the women could sometimes even leave the trucks. Some of the women tried to escape when the train stopped. Others were actually afraid that they wouldn't get back into the train in time after a stop. The conditions on the way were dreadful, especially because there was now hardly any food left at all. Ellen Daniel remembers that the women used the stops to lift the dead bodies outside and try to find something to eat and drink:

> We'd be standing there at a station and sometimes we'd be outside where we could get out of the truck for a while,

and we'd have to carry out the dead because a few people died on the way from time to time – and then you could go to the toilet between the rails.[25]

The survivors of the transport arrived in Theresienstadt on 16 April 1945. They were liberated there by the Russians on 8 May 1945.

More than sixty women died on the way from hunger, hypothermia and exhaustion; another fifteen died after arrival in Theresienstadt, most from the typhus epidemic which had broken out amongst the prisoners. One of them was Auguste van Pels. The witness statements about the exact circumstances of her death differ slightly. After the liberation, Bertha Kaas-Hekster said: "I remember […] Gusta van Pels – originally from Germany but deported from Amsterdam, […] who died of typhus or on the transport to Theresienstadt."[26] Rachel Frankfoorder told the NRK on 28 September 1945: "During the journey from Raguhn to Theresienstadt Mrs. Gusti van Pels-Roettgen, about 42 years old, was thrown under the train by the Germans and therefore killed."[27]

However, there are no other witnesses who can confirm Rachel Frankfoorder's account, and Annelore Daniel and Bertha Kaas-Hekster explicitly contradict the idea that Auguste van Pels was thrown under a moving train by the German soldiers. Annelore Daniel, who knew Auguste van Pels from the barracks in Bergen-Belsen, declared that Auguste had typhus and died next to her during the transport from Raguhn to Theresienstadt. She lifted her out of the train together with someone else and laid her down on the bank next to the rails. Annelore Daniel had already told this story to Otto Frank in 1945 when he visited Nanette Blitz in the sanatorium in Santpoort to

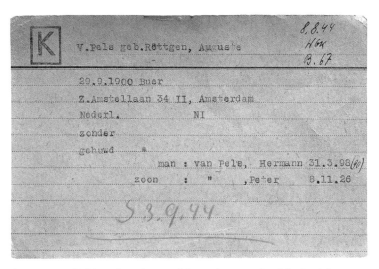

K

v.Pels geb.Röttgen, Auguste

8.8.44
HGK
B.67

29.9.1900 Buer
Z.Amstellaan 34 II, Amsterdam
Nederl.   NI
zonder
gehuwd   *
                    man : van Pels, Hermann 31.3.98(40)
          zoon   :   "   ,Peter   8.11.26

5.3.9.44

Auguste van Pels's registration card from the records of the Jewish Council.

ask her about his two daughters' last days. Annelore Daniel was in the bed next to Nanette Blitz in Santpoort and was able to add details to Blitz's story about the last meetings with Anne, Margot and Auguste.[28]

CHAPTER SEVEN

"They never came back"
Peter van Pels in Mauthausen and Melk

THE DEATH MARCH FROM AUSCHWITZ TO MAUTHAUSEN

In mid-January 1945, hundreds of thousands of people from the Auschwitz area were on the roads, leaving the area, including 58,000 prisoners from Auschwitz, thousands of English and Russian prisoners of war, enormous columns of military vehicles, retreating Wehrmacht and SS troops, and German citizens fleeing the Russian army.[1] The evacuation routes pre-planned by the SS were often impossible to follow because the roads were overcrowded and were now within reach of the Red Army. The prisoners from Auschwitz had to walk for 55 kilometers in long columns to Gleiwitz (Gliwice), or 63 kilometers to Loslau (the current Wodzislaw Śląski on the Czech–Polish border). From there they had to continue in open freight wagons to other camps such as Mauthausen, Groß-Rosen, Buchenwald, Bergen-Belsen, Flossenbürg, Mittelbau-Dora, Ravensbrück, Sachsenhausen and Dachau. Between 9,000 and 15,000 people died during these so-called "death marches".[2]

Long columns of prisoners departed from midnight on 18 January 1945 until the following afternoon.[3] For Peter van Pels and approximately 5,700 others, the destination was the Mauthausen camp in Austria. They included the above-mentioned Max Rodriques Garcia and, as revealed in the

Prisoners had to join the "death marches" when the Dachau concentration camp was evacuated, January 1945.

Max Moszkowicz, 1941.

biography by Marcel Haenen, also the future lawyer Max Moszkowicz.[4] Like Peter Moszkowicz, Max had managed to survive up to then by securing a relatively privileged position

Leen Sanders in about 1938.

while he was in Auschwitz. He had done this by taking part in boxing matches organized for the entertainment of the SS guards. The professional boxer Leen Sanders was regularly given extra food rations for this by the guards, and he shared them with other boxers such as Moszkowicz. We don't know whether Peter van Pels and Max Moszkowicz, who were about the same age, knew each other, but they went on the same death march, and mostly ended up in the same places.[5]

The first 60 kilometers towards the west were on foot.[6] It was a dreadful journey. Even before they started, many of the prisoners were already seriously weakened, and the SS guards unceremoniously shot anyone who couldn't keep up or tried to escape. Coen Schimmer also went on the same route as Peter van Pels. In his postwar account, he described how the first people died less than an hour after leaving and that he saw their dead bodies by the roadside – at first, these were mainly women, but sometimes they included children. They had been shot in the head.

The marchers had to walk for days on end through the cold and the snow. At night, they slept in a hay barn under a few planks or outside in the snow, huddled close together.[7]

After five days, they reached Loslau on 22 January 1945.[8] From there they were loaded onto open coal or freight wagons full of ice and snow, a hundred at a time.[9] The train did not leave until the next morning. It was minus 20 degrees, and the prisoners were not given anything to eat or drink. Max Rodriques Garcia says that during this trip he only survived thanks to the physical reserves he had built up when he was working at the *Paketstelle* in Auschwitz.[10] Samuel Kropveld also describes how cruelly he was treated by the guards on the train journey to Mauthausen:

Those Germans were such thugs! Those open cattle trucks that we were in for the last part of the trip would stop every now and again and we'd use the opportunity to go to the toilet. That was permitted. Once when I wanted to climb back into the truck, I was hanging from the top of the truck but I had so little strength I couldn't get in straight away. An SS officer who saw this came up to me and started beating me with his rifle. What was that all about? I was doing something and that was permitted, and I could explain and there was no hurry. He just did it because he enjoyed beating people up. He really took it out on me! He beat me all over, and if the others hadn't helped me, he would certainly have beaten me to death.[11]

Many people died of hypothermia and exhaustion during the journey, and whenever the train stopped, the dead bodies were thrown out. Kropveld says that some of the bodies had frozen to the floor of the trucks and that many prisoners suffered psychoses as a result of hunger, and especially thirst. "At night, a large proportion of those people would be completely delirious. They had no awareness of space and if it hadn't been dark, they would have beaten me black and blue".[12] After three days, they arrived at the station in Mauthausen, and from there the prisoners walked in a long column along a road that went through the town to the northwest for 6 kilometers, winding up towards the concentration camp.

Mauthausen had been established as a concentration camp for male prisoners in August 1938, five months after the Anschluss of Austria. The location had been chosen because the area was rich in granite and there had traditionally been many quarries there. Granite and the production of building materials were essential for the huge construction projects of the German Empire under the direction of Hitler's master builder, Albert Speer. In addition, the Danube made it easy to transport materials.

The Deutsche Erd- und Steinwerke GmbH (DEST), which was established by the SS in Berlin in April 1938 and run by the above-mentioned SS officer Oswald Pohl, acquired a number of quarries at Mauthausen.[13] The Gusen subcamp was built about 8 kilometers from Mauthausen in May 1940 after the DEST had taken over quarries there. The first group of prisoners came from Dachau in 1938 and consisted mainly of criminals

Prisoners working the quarry of the Mauthausen concentration camp.

and *Asoziale*. From May 1939 it was mainly used for political prisoners, prisoners of war from various countries, and all sorts of other groups which the Nazis considered to be enemies, including many Dutch and Hungarian Jews.[14] The 427 Jewish men who had been picked up in the razzia in the Jewish quarter of Amsterdam on 22 and 23 February were all transported to Mauthausen. Hardly any of them survived.[15] Apart from this, Jews were in the minority in Mauthausen, and they came last in the hierarchy of prisoners.[16]

Mauthausen was one of the worst camps.[17] The prisoners worked in the quarries of Mauthausen and Gusen as forced labor. Because of the severe regime and the heavy work in the quarries, the mortality rate was extremely high, a result of the combination of work and eradication, with many prisoners literally working themselves to death. It was standard for Jewish prisoners to be sent to the punishment *kommando* as stone carriers in the infamous Mauthausen quarry, where they carried granite boulders on their backs up steep steps in a wooden carrier. They would be kept standing for roll call for hours at a time, and any medical care was inadequate. The prisoners' diet was calculated on a life expectancy of three to four months.[18]

The camp was run by the camp commandant, *SS-Standartenführer* Franz Ziereis, who was in charge of approximately 600 men, mainly members of the *Waffen-SS*, supplemented with a number of marines, police officers and sixty-five female SS guards.[19] Zieries was merciless, and mistreatment and executions were everyday events. In September 1941, after he had attended a demonstration of an installation for shooting people in the neck, he built a comparable installation for mass executions in Mauthausen to execute Russian prisoners of war as efficiently as possible.[20] From 1941, prisoners were transported

Franz Ziereis.

to the neighboring castle of Hartheim, one of the locations of the secret euthanasia program T4, to be murdered in the gas chamber that had been built there. In addition, the SS made use of a mobile gassing installation from the autumn of 1941. In the spring of 1942, a gas chamber camouflaged as a shower area was also put into operation where thirty to eighty people could be murdered at a time with Zyklon B. There was also a crematorium where the bodies were burnt.[21]

In 1943, with Germany's prospects in the war deteriorating and prisoners increasingly used as slave labor in the war industry, a total of forty-six subcamps and *kommandos* across Austria were placed under Mauthausen's control. Towards the end of the year, the increase in Allied aerial bombardments forced airplane and arms factories to be moved to secret underground locations so that production for the war could continue. Prisoners worked on the construction of these underground factories under terrible conditions.

The main camp at Mauthausen increasingly became an administrative center from which the prisoners would be distributed across an extensive network of subcamps after they had been registered and completed a period of quarantine. Around the same time, Mauthausen became a so-called *Sterbelager*, where prisoners who were too sick or weak to carry out the heavy forced labor would be sent. Approximately 190,000 people were deported to Mauthausen, of whom more than 90,000 died.[22]

A CABINETMAKER WITH AN OVAL FACE

When Peter van Pels arrived in the Mauthausen concentration camp on 25 January 1945 he was eighteen years old. His name appears on the list of 5,714 prisoners who arrived from Auschwitz on that date.[23] The registration procedure after their arrival took a long time.[24] Considering the size of the transport, this operation could have taken the whole of the night and the next day.

When they arrived in the camp, the prisoners had to get undressed. It was winter and it was freezing. They had to go to the shower area in groups before being disinfected and shaved. Then they had to wait outside to be registered, either naked or wearing just underpants or a shirt. A former prisoner, Coen Schimmer, remembers that the bath and disinfection were "really primitive" and that there were hardly any clothes to put on afterwards.[25]

The prisoners on Peter's transport were numbered in a series from 116,501 to 122,225. The numbers of the prisoners on the list reveals that the registration was carried out in five groups of a thousand or more prisoners, and in alphabetical order.[26] Peter van Pels belonged to the third group. The prisoners were given their number printed on an iron plate that they had to wear around the wrist with a wire thread. The deportation history of

The main entrance of Mauthausen, just after the liberation in May 1945.

Prisoners in barracks in Mauthausen, one day after the liberation, 6 May 1945.

Mauthausen identity plate.

Peter van Pels is shown on a copy of his registration in Maut-hausen: "Dutch Jew, sent to Auschwitz on 3 September 1944, arrived in Mauthausen on 25 January 1945, prisoner number 119162". His registration card also shows that he was in quarantine in Mauthausen until 29 January 1945, and it says that he was a *Tischler* (cabinetmaker), height 1.73 meters and slim build. His face was oval, he had green eyes, close set ears, a straight nose, full mouth, good teeth and black hair. According to the card, he spoke Dutch, English and German. The "special characteristic" noted on his card also mentions that he had a tattoo, which was his Auschwitz number.[27]

After the registration, the prisoners were crowded into quarantine barracks en masse. There were no beds, so they slept side by side on the ground.[28] They remained there for several days, scantily clad and with little or nothing to eat. Then they were given old and used prisoners' clothes – a jacket, trousers, cap, and wooden shoes or sandals. The male prisoners had to sew their number onto their jacket at chest height and also against the seam of their right trouser leg. All the categories of prisoners had their own identifying characteristic: Jewish prisoners could be recognized by a red equilateral triangle, pointing downward with a yellow bar above it; this

Konzentrationslager Mauthausen
Verwaltung

Gef. Az. 14/2 /43/Bü

An die

Politische Abteilung des
Konzentrationslagers Mauthausen.

Der gesamte Nachlaß des oben angeführten Verstorbenen ist am

an abgesandt worden.

Der Gefangenen-Eigentumsverwalter IV:

SS-Unterscharführer.

Verfg.!
Zum Personalakt!

Benachrichtigung an die hiesige Effektenkammer zum Versand des Nachlasses an die Angehörigen. — 281 43

119162 NL Jude

van Pels
Peter
6.11.26   Osnabrück
led.
Amsterdam
Zuider-Amsterdam 44
ohne   Niederl.
            Vater
Hermann w o

    3.9.4 Au

25.1.45 KLM
NL Jude

173
schlank
oval
grün
ger.
voll

anl.
gut
schw.
holl. engl.
dtsch.

tät.

Peter van Pels's card from the records of Camp Mauthausen. The front shows his personal data; the reverse states his profession – *Tischler* (cabinetmaker) – and where he was imprisoned.

was shown next to their number.[29] There were strict rules about wearing and taking off the cap. Failing to wear a cap during the roll call was enough for the guards to shoot the person concerned.[30]

After four days in quarantine, the majority of the prisoners who had arrived on 25 January 1945 were sent on to a transport to the subcamps of Mauthausen to Ebensee, Gusen and Melk.[31] In some cases, it seems that the prisoners were selected on the basis of their profession. Coen Schimmer, a survivor, stated that "of his group of Dutch men, the metal workers were selected for Camp Gusen, Peter, who was still described as a metal worker on the transport list from Westerbork to Auschwitz, did not belong to this group." As indicated above, his card in the camp records of Mauthausen showed that he was a cabinetmaker.[32]

Most of the total of approximately two thousand men, however, were transferred to the subcamp at Melk, and their profession does not seem to have played a decisive role in this.[33] Melk had been organized as a concentration camp for male prisoners on 21 April 1944 to work as forced labor on a project with the code name Quartz: the construction of an underground factory in a mountain for the manufacture of machine parts for tanks and aircraft.[34] Up to 15 April 1945, a huge number of victims died as a result of the heavy work, the extreme working conditions and the inhuman treatment.[35] On 29 January 1945, this large group of prisoners walked down through the town to the station at Mauthausen.[36] They were transported in freight wagons to the camp in Melk, approximately 70 kilometers east of Mauthausen. The Greek Jew Moshe Ha-Elion had arrived in Mauthausen on a death march from Auschwitz on 21 January 1945 and was in the same train to Melk as Peter van Pels on

Roll call of prisoners at the camp in Melk.

29 January. In his book *The Straits of Hell*, he describes the prisoners walking from the train station to the camp through a wild snowstorm after a journey of approximately seven hours.[37]

Melk was situated in a former military barracks, high up on the southwestern edge of the town of Melk, on the banks of the Danube. Julius Ludolph was the camp commandant.[38] There were, on average, 7,000 prisoners of different nationalities in the camp.[39] The conditions when Peter van Pels arrived there were terrible. With the arrival of the transport of 29 January 1945 from Mauthausen, there were a total of 10,314 prisoners in Melk. Between January and April 1945, 3,106 people died as a result of disease, accidents, mistreatment or were simply shot.[40] In one year, approximately 5,000 of the approximately 15,000 prisoners in the camp at Melk died.[41]

Moshe Ha-Elion provides a dreadful picture of the appalling sanitary conditions in the camp: "The toilets were caked with dirt, as were the few showers here. In fact, dirt covered everything, and before long, we were infested with lice."[42] The prisoners were accommodated in primitive wooden barracks on the former military site in the camp. They slept in bunk beds with three levels and shared a bed with three others. They had no winter clothes, only a thin pair of trousers, a jacket and a cap. Many prisoners had no underclothes and sometimes no shoes. Ha-Elion remembers that although the conditions were extremely bad, the food was "surprisingly good". He said that both the quality and the quantity were better than in Auschwitz and Mauthausen, particularly because the prisoners were given a quarter of a loaf of bread twice a day. In the morning, the rations consisted of half a liter of "coffee", followed by a liter of watery cabbage soup in the afternoon, and in the evening, bread, and a piece of margarine or sausage. However, a Dutch former prisoner, H.L. Bastiaans, emphasizes that during the last months of their life in the camp at Melk, the prisoners were hungry and there was no bread for weeks at a time.[43]

It was the heavy work in particular which led to many prisoners dying. Prisoners were gathered every day for roll call before being marched out of the camp in blocks of five by five, guarded by SS officers. The prisoners were obliged to walk arm in arm to prevent anyone from escaping. If one of them made an attempt to escape, the whole line would be shot.[44] In the winter, it was dangerously slippery. At the bottom, the approximately 2,000 prisoners on the morning, day or night shift walked to an emergency platform where they had to wait for a train. The civilian workers and the SS officers were transported in passenger carriages. The prisoners were sent to the village of

Roggendorf, about twenty minutes further on, in open freight wagons with about 160 men to a wagon.[45] They had to walk another half hour from there and were then divided amongst the various work *kommandos.*

The prisoners worked day and night in three shifts, drilling, digging and shoring up the tunnels, moving quartz, manufacturing the beams that were needed to support the tunnels, loading and unloading construction materials, and working on other construction activities in the gigantic factory complex. The work was extremely heavy and difficult, as Moshe Ha-Elion emphasized: "It soon became clear to me how monstrously heavy this work was, it really was heavy labor and I hadn't experienced anything like this since my days in the punishment kommando at Auschwitz."[46]

In Melk, there was a striking number of young Jewish men under the age of twenty;[47] one group of approximately 100 prisoners from the transport of 29 January was even younger than fifteen. In general, the children in the camp did the same work as the adults, insofar as they were able to. The group of children in Melk was assigned to the kitchen *kommando* and had to peel potatoes.[48] Peter van Pels was just eighteen when he arrived in Melk. Because of his age, he would have been assigned to a work *kommando* and would have worked under comparable conditions to Ha-Elion.[49]

When the prisoners were working, they were guarded by SS officers, kapos and civilian workers. They were poorly dressed, very weak and sick, and were mistreated when they were working. Schimmer remembers that there were "extremely strict rules" and the SS officers "beat everyone mercilessly".[50] The Czechoslovakian Jewish former prisoner Miksa Mechlowitz also remembers the gratuitous violence: "Once I was beaten up because I'd fallen asleep when I was working. They beat me with sticks twenty-five times and we were constantly beaten for no particular reason. Just like that."[51] In addition, the work itself was very dangerous. There were no safety measures during the heavy work in the galleries of the mine, and there were serious, often fatal, accidents every day. The galleries were regularly flooded. In winter, many of the prisoners suffered from frozen limbs.[52] During the frequent Allied bombing raids in the area, the prisoners hid in the tunnels. "New" prisoners were regularly transported from Mauthausen to replace the dead. The huge evacuation transports provided a constant stream of forced labor, and it was above all the Jewish prisoners who were used for this.[53]

Although the exact date is not known, Peter van Pels died at a certain moment as a result of the heavy work and the atrocious living conditions. We know that he worked for at least ten weeks in the camp in Melk, in the underground factory making ball bearings, and that he also eventually became sick and was sent to the infirmary at Mauthausen. Miksa Mechlowitz was in Melk for about a year and remembers that many people fell sick at work and had to be carried back by others. A transport of sick people was sent to the infirmaries in Mauthausen every week. According to Mechlowitz, "They never came back."[54]

There was absolutely no medical treatment in Melk. If a prisoner became ill, they were left to their fate, and in some cases, gassed or shot.[55] Sick prisoners lay on their bunks, naked and without bags of straw. Coen Schimmer, who was in the infirmary at about the same time as Peter van Pels, called the situation there "indescribable". Sometimes the sick were four to a bed. Schimmer describes how an SS officer would come every morning to check who could be considered to be "cured" and ready for work. From November 1944, the bodies were burnt in the crematorium of the camp in Melk; before that, the dead were taken to Mauthausen to be burnt there.[56]

At the beginning of April 1945, with the Red Army approaching and on the point of taking Vienna, the camp in Melk was hastily evacuated. On 11 April 1945, the sick from the *Revier* and the young men in the camp (a total of 1,500) were sent back to Mauthausen by train.[57] Everyone in the *Revier* who could still stand up had to go along;[58] when they arrived in Mauthausen, many of them were gassed.[59] The others ended up in the *Sanitätslager* of Mauthausen. The other 6,000 prisoners in the camp in Melk were transported to the Außenlager Ebensee on 13 and 15 April 1945.[60]

Peter van Pels returned to Mauthausen on 11 April 1945. He was not one of the prisoners to be gassed immediately, but ended up in the *Sanitätslager*,[61] the wooden barracks outside the walls of the Mauthausen camp where Russian prisoners of war had been accommodated in the past. As in Bergen-Belsen, the *Sanitätslager* was also known as the *Russenlager*. The conditions there were abominable: the barracks were overpopulated, and prisoners were left there without any medical care, often naked and without food.[62] They lay on the ground or with four to six people to a bunk, in bunks with three levels. It was actually only a place to die. The seriously ill and weak prisoners usually did not survive long.[63] There are witnesses who have even mentioned cannibalism in the *Sanitätslager* in Mauthausen.[64]

On 5 May 1945, a reconnoitering unit of the Third United States Army entered the camp in Mauthausen and liberated it.[65] The next day, 6 May 1945, the Third Army itself arrived in the camp and started to care for the sick. The book of the dead in the infirmary of Mauthausen, which was kept up to date after the camp leaders and guards left, states that Peter van Pels died on 10 May 1945.[66] This date is also shown on an US army list, but it was probably taken from the book of the dead.[67] This means that despite the terrible conditions in the *Sanitätslager*, Peter van Pels lived for another four weeks in Mauthausen. Ironically, he therefore died after the liberation. This was the fate of thousands of other prisoners who had been liberated but who had been so weak as a result of sickness and malnourishment that they could no longer be saved by the doctors who treated them after the camps were liberated.[68]

For a long time after the war, there was some uncertainty about the date of Peter van Pels's death. Because of the enormous number of missing persons and the huge administrative chaos, the NRK was not able to ascertain the exact dates and circumstances of the deaths of the victims in detail. In some cases, the date on which the camp was liberated was shown as the date of the death of missing persons. In the case of Mauthausen, this was 5 May 1945. The Commission for the Registration of

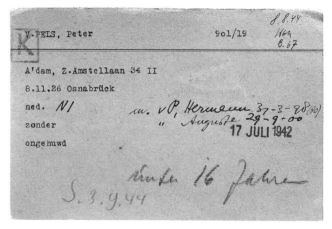

Peter van Pels's registration card from the records of the Jewish Council.

the Deaths of Missing Persons used that date, and that is why the date of 5 May 1945 is shown on Peter van Pels's death certificate.[69] When the NRK was later informed of the date of 10 May 1945 – ascertained with the help of data from the book of the dead from the infirmary at Mauthausen and the US army list – an "official" date had already been registered. As far as is known, no attempts have been made to change it.

CHAPTER EIGHT

"The largest proportion of deaths was amongst the Dutch"

Fritz Pfeffer in Neuengamme

NEUENGAMME

On the basis of the scarce information available, we must assume that Fritz Pfeffer was sent from Auschwitz I to Birkenau on foot between October and November 1944. Subsequently, he is believed to have been taken to Neuengamme on a so-called "medical" transport, as several witnesses refer to a transport of doctors and dentists who left Birkenau in October or November 1944. In an interview with the American journalist Arthur Unger, Otto Frank also mentioned that Fritz Pfeffer appeared one morning with a group of dentists.[1] Moreover, Charlotte Kaletta, Fritz Pfeffer's partner, wrote to the NRK in August 1945 that Fritz Pfeffer had been transported from Auschwitz to Neuengamme on a medical transport on 1 October 1944.[2]

Although the transport did not take place on 1 October, but in November, it is likely that it was a transport solely dedicated for doctors and dentists.[3] It often happened that prisoners were transported together with others of the same profession, such as typographers or draftsmen, or doctors, dentists and nurses. For example, Janny Hamburger-Bolle was sent from Auschwitz to the camp in Groß-Rosen together with a group of sixteen nurses,[4] and on 24 January 1944, a transport left Auschwitz for Sachsenhausen that mainly consisted of typographers and draftsmen.[5] Another example is a transport which went from Auschwitz to a subcamp of Groß-Rosen on 15 May 1944 consisting solely of doctors and nurses.[6] In this case, the prisoner numbers and registration cards show that a number of dentists and doctors arrived in Neuengamme together with Fritz Pfeffer between 10 and 18 November.[7]

We do not know with any certainty who told Charlotte Kaletta that her lover had been sent on a so-called medical transport. It is possible that she received this information from Otto Frank, who had been in quarantine block 8 in Auschwitz together with Fritz Pfeffer. After Otto's return to the Netherlands, Kaletta had a great deal of contact with him from June 1945. Another possibility is that she heard it from Barend Konijn or Fritz Simon, Pfeffer's fellow prisoners. In his declaration to the NRK, Barend Konijn, who survived Auschwitz, mentioned a transport on November 1944 "of several dentists and orthodontists going somewhere else."[8] Although it's not certain what profession all these people had, we know that eight men on the list were doctors or dentists, and so it can be assumed that it was a professionally oriented transport.[9]

The destination was Neuengamme, a village situated about 20 kilometers southeast of Hamburg, where a subcamp of the Sachsenhausen concentration camp had been established in 1938. Approximately 100 prisoners and a number of SS guards came from Sachsenhausen in the first transport.[10] Shortly after the outbreak of the Second World War, the camp in Neuengamme was enlarged and organized as an independent concentration camp. During the course of the war, a large number of external subcamps throughout Germany were placed under the control of Neuengamme, the so-called *Außenlager*

Forced labor in the Neuengamme concentration camp.

or *Außenkommandos*. Like virtually all other concentration camps, Neuengamme was also run by the SS.[11]

From 1942, the camp commandant of Neuengamme was *SS-Sturmbannführer* Max Pauly. Pauly was known as an *Alter Kämpfer*, someone who had joined the NSDAP, the SA or the SS at an early stage. He was a top officer in the SS even before Hitler took power, and during the German attack on Poland in 1939 he was placed in charge of the internment camps in the occupied territory. Shortly afterwards, he was appointed as the commandant of the Stutthof concentration camp. When he was transferred to Neuengamme, he was made responsible for a large number of public executions and crimes.[12]

Pauly was in charge of a total of 2,600 SS officers who guarded Neuengamme and the subcamps and supervised the forced labor. Up to 1945, there were more than 100,000 people imprisoned in Neuengamme and the subcamps, of which at least 42,900 did not survive.[13] They died as a result of the hard work, the terrible living conditions and mistreatment, but many

Max Pauly.

were also executed immediately or were murdered in the gas chamber that was built in one of the bunkers in October 1942.[14] That year, the SS murdered 251 Russian prisoners of war using the poisonous gas Zyklon B.[15]

The concentration camp's aim was to intern political opponents and other "enemies" of the Nazi regime such as Jews, Roma and Sinti, Jehovah's Witnesses and homosexuals. There were also Russian prisoners of war and people from the German occupied areas who had avoided labor. At first, these included many Poles, Czechs and Russian prisoners of war, but during the course of the war, thousands of prisoners from all the occupied countries of Europe were sent to Neuengamme.[16] From the summer of 1944, large groups of Jewish prisoners arrived in Neuengamme directly from Hungary and with the evacuation transports from Auschwitz.[17]

At the end of 1944, during the period that Fritz Pfeffer was in Neuengamme, there were 12,000 prisoners in the main camp and 37,000 in related subcamps. Apart from the women from Ravensbrück, who were forced into prostitution in the Neuengamme brothel, there were only men in the main camp. Approximately 10,000 women were imprisoned in the subcamps.[18]

The prisoners in Neuengamme came from all over Europe, from a total of about twenty-eight countries. In addition to the Russians, Poles, Belgians and French, there were about 5,500 Dutch prisoners in Neuengamme, including Fritz Pfeffer.[19] The Dutch prisoners who ended up in the camp in Neuengamme included anti-German police officers, Jews, Jehovah's Witnesses and all sorts of people from the Resistance such as the freedom fighter Anton de Kom from Suriname, the mayor Inus van Haersma Buma, and the poet and journalist Jan Campert.[20]

A group of more than 600 men arrived in Neuengamme in October 1944 from Putten on the Veluwe. They had been arrested by the Germans on 2 October 1944 in retaliation for an attack by a Resistance group, and had been sent to the camp in Amersfoort.[21] They were transported to Neuengamme on 11 October 1944, arriving the night of 14 October 1944. Wim Alosery, a Dutchman who was not Jewish but who had avoided labor, arrived in Neuengamme at about the same time as Pfeffer. In postwar interviews, he emphasized how difficult it was for him to find the words to describe his camp experiences in Neuengamme: "I can summarize my own history in a few lines but what I felt there is impossible to express. The fear, the cold, the hunger, the sadism. It's indescribable."[22]

The experiences of the hostages and prisoners who had avoided work from Putten, like Alosery, give an impression of the circumstances in Neuengamme, but it's important to realize that as a Jewish prisoner, Pfeffer must have had an even more difficult time. Here too, the Jews were at the bottom of the camp hierarchy. The prisoners had to carry out forced labor in very bad conditions. The above-mentioned construction company DEST, which also made use of the camp in Mauthausen, had acquired a piece of land there that included an old stone factory that had ceased operating. Through the use of the forced labor provided by the camp, the factory became operational again. The prisoners worked on the drainage of the site, and built barracks, watchtowers and fencing.

As in Mauthausen and a number of other concentration camps, DEST produced construction materials in Neuengamme for the large projects of the German Empire. In the clay soil around Neuengamme, this involved the production of bricks and blocks for the construction of monumental buildings on the banks of the Elbe in Hamburg.[23] The prisoners built a new stone factory on the extensive camp site and worked in the quarry. They were also used for building a railway connection and digging out a more navigable tributary of the Elbe, as well as digging out a side canal and a basin for the harbor. Everything was focused on the infrastructure to transport the products from the stone factory to Hamburg, and transport the necessary raw materials, such as cement, to Neuengamme.[24] The prisoners in Neuengamme also worked in different branches of the war industry, such as the manufacture of detonators for grenades and parts for weapons. They also had to sort through the rubble in Hamburg, clear unexploded bombs, dig anti-tank trenches and carry out other heavy work that was sometimes extremely dangerous.[25]

FRITZ PFEFFER IN NEUENGAMME

Fritz Pfeffer was one of the 42,000 men who did not survive Neuengamme.[26] He arrived in the camp at some point between 10 and 18 November 1944; the exact date remains unknown. As indicated above, he probably went directly from Auschwitz to Neuengamme with a transport of prisoners who all had a medical background.[27]

Based on the accounts of survivors, the arrival of Pfeffer in Neuengamme was approximately as follows. First, he had to go to an area with the other new prisoners where they had to hand in all their possessions and get undressed.[28] (Although Fritz Pfeffer came from Auschwitz and would not have had anything left to hand in, he nevertheless had to go through the same procedure.) After this, they were once again shaved, removing all body hair. Cor Bos, a Dutch police officer who had been arrested for anti-German sabotage and arrived in Neuengamme on 13 October 1944 with a group of other police officers, remembers this procedure: "This was not done very gently. I ended up with a bad cut in my groin which bled profusely. There was a large bucket with a brush with some white stuff in it and you had to apply that. It hurt like hell, but the bleeding did stop."[29] After being shaved, they were showered, checked for lice and disinfected.

Before going into the showers, the prisoners were given a metal plate with a number that they had to wear around their neck using a piece of string or steel chain. The special prisoner uniforms that had been given out in previous years were no longer available. Pfeffer was probably also given other clothes in Neuengamme, such as a few worn and ripped rags. Prisoners were not provided with underclothes and there were no socks either, but they were given cloths for their feet, wooden shoes or slippers, and a cap. The clothes were much too light and were marked on the back with a cross of yellow paint so that they would be clearly identifiable. When the prisoners had received their clothes, they had to wait at the roll call, before being allocated to a barracks. Four hundred prisoners slept in every

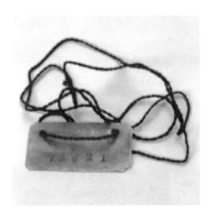

Neuengamme identification tag.

wooden barrack, often with broken windows, three to four to a bed with bunks with three levels. Mistreatment was also very common here.[30]

The average day for the prisoners in Neuengamme started at 4.30 a.m. Breakfast consisted of a slice of bread and a quarter liter of coffee. After the morning roll call, they had to work. For the midday meal there was cabbage soup, and after work there was another roll call. In the evening, the prisoners were given two slices of bread; four times a week they were given a piece of margarine and sometimes a slice of sausage, soft cheese or a cooked potato. The day finished at nine in the evening. Whenever the alarms went off because of overhead Allied bombing, the prisoners were driven into the underground shelters.

In Neuengamme, there were also increasing numbers of people who could no longer cope with the terrible conditions and seemed to give up on fighting for survival. Jaap van Wincoop, a hostage from Putten, explained how the prisoners reached the critical stage: "Most of them no longer thought about keeping themselves clean. They walked round in a filthy state with open wounds on their hands, mouth and feet."[31] The resistance fighter Han Lokker from Barneveld, who was a dentist like Pfeffer, arrived in Neuengamme at the beginning of February 1945.[32] Lokker subtitled his account of the camp: "You only got out alive if you were lucky". He described the terrible conditions which he experienced in Neuengamme:

> At first I wrote that you could only survive the camp with luck. And that's true. If you lived in the blocks and carried out the ordinary activities you needed an iron constitution to keep going, as well as a significant dose

of brutality. In general, the Russians had that. Percentage wise only a few of them died. They were not very sensitive to infections and ate everything they could get their hands on. Raw cabbage stems, potato peel etc., and in addition they understood the art of "organizing", which meant getting hold of something extra in ways that were not in accordance with the norms. The largest proportion of deaths was amongst the Dutch. 650 young men had been taken to Neuengamme from a village in the Netherlands because two German subofficers had been attacked there. [...] Of the 650, perhaps 150 were still alive when the war ended. Many simply died because they could not cope with life in the camp, did not have enough will power to fight for their existence. The first symptom of this was that in the mornings they no longer washed and slowly became totally filthy. They were too indolent to pay attention to their bread or meal at midday and others would always be grateful to have that. The law of the jungle, the idea that the strongest would prevail meant that the weaker men died.[33]

Lokker, who was not Jewish and had been arrested in Barneveld for hiding Jews, emphasized not only how hard life was in the camp, but also how unequal the chances of survival were for different groups of prisoners. The Nazi ideology and the hierarchy imposed by the camp authorities on the prisoners played an important role in this, as well as the sort of job a prisoner managed to get.[34] According to Lokker, anyone who was lucky enough to get a special job had a significantly better chance of surviving: if you were a cook, barber, writer, doctor or a member of the *Stubendienst*, for example, there was the possibility to get your hands on some extras. Han Lokker's "luck" was that he was a dentist in the *Revier* in Neuengamme, which meant he had to treat, among other things, fractured jaws. He wrote that the guards often hit the prisoners so hard that they lost their teeth. Every week he had to go to Hamburg to treat the prisoners in the *Spaldingstrasse*, a subcamp of Neuengamme where there was a so-called *Sprengkommando* of about 2,000 men who had to clear unexploded bombs in the streets of Hamburg.

The hostages from Putten who are described in Lokker's account as prisoners with a relatively low chance of survival only remained in Neuengamme for a short while before they were sent on to the various subcamps. Lokker's fellow prisoner Jaap van Wincoop concluded: "The camp served as the supply shed for workers".[35] It was mainly workers in the building trade, such as carpenters and bricklayers, who remained behind in the

The infirmary at Neuengamme.

camp. Most went from one camp to the other to carry out forced labor in different places. For example, in Hussum and Ladelund, the prisoners had to dig walls for tanks. When they were too sick to work (infected and frozen feet were very common as a result of digging in marshy soil), they were sent back to the main camp. Oftentimes, they ended up in the infirmary and died, or were sent on to the next subcamp to work as forced labor there.

The question whether Fritz Pfeffer, like Han Lokker, managed to use his profession as a dentist to acquire a relatively privileged position remains unanswered because of a lack of sources. As a Jewish prisoner, it would certainly have been much more difficult to climb up the ladder of the camp hierarchy than it was for Lokker. It is not clear either whether Pfeffer remained in the main camp the whole time. There are no testimonies from people who met him in Neuengamme or in any of the subcamps. However, it's quite possible that he was put to work in one of the external camps, as this happened to the majority of the prisoners who arrived in Neuengamme at that time. Prisoners who were doctors or dentists also worked there alongside the many prisoners carrying out forced labor.[36] We can only go by the probabilities and the scant administrative sources. However, we do know that he did not die in one of the subcamps, but in the main camp, though this could mean that he worked somewhere else temporarily and was taken back to the main camp in a very weak condition.

At some point in the winter of 1944, Pfeffer became seriously ill. The book of the dead at Neuengamme states that Fritz Pfeffer died of enterocolitis, an inflammation of the intestines, at 9 a.m. on 20 December 1944.[37] He was fifty-five years old. Enterocolitis causes diarrhea, and when this is untreated,

From the camp records at Neuengamme. A notebook with the names
of prisoners who died between 17 December 1944 and 19 January 1945.
Fritz Pfeffer died on 20 December 1944.

The Neuengamme book of the dead.

it can lead to dysentery and eventually to death.[38] Diarrhea and dysentery were the most common diseases in the *Revier* at Neuengamme and were virtually impossible to cure. The cause and time of death that is recorded in the book of the dead give the impression of a careful diagnosis and observation of the sick, as it does for the other names of prisoners who died. In fact, the cause of death was often chosen arbitrarily from a list.[39]

The conditions in the *Revier* were atrocious. It was overcrowded, there were hardly any medicines and the prisoners lay there naked, three or four to a bed. Han Lokker describes how the sick were put into beds with blankets covered in the diarrhea of other patients with dysentery.[40] Prisoners who died at night were pushed out of the bed by the others so that they had more room and didn't have to lie next to a dead body. In the

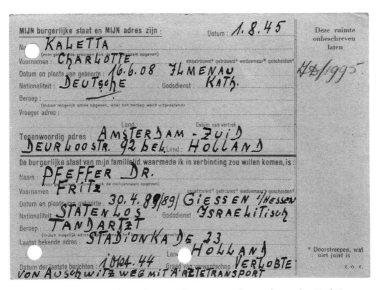

Charlotte Kaletta tried to obtain information about from the Red Cross with this card.

morning, the bodies were taken to the mortuary, where their numbers were removed, and they remained there until there were enough (approximately 200) to be taken to the crematorium to be burnt.[41]

Fritz Pfeffer's death certificate was drawn up by the Standesamt Hamburg-Neuengamme, and gives the address at the time of death as Hausdeich 60 in Hamburg Neuengamme,[42] which is the address of the Neuengamme crematorium.[43] It is therefore probable that Fritz Pfeffer was cremated. On 23 October 1945, the NRK sent an official death certificate to Charlotte Kaletta. "On the basis of a notification sent here by an assisting team of the Dutch Red Cross in Germany I have the sad duty to inform you that Mr. Fritz Pfeffer, born on 30 April 1889 and last resident in Amsterdam, died in the Neuengamme concentration camp on 20 December 1944."[44]

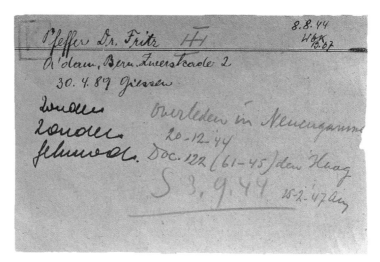

Fritz Pfeffer's registration card, taken from the records of the Jewish Council.

CHAPTER NINE

"I don't know where the children are"
Otto's search

BACK HOME

Otto Frank was the only one of the group of eight people from the Annex who survived the camps. After Auschwitz was liberated on 27 January 1945, he started the long journey home. He also started to try to find out what had happened to his wife and children, and how his friends and the others who had been in hiding with him were doing. Shortly after the arrival of the Red Army in Auschwitz, he was given a small notebook in which he noted events and names with short keywords. He was not yet capable of any detailed reflection, but he did record a large number of names of fellow prisoners who had been on the transport of 3 September. He was repatriated to the Netherlands and always kept in contact with some of them, including Sal de Liema.[1]

Otto also wrote down the names of people whose fates were unknown to him at that point.[2] For example, using short keywords, he noted in his book "Goudsmit, Watches, Rotterdam", and "Gerhard Salinger, publisher".[3] It later transpired that both had been deported to the Stutthof concentration camp on 26 October 1944 and had died there.[4]

However, it was above all the uncertainty about the fate of Edith, Margot and Anne which tormented him. While he slowly gained strength in an infirmary at the liberated camp that had

303

been organized by the Russians, he asked all the women there who had been in Birkenau whether they could tell him anything about his wife and daughters. In the beginning, this didn't lead to much information. On 23 February he wrote the first letter to his mother, Alice Frank, who had been living in neutral Switzerland since 1933:

> I hope that these lines will reach you to give you and all our loved ones the news that I was saved by the Russians, I am healthy and full of hope and being cared for well in every respect. I don't know where Edith and the children are. We've been separated since 5 September 44. I only heard that they were transported to Germany. We must hope that we will see them again, well and healthy. Please inform my brothers-in-law and my friends in Holland that I was saved. I long to see you all again and hope that this will be possible really soon. I just hope that you are all healthy as well. When can I receive some news from you? Much love and warm greetings and kisses. Your son. Otto.[5]

Not long afterwards, on 22 March, he heard that his wife Edith had died in Auschwitz. He met Rosa de Winter-Levy, whom he'd got to know in Westerbork, in Katowice, where he was waiting to be repatriated to the Netherlands. She had remained close to Edith up the end in Birkenau. Rosa told him how she had ended up in Birkenau together with Edith, Margot and Anne, and how Anne and Margot, like her own daughter Judik, had been transferred to another camp a few days earlier in October.[6] She also said that Edith had become seriously ill shortly after the departure of her daughters and had died in an infirmary in Birkenau of the consequences of malnutrition and an intestinal infection – "without suffering", she added, in an attempt to console him.[7] She remembered later: "Mr. Frank did not move at all when I told him. I wanted to look at him, but he turned away. Then he made a movement. I can't remember exactly what it was, but I believe he laid his head on the table."[8]

On 28 March he wrote to his mother Alice that he had heard that Edith had died from weakness and malnutrition which had resulted in an intestinal disorder: "In reality, also murder by the Germans". It was news that had "hit him so hard [...] that I am not quite my old self."[9] His only hope now was that his daughters had survived. In his notebook, he noted that Rosa de Winter-Levy had told him that his daughters had left in October and had added: "Very bravely, especially, Anne, I especially miss Anne." At the end of March, Otto left by train to Czernowitz (now Chernivtsi in Ukraine). On the train he met his former neighbor Eva Geringer, whom he had spoken to in Auschwitz shortly after the liberation in the vain hope that she would be able to tell him more about his wife and children.

Meanwhile, Eva had found her own mother, Fritzi Markovits, and when she met Otto Frank on the train, she introduced

Eva Geiringer, 1945.

305

them to each other. (Later, a new love blossomed between Fritzi and Otto, and they married in 1953.) Eva remembers that Otto and Fritzi had exchanged a few words when they met in the train, but "there was little that could console him and he was not interested in anything."[10] On 24 April they reached the city of Odessa, where they had to wait for a ship to take them to France. They resumed their journey on 22 May with the New Zealand ship the *Monowai*, which set sail for Marseille. After a journey by train and car through France, Belgium and the Netherlands, Otto finally arrived in Amsterdam on 3 June 1945. He knocked on the door of Miep and Jan Gies. He heard that his two non-Jewish friends Victor Kugler and Johannes Kleiman – who had been arrested together with the group who had been in hiding but from whom he had heard nothing since August 1944 – had survived their imprisonment unharmed. He also saw Charlotte Kaletta in Amsterdam. At that time, she had not had any news of Fritz Pfeffer's fate, and it was also completely unclear what had happened to the Van Pels family.[11]

In Amsterdam, Otto continued his search for Anne and Margot. To his great relief, his mother, brothers and sister had survived the war with their families, but he was unable to find out what had happened to his daughters. "I'm writing here from my office and it is all like a horrible dream" he wrote to his mother on 8 June, "I can't grasp the reality of it yet […] where [the children] are I don't know, but I think about them all the time."[12] During those months, Otto went to the Central Station almost daily to wait for trains with camp survivors who were returning, and walked around with photographs of his daughters looking for someone who would be able to tell him what had happened to them. He constantly read the lists of victims and survivors which appeared in the newspapers

Otto and Fritzi Frank, August 1954.

The *Monowai*, the ship on which Otto traveled from Odessa to Marseille.

and also placed advertisements himself in newspapers with a request for information about his daughters.

Rudi Nussbaum, who had survived the war by going into hiding but whose parents had been deported, remembers:

> My mother was still alive when the English liberated Bergen-Belsen, and to our enormous joy she was mentioned on a list of the International Red Cross as a survivor. We were very hopeful that she would return [...], and so Otto also expected to see his two girls back. We went to the Central Station virtually every day. The trains were still arriving completely arbitrarily, but there were always a few passengers on the trains from Germany with survivors from the camps and we hoped that we would find someone by walking round with those photographs and that they would say: "Yes, I saw that woman or those two girls and they will come." But the opposite

Carte de Rapatrié which Otto Frank received in upon arrival in France. It serves as a proof of identity. As his address in the Netherlands, Otto gives the address of Jan and Miep Gies.

In August 1945, Otto Frank places an appeal in the newspaper *Het Vrije Volk*. He is looking for people who can tell him something about Margot and Anne.

happened, he found someone who told him: "They are both dead". And I found someone who said: "I knew your mother and she did not survive."[13]

Nussbaum's mother had admittedly still been alive when the camp was liberated, but she died soon after from the consequences of malnourishment and poor treatment. On 18 July,

Otto also experienced another crushing blow: when he went through the Red Cross list, he saw the names of his two daughters with a cross next to them, which meant that they had died. Through the Red Cross he found out who had made those crosses, and soon afterwards he arranged to meet Lientje Brilleslijper. She told him that Anne and Margot had died in Bergen-Belsen, one soon after the other, as a result of typhus. Lientje also told him that she and her sister Janny had been in contact with his daughters up to the end and had seen for themselves how they had died. Not long afterwards, Miep Gies handed him his daughter's diary that she'd kept for Anne.

In the following months, Otto Frank heard that the others who had been in hiding with him – Auguste, Hermann and Peter van Pels, as well as Fritz Pfeffer – had also died in the camps. Although he now knew what had happened to them, he continued to look for people who had met his wife and

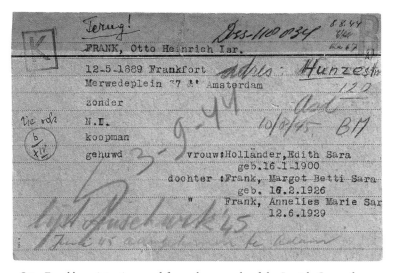

Otto Frank's registration card from the records of the Jewish Council.

310

daughters in the camps and who could tell him more about them. As mentioned in the introduction, many of the witnesses who have been quoted in this book told their story for the first time during those months in 1945 and 1946 when Otto was trying to find out as much as possible about the experiences of his wife and children in the camps after they had been separated.

EVERY CRUMB

After the Annex has in a sense become a continuation of the search Otto Frank started in 1945. It shows how difficult it is to gain an accurate picture of the experiences which individual victims like Anne, Margot, Edith and the others who had been in hiding had of the camps. While we have a relatively large amount of information about their lives during the period up to August 1944, partly as a result of Anne's diary, the picture of the period afterwards has always been rather opaque and fragmented.

This book has attempted to fill these gaps as far as possible, and this has sometimes led to new insights. For example, we now know that Anne and Margot Frank were already so sick at the beginning of February 1945 that they probably died in that month and not on 31 March 1945, as has been assumed. A similar correction can be made with regard to the day on which Anne and Margot were deported to Bergen-Belsen and the date of the arrival of Fritz Pfeffer in Neuengamme. We now know with some certainty that he must have arrived in Neuengamme between 10 and 18 November 1944, and that this was almost certainly during a so-called medical transport, when a large group of dentists and doctors were taken to Neuengamme from Auschwitz together. More information has also come to light about the death of Hermann van Pels. For a long time it was assumed that he was either gassed immediately upon his arrival in Auschwitz, or possibly died in the camp in Stutthof somewhere between 1 October 1944 and 9 May 1945. However, our research has shown that Van Pels was missing from the transport lists to that camp and was almost certainly murdered in one of the gas chambers in Auschwitz on 3 October 1944. He ended up there because he had been injured during the forced labor and was probably considered unsuitable for work for that reason during a large selection on 2 October 1944.

In many cases, we have to make do with scant information: times of arrival and departure, camp numbers and the layout of the barracks. Sometimes we find out a little more; for example, about the sort of work that the group of eight had to carry out in the concentration camps, the other prisoners they shared the barracks with, and when and under what circumstances they were selected to be sent on to another camp. In the case of Peter van Pels, the job that he had in the *Paketstelle* in Auschwitz not only turned out to be very important for his own imprisonment, but also for Otto Frank, who was able to get enough food as a result.

However, it is much more difficult to answer the question exactly what these eight individuals experienced, and how they dealt with the hardships in the camp in their attempts to survive. The most important sources which really have something to say about this are still the eyewitness accounts of survivors, although these are limited as a historical source in a number of respects, and are sometimes simply lacking. For example, witnesses such as Rosa de Winter-Levy, Nanette Blitz, the Brilleslijper sisters and Hanneli Goslar provide a picture of the conditions in which Edith, Anne and Margot died, but there

312

are no eyewitnesses who could say anything about the experiences of Fritz Pfeffer in Neuengamme or about Auguste van Pels in Raguhn. Nevertheless, the witnesses do give us a picture of the conditions in which these eight people lived in the punishment barracks at Westerbork, how they were separated from each other at Auschwitz, and what daily life was like for the men and women in the camps.

We have to accept that we will simply never know about certain things: exactly what Anne and Margot went through during the last days of their lives, how they tried to support each other, or when they lost their fight for life as a result of their illness and exhaustion. However, it is certainly possible to get to know more about their experiences of the camp indirectly and by making considered assumptions. For example, on the basis of some medical insights into the way that typhus develops, it is possible to make a more exact estimate of the date of Anne and Margot's deaths. The time of arrival, especially at the camps of Auschwitz and Bergen-Belsen, was crucial for the living conditions and chances of survival of the prisoners. The fact that all eight people in hiding in the Annex – including Anne Frank, who was only fifteen, and Otto Frank and Fritz Pfeffer, who were in their fifties – got through the selection on the platform of Birkenau in August 1944 is related to the increased pressure on the SS to maintain an adequate workforce and carry out the selections less strictly than previously. At the time that they arrived, the relative importance which Himmler attributed to forced labor in relation to mass extermination had increased, and proportionally fewer people were sent directly to the gas chambers.

There are also the eyewitness accounts about other prisoners who were in the concentration camps with our group of eight during the same period, but who did survive. They provide a "horizon" of experiences which give an insight into the probable experiences of the eight from the Annex, or what they certainly went through. It is therefore possible to imagine, through their eyes, what they must have suffered during the last months in the camps.

This book is about eight people – Anne, Margot, Edith and Otto Frank, Hermann, Auguste and Peter van Pels, and Fritz Pfeffer – who became the protagonists of perhaps the best-known story of war in western history as a result of a special coming together of circumstances. Their experiences in the Annex have reached millions of people all over the world as a result of the publication of the diary and films about the Annex. This is exceptional. But the story that is not told in Anne's diary and that followed the period in hiding – all those inhuman humiliations, brutality, hunger, cold, sickness and other horrors which they suffered in Auschwitz, Bergen-Belsen, Mauthausen, Neuengamme and Raguhn – is a story that can be told millions of times with slight variations. The fact that there are so few details known about the events which took place after their arrest confronts us with how difficult it is to distinguish individuals in the masses. The genocide of the European Jews carried out by the Nazis not only took away all their dignity, but was also an attempt to eradicate all traces of their individual fates, experiences and memories. This means that every crumb, no matter how small, that brings this experience closer and gives more insight into the individual experiences and victims of the Holocaust is of great value, not only in an historical but also in a human respect.

Badges used to identify groups of prisoners in concentration camps, 1936

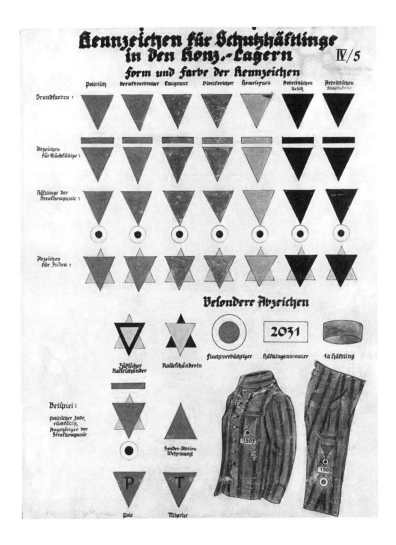

(See also endpapers for colour version)

Camps across Europe associated with the 'eight'

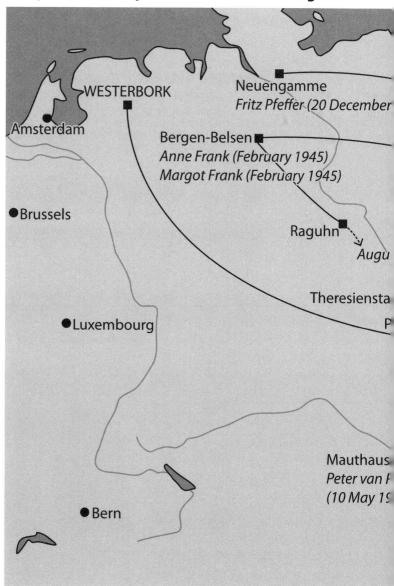

WESTERBORK

Amsterdam

Neuengamme
Fritz Pfeffer (20 December

Bergen-Belsen
Anne Frank (February 1945)
Margot Frank (February 1945)

Brussels

Raguhn

Augu

Theresiensta

Luxembourg

P

Mauthaus
Peter van F
(10 May 19

Bern

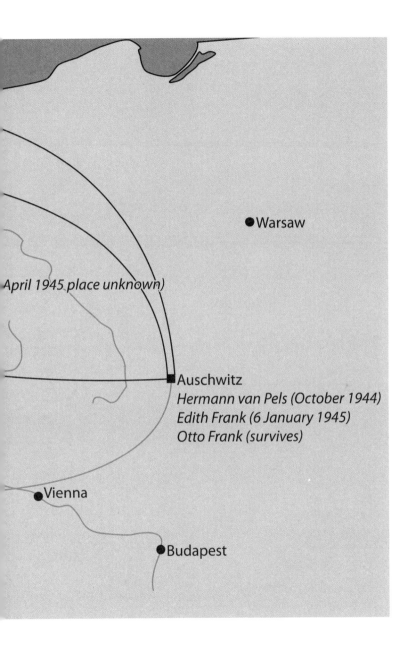

April 1945 place unknown)

●Warsaw

■Auschwitz
Hermann van Pels (October 1944)
Edith Frank (6 January 1945)
Otto Frank (survives)

●Vienna

●Budapest

Westerbork Transit Camp, 1942

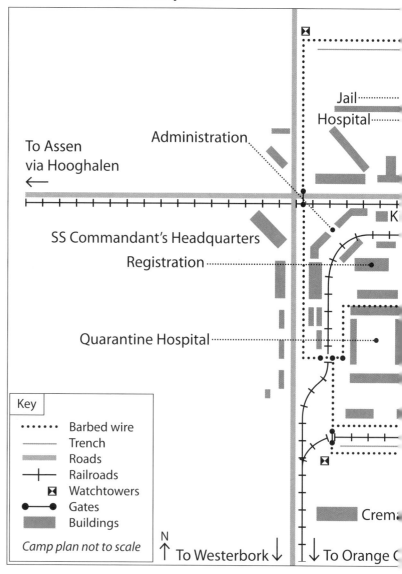

To Assen
via Hooghalen
←

Administration

Jail
Hospital

K

SS Commandant's Headquarters

Registration

Quarantine Hospital

Crem

Key

- ⋯⋯ Barbed wire
- ——— Trench
- ▬▬ Roads
- ─┼─ Railroads
- ☒ Watchtowers
- •——• Gates
- ▬▬ Buildings

Camp plan not to scale

N
↑ To Westerbork ↓   ↓ To Orange C

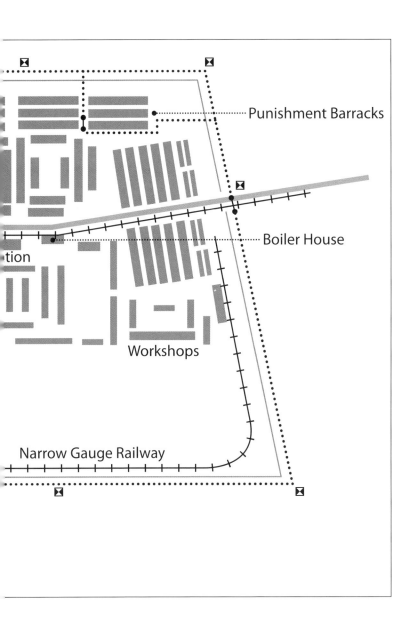

Punishment Barracks

Boiler House

tion

Workshops

Narrow Gauge Railway

Auschwitz I Concentration Camp, 1944

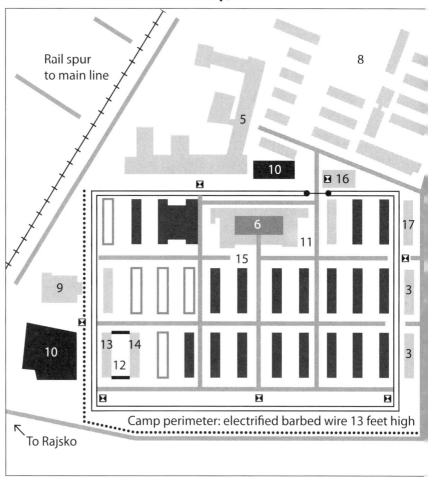

Rail spur to main line

8

5

10

16

6

11

17

15

9

3

13 14

12

10

3

Camp perimeter: electrified barbed wire 13 feet high

To Rajsko

320

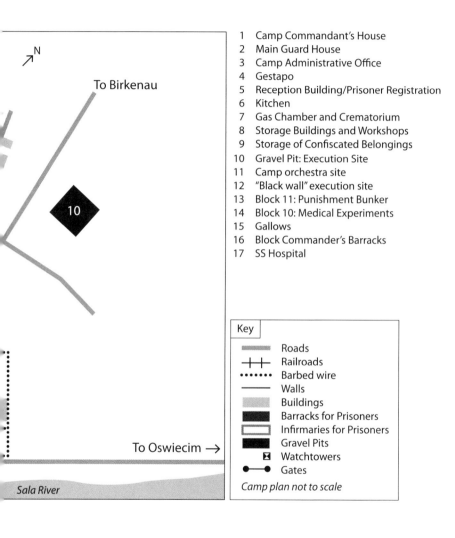

1   Camp Commandant's House
2   Main Guard House
3   Camp Administrative Office
4   Gestapo
5   Reception Building/Prisoner Registration
6   Kitchen
7   Gas Chamber and Crematorium
8   Storage Buildings and Workshops
9   Storage of Confiscated Belongings
10 Gravel Pit: Execution Site
11 Camp orchestra site
12 "Black wall" execution site
13 Block 11: Punishment Bunker
14 Block 10: Medical Experiments
15 Gallows
16 Block Commander's Barracks
17 SS Hospital

Key

Roads
Railroads
Barbed wire
Walls
Buildings
Barracks for Prisoners
Infirmaries for Prisoners
Gravel Pits
Watchtowers
Gates

Camp plan not to scale

321

Auschwitz II (Birkenau) Concentration Camp, Summer 1

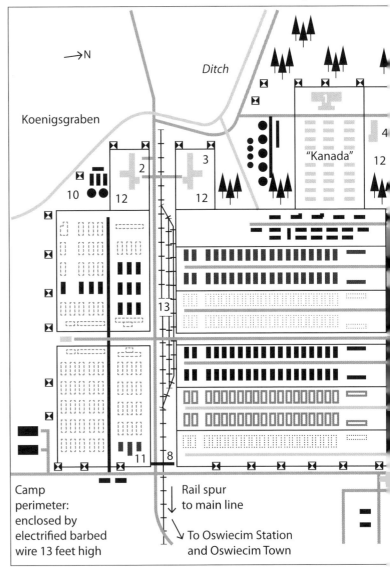

→N

Ditch

Koenigsgraben

"Kanada"

4

12

10   12

2

3

12

12

13

11   8

Camp
perimeter:
enclosed by
electrified barbed
wire 13 feet high

Rail spur
to main line

To Oswiecim Station
and Oswiecim Town

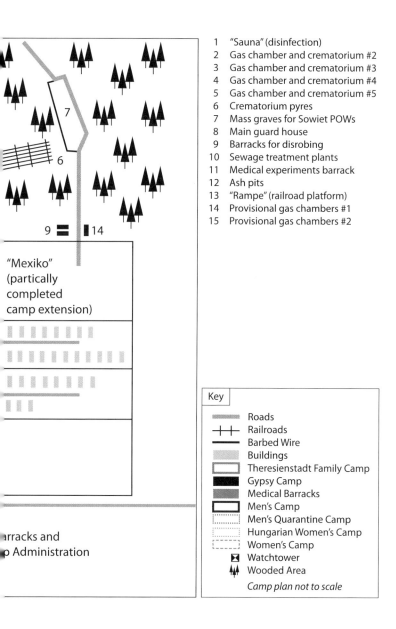

1   "Sauna" (disinfection)
2   Gas chamber and crematorium #2
3   Gas chamber and crematorium #3
4   Gas chamber and crematorium #4
5   Gas chamber and crematorium #5
6   Crematorium pyres
7   Mass graves for Sowiet POWs
8   Main guard house
9   Barracks for disrobing
10 Sewage treatment plants
11 Medical experiments barrack
12 Ash pits
13 "Rampe" (railroad platform)
14 Provisional gas chambers #1
15 Provisional gas chambers #2

"Mexiko"
(partically
completed
camp extension)

9   14

arracks and
o Administration

Key

	Roads
┼┼	Railroads
▬	Barbed Wire
	Buildings
☐	Theresienstadt Family Camp
◼	Gypsy Camp
	Medical Barracks
☐	Men's Camp
⋯	Men's Quarantine Camp
	Hungarian Women's Camp
╌	Women's Camp
⊠	Watchtower
♠	Wooded Area

Camp plan not to scale

323

Bergen-Belsen Concentration Camp, 1944

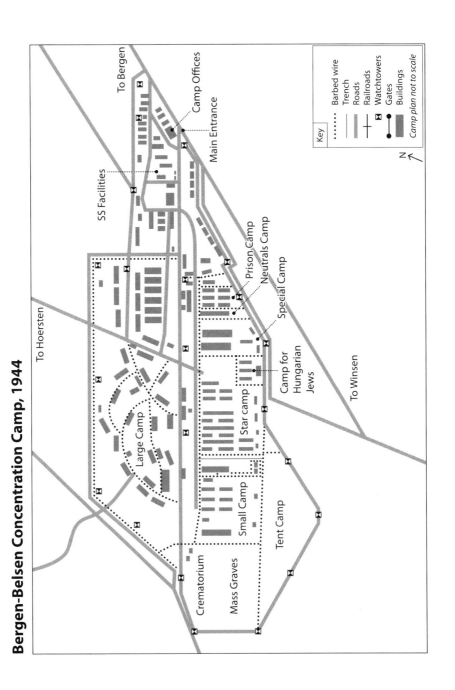

Key
.... Barbed wire
——— Trench
——— Roads
—|—|— Railroads
⊠ Watchtowers
●—● Gates
▬ Buildings
Camp plan not to scale

N

To Bergen

Camp Offices

Main Entrance

SS Facilities

Prison Camp

Neutrals Camp

Special Camp

Camp for Hungarian Jews

Star camp

To Hoersten

Large Camp

Small Camp

Tent Camp

Crematorium

Mass Graves

To Winsen

Mauthausen Concentration Camp, April 1945

Key

Barbed wire	
Trench	
Roads	
Railroads	
Watchtowers	
Gates	
Buildings	
Reservoir	

Camp plan not to scale

N

Execution Site

Armoury

SS Facilities

To town of Mauthausen

Entrance ⊠ Roll Call Square

Entrance

Garage Yard

Fruit Garden

Entrance Road

SS Barracks

Tent Camp

Quarry Road

Warehouse and Workshops

Quarry

Command Area

Russian Camp (Hospital Camp)

Quarry Rim

325

Neuengamme Concentration Camp, 1942–1945

DAW

Crematorium

Construction Materials Storage and Offices

Walther Factory

Cancl

DAW German Armament Works

Commandant's Villa

Prisoner Camp

Detention Center (bunker)

Roll Call Square

SS Camp Facilities

Harbour Warehouse

Brickworks

Workshops

Farmland

Greenhouse and Gardens

Old Brickworks

Key

Barbed wire
Trench
Roads
Railroads
Watchtowers
Gates
Buildings

Camp plan not to scale

N ←

Notes

Insofar as there are no official translations available, the translations of the German quotations have been provided by the author. In addition, it was decided to use the quotations as shown in the original source, and not to correct spelling mistakes, such as those which occur, for example, in Anne Frank's *Diary*.

CHAPTER ONE

1. Anne Frank House (AFH), Anne Frank Collection (AFC), Otto Frank Archief (OFA), inv. no. 058, "Lebenslauf" Otto Frank. The St. Quentin spring offensive started on 21 March 1918. According to the correspondence of 28 March 1918, Otto Frank was still with the Lichtmesstrupp 13 at the time. See also Anne Frank Fund (AFF), Basel, the Frank-Elias family archive, Robert Frank (RoF), corr. 01; and Otto Frank, AFF, Otto Frank (OtF), pdoc 14.

2. Original quotation: "Ich erinnere mich schon 1932, daß sa-Gruppen vorbeigezogen sind und gesungen haben 'Wenn das Judenblut am Messer spritzt'. Also das war schon sehr deutlich sichtbar. Und ich habe gleich mit meiner Frau besprochen 'Wie können wir wegkommen?', aber es ist ja schließlich die Frage 'Wie kann man einen Lebensunterhalt verdienen, wenn man weggeht und alles mehr oder weniger aufgibt?'" Birgit Kienzle (director), *Lasst mich so sein wie ich will. Anne Frank*, television documentary (1979). See also Menno Metselaar, *Anne Frank. Dromen, denken, schrijven* (Amsterdam, 2016), p. 27; and Carol Ann Lee, *The Hidden Life of Otto Frank – The Biography* (New York, 2003).

3. Julius H. Schoeps, *Neues Lexikon des Judentums* (Gütersloh, 2000), p. 261; Jürgen Steen and Wolf von Wolzogen (eds), *Die Synagogen brennen. Die Zerstörung Frankfurts als jüdische Lebenswelt* (Frankfurt am Main, 1988), pp. 2–4.

4. Original quotation: "Frankfurt soll Deutsch werden. […] Ihr Juden braucht nicht zu zittern. Wir bleiben legal. So legal, dass es euch vor so viel Legalität noch unbehaglig wird." Steen and von Wolzogen, *Die Synagogen brennen*, p. 60.

5. Amsterdam City Archive (SAA), access number 30238: Archive cards Otto, Edith, Anne and Margot Frank.

6. We know for sure that Anne and Margot were in Aachen between August and December 1933, and visited their grandmother after that in the summer of 1934 and the Christmases of 1935–7. They often stayed there together, but sometimes Otto took one of them to Basel for a few days, while the other one stayed in Amsterdam or in Aachen with grandmother Holländer. In this respect, see, inter alia, Carol Ann Lee, *Anne Frank 1929–1945. Roses from the Earth: The Biography of Anne Frank* (Penguin, 2000); Lee, *The Hidden Life of Otto Frank*; Melissa Müller, *Anne Frank: The Biography* (Macmillan, 2013), p. 75; Wouter van der Sluis and Menno Metselaar (eds), *Anne Frank's Life in Letters*, exhibition guide of Amsterdam Historical Museum (Amsterdam, 2006); Otto Frank to Gertrud Naumann, 4 September 1933; Edith Frank to Gertrud Naumann, undated (1934); AFH, Maly collection; Edith Frank to Gertrud Naumann, 27 December 1936; Edith Frank to Gertrud Naumann, 18 January 1938; Edith to Hedda Eisenstedt, 24 December 1937; and AFH, AFC, OFA, inv. no. 1, Otto Frank's diary, 1937.

7. See Herbert Lepper, *From Emancipation to the Holocaust. The Israelite Synagogue Community in Aachen 1801–1942* (Aachen, 1994); and various statements regarding the Holländer family in Landesarchiv NRW BR 3000 no. 1025, Entschädigungsakte Julius Holländer. In about 1930, the population of Aachen was over 150,000, the large majority of which was Roman Catholic. There were about 1,350 Jews, together accounting for

less than 1 per cent of the total number of inhabitants. Bettina Klein, *Spuren jüdischen Lebens in Aachen von 1850 bis 1938. Eine Anschauungsmappe* (Aachen, 1997), p. 7. See: Landesarchiv NRW BR 3000 no. 1025, Entschädigungsakte Julius Holländer.

8. See also Landesarchiv NRW BR 3000 no. 1025, Entschädigungsakte Julius Holländer; declaration of Karl Löwenstein, 7 July 1955; and Lepper, *From Emancipation*, p. 95.

9. Lepper, *From Emancipation*, p. 95.

10. Landesarchiv NRW BR 235 no. 2150, Entschädigungsakte Firma Holländer.

11. See, inter alia, www.welt.de/regionales/berlin/article2696028/Woherkommt-der-Begriff-Reichskristallnacht.html (accessed 30 July 2020); www.deutschlandfunk.de/nachgefragt-warum-ist-der-begriffkristallnacht-verschwunden.2852.de.html?dram:article_id=432858 (accessed 30 July 2020). The English literature largely uses the term "Kristallnacht" (with or without quotation marks). A recent collection of conference documents edited by Steven Ross and Wolf Runer prefers the use of the term "Kristallnacht" to "November pogrom", because they suggest that the use of the term "pogrom" implies a spontaneous and locally based eruption of anti-Jewish sentiment, whereas the event in November 1938 was a campaign of violence coordinated by the state. See, inter alia, Steven Ross and Wolf Runer, *New Perspectives on Kristallnacht: After 80 Years the Nazi Pogrom in Global Perspective* (West Lafayette, 2019), and an interview with the editors available from www.newbooksnetwork.com/ steven-ross-and-wolf-gruner-new-perspectives-on-krystallnacht-purdue-up-2019/ (accessed 6 August 2020).

12. Lepper, *From Emancipation*, p. 128; Müller, *Anne Frank*, p. 120.

13. Anne Frank, *Diary* (A), 15 June 1942. The complete edition, which was published by the National Institute for War Documentation (RIOD; the current NIOD Institute for War, Holocaust and Genocide Studies) in 1986, distinguishes three versions of Anne Frank's diary. Version A is the original version of her personal notes. Anne started to rewrite this diary on 20 May 1944. She was inspired by a speech made by a government minister, Gerrit

Bolkestein, on Radio Orange, in which he called on the population of the Netherlands to keep diaries and other personal documents to serve as documentation of the occupation. The section reviewed and rewritten by Anne is referred to as version B. She herself described this as the novel she wanted to publish after the war entitled "The Annex". Finally, there is version C, the diary as it was published by Otto Frank in 1947. Otto Frank based this edition on both the A and the B versions, and made a number of changes. He also censored it in a number of places, as well as changing the names of the main characters: the Van Pels family were now called Van Daan and Fritz Pfeffer became Albert Dussel. The quotations from Anne's diary used here are based on the edition extended in 1986 of the academic edition published in 1986 by the RIOD. Harry Paape, Gerrold van der Stroom and David Barnouw (eds), *The Diaries of Anne Frank* (Amsterdam, 1990). In these notes, they will be referred to as: Anne Frank, *Diary* (A), (B) or (C – The Annex).

14. Gertjan Broek and Rebecca Erbelding, "German bombs and US bureaucrats: How escape lines from Europe were cut off" (USHMM and Anne Frank House, 2016), available from www.annefrank.org/en/downloads/filer_ public/94/3e/943ed001-ba04-4e2a-9360-e642d0d82006/ushmm_afh_july2018.pdf (accessed 18 August 2020), pp. 4–6.

15. YIVO Institute for Jewish Research, New York: three personal letters from Otto Frank as found in National Refugee Service Case File A-23007: Otto Frank to Charley Straus, 30 April 1941.

16. Edith's mother, Rosa Holländer-Stern, was also counted as a member of the family at that time. Broek and Erbelding, "German bombs", pp. 4–6.

17. YIVO, Otto Frank file, telephone message for Miss Augusta Mayerson, 11 December 1941.

18. Anne Frank, *Diary* (A), 8 July 1942. On Saturday 4 July 1942, the *Zentralstelle für jüdische Auswanderung* sent the summons to 1,000 mainly German and some very young Jews. These young Jews had to leave without their parents. Loe de Jong, *Het Koninkrijk*

der Nederlanden in de Tweede Wereldoorlog, 14 vols (The Hague, 1969–91), vol. 6/1, p. 5. According to Eva Schloss, her brother Heinz Geiringer, as well as Henk and Marcel, also received a summons on that day. Eva Schloss, *Eva's Story: A Survivor's Tale* (W.H. Allen & Co Ltd, 1988), p. 33.

19. See Müller, *Anne Frank*, pp. 143–58; and Lee, *The Hidden Life of Otto Frank*.

20. Deutsches Literaturarchiv/Schiller-Nationalmuseum (DLA), Ernst Schnabel collection. Kugler to Schnabel, 17 September 1957; Anne Frank, "Freedom in the Annex" (6 August 1943), in Anne Frank, *Tales from the Secret Annex* (New York, 2003).

21. Anne Frank, *Diary* (C – The Annex), 8 and 10 July 1942; *Diary* (A), 14 August and 30 September 1942.

22. Anne Frank, *Diary* (A), 8 July 1942.

23. Standesamt Elberfeld (Wuppertal), Register of marriages no. 1767, License number 1374: Copy (dated 14 February 1996) of the marriage license of Hermann van Pels and Auguste Röttgen, 5 December 1925.

24. Cologne University Archive, Zugang 600, Prüfungsaktenbestand der Wirtschafts- und Sozialwissenschaftlichen Fakultät, inv. no. 64, Anmeldekarte Auguste Röttgen, 28 April 1921. Other details about Auguste Rötggen's career in the letter of the lawyer Elisabeth Späth to the President of the Governor of Hannover, 7 April 1960 in Landesarchiv NRW – Standort Hannover, Nds 110 W Akz 105/93 No. 959, Entschädigungsakte Auguste van Pels. Archiv zur Geschichte Essener Juden, archive databank refers to Auguste Röttgen as a pupil of the Viktoria Gymnasium in 1914.

25. Standesamt Elberfeld (Wuppertal), Register of marriages no. 1767, License number 1374: Copy (dated 14 February 1996) of the marriage license of Hermann van Pels and Auguste Röttgen, 5 December 1925.

26. Fritz Löwenstein, quoted by Peter Junk and Martina Sellmeyer, *Stationen auf dem Weg nach Auschwitz. Entrechtung, Vertreibung, Vernichtung Juden in Osnabrück 1900–1945. Ein Gedenkbuch* (Osnabrück, 1988), p. 56.

27. See also Miep Gies, *Anne Frank Remembered. The Story of the Woman Who Helped to Hide the Frank Family* (New York, 1987); AFH, AFC, Archive of Witnesses,

interview with Jan and Miep Gies, May 1992; DLA, Schnabel collection, Victor Kugler to Ernst Schnabel, 17 September 1957; and Eda Shapiro and Rick Kardonne, *Victor Kugler: The Man Who Hid Anne Frank* (Jerusalem, 2008). AFH, AFC, OFA, inv. no. 104, Bep Voskuijl's declaration before the examining magistrate in Lübeck, made in Rheine, 29 September 1959.

28. Anne Frank, *Diary* (A), 21 September 1942.

29. Anne Frank, *Diary* (A), 13 November 1942, and *Diary* (B), 17 November 1942. In the B version of her diary, Anne notes that 17 November was the day Pfeffer arrived in the Annex.

30. They had other friends in common. For example, Pfeffer was a witness at the wedding of Paul Wronker, one of the tenants who lived with the Franks. AFH, museum collection, object no. A_OFrank_i_015, "Erklärung" Otto Frank, 4 September 1951.

31. Jürgen Dauernheim, "Dr. Pfeffer aus Gießen – Anne Franks 'Dr. Dussel' (Eine Ergänzung)", *Mitteilungen des Oberhessischen Geschichtsverein Giessen 97* (Giessen, 2012), pp. 221–7, in particular p. 223.

32. Because of a treaty dating from 1902, German subjects could not marry in the Netherlands without a declaration of no objection from the German authorities. After the introduction of the Nuremburg laws in September 1935, such declarations were no longer issued for marriages between a Jewish and a non-Jewish partner. See also "Het Duitsche Ariërshuwelijksverbod sluit een huwelijk in Nederland uit", *Het Vaderland*, 17 September 1935 (evening edition).

33. Beate Meyer, Hermann Simon and Chana Schütz (eds), *Jews in Nazi Berlin: From Kristallnacht to Liberation* (Chicago, 2009), p. 17.

34. See also David Clay Large, *Berlin* (New York, 2000), pp. 255–317; Berlin Museum (ed.), *Synagogen in Berlin. Zur Geschichte einer zerstörten Architektur*, vol. 2 (Berlin, 1983), pp. 29–31; *Tageszeitung* (Taz) 9 November 1990. See also the interactive map of the November pogrom in Berlin of RBB-24. This shows how many incidents took place in the immediate area where Fritz Pfeffer lived: www.rbb24.de/politik/thema/ 2018/80-jahre-pogromnacht/

beitraege/synagogen-berlin-brandenburg-novemberpogrome-1938-karte-.html.

35. Goebbels noted this in his diary. See also Meyer et al. (eds), *Jews in Nazi Berlin*, p. 9.

36. National Archives (Kew), Home Office, ho/396/67/439: Appeal decision, 13 October 1943. See also Vera Fast, *Children's Exodus. A History of the Kindertransporten 1938–1948* (London, 2010).

37. Landesarchiv Berlin C "Hauptausschuss Opfer des Faschismus" 118-01, inv. no. 23059, witnesses W. Ungar, V. Stolzmann and A. Casper.

38. Original quotation: "Die Holländer konnten sich nicht vorstellen, dass die Deutschen so seien. […] Sie haben die Geschichten nicht geglaubt, die die deutsche Migranten mitbrachten. […] Nicht einmal die Juden in Holland konnten es glauben." First part of the quotation based on Schnabel's notes in the archive in Ernst Schnabel, *The Footsteps of Anne Frank* (London, 1972). Katja Happe also shows that in the Netherlands there was little awareness of how serious the conditions were when German Jews fled their country in November 1938. See Katja Happe, *Veel Valse Hoop. De Jodenvervolging in Nederland 1940–1945* (Amsterdam, 2018).

39. Anne Frank, *Diary* (A), 16 March 1944.

40. Anne Frank, *Diary* (A), 28 August–1 September 1942.

41. Original quotation: "[D]a kam plötzlich jemand die Treppe heraufgerannt (...) da ging schon die Tür auf, und ein Mann stand vor uns und hielt mir die Pistole vor die Brust (...) Unten waren sie schon alle beisammen. Meine Frau und die Kinder und van Daans standen da mit erhobenen Händen", Ernst Schnabel, *Anne Frank, Spur eines Kindes. Ein Bericht* (Frankfurt am Main, 1958), p. 107.

42. Otto Frank himself repeatedly said that after his arrest they were brought to the *Aussenstelle* (the regional office) of the *Sicherheitsdienst* on the Euterpestraat by the SD. However, the *Zentralstelle für jüdische Auswanderung*, the department that was responsible for tracing and interrogating Jews who had gone into hiding, was at Adama van Scheltemaplein 1, opposite the *Aussenstelle*. Moreover, *SS-Hauptscharführer* Karl Joseph Silberbauer, who was in charge of the arresting

team, stated that he had taken the members of the group in hiding to his office at Adama van Scheltemaplein 1. National Archive, The Hague (NL-HaNa), 2.09.09, Central Archives for Special Jurisdiction (CABR), inv. no. 23892, dossier W.G. van Maaren, official report, 3 November 1964: interrogation of Otto Frank, 2–3 December 1963, p. 3.

43. David Barnouw and Gerrold van der Stroom, *Wie verraadde Anne Frank?* (Amsterdam, 2003); Lee, *Anne Frank*; Lee, *The Hidden Life of Otto Frank*; Müller, *Anne Frank*, p. 8.

44. Gertjan Broek, "Verraad & arrestatie van de onderduikers in het Achterhuis", online publication Anne Frank House 2016, https:// www.annefrank.org/nl/downloads/filer_public/99/b9/99b9c19f-182e-416d-baba-e0bb228994d9/nl_onderzoeksverslag_arrestatie.pdf (accessed 18 August 2020).

45. Rosemary Sullivan, The Betrayal of Anne Frank: A Cold Case Investigation. The most fundamental criticism regarding the investigation can be found in: Bart Wallet e.a., Report The Betrayal of Anne Frank: A Refutation Critical Analysis of the Argumentation and Use of Historical Sources (NIOD, March 2022). https://www.niod.nl/en/news/research-report-book-about-betrayal-anne-frank-based-assumptions-and-lack-historical-knowledge and Natasha Gerson, 'Less a mystery solved than a scam well played' https://jonet.nl/wp-content/uploads/2022/08/Less-a-mystery-solved-factcheck-betrayal-anne-frank-DEF-15.8.22.pdf For a reconstruction also view: https://www.volkskrant.nl/kijkverder/v/2022/reconstructie-het-verraad-van-anne-frank~v568314/ (all websites reviewed on 3 October 2022).

46. The term "Holocaust" comes from the Ancient Greek word *holocaustum*, which means "burnt offering". It was used by the Church Fathers to refer to the offerings made by the Jews. Even before the Second World War, the term was sometimes used to describe the death of a large group of people, and after the war – especially since the 1980s – it has been used to refer to the murder of the European Jews during the Second World War. The term "Shoah" is another widely used synonym. This Hebrew term also has a biblical

origin and can mean "catastrophe", or "day of retaliation". Because of the strong religious background, the two terms have obvious limitations. In his introduction to the recently published anthology *Bij ons in Auschwitz. Getuigenissen*, Arnon Grunberg strikingly states that the term "Holocaust" suggests that it concerns a sacrifice to God, whereas "Shoah" implies a punishment by God. This book opted for the more common term "Holocaust". For a discussion on this, see, inter alia, Victor Petrie, "The secular word 'Holocaust': Scholarly myths, history, and twentieth century meanings", *Journal of Genocide Research* 2/1 (2000), pp. 31–63; and Arnon Grunberg (ed.), *Bij ons in Auschwitz. Getuigenissen* (Amsterdam, 2020), pp. 9–10.

47. For this text, it was decided to use, as far as possible, the maiden names of the women who were not yet married in the period 1940–45, and therefore did not have a double surname, and to refer to married women with both their names. For the sake of simplicity, it was decided to call both the Brilleslijper sisters by their maiden name (though Janny was married during this period, Lientje was not yet married). For the same reason, Edith Holländer-Frank is always referred to as "Edith Frank". The footnotes that refer to postwar interviews give complete surnames.

48. Willy Lindwer, *The Last Seven Months of Anne Frank*, documentary (1988); and the accompanying book, Willy Lindwer, *The Last Seven Months of Anne Frank* (London, 1988); Schnabel, *Anne Frank*; Lee, *Anne Frank*; Lee, *The Hidden Life of Otto Frank*; Müller, *Anne Frank*.

49. Erika Prins, "Onderzoeksverslag naar het verblijf van de acht onderduikers in de kampen", research report Anne Frank House, Amsterdam (April 2016).

50. Nikolaus Wachsmann, *KL: A History of the Nazi Concentration Camps* (New York & London, 2015).

51. This book deliberately opted for the term "slave labor/laborers". Although the Dutch literature often refers to forced labor to include both Dutch civilian workers in the *Arbeitseinsatz* (labor deployment) and Jewish prisoners who had to work in camps such as Auschwitz, this book follows the English

literature, which emphasizes the distinction between these forms of forced labor: on the one hand, forced labor; and on the other hand, slave labor/laborers with respect to the Jews. The advantage is that this emphasizes the distinction between the position of the Jews and that of the other prisoners more clearly. Jews were at the bottom of the camp hierarchy everywhere and could be executed at any time or forced to literally work themselves to death. The working conditions of the German prisoners or of western civilian laborers and prisoners of war were in most cases fundamentally different. Some academics have a problem with the use of the term "slave labor", arguing that it is in the interests of slave owners for their slaves to survive, which was not the case with regard to the treatment of the Jewish prisoners. Nevertheless, Nikolaus Wachsmann justifiably states that a broad definition of the term slavery as a system of domination based on violence and terror, aimed at economic gain with the subjugation of social outcasts, certainly does apply to the Jewish prisoners in the concentration camps. Wachsmann, *KL*, pp. 574–5. For a summary of the different categories of forced labor in the Third Reich, see Ulrich Herbert, "Forced laborers in the Third Reich: An overview", *International Labor and Working-Class History* 2 (2000), pp. 192–218.

52. See, for instance, the above-mentioned biographies of Schnabel, Lee and Müller and the academic literature on the persecution of the Jews and the Second World War. For the Dutch perspective, these are the standard works by Loe de Jong and Jacques Presser, and a number of more recent studies on the individual topics of history of the Netherlands in the Second World War, such as Eva Moraal's study on the camp at Westerbork and the most important studies of the persecution of the Jews in the Netherlands by Bob Moore, Katja Happe, Pim Griffioen and Ron Zeller. See Jacques Presser, *Ondergang. De vervolging en verdelging van het Nederlandse Jodendom, 1940–1945*, vol. 2 (The Hague, 1965), p. 295; Raymund Schütz, "Vermoedelijk op transport. De Joodsche Raadcartotheek als informatiesysteem binnen sterk veranderende kaders: repressie, opsporing en herinnering: een archiefwetenschappelijk onderzoek naar

de herkomst, het gebruik en het beheer van een bijzondere historische bron", master's thesis (University of Leiden History Institute, 2010); Pim Griffioen and Ron Zeller, *Jodenvervolging in Nederland, Frankrijk en België 1940–1945. Overeenkomsten, verschillen, oorzaken* (Amsterdam, 2011); Eva Moraal, *Als ik morgen niet op transport ga… Kamp Westerbork in beleving en herinnering* (Amsterdam, 2014); Happe, *Veel valse hoop*. For the international context of the persecution of the Jews and the Holocaust, use is made of the studies by Nikolaus Wachsmann, and Debórah Dwork and Robert Jan van Pelt, as well as the most important monographs about the individual camps. See Debórah Dwork and Robert Jan van Pelt, *Auschwitz*, rev. edn (London, 2008); Wachsmann, *KL*. The description of the Auschwitz complex is based, inter alia, on the publications of different researchers affiliated to the Polish National Museum Auschwitz-Birkenau. The study by Alexandra-Eileen Wenck proved to be very valuable for Bergen-Belsen, and the extensive and encyclopedic works by Wolfgang Benz and the United States Holocaust Memorial Museum (USHMM) were used for smaller camps such as Melk and Raguhn. See Aleksander Lasik et al. (eds), *Auschwitz, 1940-1945: Central Issues in the History of the Camp*, 5 vols (Oświęcim, 2000); Franciszek Piper, Teresa Swiebocka and Danuta Czech (eds), *Auschwitz: Nazi Death Camp* (Oświęcim, 2007); Alexandra-Eileen Wenck, *Zwischen Menschenhandel und "Endlösung". Das Konzentrationslager Bergen-Belsen* (Paderborn, 2000); Wolfgang Benz and Barbara Distel (eds), *Der Ort des Terrors. Geschichte der nationalsozialistische Konzentrationslager*, 9 vols (Munich, 2005–9); Geoffrey P. Megargee (ed.), *Encyclopedia of Camps and Ghettos, 1933–1945*, vol. 1 (Bloomington, 2009).

53. Some of the archives of the various concentration camps were collected together in the postwar years by the RIOD, NIOD Institute for War, Holocaust and Genocide Studies, access no. 250d, Kampen en gevangenissen; and idem, 804, Onderzoek vernietigingskamp Sobibor. The NIOD also has a reasonably extensive collection about Theresienstadt (250k and 250n). In addition, there was a search through the archives of

the Dutch Red Cross (NRK), which was charged with establishing what happened to the many missing persons after the war, as well as the Bad Arolsen Archives (formerly the International Tracing Service [ITS]). After the war, these two institutions brought together all sorts of administrative sources on the deportation and deaths of prisoners. See Dutch Red Cross, The Hague: 2050, NRK Collectie Vervolging (Westerbork camp); Kampen en Gevangenissen bij oorlogsnazorg; Persoonsdossiers; Joodsche Raad Cartotheek; Arolsen Archives-International Center on Nazi Persecution Bad Arolsen Duitsland (formerly the ITS). There was also a search though the archives of the memorial centers and museums in Bergen-Belsen, Neuengamme, Mauthausen, Westerbork and Auschwitz-Birkenau. The archives of the Commission for the Declaration of the Deaths of the Missing (COAV) and the Central Archives for Special Jurisdiction (CABR) can be found in the National Archive (NL-HaNa) in The Hague.

54. Wachsmann, *KL*, p. 36. In 1993, an NIOD delegation looked through the Russian archives in Moscow for materials about the German occupation of the Netherlands and the persecution of Dutch nationals in the concentration camps that had been confiscated by the occupying forces. Copies of these can be found in the NIOD archive. However, this material mainly relates to the period 1938–42 and has not resulted in any additional information for his study. NIOD, 206, Moscow collection.

55. AFH, AFC, inv. no. A_OFrank_i_011, "Raucherkarte" 1944–45. Häftlingkantine 1. Auschwitz Haftl. no. B9174 Block 5A. Documents have also been provided from the camp records with some information about the period when the group of eight were there, including *Lagerbefehle* (camp regulations), documents about the camp numbers, etc.

56. The above-mentioned archives in the various *Gedenkstätten* and memorial centers, NRK and the NIOD also provide access to witnesses' testimonies. Both the NRK and the RIOD (as it was known then) recorded and collected numerous witness statements at the time. Finally, some personal collections were consulted, in the first place the Otto Frank Archive, but also the collections of Juan

Goudsmit, the Frank-Elias Family Archive and the Ruth Wiener collection.

57. Arnon Grunberg, "Nee", 4 May 2020 speech (publication of the National Committee, Amsterdam, 4 and 5 May 2020), p. 10.

58. As described later, there are two contemporary written statements by witnesses confirming the presence of the girls in the camp. These both come from children who were at the Jewish Lyceum with Anne and Margot: namely a letter from Bram Asscher from Westerbork (August 1942) and a note in the diary of Ruth Wiener from Bergen-Belsen (December 1944).

59. Rosa de Winter-Levy, *Aan de gaskamer ontsnapt! Het Satanswerk van de ss. Relaas van het lijden en de bevrijding uit het concentratiekamp "Birkenau" bij Auschwitz* (Doetinchem, 1945). See also Izaak van Nierop and Louis Coster, *Westerbork. Het leven en werken in het kamp* (The Hague, 1945); M. Frankenhuis, *Westerbork en een vraaggesprek met zijn commandant Gemmecke in 1948* (The Hague, 1948). The diary letters written by Mirjam Bolle in Westerbork and Bergen-Belsen are another example, and were published in book form in 2003. Mirjam Bolle, *Ik zal je beschrijven hoe een dag er hier uitziet. Dagboekbrieven uit Amsterdam, Westerbork en Bergen-Belsen* (Amsterdam, 2003).

60. AFH, AFC, OFA, inv. no. 40, Otto Frank's notebook, 194, and family correspondence in OFA, inv. nos. 68–74 and afs_AlF_corr_10.

61. AFH, AFC, OFA, inv. no. 70, Otto Frank, "Bitte schreiben Sie".

62. Rosa de Winter-Levy was on the transport of 3 September 1944 and was in Auschwitz with Edith, Anne and Margot Frank. She described her experiences in Auschwitz in August 1945: De Winter-Levy, *Aan de gaskamer ontsnapt!*; AFH, AFC, inv. no. 01204: R. Rebling-Brilleslijper, 11 November 1945.

63. AFH, AFC, Witnesses' archives, letter from Nanette Blitz to Otto Frank, 31 October 1945 (digital copy, the original is with the Anne Frank Fund, Basel).

64. AFH, AFC, Witnesses' archives. In addition to the above-mentioned interviews, other oral history projects were also consulted, in particular the extensive collection of the

USC Shoah Foundation Visual History Archive (USC-SF, VHA) and of the Memorial Center at Camp Westerbork (HCKW).

65. R. Samuel and P. Thompson, "Introduction", in R. Samuel and P. Thompson (eds), *The Myths We Live By* (London, 1990), pp. 8–10.

66. Selma Leydesdorff, *De mensen en de woorden. Geschiedenis op basis van verhalen* (Amsterdam, 2004), pp. 113–14.

67. Primo Levi in Grunberg, *Bij ons in Auschwitz*, pp. 14–15.

68. On the influence of films, novels and other media on individual memories of the Holocaust, see Harald Welzer, Sabine Moller and Karoline Tschuggnall, *"Opa war kein Nazi". Nationalsozialismus und Holocaust im Familiengedächtnis* (Frankfurt am Main, 2002), pp. 105–33.

69. For example, see AFH, AFC, Witnesses' archive, interview with Bloeme Evers-Emden, 11 March 2010, and the interview with Albert Gomes de Mesquita, 1 April 2009.

70. AFH, AFC, Witnesses' archive, interview with Freda Wineman-Silberberg, 24 August 2015. Hanneli Goslar, Anne's school friend, who met her once more just before her death in the camp in Bergen-Belsen, also emphasizes the important of Anne's story: "Here I am, a more or less happy great-grandmother, and Anne didn't even reach the age of sixteen. For just one reason. She was a Jewish girl. And that's why I feel obliged to talk about her as much as possible. Most of it is already known, but there's always a bit more to say, and I think it's important that that whole story is never forgotten." AFH, AFC, Witnesses' archive, interview with Hanneli Goslar, 6–7 May 2009.

71. "The moral witness plays a special role in uncovering the evil he or she encounters. Evil regimes try hard to cover up the enormity of their crimes, and the moral witness tries to expose it." Avishai Margalit, *The Ethics of Memory* (Cambridge, 2003), p. 165. See also the introduction in Grunberg, *Bij ons in Auschwitz*, pp. 26–27.

72. Leydesdorff, *De mensen en de woorden*, p. 47.

73. Approximately 500 witnesses were consulted for this research: NRK, 2050, NRK-Collectie Vervolging (Camp Westerbork),

inv. nos. 1237-1309; NIOD, 250d, Statements by former prisoners about their experiences, inv. nos. 90-1219 (selection); witness statements Memorial Center Westerbork, Gedenkstätte Bergen-Belsen, Mauthausen and Neuengamme.

CHAPTER TWO

1. Jaques Presser, *Ondergang*, pp. 249–51. The size of this group is not completely clear, although figures between 375 and 800 have been mentioned.

2. Anne Frank, *Diary* (A), 8 July 1942.

3. According to Pim Griffioen and Ron Zeller, forty-two transports left from Westerbork to Auschwitz in 1942; a total of thirty-six transports left in 1943, of which fifteen went to Auschwitz, nineteen to Sobibor and two to Theresienstadt; a total of twenty transports left in 1944, of which seven went to Auschwitz, eight to Bergen-Belsen and five to Theresienstadt. Griffioen and Zeller, *Jodenvervolging*, pp. 893–5. However, new research indicates a total of 101 transports from Westerbork, two from Vught and nine from other places. See David Barnouw, Dirk Mulder and Guus Veenendaal, *De Nederlandse Spoorwegen in oorlogstijd 1939–1945. Rijden voor Vaderland en Vijand* (Zwolle, 2019), pp. 116–18.

4. The so-called Cosel transports also took place in 1942, for which men aged between the ages fifteen and sixty were taken off the train for Organization Schmelt, about 80 kilometers from Cosel. For details on this, see Herman van Rens and Annelies Wilms, *Tussenstation Cosel. Joodse mannen uit West-Europa naar dwangarbeiderskampen in Silezië, 1942–1945* (Hilversum, 2020).

5. Danuta Czech, "Origins of the camp, its construction and expansion", in Piper et al., *Auschwitz*, pp. 21–42, in particular pp. 36–38.

6. See Griffioen and Zeller, *Jodenvervolging*, pp. 893–5, which provides summary of the deportations showing the number of survivors in May 1945.

7. Nineteen survivors from a total of nineteen transports (34,293 people). Griffioen and Zeller, *Jodenvervolging*, p. 894.

8. Griffioen and Zeller, *Jodenvervolging*, pp. 899–900.

9. Figures based on Griffioen and Zeller, *Jodenvervolging*, pp. 561–3 (figure 16): summary of when and how Jews fell into German hands.

10. On 29 September 1943, the leaders of the Jewish Council were sent on a transport to Camp Westerbork with their families and dependents, and it was effectively disbanded. Schütz, *Vermoedelijk op transport*, p. 14.

11. NRK 2050, inv. no. 191.

12. Whether Pfeffer and Van Pels were also interrogated is not known.

13. NL-HaNa, CABR, inv. no. 23892, dossier W.G. van Maaren, official report, 3 November 1964: interrogation of Otto Frank, 2–3 December 1963, p. 3.

14. HCKW, Jacob Swart's diary, p. 9.

15. HCKW, interview with Ronnie Goldstein-van Cleef, 11 March 2002; HCKW, interview with Frieda Menco-Brommet by Eva Moraal, 27 February 2008; HCKW, interview with B. de Brave-Schelvis by Guido Abuys, 26 July 2006; HCKW, interview with Leny Boeken-Velleman, 12 December 2000; HCKW, Jacob Swart's diary, pp. 11–15 and pp. 20–23.

16. HCKW, Jacob Swart's diary, p. 9.

17. HCKW, interview with Ronnie Goldstein-van Cleef, 11 March 2002. See also Ralf Futselaar, *Gevangenissen in oorlogstijd. 1940–1945* (Amsterdam, 2015).

18. On the basis of testimonies about earlier and later transports, it was concluded that the prisoners went to the Central Station by tram. HCKW, interviews with Ronnie Goldstein-van Cleef and Frieda Menco-Brommet (both went to the Central Station by tram on 1 July 1944), B. de Brave-Schelvis and Sonja Wagenaar-van Dam (from the Weteringschans to the Central Station by tram), Leny Boeken-Velleman (from the Weteringschans to the Central Station on approximately 14 August 1944 by tram). See Schloss, *Herinneringen*, p. 58.

19. Cf. Lee, *Anne Frank*, p. 182; Janny Brilleslijper is not shown on the transport list of 8 August 1944, and according to the camp records, she arrived in Westerbork on 20 July 1944: NRK, dossier 190.262, Rebling-Brilleslijper, Rebekka.

20. AFH, AFC, OFA, inv. no. 70, Otto Frank, "Bitte schreiben Sie"; Schnabel, *Anne Frank*, pp. 119–20.

21. DLA, Schnabel collection, typed notes, p. 147. Earlier and later transports were also carried out with ordinary passenger trains. HCKW, interviews with Sonja Wagenaar-van Dam and Frieda Menco-Brommet; AFS, AFC, Archive of testimonies, interview with Eva Schloss-Geiringer, 12 and 13 November 2008.

22. See www.projects.knmi.nl/klimatologie/daggegevens/index.cgi (accessed October 2015).

23. AFH, AFC, OFA, inv. no. 70, Otto Frank, "Bitte schreiben Sie".

24. Moraal, *Als ik morgen niet*, pp. 112–13; Mirjam Bolle, *Dagboekbrieven*, pp. 133–5. A timetable for 4 June 1943 shows that at an average speed of 60 kilometers per hour, the train took over four hours to travel from Amsterdam to Camp Westerbork. Timetable of NV Nederlandsche Spoorwegen, Utrecht, 4 June 1943; HCKW, Jacob Swart's diary, p. 23.

25. See also Barnouw et al., *De Nederlandse Spoorwegen*, pp. 62–75. There were also trains to Westerbork from Amsterdam Muiderpoort and the Amstel station. Email from Jos Zijlstra, (curator of the Railway Museum in Utrecht) to Erika Prins, 26 October 2015. According to Zijlstra, the route has always remained the same for larger transports since November 1942. In the case of smaller transports, the train went to Assen, and prisoners either had to walk to the camp, or there were trucks waiting to take them.

26. Frank van Riet, *De bewakers van Westerbork* (Amsterdam, 2016), pp. 27–62; Presser, *Ondergang*, pp. 295–6.

27. This special unit in the Dutch police, based on the German military example – and established by the German occupying forces in May 1941 – was widely used for the persecution of the Jews. The training battalion was in Schalkhaar. For this, see Guus Meershoek, *Dienaren van het gezag. De Amsterdamse politie tijdens de bezetting* (Amsterdam, 1999).

28. Presser, *Ondergang*, p. 287.

29. The registration procedure was reconstructed on the basis of Bolle, *Dagboekbrieven*, pp. 145–8; Schütz,

Vermoedelijk op transport, pp. 21–27; Presser, *Ondergang*, p. 355; NRK 2050, inv. no. 192.

30. Lindwer, *The Last Seven Months of Anne Frank*, p. 118. See also Van Riet, *Bewakers*, pp. 117–25; Moraal, *Als ik morgen niet*, pp. 240–64.

31. Van Riet, *Bewakers*, pp. 118–21.

32. For the description of the camp organization, see Van Riet, *Bewakers*, pp. 306–27 and pp. 332–64; Schütz, *Vermoedelijk op transport*, pp. 19–21.

33. See, inter alia, Lotte Bergen, *Albert Konrad Gemmeker. Commandant van Westerbork* (Soesterberg, 2013); and Ad van Liempt, *Gemmeker. Commandant van Westerbork* (Amsterdam, 2019).

34. Presser, *Ondergang*, p. 307.

35. The film was made by a prisoner in the camp, Rudolf Breslauer, and the recording started on 5 March 1944. The film is kept in the archives of Beeld en Geluid, and can be seen on: http://in.beeldengeluid. nl/kanaal/4142-westerbork (accessed 2 September 2020). See also Presser, *Ondergang*, p. 290.

36. Presser, *Ondergang*, pp. 324–5.

37. In the scrapyard, parts of aircraft that had crashed were removed. They were brought to the camp from the Oranjekanaal by a freight train on a narrow-gauge railway. Presser, *Ondergang*, pp. 324–5.

38. The camp commandant of Westerbork made announcements regarding obligations, rules and changes to the daily camp regimen with a large number of (consecutively numbered) camp orders. *Lagerbefehl 86* of 3 August 1944 concerns "the increase of the labor force and improving performance at work." HCKW, *Lagerbefehl* 86, 3 August 1944.

39. The prisoners in the "free part of the camp" were Jews who had been in Westerbork for some time or had only received a summons at a relatively late stage and were exempt from deportation for some time on the basis of a *Sperre*.

40. Van Riet, *Bewakers*, pp. 117–25; HCKW, *Lagerbefehl* 87, 10 August 1944.

41. Van Riet, *Bewakers*, pp. 65–67 and pp. 89–98; and Moraal, *Als ik morgen niet*, p. 165. However, from July 1942, the SS-*Wachbataillon Nordwest*, consisting of approximately eighty men, was stationed in the nearby *SS-Lager*

Hooghalen (1 kilometer from Westerbork).
These men were responsible for guarding
prisoners outside Westerbork and were not
allowed to interfere with the internal guard. In
March 1943, their task was taken over by the
Dutch police.

42. Van Riet, *Bewakers*, pp. 27–50.

43. Van Riet, *Bewakers*, pp. 152–57. The OD
had to take 1,200 Jewish patients from there
to the station in Apeldoorn in a truck and put
them onto a freight train that went directly to
Auschwitz. Once there, they were murdered
immediately.

44. Philip Mechanicus, *In dépôt. Dagboek uit
Westerbork* (Amsterdam, 1989), p. 179 (30
August 1943).

45. Mechanicus, *In dépôt*, p. 337 (12 February
1944).

46. Vera Cohn, "The day I met Anne Frank",
Anti-Defamation League Bulletin 13/6 (June
1956), pp. 7–8.

47. For the way in which this system worked
in Westerbork, see Moraal, *Als ik morgen niet*,
pp. 264–9.

48. For this, see also Revital Ludewig-Kedmi,
*Opfer und Täter zugleich? Moraldilemmata
jüdischer Funktionshäftlinge in der Shoah*
(Giessen, 2001), pp. 38–40; Moraal, *Als ik
morgen niet*, pp. 264–74; Wachsmann, *KL*,
pp. 712–30; Samuel Schalkowsky (ed.), *The
Clandestine History of the Kovno Jewish Ghetto
Police* (Bloomington, 2014).

49. Van Riet, *Bewakers*, pp. 125–6.

50. Van Riet, *Bewakers*, pp. 278–9. According
to Van Riet, it is not clear why these particular
thirty-two members of the OD were not
deported.

51. Cf. Bolle, *Dagboekbrieven*, pp. 145–6;
Moraal, *Als ik morgen niet*, pp. 112–13; HCKW,
Jacob Swart's diary, p. 20.

52. Written explanation by Guido Abuys,
curator at the Memorial Center Camp
Westerbork.

53. Schütz, *Vermoedelijk op transport*, p. 33.

54. Schütz, *Vermoedelijk op transport*, p. 22.

55. NRK 2050, inv. no. 650, transport list 3
September 1944. The cards of the *Zentralkartei*
have not survived. Only the approximately
800 people who were still in the camp at the
time of the liberation have survived; Schütz,
Vermoedelijk op transport, p. 25.

56. For Ottenstein, see Moraal, *Als ik morgen
niet*, pp. 106–7, and pp. 177–200; Schütz,
Vermoedelijk op transport, p. 20.

57. Ten per cent of the approximately 100,000
prisoners were criminal cases during the
period from July 1942 to May 1945. Of these
10,000 prisoners, 1,740 lost their status of
criminal prisoner. Presser, *Ondergang*, p. 315.

58. Schütz, *Vermoedelijk op transport*, p. 24.

59. NRK, Jewish Council cards of Otto Frank
(doss. no. 118834), Edith Frank-Holländer
(117265), Margot Frank (117267), Anne
Frank (117266), Auguste van Pels-Röttgen and
Hermann van Pels (103586), Peter van Pels
(135177), Fritz Pfeffer (7500).

60. Van Nierop and Coster, *Westerbork*, p. 8.
HCKW, document in the collection about the
criminal barracks, Witness 195: Weinberg.

61. There are several testimonies that confirm
that the male prisoners were shaved bald.
HCKW, Hans Goudsmit, *Vijf clandestiene
brieven uit Westerbork van Hans Goudsmit
aan zijn vrouw Gerry*, letter dated 13 July
1944; Willem Willing and Edgar Weinberg
(transport 4 September), in Moraal, *Als ik
morgen niet*, pp. 108–9; Rosa de Winter-Levy,
in Schnabel, *Anne Frank*, p. 129; Van Nierop
and Coster, *Westerbork*, p. 8.

62. Although Hans Ottenstein later stated
that the hair of the women in Westerbork was
cut short, this was explicitly denied by several
witnesses. NIOD, 250d, "Camps and prisons
outside the Netherlands", p. 731, Ottenstein.
Cf. HCKW, RA 1850, interview with Lies van
der Kolk-Cohen by Guido Abuys, 2 November
1999; HCKW, interviews with Henriëtte
van Bekkum-Sachs, Sonja Wagenaar-van
Dam, Ronnie Goldstein-van Cleef and B. de
Brave-Schelvis; Edgar Weinberg, in Moraal,
Als ik morgen niet, pp. 54–7. Cloths soaked
in petroleum were used in the past to combat
head lice.

63. HCKW, Jacob Swart's diary, p. 24. Other
times of day are mentioned in other sources
(varying from 9 p.m. to 10.30 p.m.).

64. Anita Mayer, *Als ik Hitler maar kan
overleven* (Nieuwkoop, 1990), p. 71.

65. Schnabel, *Anne Frank*, pp. 109–10. Furthermore, Anne wrote that she had prepared an escape bag in case she suddenly had to flee.

66. HCKW, RA 2022, letter dated 9 July 1944 from Greet Schoemaker-Lisser to the R. van Sitteren family. Greet wrote from the criminal barracks to ask for a blanket, underclothes, a spoon, fork and knife, and a towel, because she had arrived in the camp with nothing. She was sent on the transport of 3 September 1944 and died in the camp in Flossenbürg on 17 March 1945. See www.joodsmonument.nl/nl/page/32046/margaretha-schoemaker-lisser (accessed 31 July 2020). See also HCKW, Jacob Swart's diary, p. 24.

67. Moraal, *Als ik morgen niet*, pp. 233–40.

68. Moraal, *Als ik morgen niet*, p. 394 and p. 414.

69. See also Van Riet, *Bewakers*, p. 124.

70. Van Riet, *Bewakers*, pp. 117–25. There were many German Jewish refugees and privileged Jews in the transport to Theresienstadt.

71. Moraal, *Als ik morgen niet*, pp. 83–5.

72. Presser, *Ondergang 2*, pp. 324–5.

73. Moraal, *Als ik morgen niet*, pp. 127–31.

74. Lindwer, *The Last Seven Months of Anne Frank*, p. 76 and p. 144; Schnabel, *Anne Frank*, p. 129.

75. Lindwer, *The Last Seven Months of Anne Frank*, p. 76.

76. Lindwer, *The Last Seven Months of Anne Frank*, pp. 106–7.

77. AFH, AFC, Witnesses' archive, interview with Rose de Liema-van Gelder by David de Jongh, 11 June 2009.

78. AFH, AFC, OFA, inv. no. 70, Otto Frank, "Bitte schreiben Sie", p. 4.

79. HCKW, interview with H.J. van Collem by Guido Abuys, Schoonhoven, 5 July 2000.

80. Ben Nijhuis, *Breekbaar maar niet gebroken* (Laren, 2008), p. 68.

81. Ad van Liempt, *Frieda. Verslag van een gelijmd leven. Herinneringen aan kamp Westerbork* (Hooghalen, 2007), p. 46.

82. AFH, AFC, OFA, inv. no. 70, Otto Frank, "Bitte schreiben Sie", p. 4.

83. HCKW, RA 1090, Bram Asscher to the D.L. Tollenaar family, 24 August 1944; Moraal, *Als ik morgen niet*, p. 363.

84. AFH, AFC, Witnesses' archive, interview with Bloeme Evers-Emden, 13 November 2010.

85. Lee, *Anne Frank*, p. 185; Cohn, "The day I met Anne Frank", pp. 7–8.

86. HCKW, interview with Ronnie Goldstein-van Cleef, 11 March 2002; and RA 1821, Ronnie Goldstein-van Cleef, *Werkelijkheid en Mythe*, 2003.

87. Original quotation: "Auch Margot war schweigsam, aber Edith Frank war wie stumm. Sie sagte nichts bei der Arbeit, und abends wusch sie immer Wäsche, in schmutzigem Wasser und ohne Seife, aber immer musste sie waschen. Annes Vater war ja auch still, aber das war eine beruhigende Stille […]." Schnabel, *Anne Frank*, p. 130.

88. Original quotation: "Ich habe Anne Frank und Peter van Daan jeden Tag in Westerbork gesehen. Sie waren immer beisammen, und ich sagte oft zu May nem Manne: Schau' dir diese beiden schönen jungen Menschen an […] Anne war schön in Westerbork, so strahlend, dass es sogar auf Peter überging. Sie war sehr blass in der ersten Zeit, aber von ihrer Zartheit und ihrem ausdrucksvollen Gesicht ging eine Anziehungskraft aus, so gross dass sich Judy zuerst gar nicht an sie heranwagte. Vielleicht darf ich es nicht sagen, dass Annes Augen strahlten. Aber sie hatten einen Schein, verstehen sie mich? Und sie war so frei in ihren Bewegungen und Blicken, dass ich mich oft fragte: ist Sie glücklich? Sie war glücklich in Westerbork, wenn es auch kaum zu begreifen ist, denn wir hatten es ja nicht gut im Lager." Schnabel, *Anne Frank*, p. 129; Cohn, "The day I met Anne Frank", pp. 7–8.

89. See Chapters 1 and 3.

90. AFH, AFC, OFA, inv. no. 70, Otto Frank, "Bitte schreiben Sie", p. 4.

91. AFH, AFC, A_OFrank_iv_011, documentary on Radio Canada, 1970. It is possible that he's referring to Lientje Brilleslijper, who was a singer and also said herself that she had sung Yiddish songs with accompaniment in Westerbork. See also HCKW, interview with H.J. van Collem. In this interview, he said that he sang in a male voice

choir and wrote out the musical pieces for this from memory.

92. AFH, AFC, Witnesses' archive, interview with Rose de Liema-van Gelder, 11 June 2009.

93. HCKW, interview with Frieda Menco-Brommet.

94. Liberation portrait of Benny Behr, bevrijdingsportretten.nl/portret/benny-behr/. See also HCKW, interview with H.J. van Collem.

95. See also the comment by Eva Moraal that this group of prisoners thought much less about the tensions between the different groups of prisoners. Moraal, *Als ik morgen niet*, pp. 230–3.

96. Schelvis, cited in www.tracesofwar.nl/articles/1427/Kamp-Westerbork.htm?c=gw.

97. AFH, AFC, Witnesses' archive, interview with Rose de Liema-van Gelder, 11 June 2009.

98. AFH, AFC, OFA, inv. no. 70, Otto Frank, "Bitte schreiben Sie", p. 4.

99. Presser, *Ondergang*, p. 304; HCKW, interview with H.J. van Collem; HCKW, interview with A. Lobsteyn by Guido Abuys, Leeuwarden, 24 January 1995; Schnabel, *Anne Frank*, p. 131; NRK 2050, NRK-Collectie Vervolging (Camp Westerbork), inv. no. 309, Meldezettel no. 550, 1 September 1944.

100. On 3 June 1944, a transport had left from Vught to Auschwitz-Birkenau with 496 people who were all in the Philips-Kommando. Transports left from Westerbork to Bergen-Belsen and Theresienstadt on 31 July 1944: NRK 2050, inventory, p. 55. In June 1944, the criminal barracks were almost empty: HCKW, interview with Henriëtte van Bekkum-Sachs, 28 September 2004.

101. Presser, *Ondergang*, p. 305; HCKW, interview with Ronnie Goldstein-van Cleef, 11 March 2002; De Winter-Levy, *Aan de gaskamer ontsnapt!*, p. 10.

102. Presser, *Ondergang*, p. 304; Lindwer, *Kamp van hoop en wanhoop. Getuigen van Westerbork, 1939–1945* (Amsterdam, 1990), p. 44; De Winter-Levy, *Aan de gaskamer ontsnapt!*, p. 11.

103. L. Landsberger, A. de Haas and K. Selowsky (NRK) (eds), *Auschwitz*, 6 vols (The Hague, 1953), vol. 6: "The transports from Auschwitz and the surrounding

areas to the north and west and the big evacuation transports", p. 3; Wenck, *Zwischen Menschenhandel*, p. 338.

104. About sixty criminal cases were dismissed from the criminal barracks just before 3 September: HCKW, interview by Guido Abuys with A. Lobsteyn.

105. Presser, *Ondergang*, p. 304; Lindwer, *Kamp van hoop en wanhoop*, p. 44; De Winter-Levy, *Aan de gaskamer ontsnapt!*, p. 11.

106. NRK 2050, inv. no. 650, transport list 3 September 1944.

107. NRK 2050, inv. no. 650, transport list 3 September 1944. See also Landsberger et al. (eds), *Auschwitz*, vol. 6, p. 15. Prisoners were classified as "normal" prisoners, *Häftlinge* (criminal cases) and *Schutzhäftlinge*.

108. It has never been examined precisely how the prisoners were distributed in the wagons. As the *Schutzhäftlinge* were read from a different list when they arrived in Auschwitz (they went through a different registration procedure there), it is likely that they were placed in separate wagons when they left Westerbork. It would have been virtually impossible to select the approximately 195 *Schutzhäftlinge* from more than 1,000 prisoners who arrived in Auschwitz in the dark. Most of the witness statements also suggest that the different categories of prisoners were in different wagons. Rosa de Winter-Levy, Lenie de Jong-van Naarden and Anita Mayer-Roos all state that they were in the wagon with the Franks. Anita Mayer also mentioned the Van Pels family. Rosa de Winter-Levy mentions the Van Pels family as well as Fritz Pfeffer. Henriëtte van Bekkum-Sachs says that the wagon was allocated. HCKW, interview with Henriëtte van Bekkum-Sachs, 28 September 2004; HCKW, letters from Hans Goudsmit to his wife, 30 July 1944 and 2 September 1944. Janny Brilleslijper made a similar statement, but because she was in a mixed marriage and registered as a *Schutzhäftling*, and the Franks were Jewish criminal cases, it's unlikely that they were in the same wagon. She also remembers that, as a *Schutzhäftling*, she was separated from her parents and her little brother, and mentions that the list of names was read out so that it was not possible to go in a different wagon. Lindwer, *The Last Seven*

Months of Anne Frank. See also NRK 2050, inv. no. 650, transport list 3 September 1944.

109. HCKW, letter from Hans Goudsmit, 2 September 1944.

110. HCKW, interview with Henriëtte van Bekkum-Sachs, 28 September 2004.

111. See www.drentheindeoorlog. nl/?pid=47&Jodenvervolging; Schnabel, *Anne Frank*, p. 131; AFH, AFC, Witnesses' archive, Witnesses' stories, Witnesses of the history of Anne Frank, p. 17, interview with Lenie de Jong-van Naarden, 22 March 2010; Lenie de Jong-van Naarden in Lindwer, *The Last Seven Months of Anne Frank*; Mayer, *Als ik Hitler maar kan overleven*, p. 23.

112. NRK 2050, inv. no. 675, arrangements in the trains and distribution of jobs.

113. Bolle, *Dagboekbrieven*, p. 149; HCKW, interview with Sonja Wagenaar-van Dam, 19 February 2010.

114. Barnouw et al., *De Nederlandse Spoorwegen*, p. 94.

115. NRK 2050, inv. no. 675, arrangements in the trains and distribution of jobs.

116. NRK 2050, inv. no. 309. One of them was Samuel Kropveld, who later made sure that Otto Frank went to the infirmary in Auschwitz. See also NIOD, 250d, inv. no. 646, statement by S.M. Kropveld.

117. Janny Bolle was married to Meijer Hamburger between 1943 and 1973. She remarried in 1979 and since then her name has been Moffie-Bolle.

118. NRK 2050, inv. no.1091, statement by Janny Hamburger-Bolle, 29 March 1951 (transport 2 February 1944).

119. Transports to Bergen-Belsen and Theresienstadt continued to be carried out in passenger carriages in most cases, even after March 1943. Barnouw et al., *De Nederlandse Spoorwegen*, pp. 90–4 and pp. 123–4 (for the number of people per carriage). See also Lindwer, *The Last Seven Months of Anne Frank*; Saar Roelofs, *Nog altijd. Ronnie Goldstein-van Cleef over jeugd, verzet, concentratiekampen en het leven daarna* (Kampen, 2005), p. 61. Presser wrote that, according to the minutes of the Jewish Council of 4 June 1943, "3.6 Jews were transported per m2 in June 1943." Presser, *Ondergang*, p. 372.

120. Lindwer, *The Last Seven Months of Anne Frank*; Rose de Liema-van Gelder in: Collection, "Anne Frank remembered", 1995 (transcript of raw material), tab. Westerbork 2; Van Liempt, *Frieda*, p. 55.

121. The original Dutch edition of this book stated that the transport took the usual route via Assen and Nieuweschans. However, other sources reveal that a few prisoners managed to escape from this train near Zwolle. This means we must assume that the train traveled along that route. See, inter alia, "Moedige joodse groep ontvluchtte de dodentrein naar Auschwitz" in *Zwols Nieuws-en Advertentieblad*, 23 June 1945. See also Tanja von Fransecky, *Escapees: The History of the Jews Who Fled Nazi Deportation Trains in France, Belgium and the Netherlands* (Oxford, 2019), pp. 234–239.

122. Wim A.H. Rozema, "Treinen naar het eindstation van de beschaving… 'In het midden stond een vent…, die beschikte over je leven…'", 23 April 2015, Historische vereniging Hoogezand-Sappemeer and Noord-Nederlands Trein & Tram Museum, Zuidbroek; interview with Henriëtte van Bekkum-Sachs, 28 September 2004.

123. The train did not stop in the camp itself initially, but some distance before it, on a separate platform at the freight station near the town of Oświęcim (Auschwitz in German), which was 1 kilometer from Birkenau. This platform is now referred to as "die alte Rampe" or "Judenrampe". From May 1944, the trains traveled directly to the new platform in Birkenau; this applied to the transports of 19 May, 3 June and 3 September 1944. De Jong, *Het Koninkrijk*, vol. 8, p. 763; Herman van Rens, *Vervolging in Limburg. Joden and Sinti in Nederlands-Limburg tijdens de Tweede Wereldoorlog* (Hilversum, 2013), p. 150. See also Barnouw et al., *De Nederlandse Spoorwegen*, p. 104; AFH, research collection, email from Jos Zijlstra, curator of the Railway Museum in Utrecht to Erika Prins, 26 October 2015.

124. Rachel van Amerongen-Frankfoorder in Lindwer, *The Last Seven Months of Anne Frank*, pp. 118–19. Ronnie Goldstein-van Cleef also says that they only knew they were going to Auschwitz when they passed Katowice; Ronnie

Goldstein-van Cleef in Lindwer, *The Last Seven Months of Anne Frank*.

125. AFH, AFC, research collection, Jos Zijlstra to Erika Prins, 26 October 2015.

126. Lindwer, *The Last Seven Months of Anne Frank*; Bloeme Evers-Emden, *Als een pluisje in de wind* (Amsterdam, 2012), p. 98; Roelofs, *Nog altijd*, p. 64; Van Liempt, *Frieda*, p. 55; Henriëtte Sachs, born in 1922 in Vlagtwedde; see Rozema, *Treinen*, p. 18.

127. Rozema, *Treinen*, p. 18.

128. Lenie de Jong-van Naarden, in Lindwer, *The Last Seven Months of Anne Frank*, p. 171.

129. De Winter-Levy, *Aan de gaskamer ontsnapt!*, p. 11; HCKW interviews with Leny Boeken-Velleman, B. de Brave-Schelvis, Lies van der Kolk-Cohen, Frieda Menco-Brommet; Presser, *Ondergang*, p. 409; Piper et al., *Auschwitz: Nazi Death Camp*, p. 59, Lenie de Jong-van Naarden in Lindwer, *The Last Seven Months of Anne Frank*.

130. See also Barnouw et al., *De Nederlandse Spoorwegen*, pp. 97–111; Simone Gigliotti, *The Train Journey: Transit, Captivity, and Witnessing in the Holocaust* (New York, 2009), which reveals that the deported prisoners were given food for the journey, which was arranged by the Jewish Council. Lenie de Jong-van Naarden in Lindwer, *The Last Seven Months of Anne Frank*; HCKW, interviews with Lies van der Kolk-Cohen, Ronnie Goldstein-van Cleef; Rozema, *Treinen*, p. 18 (interview with Henriëtte van Bekkum-Sachs, 28 September 2004).

131. De Winter-Levy, *Aan de gaskamer ontsnapt!*, p. 11. Sara Boektje also mentions a small jar of jam: NIOD, 250d, inv. no. 439.

132. HCKW, interviews with Henriëtte van Bekkum-Sachs, 28 September 2004; interviews with Lies van der Kolk-Cohen and B. de Brave-Schelvis.

133. NIOD, 250d, inv. no. 583, I. Salomon; De Winter-Levy, *Aan de gaskamer ontsnapt!*, p. 11; HCKW, interviews with Leny Boeken-Velleman, Ronnie Goldstein-van Cleef; De Jong, *Het Koninkrijk*, vol. 8, pp. 748–9.

134. Between 230 and 300 prisoners escaped from Camp Westerbork during the occupation, often with the help of Resistance organizations. The number of prisoners who managed to escape from the deportation train remains unknown, but is probably much lower. See also Guido Abuys and Dirk Mulder, *Een gat in het prikkeldraad. Kamp Westerbork, ontsnappingen en verzet* (Hooghalen, 2003), pp. 37–58 and pp. 65–8; and Van Riet, *Bewakers*, pp. 126–34.

135. Carry van Lakerveld and Victor Levie, *"Ze doen ons niets". Vervolging and deportatie van de Joden in Nederland 1940–1945* (Amsterdam, 2016), p. 186; NRK, Isidor Stoppelman's Jewish Council card; Leny Bocken Velleman, *Breekhaar*, pp. 78–82; "Vermetele ontsnapping uit Westerbork", *De Waarheid*, 4 May 1966.

136. NRK 2050, inv. no. 1291, Rica Rozenthal, transport 3 September 1944. Salomon Tas is not shown on the list of names of wagon leaders, but is shown on the transport list. NRK 2050, inv. no. 675; Otto Frank made a note of Tas in his list of important addresses in his diary in 1946: "Tass [Otto Frank wrote "Tas" with a double s] Staringlaan 19, 02950-5545", AFH, AFC, OFA, inv. no. 3, Otto Frank's diary, 1946.

137. NIOD, 250d, inv. no. 475, E.A. Cohen.

138. Presser, *Ondergang*, p. 373; NRK 2050, inv. no. 1012, E. de Wind, transport of 14 September 1943.

139. NRK 2050, inv. no. 675, arrangement of the trains and summary of jobs, 3 September 1944. Kropveld, who described his subsequent experiences in quite a lot of detail, did not say much about this transport. See NIOD, 250d, inv. no. 646, statement by S.M. Kropveld.

140. Eddy de Wind, *Eindstation Auschwitz. Mijn verhaal vanuit het kamp (1943–1945)*, rev. edn (Amsterdam, 2020), p. 14. This concerns an edited version of De Wind's eponymous account published in 1946. See www.joodsmonument.nl/nl/page/225527/joel-van-der-kous (accessed 15 April 2019).

141. NIOD, 250d, inv. no. 700, D. Moffie.

142. NRK 2050, inv. no.1284, Leo Maurits Muller, transport of 3 September 1944. Leo Muller was the wagon leader of *Krankenwaggon* C. There was a total of five wagons for the sick, see: NRK 2050, inv. no. 675.

143. Janny Moffie-Bolle was deported to Auschwitz-Birkenau on 10 February 1944. Esther Göbel, *Een hemel zonder vogels. Het*

aangrijpende levensverhaal van Janny Moffie-Bolle (Amsterdam, 2010), p. 68.

144. For an attempt, see Simone Gigliotti, *The Train Journey: Transit, Captivity, and Witnessing in the Holocaust* (New York, 2009).

145. AFH, AFC, Witnesses' archive, interview with Lenie de Jong-van Naarden, 22 March 2010.

146. AFH, AFC, Witnesses' archive, interview with Lenie de Jong-van Naarden, 22 March 2010.

147. Moraal, *Als ik morgen niet*, pp. 167–73; Lindwer, *The Last Seven Months of Anne Frank*, p. 204 and p. 145; HCKW , inv. no. RA 1534, transcription of interview with Henriëtte van Bekkum-Sachs by Guido Abuys, 28 September 2004.

148. AFH, AFC, OFA, inv. no .70, Otto Frank, "Bitte schreiben Sie", p. 4.

149. Lindwer, *The Last Seven Months of Anne Frank*; USC-SF, VHA, interview with Sera Wagenaar (Sonja Wagenaar-van Dam), 10 June 1996.

150. Lindwer, *The Last Seven Months of Anne Frank*.

151. USC-SF, VHA, interview with Sera Wagenaar (Sonja Wagenaar-van Dam), 10 June 1996; Hannah van den Ende, "Vergeet niet dat je arts bent", *Joodse artsen in Nederland 1940–1945* (Amsterdam, 2015), pp. 322–3; NRK, Isidor van der Hal's Jewish Council card; NRK, report of the witness statement by R. Corper-Blik, 24 April 1947, p. 7. See also Lindwer, *The Last Seven Months of Anne Frank*, pp. 134–5.

152. Bart van der Boom, *"Wij weten niets van hun lot". Gewone Nederlanders en de Holocaust* (Amsterdam, 2012), pp. 313–416.

153. See also Evelien Gans and Remco Ensel, "Nivellering in de geschiedenis. 'Wij weten iets van hun lot'", *De Groene Amsterdammer*, 12 December 2012, available from www.groene.nl/artikel/wij-weten-iets-van-hun-lot (accessed 17 June 2020); and idem, "Commentaar op 'Wij weten iets van hun lot'", *De Groene Amsterdammer*, 6 February 2013, available from www.groene.nl/artikel/ over-wij-weten-iets-van-hun-lot (accessed 17 June 2020); Jaap Cohen, "Hoe cruciaal is onwetendheid", *NRC Handelsblad*, 9 April 2013, available from www.nrc.nl/nieuws/2013/04/09/hoe-cruciaal-is-onwetendheid-1226995-a520763 (accessed 17 June 2020).

154. Gans and Ensel, "Nivellering" and "Commentaar"; Guus Meershoek, "Een aangekondigde massamoord", *De Groene Amsterdammer*, 30 January 2013, available from www.groene.nl/artikel/ een-aangekondigde-massamoord.

155. For the dissemination of knowledge about the Holocaust in occupied Europe, see Peter Fritzsche, *An Iron Wind: Europe under Hitler* (New York, 2016), pp. 159–202; for Poland, see Samuel D. Kassow, *Who Will Write Our History: Emanuel Ringelblum, the Warsaw ghetto and the Oyneg Shabes Archive* (Bloomington, 2007).

156. For example, see Wachsmann, *KL*, pp. 686–90; Peter Fritzsche, *Life and Death in the Third Reich*, pp. 235–52; Beate Kosmala, "Zwischen Ahnen und Wissen: Flucht vor der Deportation (1941–1943)", in Birthe Kundrus and Beate Meyer (eds), *Deportation der Juden aus Deutschland: Pläne – Praxis – Reaktionen 1938–1945* (Göttingen, 2012), pp. 135–59.

157. There is still a lot of discussion about the extent to which the Dutch had specific knowledge about what was taking place in the German extermination camps in Poland. For example, see Ies Vuijsje, *Tegen beter weten in. Zelfbedrog en ontkenning in de Nederlandse geschiedschrijving over de Jodenvervolging* (Amsterdam, 2006), and Gans and Ensel, "Nivellering". Cf. also Van der Boom, *"Wij weten niets van hun lot"*, in which the author argues against Vuijsje, and a collection of the most important documents in this discussion and Van der Boom's response to them at wijwetennietsvanhunlot.blogspot.com/ (accessed 30 August 2019). See also Christina Morina and Krijn Thijs (eds), *Probing the Limits of Categorization: The Bystander in Holocaust History* (New York, 2018).

158. Anne Frank, *Diary* (A), 3 February 1944.

159. Anne Frank, *Diary* (B), 9 October 1942.

160. Junk and Sellmeyer, *Stationen*, p. 160.

161. See also Chapter 1, pp. 40–41.

162. De Jong, *Het Koninkrijk*, vol. 4, p. 739, p. 929 and p. 934; Peter Romijn, *Burgemeesters in oorlogstijd. Besturen tijdens de Duitse bezetting* (Amsterdam, 2006), pp. 250–63.

163. See, inter alia, De Jong, *Het Koninkrijk*, vol. 4, pp. 548–50. For the impact of the razzia on the residents of the Merwedeplein, see Rian Verhoeven, *Anne Frank was niet alleen. Het Merwedeplein 1933–1945* (Amsterdam, 2019), pp. 145–72; and www.annefrank.org/nl/anne-frank/verdieping/de-tweede-razzia-amsterdam/# source-396717.

164. Verhoeven, *Anne Frank was niet alleen*, pp. 158–61; and www.annefrank. org/nl/anne-frank/verdieping/de-tweede-razzia-amsterdam/#source 396717.

165. NIOD, archive of the Jewish Council (entry 182), inv. no. 263, list of the Jewish men arrested on 11 June 1941; after the war, Otto Frank sent a copy of *Het Achterhuis* to Lewkowitz's father. AFH, AFC, OFA, inv. no. 100, list of names and addresses.

166. Kienzle, *Lasst mich so sein*.

167. Suzanne Heim (ed.), *Deutsches Reich und Protektorat Böhmen und Mähren Oktober 1941-März 1943. Verfolgung und Ermordung der Europäischen Juden durch das nationalsozialistische Deutschland 1933–1945*, vol. 6 (Oldenburg, 2019), pp. 199–204.

168. Mark Mazower, *Hitler's Empire: Nazi Rule in Occupied Europe* (London, 2008), p. 175.

169. Original quotation: "Die Juden waren um diese Zeit ziemlich weich, da der Zug unbeheizt liegengeblieben war und vor allem seit Einfahrt ins russische Gebiet keine Möglichkeit mehr gegeben war, Wasser zu fassen, weil dort das Wasser nur gekocht verwendet werden darf, ich anderseits aber keine Abkochmöglichkeit für fast 1000 Personen hatte und nicht bereits während der Fahrt schon Ruhr-oder Typhusanfälle im Zuge haben wollte." "Vertraulicher Bericht des Hauptmanns der Schutzpolizei Wilhelm Meurin betr. Evakuierung von Juden nach Minsk", 22 November 1941, in Heim (ed.), *Deutsches Reich*, vol. 6, pp. 199–204.

170. Original quotation: "[…] die ein entsprechend deutliches tempobeschleunigend Verhalten an den Tag legte." "Evakuierung von Juden nach Minsk", 22 November 1941, in Heim (ed.), *Deutsches Reich*, vol. 6, 199–204.

171. Heim (ed.), *Deutsches Reich*, vol. 6, pp. 199–204.

172. This expression was based on Barnouw et al., *De Nederlandse Spoorwegen*, p. 108, in which the authors find that "swinging back and forth between hope and despair" is a recurring theme in the diaries and letters that have survived.

CHAPTER THREE

1. Leaving on 3 September at about noon, and arriving at midnight on the night of 5–6 September comes to sixty hours.

2. From May 1944, the trains traveled on directly to this new platform; this applied for the transports of 19 May, 3 June and 3 September 1944. Before that, the transports had stopped on a separate platform of the freight station near the town of Oświęcim, which was 1 kilometer away from Birkenau. This platform is now known as "die alte Rampe" or "Judenrampe". De Jong, *Het Koninkrijk*, vol. 8, p. 763; Van Rens, *Vervolging in Limburg*, p. 150.

3. See also Esther Göbel, "Nederlandse Joden in dwangarbeid. Rapport over het kwantitatieve, kwalitatieve en museale onderzoek naar de inzet van Joodse dwangarbeiders uit Nederland, in kampen in Nederland en daarbuiten, tijdens de Sjoa", JCK, 2015, digital, inv. no. 20170344.

4. Benz and Distel, *Der Ort des Terrors*, vol. 5, pp. 175–236.

5. Most of these work camps were established from mid-1944. In the spring of 1944, Auschwitz III still consisted of fourteen subcamps. Wachsmann, *KL*, p. 403, p. 477 and pp. 482–5.

6. For the WVHA, see Wachsmann, *KL*, p. 405.

7. It was necessary to appoint an expert in Auschwitz for the deportations from Hungary, and Liebehenschel had fallen out of favor because of a private matter with his fiancée. Wachsmann, *KL*, pp. 640–2.

8. See Robert Jay Lifton, *The Nazi Doctors: A Study in the Psychology of Evil* (London, 1986), pp. 271–8; Daan de Leeuw, "In the Name of Humanity. Nazi Doctors and Human Experiments in German Concentration Camps, 1939–1945", MA thesis (University of Amsterdam, 2013), pp. 83–7.

9. The phrase had been used by the Nazis since 1933 and was also used in other

concentration camps such as Oranienburg, Dachau, Groß-Rosen and Theresienstadt.

10. Van Pelt and Dwork show that the construction of a concentration camp in Upper Silesia was connected with the special status of this highly industrialized area in the Nazi policy on population. While the Polish population in other parts of the Generaal Gouvernement were subjected to forced removals, this policy did not fit in with Himmler's plans for Silesia, where there was a relatively high number of Polish Germans, as well as many workers who were essential for the German war industry. In order to combat the Polish resistance in this region effectively, the *Höhere SS-Führer* for Silesia, Erich von dem Bach-Zelewski, insisted that a concentration camp should be built near Katowice. Dwork and Van Pelt, *Auschwitz*, p. 166.

11. Sybille Steinbacher, *Auschwitz. Een geschiedenis* (Utrecht, 2005), pp. 27–9; Dwork and Van Pelt, *Auschwitz*, pp. 168–71.

12. See www.Auschwitz.org/en/history/prisoner-classification/markingof-jewish-prisoners (accessed 4 September 2020).

13. Wachsmann, *KL*, pp. 359–60; Christopher Browning, *The Origins of the Final Solution: The Evolution of Nazi Jewish Policy, September 1939-March 1942* (Lincoln, 2004); Waitman Beorn, *Marching into Darkness: The Wehrmacht and the Holocaust in Belarus* (London, 2018); and idem, *The Holocaust in Eastern Europe: At the Epicentre of the Final Solution* (Cambridge, MA, 2014).

14. Steinbacher, *Auschwitz*, p. 71; Mazower, *Hitler's Empire*, p. 176.

15. Wachsmann, *KL*, pp. 371–3 and p. 421; Steinbacher, *Auschwitz*, pp. 76–7. Christopher Browning also stated that particular decisions that resulted in Auschwitz being organized as a camp with the primary aim of murdering large numbers of people were only taken in September and October 1941. Browning, *The Origins*, pp. 352–73.

16. Franciszek Piper, "Gas chambers and crematoria", in Yisrael Gutman and Michael Berenbaum (eds), *Anatomy of the Auschwitz Death Camp* (Bloomington, 1998), pp. 157–82; see in particular pp. 157–60.

17. This program was aimed at murdering the sick and weak prisoners who were no longer able to work, with the use of methods that had been developed earlier in 1939 for the Aktion T-4, a secret euthanasia program in which the mentally handicapped and others were murdered. There was a lot of opposition to Aktion T-4 in German society, and it was officially stopped in 1939, but then continued in the concentration camps as Aktion 14f13.

18. Wachsmann, *KL*, p. 372 and p. 402.

19. Yitzhak Arad, *The Operation Reinhard Death Camps: Belsec, Sobibor, Treblinka*, rev. edn (Indiana, 2018), pp. 32–3; Mazower, *Hitler's Empire*, pp. 368–83.

20. See also Arad, *The Operation Reinhard Death Camps*, pp. 32–3; Browning, *The Origins*, pp. 277–308; Christian Gerlach, *The Extermination of the European Jews* (Cambridge, 2016), pp. 66–88; Wachsmann, *KL*, pp. 407–8; Saul Friedländer, *Nazi-Duitsland en de Joden, De jaren van vervolging 1933–1939*, vol. 1 (London, 1997), p. 245; and *De jaren van vernietiging 1939–1945*, vol. 2 (London, 1997), pp. 292–3; Steinbacher, *Auschwitz*, p. 70; Browning, *Initiating the Final Solution*, p. 7.

21. Mark Roseman, *The Wannsee Conference and the Final Solution: A Reconsideration* (New York, 2002), pp. 109–13; Wachsmann, *KL*, pp. 411–18; Shmuel Krakowski, "The satellite camps", in Gutman and Berenbaum (eds), *Anatomy of the Auschwitz Death Camp*, pp. 50–51. The term "Vernichtung durch Arbeit" led to some discussion amongst historians after the war. Although "annihilation through labor" is often described as a specific policy to murder Jews with slave labor, some historians recently modified this view. After all, forced labor had been part of the concentration camp system from the beginning, and this continued when the persecution of the Jews developed to become genocide. Recent research assumes that the Nazi leaders never implemented an unequivocal policy of "annihilation through labor" with regard to the Jews, although that's certainly what happened in practice. The starting point for slave labor in the SS camps was not so much to work the Jews to death, as to use their work as long as this was necessary. If Germany won the war, and Jewish slave

labor was no longer necessary, would the Jews who were still alive, still be murdered? At the same time, in Hitler and Himmler's policy, the extermination of Jews was more important than making use of their labor. This contributed to the fact that the conditions in the camps were so bad that enormous numbers of prisoners died during the slave labor. Thus the Holocaust and "Vernichtung durch Arbeit" were two sides of the same coin. See Wolf Gruner, *Jewish Forced Labor under the Nazis: Economic Needs and Racial Aims 1938-1944* (Cambridge, MA, 2006), pp. 289–93; Nikolaus Wachsmann, "Annihilation through labour: The killing of state prisoners in the Third Reich", *Journal of Modern History* 3 (1999), pp. 624–59; Jens Christian Wagner, "Work and extermination in the concentration camps", in Jane Caplan and Nikolaus Wachsmann (eds), *Concentration Camps in Nazi Germany: The New Histories* (London, 2010), pp. 127–48, in particular p. 140; Dieter Pohl, "The Holocaust and the concentration camps", in Caplan and Wachsmann (eds), *Concentration Camps in Nazi Germany*, pp. 149–66, in particular p. 151 and p. 161.

22. Arad, *The Operation Reinhard Death Camps*, pp. 7–33.

23. The name Aktion T4 (also known as Operation T4) refers to the address, Tiergartenstrasse 4 in Berlin, the headquarters of the eugenics program established by Hitler's doctor, Karl Brandt, in which large numbers of psychiatric patients were murdered from October 1939. See also Wachsmann, *KL*, pp. 336–8.

24. Arad, *The Operation Reinhard Death Camps*, pp. 421–33.

25. Wachsmann, *KL*, pp. 396–403.

26. Steinbacher, *Auschwitz*, pp. 77–8.

27. Kinna report, quoted in Wachsmann, *KL*, p. 485. See also the Red Cross report on the transports to Auschwitz II, pp. 4–8.

28. Landsberger et al. (eds), *Auschwitz*, vol. 5, pp. 20–23.

29. Wachsmann, *KL*, pp. 415–25.

30. Red Cross report on the transports to Auschwitz II, 3, p. 18.

31. In addition, preparations were made for the arrival of large numbers of Jewish women

with the idea of using them as slave labor. Wachsmann, *KL*, p. 400 and pp. 412–14.

32. Wachsmann, *KL*, p. 19; and Irena Strzelecka, "Women", in Gutman and Berenbaum (eds), *Anatomy of the Auschwitz Death Camp*, p. 395.

33. Wachsmann, *KL*, pp. 413–17, Dwork and Van Pelt, *Auschwitz*, pp. 304–5.

34. Wachsmann, *KL*, p. 421 and p. 982, footnote 57; Dwork and Van Pelt, *Auschwitz*, p. 304; Steinbacher, *Auschwitz*, p. 83.

35. Wachsmann, *KL*, p. 424; Dwork and Van Pelt, *Auschwitz*, p. 306.

36. The gas chambers of Crematorium II and II were underground, whereas those of Bunker I and II and Crematorium IV and V were above ground. Dwork and Van Pelt, *Auschwitz*, pp. 307–48.

37. In addition, camp BII consisted of BIID (the men's camp), BIIE (the *Zigeunerlager*, which was the Roma and Sinta camp), BIIF (the male sick bay) and BIIG, which accommodated the members of the *Kanada kommando*.

38. Wachsmann, *KL*, pp. 413–14 and p. 481; Strzelecka, "Women", pp. 393–4.

39. Steinbacher, *Auschwitz*, p. 74; Strzelecka, "Women", p. 394.

40. Strzelecka, "Women", p. 394.

41. The construction of Crematoria II–V started in 1942, and went into operation between March and June 1943. Treblinka and Sobibor were closed down in the summer and the autumn respectively. Dwork and Van Pelt, *Auschwitz*, pp. 321–5; Steinbacher, *Auschwitz*, p. 83 and p. 85; Wachsmann, *KL*, p. 407, pp. 402–23 and p. 429.

42. Dwork and Van Pelt, *Auschwitz*, p. 348.

43. Wachsmann, *KL*, pp. 418–20; Dwork and Van Pelt, *Auschwitz*, p. 304.

44. Wachsmann, *KL*, pp. 403–6.

45. Wachsmann, *KL*, p. 581, p. 588 and pp. 590–3.

46. Wachsmann, *KL*, pp. 590–3; Irena Strzelecka, "Hospitals", in Gutman and Berenbaum (eds), *Anatomy of the Auschwitz Death Camp*, p. 383 and p. 386.

47. Strzelecka, "Women", p. 402.

48. Wachsmann, *KL*, p. 592; Strzelecka, "Hospitals", p. 386.

49. Wolf Gruner, *Jewish Forced Labor under the Nazis: Economic Needs and Racial Aims, 1938-1944* (Cambridge, MA & New York, 2006), p. 3.

50. Wachsmann, *KL*, p. 488, p. 625, p. 631 and pp. 633–4.

51. This also applied for Poles with a sentence of three or four years, and for Czechs and Germans with a life or death sentence. See Krakowski, "The satellite camps", pp. 50–51; Yehuda Bauer, "Gypsies", in Gutman and Berenbaum (eds), *Anatomy of the Auschwitz Death Camp*, pp. 441–55, in particular p. 446; Wachsmann, *KL*, p. 586.

52. Bauer, "Gypsies", pp. 447–50; Wachsmann, *KL*, pp. 643–6; Wichert ten Have et al., *De Holocaust en andere genociden*, available from https://www.niod.nl/sites/niod.nl/files/Holocaust%20en%20andere%20genociden.pdf (accessed 4 September 2020).

53. See www.kampwesterbork.nl/geschiedenis/tweede-wereldoorlog/vervolging-sinti-en-roma (accessed 13 August 2020). See also Wachsmann, *KL*, pp. 743–7.

54. Wachsmann, *KL*, p. 624, p. 631, pp. 633–4 and pp. 636–8.

55. Landsberger et al. (eds), *Auschwitz*, vol. 6, p. 3 and p. 15; Wenck, *Zwischen Menschenhandel*, p. 339 and p. 343; Andrzej Strzelecki, "Evacuation, liquidation and liberation of the camp", in Piper et al., *Auschwitz*, pp. 269–92, in particular pp. 269–70.

56. Wenck, *Zwischen Menschenhandel*, p. 343 and p. 346.

57. Marc Buggeln, *Slave Labor in Nazi Concentration Camps* (Oxford, 2014), pp. 44–5.

58. Wenck, *Zwischen Menschenhandel*, p. 338; Gedenkstätte Bergen-Belsen, discussion between Erika Prins and Klaus Tätzler, November 2013; Strzelecki, "Evacuation, liquidation and liberation of the camp", pp. 269–92, in particular p. 269.

59. Franciszek Piper, "The mass extermination of Jews in the gas chambers", in Piper et al, *Auschwitz*, pp. 165–73, in particular p. 172.

60. Piper, "The mass extermination", p. 173.

61. The prisoners who were sent on the death march also included Peter van Pels. See Chapter 7 of this book.

62. Lindwer, *The Last Seven Months of Anne Frank*.

63. Wachsmann, *KL*, p. 710.

64. Wachsmann, *KL*, pp. 118–35.

65. See www.duden.de/rechtschreibung/Kapo_Haeftling_Arbeiter (accessed 4 September 2020).

66. Wachsmann, *KL*, pp. 118–35; Wolfgang Sofsky, *The Order of Terror: The Concentration Camp*, English translation (New Jersey, 1997), p. 117, p. 121 and p. 130.

67. Abel Herzberg, *Amor fati & Tweestromenland, Bergen-Belsen 1944–1945* (Amsterdam, 2016).

68. Danuta Czech, "The Auschwitz prisoner administration", in Gutman and Berenbaum (eds), *Anatomy of the Auschwitz Death Camp*, p. 363.

69. De Wind, *Last Stop Auschwitz*.

70. In his book, De Wind refers to himself in the third person and uses the name "Hans".

71. De Wind, *Last Stop Auschwitz*.

72. Wachsmann, *KL*, pp. 436–41.

73. This problem returns in the work of Primo Levi, but was introduced in the academic debate by Lawrence Langer in "The dilemma of choice in the deathcamps", *Centerpoint: A Journal of Interdisciplinary Studies* 4:1 (1980), pp. 53–8.

74. Wachsmann, *KL*, p. 735. René Kok and Erik Somers, *The Persecution of the Dutch Jews in Photographs. The Netherlands 1940–1945* (Zwolle, 2019), p. 268. Errera did not survive the war, as he was beaten to death for attempting to escape Auschwitz.

75. For countless other examples of Jewish resistance in concentration camps, see, inter alia, Arad, *The Operation Reinhard Death Camps*, pp. 289–417; Patrick Henry (ed.), *Jewish Resistance against the Nazis* (Washington DC, 2015). This literature clearly and convincingly undermines the image of Jews allowing themselves to be driven like "sheep to the slaughter".

76. Wachsmann, *KL*, pp. 489–94 and pp. 732–50. See also Shlomo Venezia, *Inside the Gas Chambers: Eight Months in the*

Sonderkommando of Auschwitz (Cambridge, MA, 2009).

77. Wachsmann, *KL*, p. 596.

78. From the beginning of May 1944, the transports arrived in Auschwitz-Birkenau on the loading platform between parts BI and BII of the camps. Before that (from 1942) the trains arrived at the "Judenrampe" at the Oświęcim station near Auschwitz-Birkenau. Tadeusz Iwaszko, "Reasons for confinement in the camp and categories of prisoners", in Lasik et al. (eds), *Auschwitz, 1940–1945*, p. 2 and p. 17. The arrival during the night from Tuesday to Wednesday was specifically mentioned by I. Salomon, NIOD, 250d, inv. no. 538, I. Salomon; Presser, *Ondergang*, p. 407. In relation to the three days in locked wagons, see AFH, AFC, OFA, inv. no. 70, Otto Frank, "Bitte schreiben Sie"; De Winter-Levy, *Aan de gaskamer ontsnapt!*, p. 12.

79. Lindwer, *The Last Seven Months of Anne Frank*.

80. For example, NIOD, 250d, inv. no. 439, Sara Boektje; HCKW, interviews with B. de Brave-Schelvis and Ronnie Goldstein-van Cleef.

81. Landsberger et al. (eds), *Auschwitz*, vol. 2, p. 18; NRK 2050, inv. no. 1293.

82. AFH, AFC, OFA, inv. no. 070; for example, Frieda Menco-Brommet, interview with AFH, about not being able to say goodbye to her father. Rosa de Winter-Levy's statement to Schnabel many years later about how she saw Otto Frank, Hermann and Peter van Pels, and Fritz Pfeffer being sent the "right" way is not really credible in view of the masses present at the time. See also Schnabel, *Anne Frank*, p. 133.

83. Landsberger et al. (eds), *Auschwitz*, vol. 5, pp. 20–23.

84. Ronnie Goldstein-van Cleef in Lindwer, *The Last Seven Months of Anne Frank*.

85. Mengele was mentioned by, inter alia, Ronnie Goldstein-van Cleef in Lindwer, *The Last Seven Months of Anne Frank*; Lenie de Jong-van Naarden, ibidem; Rachel van Amerongen-Frankfoorder, ibidem; HCKW, interview with Henriëtte van Bekkum-Sachs; NRK 2050, inv. no. 1294, Sientje Spiekerman-de Zwarte.

86. Langbein, *People in Auschwitz*, p. 295. See also Wachsmann, *KL*, pp. 611–13.

87. Lifton, *The Nazi Doctors*, pp. 173–5.

88. Lifton, *The Nazi Doctors*, pp. 173–5.

89. See De Jong, *Het Koninkrijk*, vol. 8, p. 708 and p. 888; Wagner, "Work and extermination in the concentration camps", pp. 127–48, in particular p. 154; Dwork and Van Pelt, *Auschwitz*, pp. 347–8.

90. Landsberger et al. (eds), *Auschwitz*, vol. 5, p. 3.

91. A total of 477 people of the *Normal* and *Häftlinge* transport (the ordinary prisoners and the criminal cases, including the eight from the Annex) were not selected for the gas chambers: 221 women and 256 men. In total, there were 195 *Schutzhäftlinge* (political prisoners, mixed marriages and half-Jews: 144 men and 51 women) who were not subjected to the selection for the gas chambers. NRK 2050, inv. no. 650, transport list, 3 September 1944. The distinction between criminal cases, such as the eight from the Annex, and "ordinary prisoners" did not play any role at all after their arrival in Auschwitz. On the other hand, the reception, registration and numbering of the *Schutzhäftlinge* was different when they arrived. Landsberger et al. (eds), *Auschwitz*, vol. 5, pp. 20–23. This Red Cross brochure does not claim to be complete and does not take into account the eight people who escaped from the transport or those who died during the journey.

92. Herman Frijda (1887), Philip Grishaver (1886), Willem Swaap (1888) and even Joseph Matthijs Wolf (1878). NRK 2050, inv. no. 650, transport list, 3 September 1944.

93. Landsberger et al. (eds), *Auschwitz*, vol. 2, p. 19; De Winter-Levy, *Aan de gaskamer ontsnapt!*, p. 12.

94. Roelofs, *Nog altijd*, p. 69; Fia Polak, *Oorlogsverslag van een zestienjarig joods meisje* (Amsterdam, 1995), p. 62; Lindwer, *The Last Seven Months of Anne Frank*; Schloss, *Herinneringen*, p. 65.

95. Boeken-Velleman, *Breekbaar*, p. 89.

96. NRK 2050, inv. no. 1291, Rica Rozenthal, and inv. no. 1301, Mrs. S. Weisz. Both say that they met the men once more, but most did not see their husbands again after the selection.

97. "Aan Bureau Inlichtingen (of the Rode Kruis) verschaft ooggetuigenverslag van een jong meisje, teruggekeerd uit kamp Auschwitz", JHM collection, no. D001088.

98. Landsberger et al. (eds), *Auschwitz*, vol. 2, pp. 19–22; Tadeusz Iwaszko, "Deportation to the camp and registration of prisoners", in Piper et al., *Auschwitz*, pp. 54–69, in particular pp. 59–62; AFH, AFC, Witnesses' archive, interviews with Bloeme Evers-Emden, Ronnie Goldstein-van Cleef, Frieda Menco-Brommet, Lenie de Jong-van Naarden, B. de Brave-Schelvis. This order is also in accordance with the explanation during a visit to Auschwitz by Teresien da Silva, Gertjan Broek and Erika Prins in 2009. On the other hand, Auschwitz's own publications give a different order, but only provide a general description of the whole period, without specifically focusing on September 1944.

99. HCKW, interview with Ronnie Goldstein-van Cleef, 11 March 2002; Lindwer, *The Last Seven Months of Anne Frank*.

100. Lindwer, *The Last Seven Months of Anne Frank*, pp. 190–91. See also Iwaszko, "Deportation", p. 60; and Landsberger et al. (eds), *Auschwitz*, vol. 2, p. 21.

101. NIOD, 250d, inv. no. 439, Sara Boektje, and NRK 2050, inv. no. 1301, Mrs. S. Weisz.

102. Iwaszko, "Deportation", p. 59; AFH, AFC, OFA, inv. no. 85: József Spronz, "Ich war ein Haeftling in Auschwitz" (from József Spronz, *Fogoly voltam Auschwitzban*, unpublished German translation [Budapest, 1946], p. 4); Strzelecka, "Woman", pp. 399–400.

103. Lindwer, *The Last Seven Months of Anne Frank*.

104. NIOD, 804, Sobibor research: inv. no. 18, Cato Polak, declaration of 20 October 1947; NRK 2050, inv. no. 1301, Mrs. S. Weisz; Iwaszko, "Deportation", pp. 58–60.

105. Strzelecka, "Women", p. 400; eyewitness account by a young girl, JHM, no. D001088.

106. Boeken-Velleman, *Breekbaar*, p. 90.

107. Andrzej Strzelecki, "The plunder of victims and their corpses", in Gutman and Berenbaum (eds), *Anatomy of the Auschwitz Death Camp*, p. 253; Lindwer, *The Last Seven Months of Anne Frank*.

108. According to the literature, the men were registered in Auschwitz I, but Max Frankfort, amongst others, said that he went to Auschwitz I after the registration. Rica Rozenthal and Mrs. Weisz met the men a few times at the *Zentralsauna* during the procedure.

109. AFH, Sal de Liema, Jon Blair Collection, "Anne Frank remembered", 1995 (transcript of raw material).

110. De Wind, *Last Stop Auschwitz*.

111. NRK, inv. no. 3281, International Committee of the Red Cross, Häftlings-Nummerzuteilung, 26. See also Piper et al., *Auschwitz*, p. 61.

112. Landsberger et al. (eds), *Auschwitz*, vol. 2, pp. 25–7.

113. AFH, Collection of research materials, statement made by Eva Schloss-Geiringer to Erika Prins, January 2016. See also www.auschwitz.org/en/history/life-in-the-camp/ (accessed 4 September 2020).

114. De Wind, *Last Stop Auschwitz*; De Jong, *Het Koninkrijk*, vol. 6, p. 6, p. 424 and p. 436; NRK 2050, inv. no. 1274, Barend Konijn; NRK 2050, inv. no. 1264, statement of Abraham Hakker; Odette Abadi, *Terre de détresse. Birkenau-Bergen-Belsen* (Paris, 2012), p. 41.

115. Tadeusz Iwaszko, "The daily life of prisoners", in Piper et al., *Auschwitz*, pp. 70–87, in particular, p. 70; De Jong, *Het Koninkrijk*, vol. 6, p. 436.

116. De Jong, *Het Koninkrijk*, vol. 6, p. 436 and p. 826; Landsberger et al. (eds), *Auschwitz*, vol. 2, p. 25; Krakowski, "The satellite camps", p. 52; Strzelecka, "Women", p. 400.

117. De Jong, *Het Koninkrijk*, vol. 8, pp. 824–7.

118. NRK 2050, statements of Abraham Hakker (inv. no. 1264), Philip Felix de Jong (inv. no. 1268), Eliazer Kater (inv. no. 1271), Elias Jacob Kleerekoper (inv. no. 1272), Barend Konijn (inv. no. 1274), Richard Felix Levee (inv. no. 1276) and Aron Leyden van Amstel (inv. no. 1277).

119. De Wind, *Last Stop Auschwitz*, in particular the afterword.

120. NRK 2050, inv. no. 1284, Fritz Muller (mainly about street building and groundwork while in quarantine).

121. Original quotation: "Da ich selbst einige Zeit in einem Kieskommando war, wusste

ich über die dort verlangte schwere Arbeit gut Bescheid und die damit oft verbundenen Misshandlungen." AFH, AFC, OFA, inv. no. 85, statement of Otto Frank for his fellow prisoner, Joseph Spronz, 29 July 1962.

122. De Wind, *Last Stop Auschwitz*.

123. NRK, dossier 103586, Hermann van Pels, letter to Jansma, 20 December 1951; Landsberger et al. (eds), *Auschwitz*, vol. 5, p. 21; NRK 2050, inv. nos. 1257: Max Frankfort; 1268: Philip Felix de Jong; 1293: Fritz Bernard Simon; 1302: Jacob West: 1249: Andries Max Cats.

124. Original quotation: "Während meiner Zeit haben 2 Selektionen stattgefunden […]. Bei der ersten Selektion wurden alle Menschen heraus gesucht, die Blockschonung hatten, d.h. die wegen irgend eines Leidens von der Arbeit für einige Tage dispensiert waren. […] Diese so selektierten kamen in einen besonderen Block und wurden nach 2 Tagen offenbar zur Vergasung nach Birkenau verladen. Die 2 Tage waren schrecklich für diese Menschen, da sie genau wussten [sic], was ihnen bevorstand. Auch hierbei wurden die Mischehen schließlich wieder herausgesucht, nachdem sie zunächst die Todesangst durchgemacht hatten. Die zweite Selektion fand in ähnlicher Art statt, nur wurde hierbei in erster Linie, das Krankenhaus leergemacht." NRK 2050, inv. no. 1293, Fritz Simon.

125. De Wind, *Last Stop Auschwitz*.

126. Jetteke Frijda survived the war in hiding. In an interview, she said that Otto and Herman Frijda were not really close friends, but knew each other through their daughters. Otto Frank also told Jetteke that he had met Herman again in the camps. AFH, AFC, Witnesses' archive, interview with Jetteke Frijda, 9 March 2009.

127. De Wind, *Last Stop Auschwitz*.

128. De Wind, *Last Stop Auschwitz*; NRK, dossier EU 85.297, Herman Frijda. His Jewish Council card states "gassed in Auschwitz after a selection", NRK, Jewish Council card index, H. Frijda's card. There are a few other survivors of the transport of 3 September who mention Frijda and the two selections for the gas chambers at the beginning of October 1944. NRK 2050, statement of Leo Maurits Muller (inv. no. 1284), Philip Felix de Jong (inv. no. 1268), Andries Max Cats (inv. no. 1249).

129. NRK, dossier 103586 of Hermann van Pels, *Bescheinigung* (statement), February 1961.

130. NRK, dossier 103586 of Hermann van Pels, letter to Jansma, 20 December 1951.

131. Transport list for Stutthof of 26 October; this list was "discovered" as recently as 2005 by Juan Goudsmit, who was looking for his father, Hans Goudsmit, who died in Stutthof.

132. NRK 2050, inv. no. 1293, Fritz Simon. He is listed in Otto Frank's notebook and is also mentioned there in relation to Fritz Pfeffer.

133. AFH, AFC, OFA, inv. no. 211, William Banks, "How the end came to Anne Frank", undated; AFH, letter from Fritzi Frank to Vincent Frank-Steiner, 14 December 1990; DLA, Schnabel Collection, Schnabel notes, p. 149; *Welt am Sonntag*, interview, 4 February 1979.

134. Danuta Czech, *Kalendarium der Ereignisse im Konzentrationslager Auschwitz-Birkenau 1939–1945* (Reinbek bei Hamburg, 1989), p. 892.

135. For example, Louis Salomon de Goede, mentioned by Jacob van West. NRK 2050, inv. no. 1302, Jacob van West.

136. Filip Müller, "Hoelang jij leeft and wanneer jij crepeert, dat beslissen wij", in Grunberg (ed.), *Bij ons in Auschwitz*, pp. 366–8.

137. DLA, Schnabel collection, Schnabel notes, p. 151.

138. *Welt am Sonntag*, interview with Otto Frank, 4 February 1979.

139. Wachsmann, *KL*, pp. 765–6.

140. Road construction, groundwork and carpentry (Georg Hirsch, NRK 2050, inv. no. 1265); Petersen and the HUTA (Philip Felix de Jong, inv. no. 1268); canalization and abattoir work *kommando* (Barend Konijn, inv. no. 1274); groundwork and digging in the Petersen Kommando and potato peeling *kommando* (Max Canes, inv. no.1248); Petersen Kommando (groundwork) and HUTA, canalization for sewerage work (Jacob van West, inv. no. 1302); road construction and groundwork (canalization) and groundwork for road construction and HUTA (Fritz Bernard Simon, inv. no. 1293), see also EHRI.

141. NRK 3281, International Committee of the Red Cross, Häftlings-Nummerzuteilung;

348

Landsberger et al. (eds), *Auschwitz*, vol. 2, p. 26.

142. Landsberger et al. (eds), *Auschwitz*, vol. 5, p. 21, transports to Stutthof on 26 October 1944 and 29 November 1944. Pfeffer is not shown on the transport list of 26 October to Stutthof. The transport of 29 November 1944 is not involved, because Pfeffer went on the same transport as Willem Swaap, who died in Neuengamme on 21 November 1944. NRK, dossier 42095 of Willem Swaap.

143. Transport list from Auschwitz to Stutthof, private collection of Juan Goudsmit.

144. Braunschweig became a subcamp of Neuengamme on 5 November 1944. A significant proportion of the prisoners were Polish, particularly Polish Jews who had survived the ghetto in Lodz and had been deported to Auschwitz, where they were selected for slave labor in the Braunschweig subcamp by representatives of the Büssing-NAG company. The company was looking for metalworkers. The prisoners arrived in three transports between September and November 1944. See Buggeln, *Slave Labor*, pp. 128–31. *Der Ort des Terrors* refers to a transport to Braunschweig on 9 November 1944. See Benz and Distel, *Der Ort des Terrors*, vol. 5, p. 358.

145. We know from prisoners who were registered in Neuengamme on 10 November 1944 that they were given camp numbers from 64230 and that the lowest known camp number of a prisoner arriving on 18 November was 65105. Pfeffer (64976) was therefore registered on 10 November at the earliest and 18 November at the latest. As we do not have the complete lists, and as we cannot be certain that no other transport arrived between 10 and 18 November, Pfeffer could therefore be in the group of 10 November, but it is also possible that he arrived on 18 November or on a day in between. For the (incomplete) list of prisoners and camp numbers, see the emails from Alyn Beßmann, Archives Neuengamme Concentration Camp Memorial to Erika Prins and Gertjan Broek, 5 May 2017–6 June 2017.

146. In 1943, Jan Gies helped Stoppelman to find a place to go into hiding in Laren. Stoppelman eventually ended up in Auschwitz after being betrayed.

147. AFH, AFC, Witnesses' archive, Stoppelman.

148. On 17 January 1945, Stoppelman traveled on one of the evacuation transports. Written statement of Max Stoppelman, 9 August 1995. AFH, AFC, Witnesses' archive, documentation on Max Stoppelman. See also Lee, *Het verborgen leven*, p. 138; and Müller, *Anne Frank*, pp. 232–3.

149. Camp Westerbork Memorial Center and NOS Actueel, *Leven na de ondergang. Acht portretten van Holocaustoverlevenden*, DVD documentary, 2007. Julius Erich Anhalt (transport of 25 January 1944) stated that when they arrived, they were individually asked about their age and profession. For an external *kommando*, he had to follow so-called *Nachschule* to train as a metalworker, NRK 2015, inv. no. 1168. During the selections in the Cosel camps, the physical size, estimated physical strength and profession were assessed. See Göbel, "Nederlandse Joden in dwangarbeid", p. 20.

150. NRK, dossier 135177-3, Mauthausen camp card.

151. AFH, AFC, OFA, inv. no. 211, interview with Otto Frank by Arthur Unger, 6 February 1978. See also the quotation in Lee, *The Hidden Life of Otto Frank*.

152. Priscilla Alden Thwaits Garcia, *Auschwitz, Auschwitz… I Cannot Forget You. As Long As I Remain Alive: The Story of Max Rodrigues Garcia As Told to Priscilla Alden Thwaits Garcia* (San Jose, CA, 1979), pp. 109–23.

153. Alden Thwaits Garcia, *Auschwitz*, pp. 109–23.

154. AFH, AFC, OFA, inv. no. 211, interview with Otto Frank by Arthur Unger, 6 February 1978. See also Lee, *The Hidden Life of Otto Frank*.

155. Alden Thwaits Garcia, *Auschwitz*, pp. 109–23.

156. AFH, AFC, OFA, inv. no. 40, Otto Frank's notebook, 1945.

157. AFH, AFC, OFA, inv. no. 40, Otto Frank's notebook, 1945. See also HCK, Hans Goudsmit, five secret letters sent by Hans Goudsmit to his wife Gerry from Westerbork, introduction. Hans Citroen to Juan Goudsmit,

see email from Juan Goudsmit to Erika Prins, 16 December 2015; Juan Goudsmit's private collection, card from Office of Ex-political Prisoners Foundation 1940–1945 to Mrs. Goudsmit-ter Heegde, statement of Philip Felix de Jong, 10 September 1945.

158. Sal de Liema recounts how he looked out of the window from the first floor with Otto Frank AFH, Jon Blair Collection, "Anne Frank remembered", 1995 (transcript of raw materials); Iwaszko, "The daily life of prisoners", p. 73.

159. AFH, AFC, museum collection inv. no. A_OFrank_i_015, statement of Otto Frank about his relationship with Pfeffer, 4 September 1951.

160. AFH, Jon Blair Collection, "Anne Frank remembered", 1995 (transcript of raw materials).

161. AFH, AFC, OFA, inv. no. 85; Spronz, "Ich war ein Haeftling". Otto Frank got to know the Hungarian Jew Spronz when they were both in the hospital. The terms "hospital", "infirmary", "Krankenbau", "Revier", etc. are used interchangeably.

162. DLA, Schnabel collection, Schnabel notes, p. 150.

163. Max Canes (NRK 2050, inv. no. 1248) ended up in barracks 2 for excavation and digging work in the Petersen Kommando; then he was sent to barracks 5 for the potato peeling *kommando*. Later, he returned to block 2 for street construction, again doing excavation and digging in the Petersen Kommando.

164. DLA, Schnabel collection, Schnabel notes, p. 150.

165. AFH, AFC, OFA, inv. no. 85; Spronz, "Ich war ein Haeftling", p. 16.

166. AFH, AFC, OFA, inv. no. 011, "Raucherkarte",1944–5.

167. Otto was given the other early document, his red notebook, shortly after he was liberated. It is not known who gave it to him. It certainly dates from after his imprisonment.

168. Nicolas Roth, *Avoir 16 ans à Auschwitz. Mémoire d'un juif hongrois* (Paris, 2011), p. 297, p. 332 and p. 343.

169. AFH, AFC, OFA, inv. no. 85, Spronz, "Ich war ein Haeftling", p. 16.

170. AFH, AFC, Witnesses' archive, (telephone) interview with Hannah Pick-Goslar, 7 November 2019.

171. AFH, Sal de Liema, Jon Blair Collection, "Anne Frank remembered", 1995 (transcript of raw materials), p. 10.

172. AFH, Sal de Liema, Jon Blair collection, "Anne Frank remembered", 1995 (transcript of raw materials), p. 3.

173. AFH, Sal de Liema, Jon Blair collection, "Anne Frank remembered", 1995 (transcript of raw materials), p. 3.3. For further details, see USC-SF, VHA, interview with Sal de Liema, 25 April 1995.

174. AFH, Sal de Liema, Jon Blair Collection, "Anne Frank remembered", 1995 (transcript of raw materials), pp. 24–5.

175. Primo Levi, *If This is a Man* (New York, 2003).

176. See also the definition of "Muselmann" on the website of the Shoah Resource Center, The International School for Holocaust Studies of Yad Vashem, available from www.yadvashem.org/odot_pdf/Microsoft%20Word%20-%206474.pdf (accessed 4 September 2020).

177. Wachsmann, *KL*, pp. 292–3.

178. Miep Gies, quoted in Lee, *The Hidden Life of Otto Frank*.

179. AFH, Sal de Liema, Jon Blair Collection, "Anne Frank remembered", 1995 (transcript of raw materials), p. 3.1-2.

180. AFH, Sal de Liema, Jon Blair Collection, "Anne Frank remembered", 1995 (transcript of raw materials), p. 3.

181. AFH, Sal de Liema, Jon Blair Collection, "Anne Frank remembered", 1995 (transcript of raw materials), p. 3.

182. AFH, Sal de Liema, Jon Blair Collection, "Anne Frank remembered", 1995 (transcript of raw materials), p. 11.

183. DLA, Schnabel collection, Schnabel notes, p. 150; Rosa de Winter-Levy in Kienzle, *Lasst mich so sein*.

184. Original quotation: "Ich war in Auschwitz eines Tages sehr down und konnte nicht mehr. Ich bin geschlagen worden und das hat mich sehr, sehr auch moralisch beeindruckt. Es war ein Sonntagmorgen und da habe ich gesagt 'Ich kann nicht aufstehen'. Und da haben May

ne Kameraden, alles Holländer natürlich, ich war ja schließlich doch Deutscher unter Holländern, aber ich bin volkommen aufgenommen worden von den anderen, gesagt 'Das geht nicht, Du mußt aufstehen, sonst bist du verloren!' Und dann sind sie zu einem holländischen Arzt gegangen, der mit dem Deutschen Arzt zusammen gearbeitet hat, und dieser holländische Arzt kam zu mir in die Baracke. Er hat gesagt 'Steh auf und komme morgenfrüh an die Krankenbaracke, sozusagen. Ich werde mit dem Deutschen Arzt sprechen, daß Du aufgenommen wirst.' Und so ist es gekommen und dadurch bin ich auch gerettet worden." Kienzle, *Lasst mich so sein*.

185. NIOD, 250d, inv. no. 646, S.M. Kropveld.

186. AFH_AlF_corr_10, letter from Otto Frank to Alice Frank-Stern, 8 June 1945.

187. Otto Frank made slightly different statements about this. He told Ernst Schnabel in 1957 that he had been admitted to hospital from 19 November 1944, but in an application for benefit for Spronz, he wrote that he had been admitted to hospital from "the beginning of November 1944". Cf. DLA, Schnabel collection, Schnabel notes, p. 150. AFH, AFC, OFA, inv. no. 85; Spronz, "Ich war ein Haeftling"; Otto Frank's statement, 29 July 1962. A list drawn up by the Red Army after the liberation, which contains Otto Frank's name, appears to indicate 21 November. See NRK, camps and prisoners, inv. no. 53, list drawn up by Dr. Józef Bellert, head of the camp hospital of the Polish Red Cross.

188. Spronz, "Ich war ein Haeftling"; statement by Otto Frank, 29 July 1962. Elie Cohen provided a description of the different barracks for the sick: Block 9 was officially the *Schonungsblock*, Block 19 was intended for cases of diarrhea and internal diseases, Block 20 for infectious and skin diseases, Block 28 was for surgery (with an operating theater), and also contained the HKB-Schreibstube, and Block 28 was the *Prominentenblock* and the block for admissions, the polyclinic, laboratory, X-ray department, ear, nose and throat department and a small operation theater. Block 9 was closed down after the selection in which Professor Frijda was selected for the gas chambers. See Elie Cohen, *Beelden uit de nacht. Kampherinneringen* (Baarn, 1992), p.

64 and p. 99. Spronz wrote that this took place in mid-November. See AFH, AFC, OFA, inv. no. 85, Spronz, "Ich war ein Haeftling", p. 19. Both Elie Cohen and De Wind maintained that it was earlier. See also De Wind, *Last Stop Auschwitz*.

189. AFH, AFC, OFA, inv. no. 211, interview with Otto Frank by Arthur Unger, 6 February 1978.

190. AFH, Sal de Liema, Jon Blair Collection, "Anne Frank remembered", 1995 (transcript of raw materials), p. 3.16.

191. AFH, AFC, OFA, inv. no. 85, Otto Frank to Joseph Spronz, 26 June 1945.

192. AFH, AFC, OFA, inv. no. 85, statement by Otto Frank, 29 July 1962.

193. Stanfield, 27 July 1945; in AFH, AFC, OFA, inv. no. 71, Otto Frank to Milly Stanfield, 27 July 1945. Otto Frank's notebook mentions three musicians: Van Beem, Schraab and Bleekrode. AFH, AFC, OFA, inv. no. 40, Otto Frank's notebook, 1945.

194. Undated letter from Otto Frank, quoted in Lee, *The Hidden Life of Otto Frank*.

195. AFH, AFC, OFA, inv. no. 211, interview with Otto Frank by Arthur Unger, 6 February 1978.

196. Landsberger et al. (eds), *Auschwitz*, vol. 5, p. 25.

197. A large offensive started on 22 June 1944, with the Red Army reaching the Vistula/Weichsel on 13 July 1944. The Vistula/Weichsel-Oder offensive started on 12 January 1945, and resulted in retreat by German army.

198. NIOD, 250d, inv. no. 827, C. Schimmer, p. 25.

199. Strzelecki, "Evacuation", p. 273.

200. NIOD, 250d, inv. no. 827, statement by C. Schimmer, p. 25; Alden Thwaits Garcia, *Auschwitz*, p. 123.

201. Wachsmann states that the evacuation started on 17 January 1945; according to Daniel Blatman, it was 18 January. Cf. Wachsmann, *KL*, p. 768; Daniel Blatman, *The Death Marches: The Final Phase of Nazi Genocide* (Cambridge, MA, 2011), p. 81. Cf. Landsberger et al. (eds), *Auschwitz*, vol. 6, p. 15.

202. AFH, AFC, OFA, inv. no. 211, interview with Otto Frank by Arthur Unger, 6 February

1978; DLA, Schnabel collection, Schnabel notes, p. 150. See also Marcel Haenen, *De bokser. Biografie van Max Moszkowitz* (Amsterdam, 2018), pp. 136–63.

203. AFH, AFC, OFA, inv. no. 211, interview with Otto Frank by Arthur Unger, 6 February 1978.

204. AFH, AFC, OFA, inv. no. 211, interview with Otto Frank by Arthur Unger, 6 February 1978. See also Lee, *The Hidden Life of Otto Frank*.

205. NIOD, 250d, inv. no. 646, S.M. Kropveld.

206. KZ-Gedenkstätte Mauthausen, AMM OH/ZP1/299, interview with Jakob Maestro, 17 June 2002, p.49.

207. AFH, AFC, OFA, inv. no. 211, interview with Otto Frank by Arthur Unger, 6 February 1978. See also Lee, *The Hidden Life of Otto Frank*.

208. Spronz, quoted in Lee, *The Hidden Life of Otto Frank*.

209. AFS_AlF_corr_10, letter from Otto Frank to Alice Frank-Stern, 18 February 1945.

210. NRK 2050, statements, Georg Hirsch (inv. no. 1265), Abraham Hakker (inv. no. 1264), Philip Felix de Jong (inv. no. 1268), Barend Konijn (inv. no. 1274), Richard Felix Levee (inv. no. 1276), Sally Bernard de Liema (inv. no. 1278), Fritz Bernhard Simon (inv. no. 1293).

211. See Elie Cohen, *Beelden uit de nacht*, pp. 115–16. Elie Cohen had been deported to Auschwitz on the transport of 14 September 1943. See also De Wind, *Last Stop Auschwitz*.

212. Strzelecki, "Evacuation", p. 273.

213. AFH, AFC, OFA, inv. no. 211, interview with Otto Frank by Arthur Unger, 6 February 1978; DLA, Schnabel collection, Schnabel notes, p. 151.

214. AFS_AlF_corr_10, letter from Otto Frank to Alice Frank-Stern, 8 June 1945.

215. AFH, AFC, OFA, inv. no. 40, Otto Frank's notebook, 1945.

216. NIOD 205d, inv. no. 755, Justus Philips; NRK 2015, inv. no. 1302, Jacob van West; Joseph Spronz, 23, AFF, AFC, OFA, inv. no. 85.

217. De Wind, *Last Stop Auschwitz*.

218. AFH, AFC, OFA inv. no. 40, Otto Frank's notebook, 1945.

219. Otto Frank, "Anne Frank would have been fifty this year", *Life*, March 1979. See also Lee, *The Hidden Life of Otto Frank*.

220. Scenario from the documentary *Die Befreiung von Auschwitz* by Irmgard von zur Mühlen (Chronos-Film GmbH, West Germany), commissioned in 1986 by the United States Holocaust Memorial Council. APMAB, Scenario Fond, vols 53, 23–26, 29, 40.

221. AFS_AlF_corr_10_0021, Otto Frank to Alice Frank-Stern, 18 March 1945. See also Lee, *The Hidden Life of Otto Frank*.

222. AFH, AFC, OFA inv. no. 40, Otto Frank's notebook, 1945.

223. NRK 2050, inv. no. 1455, "List of the Dutch people present at the liberation by the Red Army in Oświęcim, Birkenau (Brzezinka), and Monowice (Dwory-Bunawerke), compiled by Dr. Bellert for the Polish Red Cross, in February 1945". See also Lee, *The Hidden Life of Otto Frank*.

CHAPTER FOUR

1. Strzelecki, "Evacuation", pp. 270–71.

2. Mayer, *Als ik Hitler maar kan overleven*, pp. 47–52.

3. USHMM RG-04.078 2000.141, KL Auschwitz-Birkenau D-Au I-IIIII-s Abteilung V-SS Standortarzt, microfilm 2252. Although Edith, Margot, Anne and Auguste were probably not in this part of the camp, it gives an impression of the circumstances that prevailed in the women's camp in Birkenau at that time.

4. USHMM RG-04.078 2000.141, KL Auschwitz-Birkenau D-Au I-IIIII-s Abteilung V-SS Standortarzt, microfilm 2252.

5. AFH, AFC, Witnesses' archive, interview with Bloeme Evers-Emden, 12 February 2010.

6. However, it is not clear whether this was in subcamp BIIa or BI.

7. Landsberger et al. (eds), *Auschwitz*, vol. 5, pp. 21–2; NRK 2050, inv. no. 1261, Bertha de Groot-Godfried remembers that the quarantine lasted until the end of October 1944.

8. Landsberger et al. (eds), *Auschwitz*, vol. 2, p. 54.

9. Dwork and Van Pelt, *Auschwitz*, pp. 265–7; Strzelecka, "Women", p. 401.

10. See www.auschwitz.nl/paviljoen/
nederlanders-in-auschwitz/overlevenden/
ronnie-goldstein/verhaal (accessed December
2015); Rosa de Winter-Levy, *Aan de gaskamer
ontsnapt!*, p. 15; NIOD, 250d, inv. no. 583, I.
Salomon; Landsberger et al. (eds), *Auschwitz*,
vol. 2, p. 46.

11. "Eyewitness account of a young girl", JHM
Collection, no. D001088.

12. AFH, AFC, Witnesses' archive, interview
with Frieda Menco-Brommet, 12 February
2010.

13. Mayer, *Als ik Hitler maar kan overleven*,
p. 30; Ronnie Goldstein-van Cleef, p. 84; Inge
Kamp, p. 30.

14. De Winter-Levy, *Aan de gaskamer
ontsnapt!*, p. 14.

15. NIOD, 250d, inv. no. 583, Inge Salomon;
De Winter-Levy, *Aan de gaskamer ontsnapt!*,
p. 15.

16. There are also former female prisoners
who say that they did not have to work, like
Henriëtte van Bekkum-Sachs. See Rozema,
Treinen, p. 19.

17. AFH, AFC, Witnesses' archive, interview
with Lenie de Jong-van Naarden, 22 March
2010.

18. Rosa de Winter-Levy in Schnabel, *Anne
Frank*, p. 136; NRK 2050, inv. no. 1297, J.
Verdoner-Cohen; *Auschwitz Bulletin* 49, 1
(January 2005; Commemorative issue of the
last witnesses). The poems and drawings of
salvation by Ronnie Goldstein-van Cleef, "Ik
draag een hoed vol dode lijven", pp. 17–22;
NIOD, 250d, inv. no. 583, I. Salomon; NRK
2015, inv. no. 1301, Mrs. S. Weisz; NIOD, 250d,
inv. no. 583.

19. Strzelecka, "Women", p. 407.

20. Landsberger et al. (eds), *Auschwitz*, vol. 5,
pp. 22–3; Czech, *Kalendarium*, pp. 90, p. 894,
p. 904 and p. 907. Nine hundred and eighty-
nine women were sent to the gas chambers on
3 October; 3,000 women were sent to the gas
chambers from the *Frauenlager*; on 14 October,
477 Jewesses were sent to the gas chambers
from the *Durchgangslager*; 3,000 from BIIc;
and 156 women from the *Frauenlager*. See also
NRK 2050, Sientje Spiekerman-de Zwarte (inv.
no. 1294), Miss De Vries (inv. no. 1298).

21. Strzelecka, "Women", pp. 402–3.

22. Polak, *Oorlogsverslag*, p. 75.

23. AFH, AFC, Witnesses' archive, interview
with Bloeme Evers-Emden, 11 March 2010.

24. Strzelecka, "Women", pp. 402–3; Göbel,
Een hemel zonder vogels, p. 76. Interview with
Celine van de Hoek-de Vries in "Auschwitz no.
A-25236. One of the stories of some of the 55
million", *De Anti Fascist*, November 2004, pp.
24–26, in particular p. 24.

25. AFH, research collection, email from Eva
Schloss to Erika Prins, January 2016; NIOD,
250d, inv. no. 583, I. Salomon.

26. NIOD, 250d inv. no. 439, Sara Boektje.

27. AFH, AFC, Witnesses' archive, interview
with Bloeme Evers-Emden, 11 March 2010.

28. Kompisch, *Täterinnen. Frauen im
Nationalsozialismus* (Cologne, 2008); Elissa
Mailänder Koslov, *Gewalt im Dienstalltag.
Die ss-Aufseherinnen des Konzentrations- und
Vernichtungslager Majdanek* (Hamburg, 2009),
pp. 482–91; Wendy Lower, *Hitler's Furies:
German Women in the Nazi Killing Fields*
(Boston, 2013).

29. Mailänder Koslov, *Gewalt im Dienstalltag*,
pp. 482–91.

30. *SS-Aufseherinnen* were not given ranks
equivalent to those of the men, but they did
have their own hierarchy: from *Aufseherin* to
Chef Oberaufseherin. For a summary of the
ranks of *Aufseherinnen*, see Daniel Patrick
Brown, *The Camp Women: The Female
Auxiliaries Who Assisted the SS in Running the
Nazi Concentration Camp System* (Atglen, PA,
2002), pp. 240–41.

31. See also Lower, *Hitler's Furies*.

32. Himmler quoted in Lower, *Hitler's Furies*.

33. Strzelecka, "Women", pp. 395–6; Monika
Müller, "Die Oberaufseherin Maria Mandel.
Werdegang, Dienstpraxis und Selbstdarstellung
nach Kriegsende", in Simone Erpel (ed.), *Im
Gefolge der ss, Aufseherinnen des Frauen-kz
Ravensbrück. Begleitband zur Ausstellung*
(Berlin, 2007).

34. Andrew Rawson, *Auschwitz: The Nazi
Solution* (Barnsley, 2015), p. 57.

35. Alexandra-Eileen Wenck, "Selbstbild und
Selbstdarstellung des ss-Personals aus dem
Konzentrationslager Bergen-Belsen", in Alfred
Gottwaldt et al. (eds), *NS-Gewaltherrschaft*.

Beiträge zur historischen Forschung und juristischen Aufarbeitung (Berlin, 2005), p. 397.

36. De Winter-Levy, *Aan de gaskamer ontsnapt!*, p. 13.

37. De Winter-Levy, *Aan de gaskamer ontsnapt!*, p. 18.

38. De Winter-Levy, *Aan de gaskamer ontsnapt!*, p. 22.

39. AFH, AFC, Witnesses' archive, interview with Bloeme Evers-Emden, 11 March 2010.

40. Annie de Levie-Cohen. See also AFS_ Witnesses by name, Annie de Levie-Cohen, notes from a telephone conversation with Teresien da Silva, November 2010.

41. AFH, AFC, Witnesses' archive, interview with Lenie de Jong-van Naarden, 22 March 2010.

42. AFH, AFC, Witnesses' archive, interview with Lenie de Jong-van Naarden, 22 March 2010.

43. De Winter-Levy, *Aan de gaskamer ontsnapt!*, p. 19.

44. Original quotation: "Und sie weinte auch, als wir an den ungarischen Kindern vorbeimarschierten, die schon einen halben Tag nackt im Regen vor den Gaskammern warteten, weil sie noch nicht an die Reihe waren. Und Anne stiess mich an und sagte: Sieh doch. Die Augen […]." Schnabel, *Anne Frank*, p. 138.

45. AFH, AFC, Witnesses' archive, interview with Lenie de Jong-van Naarden, 22 March 2010.

46. From mid-May 1944, Jewish prisoners were given registration numbers starting with an A (separate series for men and women) or B (only for men). The women were given numbers in the series between A 25063 to A 25271. As many of the numbers of this transport are known and the prisoners were numbered in the alphabetical order of the first letter of their surname, it was possible to determine that Anne, Margot and Edith had numbers between A 25109 and A 25116. Reconstruction of prisoner numbers on the basis of Landsberger et al. (eds), *Auschwitz*, vol. 2, p. 26, and idem, *Auschwitz*, vol. 5, pp. 21–2; Czech, *Kalendarium,* p. 868, NRK 3281, International Committee of the Red Cross, p. 2; NRK 2050, inv. no: transport list 3

September 1944 with postwar working notes of NRK; registration numbers from the Jewish Council card index; various interviews and the database of Juan Goudsmit.

47. Roelofs, *Nog altijd*, p. 74; Evers-Emden, *Als een pluisje*, p. 101; Steinbacher, *Auschwitz*, p. 74.

48. NIOD, 250d, Camps and prisons, inv. no. 583, I. Salomon.

49. This concerns Bloeme Evers-Emden, Ronnie Goldstein-van Cleef, Lenie de Jong-van Naarden, Frieda Menco-Brommet and Anita Mayer-Roos.

50. AFH, AFC, Witnesses' archive, interview with Bloeme Evers-Emden, 11 March 2010.

51. AFH, AFC, Witnesses' archive, interview with Lenie de Jong-van Naarden, 22 March 2010.

52. Mirjam Blitz, *Auschwitz 13917. Hoe ik de Duitse concentratiekampen overleefde*, 2nd edn (Nijmegen, 1961), p. 230; De Winter-Levy, *Aan de gaskamer ontsnapt!*, p. 25.

53. Frieda's mother, Rebecca Brommet-Ritmeester, also survived the Holocaust. AFF, AFC, Witnesses' archive, interview with Frieda Menco-Brommet, 12 February 2010.

54. AFH, AFC, Witnesses' archive, the testimonies of Frieda Menco-Brommet, Ronnie Goldstein-van Cleef and Lenie de Jong-van Naarden all tell the same story and only differ with regard to a few minor details.

55. AFH, AFC, Witnesses' archive, interview with Lenie de Jong-van Naarden, 22 March 2010.

56. HCKW, interviews with Ronnie Goldstein-van Cleef and Frieda Menco-Brommet.

57. HCKW, interviews with Ronnie Goldstein-van Cleef and Frieda Menco-Brommet.

58. AFH, AFC, Witnesses' archive, interview with Frieda Menco-Brommet, 12 February 2010.

59. Original quotation: "Und sie war es auch, die bis zuletzt sah, was ringsum geschah. Wir sahen schon längst nichts mehr. […] Aber Anne war ohne Schutz, bis zuletzt. […] Sie weinte. Und Sie können nicht wissen, wie früh schon die meisten von uns mit ihren Tränen am Ende waren." Schnabel, *Anne Frank*, p. 138.

60. Mayer, *Als ik Hitler maar kan overleven*, p. 30 and p. 36.

61. Schnabel, *Anne Frank*, p. 134.

62. NRK 3281, International Committee of the Red Cross, Häftlings-Nummerzuteilung.

63. Landsberger et al. (eds), *Auschwitz*, vol. 5, p. 21; NRK, VI, p. 15.

64. Schnabel, *Anne Frank*, p. 138.

65. Lindwer, *The Last Seven Months of Anne Frank*, p. 154; AFH, AFC, Witnesses' archive, interview with Frieda Menco-Brommet, 12 February 2010.

66. Landsberger et al. (eds), *Auschwitz*, vol. 6, p. 15. All categories of prisoners were selected; sick prisoners could recover in a *Erholungslager*, to be put back to work afterwards.

67. Landsberger et al. (eds), *Auschwitz*, vol. 6, p. 15.

68. The French woman Odette Abadi also describes the selection and the transport from Auschwitz to Bergen-Belsen on which Anne and Margot Frank and Auguste van Pels traveled. See Abadi, *Terre de détresse*, pp. 84–91.

69. De Winter-Levy, *Aan de gaskamer ontsnapt!*, p. 24.

70. Original quotation: "Wieder Blocksperre, aber diesmal mussten wir nackt auf dem Apellplatz warten, und es dauerte sehr lange. Und dann mussten wir einzeln hintereinander in die Baracke gehen, und drinnen war ein Scheinwerfer aufgestellt, und da stand der Arzt, und wir mussten ins Licht treten. Aber diesmal sahen wir, er suchte sehr viele aus, alle die nicht ganz krank oder alt waren, und da wussten wir, sie kommen weg und die Alten und Kranken werden doch noch vergast. Vor uns stand eine Frau, die war sechzig, aber sie sagte, vierzig sei sie, und sie durfte mit nach Belsen fahren. Dann kam ich dran, und ich machte mich auch zehn Jahre jünger, und ich rief dem Arzt zu: Ich bin neunundzwanzig! Und ich habe noch nie Durchfall gehabt! Aber er winkte mit dem Daumen und schickte mich zu den Alten und Kranken. Dann kam Frau Frank – und sie kam auch gleich zu uns herüber. Und dann kamen die beiden Mädchen an die Reihe: Anne und Margot. Und Anne hatte ihr Gesicht, sogar unter dem Scheinwerfer noch, und sie stieß Margot an, und Margot ging aufrecht ins Licht, und da standen sie einen Augenblick, nackt und kahl,

und Anne sah zu uns herüber, mit ihrem ungetrübten Gesicht und gerade, und dann gingen sie. Was hinter dem Scheinwerfer war, war nicht mehr zu sehen. Und Frau Frank schrie: Die Kinder! O Gott […]." Schnabel, *Anne Frank*, pp. 138–9.

71. Abadi, *Terre de détresse*, pp. 84–91. Rebecca Brommet-Ritmeester, the mother of Frieda Menco-Brommet, deliberately avoided the selection for Bergen-Belsen because she wanted to stay with her daughter, who was in the *Krätzeblock*. See Van Liempt, *Frieda*, p. 63.

72. De Winter-Levy, *Aan de gaskamer ontsnapt!*, p. 22.

73. De Winter-Levy, *Aan de gaskamer ontsnapt!*, p. 23.

74. De Winter-Levy, *Aan de gaskamer ontsnapt!*, p. 24.

75. De Winter-Levy, *Aan de gaskamer ontsnapt!*, p. 24.

76. De Winter-Levy, *Aan de gaskamer ontsnapt!*, p. 24. De Winter-Levy probably also means "to the gas chamber" here and not only "to the crematorium".

77. NRK 2015, Malka Mlynek-Wajnsztok (inv. no. 1282) and Sientje Spiekerman-de Zwarte (inv. no. 1295). Martha stayed behind; see USC-SF, VHA, interview with Claire Beim, 3 March 1996. Some of the women on the transport of 3 September 1944 were in the group that was gassed. Dina Gabay-Smeer, NRK, dossier 129414; www.joodsmonument.nl/nl/page/134622/dina-gabay-smeer (accessed 4 September 2020); Martha Culp, www.joodsmonument.nl/nl/page/152758/marthaculp (accessed 4 September 2020); Wilhelmina Haagens, Hilde Cauveren-Marx and Lieselotte Lebenberg, www.joodsmonument.nl (accessed 4 September 2020), and Jewish Council cards, NRK, Jewish Council Card Index.

78. De Winter-Levy, *Aan de gaskamer ontsnapt!*, pp. 26–9.

79. De Winter-Levy, *Aan de gaskamer ontsnapt!*, pp. 26–9.

80. De Winter-Levy, *Aan de gaskamer ontsnapt!*, p. 29.

81. AFH, AFC, OFA, inv. no. 40, Otto Frank's notebook, 1945.

82. Betje Jakobs said that Edith Frank died in January (see NRK 2050, inv. no. 1267, 2 August 1945). Mrs. M. van Dam-Teeboom also said this.

CHAPTER FIVE

1. Abadi, *Terre de détresse*, p. 86 and p. 91. The registration numbers from Bergen-Belsen have not survived. The NRK worked out that the female prisoners who arrived in Bergen-Belsen from Auschwitz on 1 November 1944 were given numbers between 7270 and 8360 when they arrived.

2. Abadi, *Terre de détresse*, p. 91; Rachel van Amerongen-Frankfoorder in Lindwer, *The Last Seven Months of Anne Frank*.

3. Lindwer, *The Last Seven Months of Anne Frank*; Abadi, *Terre de détresse*, p. 92.

4. Anita Lasker-Wallfisch, *Inherit the Truth 1939–1945* (London, 1996), p. 87; Abadi, *Terre de détresse*, pp. 84–6; AFH, AFC, Witnesses' archive, interview with Freda Wineman-Silberberg, 24 August 2015.

5. Janny Brilleslijper and Rachel van Amerongen-Frankfoorder in Lindwer, *The Last Seven Months of Anne Frank*.

6. NRK 2050, inv. no. 1282, statement by Dina Wajnsztok; De Winter-Levy, *Aan de gaskamer ontsnapt!*, p. 24.

7. Gedenkstätte Bergen-Belsen, collection of witness statements, Simone Grzybowski-Hochberg; Abadi, *Terre de détresse*, pp. 92–3. It remains difficult to determine the duration of the journey exactly. The testimonies indicate that they left in the early hours of 1 November and arrived in the daytime on 3 November; hence, three days and nights.

8. Rachel van Amerongen-Frankfoorder in Lindwer, *The Last Seven Months of Anne Frank*; Abadi, *Terre de détresse*, p. 91.

9. Rachel van Amerongen–Frankfoorder in Lindwer, *The Last Seven Months of Anne Frank*.

10. Abadi, *Terre de détresse*, p. 93; Lasker-Wallfisch, *Inherit the Truth*, p. 88.

11. See www.chroniknet.de/extra/historisches-wetter-nach-monat/?wetter-monat=November-1944&wetter-station=2014-hannover (accessed 4 September 2020).

12. Rachel van Amerongen-Frankfoorder in Lindwer, *The Last Seven Months of Anne Frank*; Abadi, *Terre de détresse*, p. 93.

13. An example of a *Vorzugslager* would be Theresienstadt and the exchange camp of van Bergen-Belsen.

14. Lindwer, *The Last Seven Months of Anne Frank*.

15. Lindwer, *The Last Seven Months of Anne Frank*.

16. Wenck, *Zwischen Menschenhandel*, p. 343.

17. Official name Stalag 311 XI C; see Wenck, *Zwischen Menschenhandel*, p. 94.

18. Hundreds of Soviet commissioners, party functionaries, etc. were transported and murdered in Sachsenhausen. Wenck, *Zwischen Menschenhandel*, pp. 97–8.

19. At least 14,600 Jewish prisoners arrived between July 1943 and the end of 1944, including 2,750 children. See https://bergen-belsen.stiftungng.de/de/geschichte/ (accessed 22 October 2020).

20. Hungarian Jews who had certificates to go to Palestine were placed in the *Ungarnlager*; they would be "sold" abroad for cash to the Allies. From August 1943 there were Greek Jews of Spanish origin in the *Neutralenlager*; Polish Jews with North, Central or South American passports and certificates for Palestine were in the *Sonderlager* or *Polenlager*. For this, see Wenck, *Zwischen Menschenhandel*, p. 14.

21. Conversation between Erika Prins and Klaus Tätzler, a researcher at the Gedenkstätte Bergen-Belsen, 4 November 2013. A total of 2,560 prisoners were exchanged in the end; only 22 Jews were exchanged to Palestine from the *Sternlager*, where the Dutch Jews were imprisoned, including Mirjam Bolle, and 300 Jews were exchanged to the United States via Switzerland and Algeria in January 1945, including Ruth Wiener.

22. For example, see AFH, AFC, Witnesses' archive, interviews with Hannah Pick-Goslar (6 May 2009), Martha Dotan-van Collem (5 May 2009), Nanette Blitz (17 July 2012), Mirjam Finkelstein-Wiener (3 June 2013).

23. Renata Laqueur, *Dagboek uit Bergen-Belsen* (Amsterdam, 1979), p. 38.

24. Such as Ruth Wiener, Renata Laqueur, Mirjam Bolle and Abel Herzberg.

25. Laqueur, *Dagboek*, p. 94; *Herzberg, Amor fati*.

26. Wenck, *Zwischen Menschenhandel*, pp. 338 and p. 346.

27. Wenck, *Zwischen Menschenhandel*, p. 339.

28. Wenck, *Zwischen Menschenhandel*, pp. 340–43.

29. Eberhard Kolb, *Bergen-Belsen, Geschichte des Aufenthaltslager, 1943–1945* (Hannover, 1962), p. 115; Wenck, *Zwischen Menschenhandel*, pp. 339–46.

30. Klaus Tätzler mentions transports on 3, 4 and 5 November 1944; Odette Abadi refers to a group of 3,000 women in Auschwitz who were locked up in a barracks after a selection; Herzberg, *Amor fati*, refers to the arrival of 3,000 women in Bergen-Belsen; Dr. Terezia Braun refers to transports of 3,000 women; Landsberger et al. (eds), *Auschwitz*, vol. 6, p. 34, refers to 7,270–7,360 for the transport that left Auschwitz on 1 November 1944; idem, Cato Polak, NRK 2050, inv. no. 926.

31. Gedenkstätte Bergen-Belsen, witness statement, Margot Vetrocova, interview, December 1986.

32. Laqueur, *Dagboek*, p. 88.

33. Laqueur, *Dagboek*, p. 89.

34. Wenck, *Zwischen Menschenhandel*, p. 338 and p. 347; Wiener Library, Ruth Wiener collection, 1962/1/3/1: diary of Ruth Wiener, 4 November 1944.

35. Wachsmann, *KL*, p. 563.

36. Archive Gedenkstätte Bergen-Belsen, Protocol Dr. Terezia Braun, Budapest, 20 July 1945, for The Jewish Agency for Palestine DEGOB, no. 659.

37. Herzberg, *Amor fati*.

38. Laqueur, *Dagboek*, p. 96.

39. NIOD, 250d, inv. no. 761, Suze and Surry Polak.

40. Herzberg, *Amor fati*.

41. Gedenkstätte Bergen-Belsen, Klara Lebowitz.

42. The interview was conducted in English. AFH, AFC, Witnesses' archive, interview with Freda Wineman-Silberberg, 24 August 2015.

43. According to Freda Silberberg, this roll call was on 1 January 1945. USC-SF, VHA, interview with Freda Wineman (Freda Wineman-Silberberg), 28 February 1996.

44. Herzberg, *Amor fati*.

45. Herzberg, *Amor fati*.

46. Herzberg, *Amor fati*.

47. Herzberg, *Amor fati*.

48. Herzberg, *Amor fati*.

49. Wenck, *Zwischen Menschenhandel*, p. 346.

50. Lasker-Wallfisch, *Inherit the Truth*, p. 87.

51. Landsberger et al. (eds), *Auschwitz*, vol. 6, p. 34.

52. Arolsen Archives 5792, seq. no. 1.1.3.1, no. 315.

53. Gedenkstätte Bergen-Belsen, statement of Simone Grzybowski; Abadi, *Terre de détresse*, pp. 93–4; Janny Brilleslijper, NIOD, 250d, inv. no. 834, F. Schrijver-Jacobs.

54. Lindwer, *The Last Seven Months of Anne Frank*.

55. Laqueur, *Dagboek*, p. 93.

56. Wiener Library, Ruth Wiener collection, 1962/1/3/1, Ruth Wiener's diary, 20 November 1944.

57. Herzberg, *Amor fati*, note in the diary on 8 November 1944.

58. Wenck, *Zwischen Menschenhandel*, p. 347.

59. Wiener Library, Ruth Wiener collection, 1962/1/3/1, Ruth Wiener's diary, 20 November 1944.

60. AFH, AFC, Witnesses' archive, interview with Ruth Klemens-Wiener, 12 January 2010.

61. Lindwer, *The Last Seven Months of Anne Frank*.

62. USC-SF, VHA, interview with Ellen Spangenthal-Daniel, 26 July 1995.

63. Wachsmann, *KL*, pp. 782–4.

64. AFH, AFC, Witnesses' archive, interview with Annelore Beem-Daniel, 19 May 2014.

65. NIOD, 804, inv. no. 18, Cato Polak.

66. Wachsmann points out that in the female variation, *Muselweiber* was also used. Wachsmann, *KL*, p. 293.

67. USC-SF, VHA, interview with Ellen Spangenthal-Daniel, 26 July 1995.

68. USC-SF, VHA, interview with Ellen Spangenthal-Daniel, 26 July 1995.

357

69. AFH, AFC, Witnesses' archive, interview with Annelore Beem-Daniel, 19 May 2014.

70. Lindwer, *The Last Seven Months of Anne Frank*.

71. Lin Jaldati and Eberhard Rebling, *Sag nie du gehst den letzten Weg. Lebenserinnerungen 1911 bis 1988* (Marburg, 1995), p. 360.

72. In contrast with some other prisoners, the Brilleslijper sisters were not trained as nurses. It's not quite clear how they obtained this position and the related privileges. Cf. Janny Brandes, *Voltooid and onvoltooid verleden tijd* (Amsterdam, 1986), pp. 32–4; Lindwer, *The Last Seven Months of Anne Frank*.

73. AFH, AFC, Witnesses' archive, statement of L. Rebling-Brilleslijper, 5 April 1951.

74. Lindwer, *The Last Seven Months of Anne Frank*. See also Roxanne van Iperen, *'t Hooge Nest* (Amsterdam, 2018), p. 334.

75. AFH, AFC, Witnesses' archive, statement of L. Rebling-Brilleslijper, 5 April 1951.

76. Lindwer, *The Last Seven Months of Anne Frank*; Brandes, *Voltooid and onvoltooid verleden tijd*, p. 32.

77. Lientje Rebling-Brilleslijper refers to the same story (under Lin Jaldati, her name as an artist), but added that the guard came by every evening and was always drunk. Jaldati and Rebling, *Sag nie du gehst den letzten Weg*, p. 359. According to Annelore Beem-Daniel, she was in contact with a number of Dutch prisoners, but has only vague memories of Janny and Lientje Brilleslijper. AFH, AFC, Witnesses' archive, interview with Annelore Beem-Daniel, 19 May 2014. Her older sister, Ellen Spangenthal-Daniel, who was interviewed by the Shoah Foundation in 1995, did not describe such a close-knit group either. USC-SF, VHA, interview with Ellen Spangenthal-Daniel, 26 July 1995.

78. Lindwer, *The Last Seven Months of Anne Frank*; Van Iperen, *'t Hooge Nest*, p. 339.

79. Lindwer, *The Last Seven Months of Anne Frank*.

80. Lindwer, *The Last Seven Months of Anne Frank*.

81. Transport list, 5 December 1944, in Hetty Verolme, *De Kleine moeder van Bergen-Belsen. Hoe een veertienjarig meisje het concentratiekamp wist te overleven* (Utrecht,

2014), p. 267; AFH, AFC, Witnesses' archive, interview with Nanette König-Blitz, 2 August 2012.

82. AFH, AFC, Witnesses' archive, interview with Nanette König-Blitz, 2 August 2012.

83. AFH, OtF, coor_014, letter from Nanette Blitz to Otto Frank, 31 October 1945.

84. Ghetto Fighters' House Museum, cat. no. 195, inv. no. 11723rm, Hol, statement of Margot Drach-Rosenthal.

85. Ghetto Fighters' House Museum, cat. no. 3907, inv. no. 03097rm, statement of Sophia (Sophie) Engelsman-Huisman, August 1966. She was in Bergen-Belsen up to 7 February and is shown on the transport list from Bergen-Belsen to Raguhn.

86. Laqueur, *Dagboek*, p. 23.

87. Wiener Library, Ruth Wiener collection, 1962/1/3/1, Ruth Wiener's diary, 4 November 1944.

88. Laqueur, *Dagboek*, p. 93.

89. NIOD, 804, inv. no. 18, Cato Polak; Ghetto Fighters' House Museum, 1966, Sophia Engelsman (Jews on the other side of the fence tried to help); Rachel van Amerongen-Frankfoorder in Lindwer, *The Last Seven Months of Anne Frank*; NRK 2050, inv. no. 923, Miss Sophia Huisman, 8 August 1945.

90. NIOD, 804, inv. no. 18, Cato Polak, p. 7.

91. Lindwer, *The Last Seven Months of Anne Frank*.

92. Lindwer, *The Last Seven Months of Anne Frank*.

93. Interview with Hanna Elisabeth Pick, "Persönliche Erinnerungen an Anne Frank", *Mitteilungsblatt*, published by the Verband der Einwanderer deutsch-jüdische Herkunft, no. 28, 12 July 1957.

94. AFH, AFC, Witnesses' archive, interview with Hannah Pick-Goslar, 6–7 May 2009. See also AFH, AFC, Witnesses' archive, interview with Nanette König-Blitz, 2 August 2012, who also remembers having met Anne at the fence.

95. AFH, AFC, Witnesses' archive, interview with Hannah Pick-Goslar, 6–7 May 2009.

96. Wenck, *Zwischen Menschenhandel*, pp. 351–2.

97. NRK 2050, inv. no. 1204, Bertha Kaas-Hekster.

98. NRK 2050, inv. no. 1204, Bertha Kaas-Hekster.

99. NRK 2050, inv. no. 949, Dutch names extracted by I.R.O. I.T.S.; transport list, 3 September 1944.

100. ITS, doc. no. 3396827#1, letter from Commission Mixte de Secours de la Croix-Rouge Internationale to Deutsches Rotes Kreuz, *Generalführer* Hartmann, 23 January 1945, with a record of fifty-one recipients.

101. Apart from the testimonies following below, see also AFH, AFC, Witnesses' archive, interview with Marion Bienes, 24 November 1993. Bienes also came from Frankfurt and went to the same elementary school as Margot. However, she only got to know Margot in Amsterdam. After being arrested at the address where she had gone into hiding, Bienes was eventually sent to Bergen-Belsen. In an interview, she said that she'd heard that Anne and Margot were in the camp in January 1945, and that they would come to the fence to meet up. However, she was completely taken up by looking after her mortally ill father, who died in the camp in January 1945.

102. This must be a retrospective addition, because Hanneli was not able to see Anne through the fence, though Anne probably told her about her condition and lack of clothes.

103. VHA, interview with Irene Butter-Hasenberg, www.irenebutter.com/about (accessed 4 September 2020).

104. AFH, AFC, Witnesses' archive, interview with Martha Dotan-van Collem, 5 May 2009.

105. Presumably, this concerns the well-known boxer Ben Bril, who was in the *Sternlager* of Bergen-Belsen at that time, together with Eva Lek-van Leeuwen. For this, see the transport list of 21 January 1945, and the list of prisoners who arrived in Bergen-Belsen on 25 January 1945 for an exchange with South America. See also the statement of Bernd Horstmann, curator for the register of names of the prisoners of the Bergen-Belsen concentration camp.

106. Original quotation: "Ja, ich habe Anne in Belsen gesehen. Sie war mit einem Transport aus Auschwitz gekommen, und zuerst brachten sie sie in Zelten unter, weil in den Baracken kein Platz mehr war. Aber als das Wetter umschlug und es Herbst in der Heide wurde, zerfetzte der Sturm eines Nachts diese Zelte und warf sie um. Da wurden sie alle auf verschiedenen Blocks verteilt, und Margot und Anne kamen in unserem Nachbarblock, und ich sah Anne hinter dem Drahtverhau auf der anderen Seite der Straße. Da drüben ging es ihnen noch schlechter als uns, denn wir hatten noch ab und zu einmal ein Paket bekommen, aber sie hatten gar nichts, und ich rief hinüber: Lauf nicht weg Anne, warte! Und ich rannte in die Baracke und packte zusammen, was ich fand, und pack in ein Bündel zusammen, was ich fand und lief zum Drahtverhau zurück. Aber es war weit bis drüben, und wir Frauen waren so schwach, und wie wir noch überlegten, wie wir das Bündel hinüberwerfen könnten, kam Herr Brill vorbei. Er war sehr gross und ich sagte: Ich habe hier ein altes Kleid und Seife und ein Stuck Brot, Herr Brill, und bitte, werfen Sie es hinüber. Dort steht das Kind! Herr Brill zögerte zuerst und wusste nicht, ob er es wagen sollte, denn der Wachtposten konnte uns sehen. Aber er überwand sich, wie er das Kind sah. […] Und er nahm das Bündel und holte aus, und dann warf er es im hohen Bogen hinüber […]." Schnabel, *Anne Frank*, p. 146.

107. Lindwer, *The Last Seven Months of Anne Frank*.

108. AFH, AFC, inv. no. 01204, statement of L. Rebling-Brilleslijper, 11 November 1945.

109. AFH, AFC, OFA inv. no. 85, Otto Frank to Mrs. Rebling-Brilleslijper, 4 October 1945.

110. AFH, AFC, inv. no. AFF.01204, statement of L. Rebling-Brilleslijper, 11 November 1945.

111. NRK, dossier 117266, Anne Frank, letter from Kleiman to the Commission for the registration of deaths of missing persons of the Ministry of Justice, on behalf of Otto Frank, 7 May 1954.

112. NRK, dossier 117266, a card from the card index of the Afwikkelingsbureau Concentratiekampen (ABC).

113. Email from Michiel Schwarzenberg (NRK) to Erika Prins (AFH), 15 March 2015.

114. SAA, Archive of the Registry of Births, Deaths and Marriages, entry 5009, inv. no. 7411, supplement 105–117, death certificate no. 46 (Anne) and 47 (Margot).

115. https://lci.rivm.nl/richtlijnen/vlektyfus (accessed 4 September 2020); Gerald L.

Mandell, John L. Bennett and Raphael Dolin,
*Bennett's Principles and Practices of Infectious
Diseases*, vol. 2, 7th edn (Philadelphia, 2010),
pp. 2217–20. Erika Prins en Gertjan Broek,
"Anne kwam nog naar het hek, Margot was al
te ziek", *NRC-Handersblad,* 31 March 2015.

116. YIVO, Otto Frank file, Otto Frank to
Julius Holländer, November 1941. Otto wrote
that they had all been inoculated against
typhoid fever.

117. https://lci.rivm.nl/richtlijnen/vlektyfus
(accessed 4 September 2020); Mandell et al.,
*Bennett's Principles and Practices of Infectious
Diseases*, pp. 2217–20.

118. Lindwer, *The Last Seven Months of Anne
Frank*.

119. AFH, AFC, Witnesses' archive, interview
with Nanette König-Blitz, 2 August 2012.

120. AFH, AFC, Witnesses' archive, interview
with Nanette König-Blitz, 2 August 2012. Janny
Brandes-Brilleslijper also said that Margot
had fallen out of bed. Lindwer, *The Last Seven
Months of Anne Frank*.

121. AFH, AFC, Witnesses' archive, statement
of L. Rebling-Brilleslijper, 5 April 1951. See
also Jaldati and Rebling, *Sag nie du gehst den
letzten Weg*, pp. 362–3.

122. Arolsen Archives, 5792, 1.1.3.1, seq. nos.
101, 315 and 216.

123. Lindwer, *The Last Seven Months of Anne
Frank*.

CHAPTER SIX

1. USC-SF, VHA, interview with Freda
Wineman (Freda Wineman-Silberberg),
28 February 1996; Wenck, *Zwischen
Menschenhandel*, p. 347; NIOD, 804, inv. no.
18, Cato Polak.

2. Gedenkstätte Bergen-Belsen, Simone
Grzybowski-Hochberg; transport list Bergen-
Belsen-Raguhn, 7 February 1945: 139 French,
100 Hungarian, 86 Polish, 67 Czech, 30 Italian,
28 Dutch women, as well as women from
Greece, Turkey, Bulgaria, Romania, Slovakia,
Yugoslavia and the United States, and a
number of stateless women.

3. NRK 2050, inv. no. 949, Dutch names
extracted by I.R.O. I.T.S.; transport list, 3
September 1944.

4. AFH, AFC, Witnesses' archive, interview
with Annelore Beem-Daniel, 19 May 2014.

5. NIOD, 804, inv. no. 18, Cato Polak. See
also NIOD, 250d, inv. no. 761, Suze and Surry
Polak.

6. NIOD, 804, inv. no. 18, Cato Polak.

7. Arolsen Archives 5792, 1.1.3.1, apostille
with the transport list Bergen-Belsen-Raguhn,
10 February 1945.

8. Lindwer, *The Last Seven Months of Anne
Frank*. Large evacuation transports and death
marches were still arriving in Bergen-Belsen in
February 1945.

9. AFH, AFC, Witnesses' archive, interview
with Freda Wineman-Silberberg, 24 August
2015.

10. Megargee (ed.), *Encyclopedia of Camps
and Ghettos*, vol. 1, pp. 409–10; Irmgard Seidel,
"Raguhn", in Benz and Distel (eds), *Der Ort des
Terrors*, vol. 3, pp. 551–2.

11. Landsberger et al. (eds), *Auschwitz*, vol.
6, p. 39.

12. Copy of list with Neuzugänge from 21
March 1945, obtained in Bergen-Belsen,
Hauptkommission zur Untersuchung der
Verbrechen am polnischen Volk, Institut des
nationalen Gedenkens in Warchau, signatur
Buchenwald, syg. 41, K.30-39.

13. NIOD, 804, inv. no. 18, Cato Polak.

14. USC-SF, VHA, interview with Ellen
Spangenthal-Daniel, 26 July 1995.

15. NIOD, 804, inv. no. 18, Cato Polak;
Holocaust survivor testimonial Freda
Wineman-Silberberg at UJIA, London,
19 November 2012, www.youtube.com/
watch?v=CVsC9jJwXfs (accessed January
2016); USC-SF, VHA, interview with Freda
Wineman (Freda Wineman-Silberberg), 28
February 1996; Ria van den Brandt, *Getuigen
van Theresienstadt*, interview with Annelore
Beem-Daniel, 20 October 2009.

16. Seidel, *Raguhn*, p. 552.

17. Projekt Außenlager des ehemaligen KZ
Buchenwald, available from www.aussenlager.
buchenwald.de, (accessed January 2016).

18. Lindwer, *The Last Seven Months of Anne
Frank*.

19. Lindwer, *The Last Seven Months of Anne
Frank*.

20. USC-SF, VHA, interview with Ellen Spangenthal-Daniel, 26 July 1995.

21. AFH, AFC, Witnesses' archive, interview with Freda Wineman-Silberberg, 24 August 2015.

22. Seidel, *Raguhn*, p. 552; Megargee, *Encyclopedia of Camps and Ghettos*, vol. 1, p. 410.

23. Statement NRK, February 1961, dossier no. 103586, Auguste van Pels-Röttgen.

24. USC-SF, VHA, interview with Ellen Spangenthal-Daniel, 26 July 1995.

25. USC-SF, VHA, interview with Ellen Spangenthal-Daniel, 26 July 1995.

26. NRK 2050, inv. no. 1204, statement of Bertha Kaas-Hekster, 8 January 1948.

27. NRK 2050, inv. no. 1237, statement of Rachel van Amerongen-Frankfoorder.

28. See AFH, AFC, Witnesses' archive, interview with Nanette König-Blitz, 2 August 2012, and interview with Annelore Beem-Daniel, 19 May 2014; Otto Frank to Rechtsanwaltin Elisabeth Späth (ref. Entschädigung Auguste van Pels), 13 April 1960.

CHAPTER SEVEN

1. Landsberger et al. (eds), *Auschwitz*, vol. 5, p. 29.

2. Strzelecki, "Evacuation", p. 274. See also Wachsmann, *KL*, pp. 760–75.

3. Landsberger et al. (eds), *Auschwitz*, vol. 5, p. 31 and p. 227; idem, *Auschwitz*, vol. 6, p. 85; NIOD, 250d, inv. no. 827, statements of C. Schimmer and A.F. van Velzen.

4. Haenen, *De bokser*, pp. 136–63.

5. NRK, List of Prisoners on 25 January 1945, Mauthausen. According to the NRK records, there was a total of 5,724 prisoners. Landsberger et al. (eds), *Auschwitz*, vol. 6, p. 85. See also Haenen, *De bokser*, pp. 136–63. Moszkowicz belonged to the same group of prisoners.

6. For example, KZ-Gedenkstätte Mauthausen, AMM OH/ZP1/299, interview with Jakob Maestro, 17 June 2002, p. 53. The description of the death march is based, inter alia, on the testimonies of Jakob Maestro, Job Jansen, Mari Sloot, Max Rodrigues Garcia, C. Schimmer and A.F. van Velzen.

7. Based on the testimonies of C. Schimmer, A.F. van Velzen, Jakob Maestro and Job Jansen.

8. KZ-Gedenkstätte Mauthausen, AMM OH/ZP1/299, interview with Jakob Maestro, 17 June 2002, p. 50; A.F. van Velzen; Mari Sloot.

9. Based on the testimony of A.F. van Velzen.

10. Alden Thwaits Garcia, *Auschwitz*, p. 125.

11. NIOD, 250d, inv. no. 646, statement of S.M. Kropveld.

12. NIOD, 250d, inv. no. 646, statement of S.M. Kropveld.

13. As the *SS-Obergruppenführer und General der Waffen-SS*, Pohl became head of the WVHA in 1942.

14. Wachsmann, *KL*, pp. 230–34.

15. See also Chapter 2. De Jong, *Het Koninkrijk*, vol. 4, 739, pp. 929–34; Peter Romijn, *Burgemeesters in oorlogstijd. Besturen onder Duitse bezetting* (Amsterdam, 2006), pp. 250–63.

16. Arolsen Archives 5792, CC Mauthausen, general report by Mr. Kanthack, former inmate etc., p. 54.

17. Camps were categorized as Stufe I, II and III, of which Stufe III had the harshest rules.

18. Ladislaus Szücs, *Zählappell. Als Arzt im Konzentrationslager* (Frankfurt am Main, 1995), p. 34. Harald Hutterberger verbally explained the calculation of calories.

19. See also Hans Maršálek, *Die Geschichte des Konzentrationslager Mauthausen* (Vienna, 1995), pp. 181–215.

20. Maršálek, *Die Geschichte*, pp. 181–93.

21. Maršálek, *Die Geschichte*, pp. 196–215; Hans Maršálek, *Die Vergasungsaktionen im Konzentrationslager Mauthausen – Gaskammer, Gaswagen, Vergasungsanstalt Hartheim, Tarnnamen Dokumentation* (Vienna, 1988); Bertrand Perz and Florian Freund, "Tötungen durch Giftgas im Konzentrationslager Mauthausen", in Günther Morsch and Bertrand Perz, *Neue Studien zu nationalsozialistischen Massentötungen durch Giftgas* (Berlin, 2011), pp. 244–57.

22. These figures do not take into account the prisoners who died after the liberation of Mauthausen; see www.mauthausen-memorial.org/de/Wissen/Das-Konzentrationslager-Mauthausen-1938-1945 (accessed 16 April 2019).

23. KZ-Gedenkstätte Mauthausen, E/13/08/01, list of 25 January 1945.

24. KZ-Gedenkstätte Mauthausen, AMM OH/ZP1/234, interview with Miksa Mechlowitz, 11 June 2002; and USHMM, Michal Kraus, *Diary*, p. 15.

25. NIOD, 250d, inv. no. 827, statement of C. Schimmer, p. 28.

26. KZ-Gedenkstätte Mauthausen, E/13/08/01, list of 25 January 1945.

27. Carbon copy of Peter van Pels's registration in Mauthausen, copy with AFH. In the story "My first interview", Anne Frank wrote that he had bluish-grey eyes. *Anne Frank*, "My first interview" (22 February 1944), in Anne Frank, *Anne Frank's Tales from the Secret Annex* (Amsterdam, 2001).

28. KZ-Gedenkstätte Mauthausen, AMM OH/ZPI/299, interview with Jakob Maestro, 17 June 2002. Maestro mentions different numbers: 1,000 in barracks meant for 100 people and 500 in barracks meant for eighty.

29. Ioan Gottlieb, *Euch werde ich's noch zeigen. Vom Ghetto Baia Mare durch Auschwitz, Mauthausen, Melk und zurück: 1929–1945* (Constance, 2006), p. 25.

30. Roman Frister, *The Cap, or the Price of a Life* (New York, 2000), p. 101.

31. Summary of the number of prisoners in Mauthausen, 27 January 1945 and 30 January 1945; Zement is the codename for the Ebensee subcamp. Arolsen Archives 5792; Peter van Pels left for Melk on 29 January 1945, the transports to Gusen and Ebensee were on about this date.

32. NRK, dossier 135177-3, Mauthausen camp card. See also p. 171 and p. 278; and NIOD, 250d, inv. no. 827, statement of C. Schimmer, p. 28.

33. Arolsen Archives 5792, Deportation list Mauthausen-Melk. Schimmer mentions no less than eight cabinetmakers in this selection, so it is possible that prisoners with the same profession were also selected together for the selection for Melk. NIOD, 250d, inv. no. 827, statement of C. Schimmer, p. 28.

34. The arms factory of Steyr-Daimler-Puch AG was the largest producer of ball bearings in the German Empire and moved its factory from Steyr-Münichholz to Melk in order to be safe from Allied bombs.

35. Das Lagersystem Mauthausen, "Hauptlager und Aussenlager, zur geschichte des Aussenlagers Melk", www.mauthausen-memorial.at (accessed October 2010); and Bertrand Perz, *Das Projekt "Quarz". Der Bau einer unterirdischer Fabrik durch Häftlinge des KZ Melk für die Steyr-Daimler-Puch AG 1944–1945* (Innsbruck, 2014).

36. Transport list for Melk, 29 January 1945. This list contains 1,971 names, which roughly corresponds with the data in the summary of the number of prisoners in Mauthausen Bad Arolsen between 27–30 January 1945. Arolsen Archives no. 5792.

37. Moshe Ha-Elion, *The Straits of Hell: The Chronicles of a Salonikan Jew in the Nazi Extermination Camps Auschwitz, Mauthausen, Melk, Ebensee* (Mannheim, 2005), pp. 58–9.

38. KZ-Gedenkstätte Mauthausen, B/30/13, Melk, p. 3.

39. KZ-Gedenkstätte Mauthausen, B/30/ii/8. According to the camp commandant Julius Ludolph during his interrogation on 22 May 1945 by Major Harolder Sullivan, these included Germans, Jews, French, Russians, Poles, Norwegians, Mohammedans, Slovenians, Italians, Spaniards and young people.

40. KZ-Gedenkstätte Mauthausen, B/30/13, Melk, p. 3.

41. Five thousand prisoners died in Melk, lost their lives in accidents or were shot. In total, there were 14,357 prisoners. The total number of prisoners from April 1944 to April 1945: 14,387 (arrivals) – 8,928 (sent back) = 5,459. 4,873 died and 85 escaped.

42. Ha-Elion, *The Straits of Hell*, p. 58.

43. NIOD, 250d, inv. no. 1185, H.L. Bastiaans.

44. NIOD, 250d, inv. no. 1185, H.L. Bastiaans.

45. NIOD, 250d, inv. no. 827, statement of C. Schimmer, p. 29.

46. Ha-Elion, *The Straits of Hell*, p. 60.

47. Bertrand Perz, "Kinder und Jugendliche im Konzentrationslager Mauthausen und seine Außenlagern", *Dachauer Hefte 9* (Tübingen, 1993), pp. 71–90.

48. KZ-Gedenkstätte Mauthausen, B/30/ii/8, interrogation of the camp commandant Julius

Ludolph on 22 May 1945 by Major Harolder Sullivan. The camp commandant repeatedly tried to send the children back to Mauthausen because he couldn't use them. Companies paid for the forced labor and children were of no use to them.

49. Peter van Pels went back to Mauthausen on 11 April, with the young and the sick from Melk. The other prisoners, approximately 6,000, went to Ebensee. KZ-Gedenkstätte Mauthausen, B/30/6/d, Aufstellung über von KL-Melk abgegangene Transporte (Evakuierung des Lagers).

50. NIOD, 250d, inv. no. 827, statement of C. Schimmer, p. 29.

51. Original quotation: "Ich wurde einmal zusammengeprügelt weil ich bei der Arbeit eingeschlafen war. Bekam 25 Hiebe dafür. Und wir wurden ständig geschlagen, aus keinem bestimmten Grund. Einfach so." KZ-Gedenkstätte Mauthausen, AMM OH/ ZPI/234, interview with Miksa Mechlowitz, 11 June 2002.

52. Some of the prisoners who did specialist work benefitted from slightly better conditions, such as the Dutchman Job Jansen (a former employee of Opekta). He had to maintain the pumps to keep the tunnels dry. USC-SF, VHA, interview with Josephus Jansen, 15 October 1996. See also Ha-Elion, *The Straits of Hell*, p. 58.

53. Arolsen Archives 5792, CC Mauthausen, general report by Mr. Kanthack, former inmate etc., p. 54.

54. KZ-Gedenkstätte Mauthausen, AMM OH/ ZPI/234, interview with Miksa Mechlowitz, 11 June 2002.

55. KZ-Gedenkstätte Mauthausen, B/30/13, Melk, 3; NIOD, 250d, inv. no. 827, statement of C. Schimmer, p. 29.

56. There was a crematorium in Melk from November 1944; before that time, the bodies were piled up and taken to Mauthausen after a period of time. KZ-Gedenkstätte Mauthausen, Abteilung IV/7, B/30-B/39.

57. Perz, *Das Projekt "Quarz"*, p. 531. A total of 1,500 were sent back to Mauthausen. Perz means young people under the age of twenty years; Peter was eighteen years old.

58. Perz, *Das Projekt "Quarz"*, pp. 531–2.

59. Perz, *Das Projekt "Quarz"*, p. 532.

60. KZ-Gedenkstätte Mauthausen, B/30/6/2, Aufstellung über von KL-Melk abgegangene Transporte (Evakuierung des Lagers).

61. KZ-Gedenkstätte Mauthausen, entry registers Y/36, Y/44, entry register (E/13/8/1), registration of Peter van Pels.

62. KZ-Gedenkstätte Mauthausen, AMM H/02/03, Václav Berdych, "Krankenhauspflege", p. 8.

63. KZ-Gedenkstätte Mauthausen, Abteilung IV/7, Archiv H/1, Die medizienische Betreuung, das Revier.

64. NIOD, 250d, inv. no. 1185, H.L. Bastiaans.

65. Ten days later, the Americans transferred power to the Red Army.

66. KZ-Gedenkstätte Mauthausen, Abteilung IV/7, "Hospital Mauth. Abgangsbuch (Tote) 5.5.45–18.5.45".

67. KZ-Gedenkstätte Mauthausen, Abteilung IV/7, List of "Verstorbene", drawn up by the Third United States Army, 1945.

68. See also Wachsmann, *KL*, pp. 823–33.

69. On 21 November 1949, the NRK passed on the date of death of 5 May 1945 to the Commission for the Registration of Deaths of Missing Persons. The date of death is shown as 10 May 1945 on the back of the card, based on r830/4. NRK, camps and prisons, inv. no. 429JRK. KZ-Gedenkstätte Mauthausen, Abteilung IV/7, Hospital Mauth. Abgangsbuch (Tote) 5 May 1945–18 May 1945.

CHAPTER EIGHT

1. NRK, dossier 122, card from Charlotte Kaletta card to NRK, 1 August 1945; DLA, Schnabel Collection, Schnabel's notes, p. 149; statement of Jakob de Vries, Mrs. Swaap in NRK, dossier 42095 (Willem Swaap). AFH, AFC, OFA, inv. no. 211, interview with Otto Frank by Arthur Unger, 6 February 1978. Ernst Schnabel also writes about this in Schnabel, *Anne Frank*, p. 138.

2. NRK, dossier 122, Kaletta's card to NRK, 8 August 1945: "[…] the last message about Pfeffer dates from 1 October, when he went on a medical transport."

3. See the paragraph "Fritz Pfeffer in Neuengamme".

4. NRK 2050, inv. no.1091, statement of Janny Hamburger-Bolle, 29 March 1951.

5. The aim was to use them for the manufacture of counterfeit banknotes. Landsberger et al. (eds), *Auschwitz*, vol. 6, p. 13.

6. Landsberger et al. (eds), *Auschwitz*, vol. 6, transport to AK (Außenkommando) Wüstegiersdorf (Commando GR). They also included Dr. Abraham Wittenburg, Max Hamburger, Dr. Izak Mannheimer, Dr. S.M. Kropveld and Dr. Kok. NRK 2050, inv. no. 1091, statement of Janny Hamburger-Bolle, 29 March 1951, and dossier 42382, Maurits van Aalst. On 15 May 1944, Janny Hamburger-Bolle went from Auschwitz to Groß-Rosen with a group of sixteen nurses (or women who claimed to be nurses). NRK 2050, inv. no.1091, statement of Janny Hamburger-Bolle, 29 March 1951. See also Göbel, *Een hemel zonder vogels*, pp. 92–3.

7. Based on the digital monument of the Neuengamme Circle of Friends, www.monument.vriendenkringneuengamme.nl (accessed 4 September 2020), the online *Totenbuch* (book of the dead) of the Gedenkstätte KZ-Neuengamme, www.kz-gedenkstaette-neuengamme.de/geschichte/totenbuch/die-toten-1940-1945/ (accessed 4 September 2020), with the addition of a written description of the *Gedenkstätte* by Alyn Beßmann: doctor Max Mosheim 64969, doctor Arthur Moser 64970, dentist Fritz Pfeffer 64971, dentist Isaac Chatt 64976, dentist Willem Swaap 64995. When he arrived in Neuengamme, Fritz Pfeffer was given number 64971. Willem Swaap was given number 64995. The numbers assigned in Neuengamme are unique. However, large gaps occur in the numbering. NRK, inv. no. 3281, Comité International de la Croix-Rouge, Häftlings-Nummerzuteilung, p. 26. It can be deduced from the prisoner numbers on some of the registration cards that have survived that they arrived between 10 and 18 November 1944. Landsberger et al. (eds), *Auschwitz*, vol. 6, pp. 13–14; Judith Schuyf, *Nederlanders in Neuengamme. De ervaringen van ruim 5500 Nederlanders in een Duits concentratiekamp, 1940–1945* (Zaltbommel, 2005), p. 187. Drawn up on the basis of the testimonies of the prisoners from "Putten", Jaap

van Wincoop (www.oktober 44.nl/het-verhaal-van-jaap-van-wincoop), Wouter Roozendaal (www.oktober44.nl/het-verhaal-van-wouter-rozendaal) and J. Vonhof (www.oktober44.nl/ik-ben-zo-weer-terug), who arrived in Neuengamme in October (all accessed March 2016).

8. NRK 2050, inv. no. 2179, Barend Konijn. One of them was Willem Swaap, who was assigned to this transport in November 1944, although he was in the infirmary in Auschwitz.

9. Information provided by Alyn Beßmann from the Gedenkstätte Neuengamme. This concerns the doctors Max Mosheim, Arthur Moser, Isaac Chatt, Michel Peterfalvi, Nikolaus Stein and Wilhelm Schert, the dentist Adalbert Raduciner and the gynecologist Dr. Adalbert Fehér.

10. Buggeln, *Slave Labor*; Hermann Kaienburg, *Das Konzentrationslager Neuengamme, 1938–1945* (Bonn, 1997).

11. See also Buggeln, *Slave Labor*; Kaienburg, *Das Konzentrationslager Neuengamme*.

12. Karin Orth, "Erziehung zum Folterer? Das Beispiel des KZ-Kommandanten Max Pauly", in Peter Burschel et al. (eds), *Das Quälen des Körpers. Eine historische Anthropologie der Folter* (Cologne, 2000).

13. www.kz-gedenkstaette-neuengamme.de/geschichte/totenbuch (accessed 18 June 2020). Cf. the higher estimate of Kaienburg, who assumed that between 40,000 and 55,000 prisoners died in Neuengamme. See Hermann Kaienburg, "*Vernichtung durch Arbeit". Der Fall Neuengamme* (Bonn, 2000), p. 268.

14. Kaienburg, "*Vernichtung durch Arbeit*", p. 371.

15. Reimer Möller, "Die beiden 'Zyklon B'-Mordaktionen im Konzentrationslager Neuengamme 1942", in Günter Morsch and Bertrand Perz (eds), *Neue Studien zu nationalsozialistischen Massentötungen durch Giftgas* (Berlin, 2011).

16. Prisoners from Belgium, Denmark, Germany, France, Greece, Hungary, Italy, Yugoslavia, Latvia, Luxembourg, the Netherlands, Norway, Austria, Poland, Russia, Spain and Czechoslovakia.

17. Approximately 13,000 Jewish prisoners were registered in Neuengamme.

18. The numbers are taken from the website of the KZ Gedenkstätte Neuengamme, www. kz-gedenkstaette-neuengamme.de (accessed 26 June 2020).

19. Schuyf, *Nederlanders in Neuengamme*, p. 33.

20. For De Kom, Haersma Buma and Campert, see Bas von Benda-Beckmann, *Het Oranjehotel. Een Duitse gevangenis in Scheveningen* (Amsterdam, 2019), p. 41, pp. 350–51 and pp. 360–61.

21. In total, 659 men were taken to Amersfoort, where 58 of them were shot; 601 men then went to Neuengamme, thirteen of whom escaped. Of the 588 prisoners who arrived in Neuengamme, forty-eight survived and returned home. See www.oktober44.nl/ weggevoerde-men and www.oktober44.nl/ razzia (accessed 4 September 2020).

22. Wim Alosery interviewed in *De Volkskrant*, 2 May 2015.

23. Kaienburg, *"Vernichtung durch Arbeit"*, p. 97. Hamburg was one of the five *Führerstädten*. Amongst other things there were plans for a 700-meter-long suspension bridge over the Elbe, a 250-meter-tall "Gauhaus", and a façade of office and industrial buildings.

24. Schuyf, *Nederlanders in Neuengamme*, p. 33.

25. Prisoners were forced to work in subcamps or *subkommandos* for industrial or private clients who paid the SS a daily rate of between 4 and 6 Reichsmark; they were commissioned to dig anti-tank trenches and defense works by the Nazi government. Schuyf, *Nederlanders in Neuengamme*, pp. 55–7.

26. Friedrich Pfeffer in www.kz-gedenkstaette-neuengamme.de/geschichte/totenbuch/ (accessed 18 June 2020).

27. NRK, dossier 7500, Fritz Pfeffer. However, it is not impossible that he came to Neuengamme from Auschwitz via Sachsenhausen. Landsberger et al. (eds), *Auschwitz*, vol. 6, pp. 13–14 and p. 20; Schuyf, *Nederlanders in Neuengamme*, p. 137. On 24 October 1944, a transport with men left Auschwitz for Sachsenhausen; Sietse Geertsema (Neuengamme Circle of Friends) also mentions Buchenwald as a possibility.

28. Drawn up in the basis of testimonies of the prisoners from "Putten" Jaap van Wincoop (www.oktober44.nl/het-verhaal-van-jaap-van-wincoop), Wouter Roozendaal (www.oktober 44.nl/het-verhaal-van-wouter-rozendaal) and J. Vonhof (www.oktober44.nl/ik-ben-zo-weer-terug), who arrived in Neuengamme in mid-October (all accessed March 2016).

29. www.vriendenkringneuengamme.nl/ media/film-cor-bos, film fragment 3 (accessed 4 September 2020).

30. You would be beaten with a stick if your bed was not made properly. This is based on NRK 2050, inv. no. 1755, "Hoe was het leven in Neuengamme. Alleen door geluk komt men er levend vanaf", p. 2.

31. www.oktober44.nl/het-verhaal-van-jaap-van-wincoop (accessed 17 August 2020).

32. Johannes Paulus Lokker (Melissant, 25 September 1902) was arrested on 18 November 1944 for activities in the Resistance and arrived in Neuengamme on 4 February 1945; www. monument.vriendenkringneuengamme.nl (accessed 4 September 2020). The anonymous and undated report found at the NRK (NRK 2050, inv. no. 1755, "Hoe was het leven in Neuengamme. Alleen door geluk komt men er levend vanaf") proved to be written by Johannes "Han" Lokker te zijn. See Schuyf, *Nederlanders in Neuengamme*, p. 47. See also the excerpt from the interview fragment, "Omkijken met Ton Lokker uit Barneveld" (Omroep Gelderland, 6 March 2017), www. youtube.com/watch?v=LrEyaWgb8ZA (accessed 25 June 2020).

33. NRK 2050, inv. no. 1755, "Hoe was het leven in Neuengamme. Alleen door geluk komt men er levend vanaf", p. 6.

34. See also Wachsmann, *KL*, pp. 707–17.

35. www.oktober44.nl/het-verhaal-van-jaap-van-wincoop (accessed 17 August 2020).

36. See, for example, www.oktober44.nl/ het-verhaal-van-wouterrozendaal (accessed 4 September 2020); NRK 2050, inv. no. 1755, "Hoe was het leven in Neuengamme. Alleen door geluk komt men er levend vanaf", p. 3.

37. Gedenkstätte Neuengamme, "Häftlings-Toten-Nachweis", 17 December 1944–19 January 1945.

38. www.menselijk-lichaam.com/besmettelijke-ziektes/enterocolitis (accessed February 2016).

39. List of prescribed diseases taken from the archives of the Auschwitz-Birkenau Staatsmuseum, no known inventory number (copy with AFH); www.monument.vriendenkringneuengamme.nl (accessed 4 September 2020).

40. NRK 2050, inv. no. 1755, "Hoe was het leven in Neuengamme. Alleen door geluk komt men er levend vanaf", p. 3.

41. Kaienburg, "*Vernichtung durch Arbeit*", pp. 161–80.

42. NRK, dossier 7500, Fritz Pfeffer's death certificate, no. IX/107.

43. www.kz-gedenkstaette-neuengamme.de (accessed March 2016). Standesamt Hamburg-Neuengamme, Copy of death certificate, AFF, museum collection, object A_Pfeffer_i_016. The place of death shown on the death certificate is Hausdeich 60 in Hamburg-Neuengamme and dated 16 February 1945. This was the crematorium of the camp.

44. NRK, Fritz Pfeffer's dossier 7500, letter to Mrs. C. Kaletta from J. van de Voss, 23 October 1945.

CHAPTER NINE

1. For example, Joseph Spronz, Sal de Liema, Bob Zadick, Barend Konijn and Rudi Meijer. AFH, AFC, OFA, inv. no. 85.

2. For example, from Johan Goudsmit, Simon Meyer, who died in Stutthof, and Nico Pimentel, who died in Groß-Rosen. Juan Goudsmit database.

3. "Otto" means Hans Goudsmit here.

4. Juan Goudsmit private collection, transport list Auschwitz-Stutthof.

5. Original quotation: "Hoffentlich erreichen Dich diese Zeilen, die Dir und all den Lieben die Nachricht bringen, dass ich durch die Russen gerettet wurde, gesund voll guten Mutes bin und in jeder Beziehung gut versorgt. Wo Edith und die Kinder sich befinden weiss ich nicht, wir sind seit 5. Sept. 44 getrennt. Ich hörte nur, dass sie nach Deutschland transportiert wurden. Man muss hoffen, sie gesund zurück zu sehen. Bitte benachrichtige meine Schwäger und meine Freunde in Holland von meiner Rettung. Ich sehne mich danach Euch Alle wieder zu sehen und hoffe,

dass dies bald möglich sein wird. Wenn auch Ihr nur Alle gesund seid. Wann werde ich wohl Nachricht von Euch erhalten können? Alles Liebe und innigste Grüsse und Küsse. Dein Sohn. Otto." AFH, OFA, inv. no. 17, Otto Frank to Alice Frank-Stern, 23 February 1945.

6. Although Rosa de Winter-Levy did not know this yet, her daughter Judik survived the camps. They found each other shortly after arriving back in the Netherlands. De Winter-Levy, *Aan de gaskamer ontsnapt!*, p. 23.

7. According to Otto Frank's notebook, where he noted: "News of Edith's death in the hospital on 6 January 1945, as a result of weakness, without suffering." AFH, AFC, OFA, inv. no. 40, Otto Frank's notebook, 1945. See also Lee, *The Hidden Life of Otto Frank*.

8. Rosa de Winter-Levy in Lee, *The Hidden Life of Otto Frank*. See also AFF, AFC, OFA, inv. no. 40, Otto Frank's notebook, 1945.

9. Original quotation: "Viel kann ich nicht schreiben, denn die Nachricht von Edith's Tod am 6. I. 45, die ich jetzt erhielt, hat mich doch so getroffen, dass ich nicht ganz der Alte bin. Der Gedanke an die Kinder hält mich aufrecht. Edith ist im Krankenhaus an Schwäche durch Unternährung gestorben, so dass ihr Körper eine Darmstörung die hinzu kam nicht aushielt. In Wirklichkeit auch ein Mord der Deutschen." AFH, AFC, OFA, inv. no. 17, Otto Frank to Alice Frank-Stern, 23 February 1945. See also Lee, *The Hidden Life of Otto Frank*.

10. Eva Schloss-Geiringer quoted in Lee, *The Hidden Life of Otto Frank*. See also Schloss, *Herinneringen*, p. 179.

11. AFH, AFC, OFA, inv. no. 40, Otto Frank's notebook, 1945.

12. Original quotation: "Ich schreibe hier im Büro, es ist alles wie ein schwerer Traum. Ich kann mich in der Wirklichkeit noch nicht zurecht finden […] Wo sie sind, weiss ich nicht und die Gedanke an sie verlässt mich nicht." AFH_AlF_corr_10_0029, Otto Frank to Alice Frank-Stern, 8 June 1945. See also Lee, *The Hidden Life of Otto Frank*.

13. AFH, AFC, Witnesses' archive, interview with Rudi Nussbaum, 22 February 2010. Nussbaum's mother was Eleonora Nussbaum-Mager. She died in Bergen-Belsen on 4 May 1945. https://www.joodsmonument.nl/en/page/171634/eleonora-nussbaum-mager.

Archives

Anne Frank House (AFH), Amsterdam
* Anne Frank Collection (AFC)
* Maly Collection
* Otto Frank Archive (OFA)
* Museum Collection
* Jon Blair Collection, "Anne Frank remembered", 1995 (transcript of raw material)

Anne Frank Fund (AFF), Basel
* Frank-Elias's Family Archive

Deutsches Literaturarchiv (DLA), Marbach am Neckar, Germany
* Ernst Schnabel Collection

Landesarchiv Berlin
* Hauptausschuss Opfer des Faschismus

Landesarchiv Nordrhein Westfalen (NRW)
* BR 235 no. 2150 Entschädigungsakte Firma Holländer
* BR 3000 no. 1025, Entschädigungsakte Julius Holländer
* Nds 110

Netherlands Red Cross (NRK), The Hague
* 2050, NRK-Collectie Vervolging (Camp Westerbork) (originally: Westerbork Collection and the reconstruction of the fate of prisoners after WW II, 1939–2007)
* Camps and Prisons for Care after the War
* Personnel dossiers
* Jewish Council Card Index

NIOD Institute for War, Holocaust and Genocide studies, Amsterdam
* 250d, Camps and prisons
* 250k, Concentration camps outside the Netherlands
* 250n, Research by H.G. Adler
* 804, Research vernietigingskamp Sobibor
* 182, Jewish Council Archives

Arolsen Archives International Centre on Nazi Persecution, Bad Arolsen, Germany
* Archive 279

Gedenkstätte Bergen-Belsen, Lohheide, Duitsland
* Witness statements and documentation

Ghetto Fighters' House Museum (Lohamei HaGeta'ot), Israel
* Interview collection

Republic of Austria, Bundesministerium für Inneres (bm.i) KZ-Gedenkstätte Mauthausen, Vienna
* Witness statements and documentation

Archive Gedenkstätte Neuengamme, Neuengamme

National Archive (NL-HaNa), The Hague
* 2.09.34.01: Archive of the Commission for the Registration of Deaths of Missing Persons (COAV)
* 2.09.09: Central Archive for Special Jurisdiction (CABR)

Memorial Center Westerbork (HCKW), Westerbork
* Witness statements and documentation

Archive Auschwitz-Birkenau State Museum, Oświęcim
* Witness statements and documentation

Amsterdam City Archive (SAA), Amsterdam
* 5009: Archive of the Civil Registry
* Archive cards and indexes of the population register
* Juan Goudsmit private collection

Wiener Library, London
* Ruth Wiener Collection

National Archives (Kew/London)
* Home Office (HO)

Cologne University archive
* 600, Prüfungsaktenbestand der Wirtschafts- und Sozialwissenschaftlichen Fakultät

YIVO Institute for Jewish Research, New York
* National Refugee Service Case File A-23007

Bibliography and other sources

Abadi, Odette, *Terre de détresse. Birkenau-Bergen-Belsen* (Paris, 2012).

Abuys, Guido and Dirk Mulder, *Een gat in het prikkeldraad. Kamp Westerbork, ontsnappingen and verzet* (Hooghalen, 2003).

Alden Thwaits Garcia, Priscilla, *Auschwitz, Auschwitz… I Cannot Forget You. As Long as I Remain Alive: The Story of Max Rodrigues Garcia as Told to Priscilla Alden Thwaits Garcia* (San Jose, CA, 1979).

Arad, Yitzhak, *The Operation Reinhard Death Camps: Belsec, Sobibor, Treblinka*, rev. edn (Indiana, 2018).

Barnouw, David and Gerrold van der Stroom, *Wie verraadde Anne Frank?* (Amsterdam, 2003).

Barnouw, David, Dirk Mulder and Guus Veenendaal, *De Nederlandse Spoorwegen in oorlogstijd 1939–1945. Rijden voor Vaderland and Vijand* (Zwolle, 2019).

Benda-Beckmann, Bas von, *Het Oranjehotel. Een Duitse gevangenis in Scheveningen* (Amsterdam, 2019).

Benz, Wolfgang and Barbara Distel (eds), *Der Ort des Terrors. Geschichte der nationalsozialistische Konzentrationslager*, 9 vols (Munich, 2005–09).

Beorn, Waitman, *The Holocaust in Eastern Europe: At the Epicentre of the Final Solution* (Cambridge, MA, 2014).

Beorn, Waitman, *Marching into Darkness: The Wehrmacht and the Holocaust in Belarus* (London, 2018).

Bergen, Lotte, *Albert Konrad Gemmeker. Commandant van Westerbork* (Soesterberg, 2013).

Berlin Museum (ed.), *Synagogen in Berlin. Zur Geschichte einer zerstörten Architektur* (Berlin, 1983).

Blatman, Daniel, *The Death Marches: The Final Phase of Nazi Genocide* (Cambridge, MA, 2011).

Blitz, Mirjam, *Auschwitz 13917. Hoe ik de Duitse concentratiekampen overleefde*, 2nd edn (Nijmegen, 1961).

Boeken-Velleman, Leny en Ben Nijhuis, *Breekbaar maar niet gebroken. Het verhaal van een Auschwitz-overlevende* (Laren, 2008).

Bolle, Mirjam, *Ik zal je beschrijven hoe een dag er hier uitziet. Dagboekbrieven uit Amsterdam, Westerbork en Bergen-Belsen* (Amsterdam, 2003).

Boom, Bart van der, *"Wij weten niets van hun lot". Gewone Nederlanders and de Holocaust* (Amsterdam, 2012).

Brandes, Janny, *Voltooid en onvoltooid verleden tijd* (Amsterdam, 1986).

Broek, Gertjan and Rebecca Erbelding, "German bombs and US bureaucrats: How escape lines from Europe were cut off" (USHMM and Anne Frank House 2016), www.annefrank.org/en/downloads/filer_public/94/3e/943ed001-ba04-4e2a-9360-e642d0d82006/ushmm_afh_july2018.pdf.

Browning, Christopher, *Ordinary Men: Reserve Police-Battalion 101 and the Final Solution in Poland* (New York, 1992).

Browning, Christopher, *Initiating the Final Solution: The Fateful Months of September-October 1941* (Washington DC, 2003).

Browning, Christopher, *The Origins of the Final Solution: The Evolution of Nazi Jewish Policy, September 1939-March 1942* (Lincoln, 2004).

Buggeln, Marc, *Slave Labor in Nazi Concentration Camps* (Oxford, 2014).

Burschel, Peter et al. (eds), *Das Quälen des Körpers. Eine historische Anthropologie der Folter* (Cologne, 2000).

Caplan, Jane and Nikolaus Wachsmann (eds), *Concentration Camps in Nazi Germany: The New Histories* (London, 2010).

Cohen, Elie, *Beelden uit de nacht. Kampherinneringen* (Baarn, 1992).

Czech, Danuta, *Kalendarium der Ereignisse im Konzentrationslager Auschwitz-Birkenau 1939–1945* (Reinbek bei Hamburg, 1989).

Dauernheim, Jürgen, "Dr. Pfeffer aus Gießen – Anne Franks 'Dr. Dussel' (Eine Ergänzung)", *Mitteilungen des Oberhessischen Geschichtsverein Giessen 97* (Giessen, 2012), pp. 221–7.

Dwork, Debórah and Robert Jan van Pelt, *The Holocaust: A History* (New York, 2002).

Dwork, Debórah and Robert Jan van Pelt, *Auschwitz*, rev. edn (London, 2008).

Evers-Emden, Bloeme, *Als een pluisje in de wind* (Amsterdam, 2012).

Fast, Vera, *Kindertransporten 1938–1948. Hoe duizenden kinderen uit de klauwen van de nazi's werden gered* (Amersfoort, 2016).

Fast, Vera, *Children's Exodus. A History of the Kindertransporten 1938–1948* (London, 2010).

Frank, Anne, Dagboeken, see: Harry Paape, Gerrold van der Stroom and David Barnouw (eds), *De Dagboeken van Anne Frank*, complete edn (Amsterdam, 1990).

Frank, Anne, *Verhaaltjes, en gebeurtenissen uit het Achterhuis. Cady's leven* (Amsterdam, 2001).

Frankenhuis, M., *Westerbork en een vraaggesprek met zijn commandant Gemmecke in 1948* (The Hague, 1948).

Friedländer, Saul, *Nazi Germany and the Jews*, 2 vols (London, 1997).

Frister, Roman, *The Cap, or the Price of a Life* (New York, 2000)

Fritzsche, Peter, *Life and Death in the Third Reich* (Cambridge, MA, 2008).

Fritzsche, Peter, *An Iron Wind: Europe Under Hitler* (New York, 2016).

Futselaar, Ralf, *Gevangenissen in oorlogstijd. 1940–1945* (Amsterdam, 2015).

Gerlach, Christian, *The Extermination of the European Jews* (Cambridge, MA, 2016).

Gies, Miep, *The Story of the Woman Who Helped to Hide the Frank Family* (New York, 1987).

Gigliotti, Simone, *The Train Journey: Transit, Captivity, and Witnessing in the Holocaust* (New York, 2009).

Göbel, Esther, *Een hemel zonder vogels. Het aangrijpende levensverhaal van Janny Moffie-Bolle* (Amsterdam, 2010).

Göbel, Esther, "Nederlandse Joden in dwangarbeid. Rapport over het kwantitatieve, kwalitatieve en museale onderzoek naar de inzet van Joodse dwangarbeiders uit Nederland, in kampen in Nederland en daarbuiten, tijdens de Sjoa", research report of the Jewish Cultural Quarter (Amsterdam, 2015).

Gottlieb, Ioan, *Euch werde ich's noch zeigen. Vom Ghetto Baia Mare durch Auschwitz, Mauthausen, Melk und zurück 1929–1945* (Constance, 2006).

Gottwaldt, Alfred, Norbert Kampe and Peter Klein (eds), *NS-Gewaltherrschaft. Beiträge zur historischen Forschung und juristischen Aufarbeitung* (Berlin, 2005).

Griffioen, Pim and Ron Zeller, *Jodenvervolging in Nederland, Frankrijk en België 1940–1945. Overeenkomsten, verschillen, oorzaken* (Amsterdam, 2011).

Grunberg, Arnon (ed.), *Bij ons in Auschwitz. Getuigenissen* (Amsterdam, 2020).

Grunberg, Arnon, *Nee. 4 May lecture 2020* (Amsterdam, 2020).

Gruner, Wolf, *Jewish Forced Labor under the Nazis: Economic Needs and Racial Aims 1938–1944*, rev. edn (Cambridge, MA, 2013).

Gutman, Yisrael, and Michael Berenbaum (eds), *Anatomy of the Auschwitz Death Camp* (Bloomington, 1998).

Ha-Elion, Moshe, *The Straits of Hell: The Chronicles of a Salonikan Jew in the Nazi Extermination Camps Auschwitz, Mauthausen, Melk, Ebensee* (Mannheim, 2005).

Haenen, Marcel, *De bokser. Het leven van Max Moszkowicz* (Amsterdam, 2018).

Happe, Katja, *Veel valse hoop. De Jodenvervolging in Nederland 1940–1945* (Amsterdam, 2018).

Heim, Suzanne (ed.), *Deutsches Reich und Protektorat Böhmen und Mähren Oktober 1941-März 1943. Verfolgung und Ermordung der Europäischen Juden durch das nationalsozialistische Deutschland 1933–1945*, vol. 6 (Oldenburg, 2019).

Henry, Patrick (ed.), *Jewish Resistance against the Nazis* (Washington DC, 2015).

Herbert, Ulrich, "Forced laborers in the Third Reich: An overview", *International Labor and Working-Class History* 2 (2000), pp. 192–218.

Herzberg, Abel J., *Amor fati & Tweestromenland, Bergen-Belsen 1944–1945* (Amsterdam, 2016).

Iperen, Roxanne van, *'t Hooge Nest* (Amsterdam, 2018).

Jong, Loe de, *Het Koninkrijk der Nederlanden in de Tweede Wereldoorlog*, 14 vols (The Hague, 1969–91).

Junk, Peter, and Martina Sellmeyer, *Stationen auf dem Weg nach Auschwitz. Entrechtung, Vertreibung, Vernichtung Juden in Osnabrück 1900–1945. Ein Gedenkbuch* (Osnabrück, 1988).

Kaienburg, Hermann, *"Vernichtung durch Arbeit". Der Fall Neuengamme* (Bonn, 1990).

371

Kaienburg, Hermann, *Das Konzentrationslager Neuengamme, 1938–1945* (Bonn, 1997).

Kassow, Samuel D., *Who Will Write Our History: Emanuel Ringelblum, the Warsaw ghetto and the Oyneg Shabes Archive* (Bloomington, 2007).

Klein, Bettina, *Spuren jüdischen Lebens in Aachen von 1850 bis 1938. Eine Anschauungsmappe* (Aachen, 1997).

Kolb, Eberhard, *Bergen-Belsen. Geschichte des Aufenthaltslager, 1943–1945* (Hannover, 1962).

Kompisch, Kathrin, *Täterinnen. Frauen im Nationalsozialismus* (Cologne, 2008).

Kosmala, Beate, "Zwischen Ahnen und Wissen: Flucht vor der Deportation (1941–1943)", in Birthe Kundrus and Beate Meyer (eds), *Deportation der Juden aus Deutschland: Pläne – Praxis – Reaktionen 1938–1945* (Göttingen, 2012), pp. 135–59.

Landsberger, L., A. de Haas and K. Selowsky (Netherlands Red Cross) (eds), *Auschwitz*, 6 vols (The Hague, 1947–53)

– Vol. 2: *De deportatietransporten van July t/m August 1942.*

– Vol. 5: *De deportatietransporten in 1944.*

– Vol. 6: *De afvoertransporten uit Auschwitz en omgeving naar het noorden en het westen, en de grote evacuatietransporten.*

Langbein, Hermann, *People in Auschwitz* (Chapel Hill, 2004).

Laqueur, Renata, *Dagboek uit Bergen-Belsen* (Amsterdam, 1979).

Large, David Clay, *Berlin* (New York, 2000).

Lasik, Aleksander et al. (eds), *Auschwitz, 1940–1945: Central Issues in the History of the Camp*, 5 vols (Oświęcim, 2000).

Lasker-Wallfisch, Anita, *Inherit the Truth 1939–1945* (London, 1996).

Lee, Carol Ann, *Anne Frank 1929–1945. Roses from the Earth: The Biography of Anne Frank* (Penguin, 2000).

Lee, Carol Ann, *The Hidden Life of Otto Frank* (New York, 2003).

Leeuw, Daan de, "In the name of humanity: Nazi doctors and human experiments in German concentration camps, 1939–1945", MA thesis (University of Amsterdam, 2013).

Lepper, Herbert, *Von der Emanzipation zum Holocaust. Die Israelitische Synagogengemeinde zu Aachen 1801–1942* (Aachen, 1994).

Levi, Primo, *If This is a Man* (New York, 1957).

Leydesdorff, Selma, *De mensen en de woorden. Geschiedenis op basis van verhalen* (Amsterdam, 2004).

Liempt, Ad van, *Frieda. Verslag van een gelijmd leven. Herinneringen aan kamp Westerbork* (Hooghalen, 2007).

Liempt, Ad van, *Gemmeker. Commandant van Westerbork* (Amsterdam, 2019).

Lifton, Robert Jay, *The Nazi Doctors: Medical Killing and the Psychology of Genocide* (London,1986).

Lindwer, Willy, *De laatste zeven maanden. Vrouwen in het spoor van Anne Frank* (Hilversum, 1988).

Lindwer, Willy, *The Last Seven Months of Anne Frank* (London, 1988)

Lindwer, Willy, *Kamp van hoop en wanhoop. Getuigen van Westerbork, 1939–1945* (Amsterdam, 1990).

Lower, Wendy, *Hitler's Furies. German Women in the Nazi Killing Fields* (Boston, 2013).

Ludewig-Kedmi, Revital, *Opfer und Täter zugleich? Moraldilemmata jüdischer Funktionshäftlinge in der Shoah* (Giessen, 2001).

Maier, Anita, *Als ik Hitler maar kan overleven* (Nieuwkoop, 1990).

Mailänder Koslov, Elissa, *Gewalt im Dienstalltag. Die ss-Aufseherinnen des Konzentrations- und Vernichtungslager Majdanek* (Hamburg, 2009)

Mandell, Gerald L., John E. Bennett and Raphael Dolin (eds), *Bennett's Principles and Practices of Infectious Disease*s, vol. 2, 7th edn (Philadelphia, 2010).

Margalit, Avishai, *The Ethics of Memory* (Cambridge, ma 2003)

Maršálek, Hans, *Die Vergasungsaktionen im Konzentrationslager Mauthausen – Gaskammer, Gaswagen, Vergasungsanstalt Hartheim, Tarnnamen Dokumentation* (Vienna, 1988).

Maršálek, Hans, *Die Geschichte des Konzentrationslager Mauthausen* (Vienna, 1995).

Mazower, Mark, *Hitler's Empire: Nazi Rule in Occupied Europe* (London, 2008).

Mechanicus, Filip, *In dépôt. Dagboek uit Westerbork* (Amsterdam, 1989).

Meershoek, Guus, *Dienaren van het gezag. De Amsterdamse politie tijdens de bezetting* (Amsterdam, 1999).

Megargee, Geoffrey P. (ed.), *Encyclopedia of Camps and Ghettos, 1933–1945*, vol. 1 (Bloomington, 2009).

Metselaar, Menno, *Anne Frank. Dromen, denken, schrijven* (Amsterdam, 2016).

Meyer, Beate, Hermann Simon and Chana Schütz (eds), *Jews in Nazi Berlin: From Kristallnacht to Liberation* (Chicago, 2009).

Moraal, Eva, *Als ik morgen niet op transport ga… Kamp Westerbork in beleving en herinnering* (Amsterdam, 2014).

Morina, Christina and Krijn Thijs (eds), *Probing the Limits of Categorization: The Bystander in Holocaust History* (New York, 2018).

Morsch, Günther and Bertrand Perz, *Neue Studien zu nationalsozialistischen Massentötungen durch Giftgas* (Berlin, 2011).

Müller, Melissa, *Anne Frank. De biografie* (Amsterdam, 1998).

Nierop, Is. van and Louis Coster, *Westerbork. Het leven in het kamp* (The Hague, 1945).

Paape, Harry, Gerrold van der Stroom and David Barnouw (eds), *De Dagboeken van Anne Frank*, extended edn (Amsterdam, 1990).

Pick, Hanna Elisabeth, "Persönliche Erinnerungen an Anne Frank", interview, Jerusalem, Mitteilungsblatt published by Die Verband der Einwander deutsch-jud Herkunft, no. 28, 12 July 1957.

Perz, Bertrand, "Kinder und Jugendliche im Konzentrationslager Mauthausen und seine Außenlagern", *Dachauer Hefte 9* (Tübingen, 1993).

Perz, Bertrand, *Das Projekt "Quarz". Der Bau einer unterirdischen Fabrik durch Häftlinge des kz Melk für die Steyr-Daimler-Puch ag 1944–1945* (Innsbruck, 2014).

373

Petrie, Victor, "The secular word 'Holocaust': Scholarly myths, history, and twentieth century meanings", *Journal of Genocide Research* 2/1 (2000), pp. 31–63.

Piper, Franciszek, "Gas chambers and crematoria", in Yisrael Gutman and Michael Berenbaum (eds), *Anatomy of the Auschwitz Death Camp* (Bloomington, 1998).

Piper, Franciszek, Teresa Swiebocka and Danuta Czech (eds), *Auschwitz: Nazi Death Camp* (Oświęcim, 2007).

Polak, Fia, *Oorlogsverslag van een zestienjarig joods meisje* (Amsterdam, 1995).

Presser, Jacques, *Ondergang. De vervolging en verdelging van het Nederlandse Jodendom, 1940–1945*, vol. 2 (The Hague, 1965).

Prins, Erika (Anne Frank House), "Onderzoeksverslag naar het verblijf van de acht onderduikers in de kampen", research report Anne Frank House, Amsterdam (April 2016).

Rawson, Andrew, *Auschwitz: The Nazi Solution* (Barnsley, 2015).

Rens, Herman van and Annelies Wilms, *Tussenstation Cosel. Joodse men uit West-Europa naar dwangarbeiderskampen in Silezië, 1942–1945* (Hilversum, 2020).

Riet, Frank van, *De bewakers van Westerbork* (Amsterdam, 2016).

Roelofs, Saar, *Nog altijd. Ronnie Goldstein-van Cleef over jeugd, verzet, concentratiekampen en het leven daarna* (Kampen, 2005).

Romijn, Peter, *Burgemeesters in oorlogstijd. Besturen tijdens de Duitse bezetting* (Amsterdam, 2006).

Rosensaft, Hadassah, *Yesterday My Story* (Washington DC, 2004).

Ross, Steven en Wolf Runer, *New Perspectives on Kristallnacht: After 80 Years, the Nazi Pogrom in Global Comparison* (West Lafayette 2019).

Roth, Nicolas, *Avoir 16 ans à Auschwitz. Mémoire d'un juif hongrois. Collection témoignages de la Shoah* (Paris, 2011).

Rozema, Wim A.H., 'Treinen naar het eindstation van de beschaving… "In het midden stond een vent…, die beschikte over je leven…"', Historische vereniging Hoogezand-Sappemeer, 23 April 2015.

Samuel, R. and P. Thompson (eds), *The Myths We Live By* (London, 1990).

Schalkowsky, Samuel (ed.), *The Clandestine History of the Kovno Jewish Ghetto Police* (Bloomington, 2014).

Schloss, Eva, *Herinneringen van een Joods meisje. 1938–1945* (Breda, 2005).

Schnabel, Ernst, *Anne Frank, Spur eines Kindes. Ein Bericht* (Frankfurt am Main, 1958).

Schoeps, Julius H., *Neues Lexikon des Judentums* (Gütersloh, 2000).

Schütz, Raymund, "Vermoedelijk op transport. De Joodsche Raadcartotheek als informatiesysteem binnen sterk veranderende kaders: repressie, opsporing en herinnering. Een archiefwetenschappelijk onderzoek naar de herkomst, het gebruik en het beheer van een bijzondere historische bron", MA thesis (University of Leiden, 2010).

Schuyf, Judith (ed.), *Nederlanders in Neuengamme. De ervaringen van ruim 5500 Nederlanders in een Duits concentratiekamp, 1940–1945* (Zaltbommel, 2005).

Sluis, Wouter van der and Menno Metselaar (eds), *Anne Frank. Haar leven in brieven: tentoongestelde brieven*, exhibition catalogue Amsterdam Historical Museum (Amsterdam, 2006).

Sofsky, Wolfgang, *The Order of Terror: The Concentration Camp* (New Jersey, 1997).

Spronz, József, "Ich war ein Haeftling in Auschwitz" (unpublished German translation of *Fogoly voltam Auschwitzban* [Budapest, 1946]).

Steen, Jürgen and Wolf von Wolzogen (eds), *Die Synagogen brennen. Die Zerstörung Frankfurts als jüdische Lebenswelt* (Frankfurt am Main, 1988).

Steinbacher, Sybille, *Auschwitz. Een geschiedenis* (Utrecht, 2005).

Strzelecka, Irena, "Women", in Yisrael Gutman and Michael Berenbaum (eds), *Anatomy of the Auschwitz Death Camp* (Bloomington, 1998).

Strzelecki, Andrzej, "The plunder of victims and their corpses", in Yisrael Gutman and Michael Berenbaum (eds), *Anatomy of the Auschwitz Death Camp* (Bloomington, 1998).

Szücs, Ladislaus, *Zählappell. Als Arzt im Konzentrationslager* (Frankfurt am Main, 1995).

Venezia, Shlomo, *Inside the Gas Chambers: Eight Months in the Sonderkommando of Auschwitz* (Cambridge, MA, 2009).

Verhoeven, Rian, *Anne Frank was niet alleen. Het Merwedeplein 1933–1945* (Amsterdam, 2019).

Verolme, Hetty, *De kleine moeder van Bergen-Belsen. Hoe een veertienjarig meisje het concentratiekamp wist te overleven* (Utrecht, 2014).

Vogelaar, Jacq, *Over kampliteratuur* (Amsterdam, 2006).

Vuijsje, Ies, *Tegen beter weten in. Zelfbedrog en ontkenning in de Nederlandse geschiedschrijving over de Jodenvervolging* (Amsterdam, 2006).

Wachsmann, Nikolaus, "Annihilation through labour: The killing of state prisoners in the Third Reich", *Journal of Modern History* 3 (1999), pp. 624–59.

Wachsmann, Nikolaus, *KL. A History of the Nazi Concentration Camps* (New York, 2015).

Welzer, Harald, Sabine Moller and Karoline Tschuggnall, *"Opa war kein nazi". Nationalsozialismus und Holocaust im Familiengedächtnis* (Frankfurt am Main, 2002).

Wenck, Alexandra-Eileen, *Zwischen Menschenhandel und "Endlösung". Das Konzentrationslager Bergen-Belsen* (Paderborn, 2000).

Wielek, H., *De oorlog die Hitler won* (Amsterdam, 1947).

Wind, Eddy de, *Last Stop Auschwitz* (London, 2020).

Winter-Levy, Rosa de, *Aan de gaskamer ontsnapt! Het Satanswerk van de SS: relaas van het lijden en de bevrijding uit het concentratiekamp 'Birkenau' bij Auschwitz* (Doetinchem, 1945).

FILM AND SOUND

* Jon Blair, *Anne Frank Remembered*, documentary 1995.

* Willy Lindwer, *De laatste zeven maanden van Anne Frank*, documentary 1988.

* Kienzle, Birgit (director), *Lasst mich so sein wie ich will. Anne Frank*, TV documentary, prod. Südwestfunk, 1979.

* Camp Westerbork Memorial Center and NOS Actueel, *Leven na de ondergang. Acht portretten van Holocaustoverlevenden*, DVD documentary, 2007.
* USC Shoah Foundation Visual History Archive (USC-SF, VHA).

INTERNET SOURCES

* www.bergen-belsen.stiftung-ng.de
* www.coldcasediary.com
* www.drentheinoorlog.nl
* www.historische-vereniging-hs.nl
* www.joodsmonument.nl
* www.kampwesterbork.nl
* www.kz-gedenkstaette-neuengamme.de
* www.mauthausen-memorial.at
* www.menselijk-lichaam.com
* www.monument.vriendenkringneuengamme.nl
* www.newbooksnetwork.com
* www.October44.nl
* www.rivm.nl/infectieziekten
* www.yadvashem.org

Photographs

(*letter key: t* = top, *b* = bottom, *l* = left, *r* = right)

Aachen City Archive, Photograph collection: p. 23

Amsterdam City Archive: p. 46

bpk-Bildagentur/Karl H. Paulmann: p. 24

bpk-Bildagentur/Abraham Pisarek: p. 40

Bundesarchiv: p. 45

Camp Westerbork Memorial Center: pp. 67, 71, 75, 80, 82, 83*t*, 86*b*, 93, 98, 99, 112

Collectie Overijssel: p. 216

Collection of the Anne Frank House, Amsterdam: pp. 17, 55, 176*b*, 243, 252, 253, 309*b*

Collection of the Jewish Historical Museum, Amsterdam: p. 152

Collection of the Rotterdam City Archive, 4140_1977-3206: p. 27*b*

Diederik Schiebergen: p. 106

Dutch Resistance Museum, Amsterdam: p. 32

Erven Janny Moffie-Bolle (copyright): p. 110

Gedenkstätte Dachau: p. 269*t*

Gedenkstätte Haus der Wannsee-Konferenz: p. 131

Gouda Resistance Museum/photograph Diederik Schiebergen: p. 27*tl*

Image bank WW2/NIOD: pp. 41, 65, 74, 77*t*, 78, 83*b*, 88, 117, 118, 290*b*

Image bank WW2/NIOD/Fotopersbureau Stapf Bilderdienst: p. 28*t*

Image bank WW2/Resistance Museum Amsterdam: p. 64

Imperial War Museum: pp. 224, 225, 235, 236

Institut für Stadtgeschichte Frankfurt, S7Z Nr. 1933-50, Photograph: Hannah Reeck:
    p. 16

Jewish Monument: p. 105

Jewish Monument/Archive Peter (Eliezer) Kropveld: p. 183

joodserfgoedrotterdam.nl, Josua Ossendrijver Collection: p. 270

KZ-Gedenkstätte Neuengamme: p. 300

Maria Austria Institute, Amsterdam/Maria Austria: pp. 33, 43, 44

Maria Austria Institute, Amsterdam/Carel Blazer: p. 12

National Museum, Copenhagen, photographs Elisabeth Halgreen: p. 295

National Archive/Jac. de Nijs/Anefo: p. 66

National Archive, The Hague, the Netherlands Red Cross: pp. 102, 103, 165, 215, 257,
    267, 279, 286, 301, 302, 309*t*, 310

Panstwowe Museum Auschwitz-Birkenau: pp. 127, 136

Photograph collection of the Anne Frank House, Amsterdam: Cover (portraits), pp. 14,
    15, 18, 20*t*, 20*bl*, 21, 22, 27*tr*, 28*b*, 35, 36, 38, 53, 54, 91, 119, 174, 242, 305, 307

Private collection, Moszkowicz family archive: p. 269*b*

Private collection: pp. 56, 89, 108, 158, 209, 230, 248

ssmaritime.com: p. 308

United States Holocaust Memorial Museum (USHMM): collection (all maps from
   Holocaust Encyclopedia), pp. 59, 137, 277, 278
Van Wijk-Voskuijl family: p. 20*br*
Wiener Holocaust Library, The: p. 232
Wikimapia: p. 221
Wikimedia Creative Commons; CC-DD-Mark: pp. 77*b*, 86*t*, 148, 190, 199, 261, 275, 281
Wikimedia Creative Commons/Bundesarchiv/Bild146-1993-051-07; CC-BY-SA 3.0:
   plate section p. I*b*
Wikimedia Creative Commons/Bundesarchiv/Bild146-1969-054-16, Hoffmann,
   Heinrich; CC-BY-SA 3.0: p. 132
Wikimedia Creative Commons/Bundesarchiv/Bild 192-269; CC-BY SA 3.0, CC BY-SA
   3.0 de: p. 273
Wikimedia Creative Commons/Bron: Delpher; CC-PD-Mark: p. 116
Wikimedia Creative Commons/Bron: geheugenvannederland.nl; CC-PD-Mark: p. 143
Wikimedia Creative Commons/Jesse Hofseth; CC-BY-SA 4.0: p. 153
Wikimedia Creative Commons/Mondadori Portfolio: p. 179
Wikimedia Creative Commons/Bron: Joods Monument; CC-PD-Mark: p. 163
Wikimedia Creative Commons/Bron: Nationaal Archief: p. 26, 72
Wikimedia Creative Commons/Bron: USHMM: pp. 124, 290*t*
Yad Vashem Auschwitz Album: pp. 149, 151, 159
YIVO Institute for Jewish Research: p. 30
Zdenko Pavelka: p. 171

Unknown source: pp. 145, 167, 176*t*, 291, 298

The publisher and the Anne Frank House have tried to trace all those with a right to the
photographs and illustrations in this publication. If you consider that your rights have
not be honored despite this, please contact the publisher. Some of the illustrations on
Wikimedia Commons, the media archive of, inter alia, Wikipedia, have been used. The
abbreviations above refer to different sorts and versions of Creative Commons licenses.
The complete texts of these licenses can be found online in the following URLs:

(cc) **creative**
commons

– CC PD-Mark 1.0, Creative Commons, public domain https://creativecommons.org/
   publicdomain/mark/1.0/
– CC BY-SA 3.0, Creative Commons Naamsvermelding Gelijk-Delen, version 3.0.
Unported: https://creativecommons.org/licenses/by-sa/3.0/
 – CC BY-SA 3.0 de, Creative Commons Naamsvermelding Gelijk-Delen, versie 3.0.
   Duitsland. https://creativecommons.org/licenses/by-sa/3.0/de/deed.en
– CC BY-SA 4.0, Creative Commons Attribution-ShareAlike, version 4.0. https://
   creativecommons.org/licenses/by-sa/4.0/

Index

Page numbers in *italics* denote photographs.

Aachen 13, 17, 20–24, *23*, 25
Aktion 14f13 129, 138
Alosery, Wim 293
Amersfoort 69, 293
Amsterdam 17–19, *18*, *28*, 37, 42, 46, *46*,
    54–55, 62, 70, 306
  Central Station 68–69, 306, 308
  Havenstraat detention centre 66–68
  razzias 64–65, *64*, *65*, 76, 115–117, *117*,
    118
Annex, The (book) *see Tales from the Secret*
    Annex
Annex, The (building) 19, 31–34, *33*, 37,
    42–45, *43*, *44*, 313–314
Apeldoornsche Bosch (psychiatric
    institution) 76
Arad, Yitzhak 129–130
Asoziale 127–128, 274
Asscher, Bram 92–94, *93*
Asscher, Jeannot 92
Aufnahmekommando 155–156
Aufseherinnen (female camp guards)
    199–202, 224, 227, 228, 239, 261
Auschwitz 123–141, *127*, *148*, *159*, 160–161,
    173–183, *190*
  sickbay 183–191
  transportation to 100–111, 149–160
  work in 141–148, 160–161, 168–173
Auschwitz-Birkenau *136*, *149*, *151*, 193–198,
    204–207
  guards and violence in 198–204
Auschwitz-Monowitz 124, 137, *137*, 178

Baer, Richard *124*, 125
Bastiaans, H.L. 282
Behr, Benny 98, *99*
Bekkum-Sachs, Henriëtte van 108
Bellert, Józef 192
Belzec 130, 136
Bergen-Belsen 219–228, *221*, 229–250, *235*,
    236
  transportation to 207–210, 217–218

Berlin *24*, 39, *40*, 107, 115, 125, 272
Berman, Harold 94
Berufsverbrecher 127, 142
Birkenau *see* Auschwitz-Birkenau
Bischoff, Karl 133
Bismarckhütte 140
Blair, Jon 177
Blitz, Mirjam 205
Blitz, Nanette 49, 56, 241–242, *242*, *243*,
    254–256, 258, 266–267, 312
Boeken-Velleman, Leny 157, *158*
Boom, Bart van der 113
Bos, Cor 294
boycott, of Jewish businesses 14–17, 36
Brandes, Bob *209*
Brandes-Brilleslijper, Janny *see* Brilleslijper,
    Janny
Braunschweig (Lower Büssing-NAG) 169
Bremen 106, 107
Bremerhaven 41
Breslau 107
Breslauer, Rudolf *86*
Brilleslijper, Janny 49, 68, 88, 112–113, 141,
    208, 217, 229, 238–241, 251, *253*, 257,
    310, 312
Brilleslijper, Rebekka (Lientje) 49, *209*,
    238–241, 250–251, *252*, 256, 310, 313
Broek, Gertjan 47
Brommet (Menco), Frieda 97, *98*
Browning, Christopher 129, 130
Bruck, Hans 173
Buchenwald 25, 39, 209, 220, 259, 261–262,
    265, 268
Buer 35
Bynthiner, Vera 39

Campert, Jan 292
Chatt, Isaac 169
Chelmno 130
Citroen, Hans 173
Clauberg, Carl 126
Cleef, Ronnie Goldstein-van 68, 95, 152,
    152, 155, 156–157, 195–196, 204, 206,
    207, 208

Cohen, Elie 184, 188
Cohen, Jaap 113
Cohn, Vera 94–95, 97
Collem, Martha van 248–249, *248*, 256
Cologne, University of 35
crematoria 133–136, 140, 146–147, 150,
    166–168, 178, 203, 211–212, 220, 275,
    285, 302
criminal prisoners 64, 66, 70, 73–74, 76,
    81–105, 111, 272
Cuba 31
Czech, Danuta 165

Dachau 25, 268, *269*, 272
Dam, Sonja Wagenaar-van 112, *112*
Daniel, Annelore 49, 229, *230*, 234, 237–241,
    256, 259, 263, 266–267
Daniel, Ellen 49, 229, 234, 237–241,
    262–266
death marches 141, 185, 188, 268–270, 280
Deutsche Erd- und Steinwerke (DEST) 272,
    293
Deutsche Forschungsgemeinschaft 125
Diary of Anne Frank see Frank, Anne, diary
Dieckmann, Herbert 261
Drach-Rosenthal, Margot (Monika) 57,
    242
Düsseldorf 120, 121
Dutch Communist Party 115
dysentery 219, 230, 237, 264, 301

Ebensee 280, 285
Einsatzgruppen 114, 120, 128
Elias, Erich 17
Emden, Bloeme 59, *60*, 94, 194, 197–198,
    202, 204, 207–208
England 29, 41
Ensel, Remco 113
Errera, Alberto 147, *148*
Essen 35, 120
euthanasia programs (T4 and 14f13)
    129–131, 138, 275

Fasanenstrasse (synagogue) 40
February strike 115–117, *117*, *118*, 119
First World War 13, 25, 87
Fischer, Dr. 182–183
Fischer, Stephanie 92
Flossenbürg 209, 268
France 140, 262, 306
Frank, Alice 304–306

Frank, Anne 13–34, *15*, *18*, *257*
    diary 11–13, 25–26, 37, 42–47, 59–60, 114,
        209, 310, 311, 314
    *Tales from the Secret Annex (Het
        Achterhuis) 55, 56, 97*
    at Westerbork 79–84
    at Auschwitz 100–111, 149–160
    at Auschwitz-Birkenau 193–198, 204–207
    at Bergen-Belsen 207–210, 217–218,
        229–250
    death 250–258
Frank, Edith *née* Holländer 13–34, *14*, *15*,
    18, *21*
    in hiding and arrest 42–47
    at Westerbork 79–84
    at Auschwitz 100–111, 149–160
    at Auschwitz-Birkenau 193–198, 204–207,
        215
    death 209–216, 304
Frank, Fritzi *née* Markovits *54*, 305–306,
    307
Frank, Margot 13–34, *15*, *18*, *257*
    in hiding and arrest 42–47
    at Westerbork 79–84
    at Auschwitz 100–111, 149–160
    at Auschwitz-Birkenau 193–198, 204–207
    at Bergen-Belsen 207–210, 217–218,
        229–250
    death 250–258
Frank, Otto 13–34, *14*, *15*, *18*, *20*, *54*, *174*,
    307
    in hiding and arrest 42–47
    at Westerbork 79–84
    transportation to Auschwitz 100–111,
        149–160, *176*, *193*
    life in Auschwitz 160–161, 168–173,
        174–183
    in sickbay and liberation 183–192,
        303–306
    searches for family *252–253*, 306–314
    prior knowledge of death camps 112–113,
        119
Frankfoorder, Rachel 89, *89*, 107, 153, 208,
    218, 229, 233–234, 238, 241, 245, 254,
    256, 263–264, 265, 266
Frankfurt am Main 13–17, *16*, 39
Frijda, Herman 162–164, *163*, 166
Frijda, Jetteke 163
Funktionshäftlingen (kapos) 78, 141–148,
    158, 160–161, 175, 180, 197, 200, 201,
    225, 262, 283

Gans, Evelien 113
gas chambers 63, 110, 114–115, 128–140,
  146–147, *148*, 151, 155, 160, 179, 184,
  200, 203–204, 213, 217, 219, 231, 275,
  284–285, 292, 312, 313
  murder of Hermann van Pels 162–169
Geiringer, Eva 159, 305–306, *305*
Gelsenkirchen 35
Gemmeker, Albert Konrad 72–74, *72*, 79,
  86, 101
Gies, Jan 19, *20*, 28, 170, 306, *309*
Gies, Miep *née* Santrouschitz 19, *20*, 31, 37,
  42, 45, 46, 170, 180, 306, *309*, 310
Giessen 39
Gleiwitz 140, 268
Glücks, Richard 132
Goebbels, Joseph 40
Goldstein-van Cleef, Ronnie *see* Cleef,
  Ronnie Goldstein-van
Goslar, Hanneli 49, 56, *56*, 176–177, 239,
  245–247, 256, 258, 312
Goudsmit, Johan (Hans) 104, *105*, 173, 303
Greece 140
Grese, Irma 198, 200, 225, *225*, 228
Gross, Aron 169
Groß-Rosen 268, 288–289
Grossmann, Hermann 261, *261*
Grunberg, Arnon 11, 52
Gusen 272, 274, 280
Gutmann, Max 120, 121

Haarlem 116
Haas, Adolf 220, 223
Ha-Elion, Moshe 280, 282, 283
Haenen, Marcel 269
Haersma Buma, Inus van 292
Halle an der Saale 261
Hamburg 107, 289, 294, 298, 302
Hamburger, Max 110
Hamburger-Bolle, Janny 106, 110–111,
  288
Harjenstein, Fritz 134
Hartheim Castle 275
Harwich 41, *41*
Hasenberg, Irene 247
Havenstraat detention centre 66–68
Herzberg, Abel 143, *143*, 221, 227–228, 229,
  231, 233
Het Achterhuis (*Tales from the Secret Annex*)
  55, 56, 97
Heydrich, Reinhard 130, *132*

Hilversum 69, 116
Himmler, Heinrich 120, 126, 128, 132, 133,
  137, *137*, 138–139, 154, 199, 313
Hitler, Adolf 14, 36, 120, 272, 291
Hitlerjugend (Hitler Youth) 37
Hochund Tiefbau Aktiengesellschaft (HUTA)
  168
Holländer, Edith *see* Frank, Edith *née*
  Holländer
Holländer, Julius 22, 25, 29, 115
Holländer, Walter *21*, 22, 25, 29
Holländer-Stern, Rosa 22, *22*, 25
Hooghalen 69
Höss, Rudolf *124*, 125, 126, 133, 199
Hössler, Franz 199
Huisman, Sophie 242, 244, 256
Hungary 125, 140, 196, 217, 203–204, 222,
  262, 274, 292

Italy 140, 262

Jacobson, Abraham 109
Jakobs, Betje 216, *216*
Jehovah's Witnesses 128, 261, 292
Jewish Council 31, 51, 78
  registration cards *165*, *215*, *267*, *286*, *302*,
  310
Jong, Philip Felix de 173
Jong-van Naarden, Lenie de 108, *108*, 111,
  149–150, 173, 196, 202–204, 205–206
Joodse Ordedienst (OD) 74–79, *74*, 80, 84, 89,
  92, 104, 107

Kaas-Hekster, Bertha 266
Kaletta, Charlotte 38, 39, 40–42, 288–289,
  301, 302, 306
Kanada depots 157, *159*
kapos *see Funktionshäftlingen* (kapos)
Katowice 107, 168, 215, 304
Katz-Goldsmit, Kaatje *80*
kindertransports 38, 41
Kinna, Heinrich 133
Kleiman, Johannes 19, *20*, 28, 31, 34, 46,
  65–66, 68, 306
Kneiberg, Klara 213
Koch, Ilse 198
Kom, Anton de 292
Kompisch, Kathrin 198
Konijn, Barend 289
Kous, Joël van der 109
Kramer, Josef 134, 223–224, *224*, *225*, 227

Krätzeblock (scabies block) 196, 204–205, 206, 208
Krebs, Friedrich 15
Kremer, Johann Paul 126
Kristallnacht (November pogrom) 24, *24*, 39, 40, 69, 115
Kropveld, Samuel 109, 182, *183*, 186–187, 271–272
Kugler, Victor 19, *20*, 28, 31, 45, 46, 65–66, 68, 306

Lages, Willy 116
Landmann, Ludwig 15
Langbein, Hermann 153
Langefeld, Johanna 199
Laqueur, Renata 221, 223, 231, 244
Lasker, Anita 229
Lee, Carol Ann 47, 49, 95
Lek, Trees 92, *93*
Lek-van Leeuwen, Eva 249
Levi, Primo 58, 178–179, *179*
Lewkowitz, Karl 119
liberation 100, *136*, 190–191, *190*, *221*, *235*, 266, *277*, 285, 286, 303, 309
lice 82, 84, 183, 213, 223, 254, 255, 264, 282, 295
Liema, Sal de 90, *91*, 158, 173, 177–178, 179–181, 184, 303
Liema-van Gelder, Rose de 90, *91*, 100, 207
Lifton, Robert Jay 153–154
Lindwer, Willy 49, 98, 254
little red house (Bunker I) 134, 136
Lokker, Han 296–299, 301
Lopes Cardoso, Sonja 240
Löwenstein, Karl 22
Lower, Wendy 198
Ludolph, Julius 281

Mad Tuesday 103
Mailänder, Elissa 198
Mandel, Maria 199–200, *199*
Margalit, Avishai 61
Markovits, Fritzi, *see* Frank, Fritzi *née* Markovits
Mauthausen 268–287, *273*, *277*, *278*
Mayer-Roos, Anita 193, 207
Mazower, Mark 129
Mechanicus, Philip 76, 86, *86*
Mechlowitz, Miksa 283–284
medical experiments 50, 125–126
Meershoek, Guus 113

Melk 280–287, *281*
Menco (Brommer), Frieda 97, *98*
Mengele, Josef *124*, 125–126, 152–154, 155, 200, 214
Meppel 69
Merwedeplein, Amsterdam 17, *18*, 25, *65*, 116, 117
Messmer-Hoeft, Else 41
Meurin, Wilhelm 120–121
Minehead 41
Minsk 120–121
Mittelbau-Dora 268
Moffie-Bolle (Hamburger-Bolle), Janny 106, 110–111, 288
Monowitz *see* Auschwitz-Monowitz
Moraal, Eva 85, 86, 88
Moszkowicz, Max 269–270, *269*
Müller, Filip 166, *167*
Muller, Leo Maurits 110
Müller, Melissa 47, 49
Muselmänner 178–179, 237

National Refugee Service (NRS) 29
National Socialist German Workers Party (NSDAP) 14–16, 22, 25, 142, 198, 291
Netherlands *see* Amsterdam
Netherlands Red Cross (NRK) 51, 106, 164, 216, 229, 251, 266, 286–287, 288, 289, 302
Neuengamme 288–302, *290*, *295*, *298*
November pogrom (*Kristallnacht*) 24, *24*, 39, 40, 69, 115
Nuremberg race laws 39
Nussbaum, Rudi 308–309

Opekta 11, 17, *17*, 19, 28, 34, 37, 216
Operation Höss 125
Ordnungspolizei (order police) 106, 116
Osnabrück 35–37, *36*, 115
Ottenstein, Hans 81, 85

Paketstelle depot (Auschwitz) 171–173, 184–185, 271, 312
Palestine 81, 241
Pankoke, Vince 47
Pauly, Max 291, *291*
Pectacon 19, 28, 34
Pels, Auguste van *née* Röttgen 34–37, *35*, 120, *267*
   in hiding and arrest 42–47
   at Westerbork 79–84

at Auschwitz 100–111, 149–160
at Auschwitz-Birkenau 193–198, 204–207
at Bergen-Belsen 207–210, 217–218, 229–250
at Raguhn 259–265
death 266
Pels, Hermann van 34–37, *35*, 120
in hiding and arrest 42–47
at Westerbork 79–84
at Auschwitz 100–111, 149–160
death 162–168
Pels, Peter van 34–37, *35*, *36*, 120, *286*
in hiding and arrest 42–47
at Westerbork 79–84
at Auschwitz 100–111, 149–160, 168–172
at Mauthausen and Melk 184–187, 268–271, 276–284, 285
death 284–287
Pepper, Peter *38*
Pfeffer, Fritz 37–42, *38*, 120, *302*
in hiding and arrest 42–47
at Westerbork 79–84
at Auschwitz 100–111, 149–160, 168–169
at Neuengamme 288–299
death 299–302, *300*
Pfeffer, Werner *38*
Philips, Justus 189
Pick-Goslar, Hannah *see* Goslar, Hanneli
Pimentel, Nico 173
Piper, Franciszek 128, 130
Pisk, Arthur 76, *77*, 79, 85
Pohl, Oswald 125, 272
Polak, Cato 237, 244, 259–260, 262
Polak, Suze 225
Prins, Erika 49
Prinsengracht, Amsterdam 11, *12*, 19, 45, 87
Annex, The (building) 19, 31–34, *33*, 37, 42–45, *43*, *44*, 313–314
prison, in Amsterdam 63–69
prisoners of war 126–129, 132, 195, 219–220, 241, 261, 268, 274, 285, 292
Provincial Hospital, Santpoort 57, *230*, 266–267

quarantine 135, 139, 158–161, 164–166, 168–169, 173–174, 193–196, 204, 276, 278, 289

Raguhn 52, 62, 247, 256, 259–265, 313, 314
Randwijk, Henk van 113
Ravensbrück 198, 199, 268, 292

razzias 64–65, *65*, 76, 115–120, *116*, *118*, 274
Rebling-Brilleslijper, Rebekka, *see* Brilleslijper, Rebekka (Lientje)
Recklinghausen 35
Red Cross 50–51, 195, 204, 256, 308, 310
Netherlands (NRK) 51, 106, 164, 216, 229, 251, 266, 286–287, 288, 289, 302
parcels 221, 246–247, 256
Religionsverein Westen (synagogue) 40
Resistance, the 104, 113, 116, 147, 292–293
Riet, Frank van 79
Rodrigues Garcia, Max 171–173, *171*, 268, 271
Roma 128, 139–140, 261, 292
Rosenthal, Margot Drach- 57, 242
Röttgen, Auguste *see* Pels, Auguste van *née* Röttgen
Röttgen, Lotte *119*, 120–121
Rozenthal, Rica 109

Sachs, Henriëtte 105
Sachsenhausen 25, 39, 115, 268, 288–289
Salden, Helmut *55*
Salinger, Gerhard 303
Salomon, I. 204
Sanders, Leen 270, *270*
Santrouschitz, Miep *see* Gies, Miep *née* Santrouschitz
scabies 196, 204, 205, 206, 212
scarlet fever 204
Schelvis, Jules 100
Schimmer, Coen 271, 276, 280, 283–284
Schloss, Eva *see* Geiringer, Eva
Schnabel, Ernst 42, 49, 68, 95–96, 167, 182, 203, 209, 249
Schol, Jacques 69
Schoorl 117
Schutzhaft (protective custody) 22, 104, 199, 208
Seidel, Irmgard 263
Seyss-Inquart, Arthur 25, *26*, 64
Sicherheitspolizei (security police) 11, 45, 63–65, 69, 116
Silberbauer, Karl Joseph *45*, 46–47, 65, 85, 87
Silberberg, Freda 60, 226, 260, 262–264
Simon, Fritz 162, 165, 289
Sinti 128, 139, 261, 292
Slovakia 140
Sobibor 64, 70, 100, 107, 130, 136

Sola River 190
Sonderkommando 146–148, *148*, 166–168
Spain 31
Speer, Albert 272
Sperre 81, 82, *82*, 85–86, 92
Spronz, Joseph 161, 174–175, *174*, 184,
    188–189
Stanfield, Milly 184
Star of David 26, *28*, 70, 84, *91*, 128, 220
Sterzenbach, Werner *82*
Stoppelman, Max 169–171
Straus, Nathan 29, 31
Stutthof 164, 169, 291, 303, 312
Swart, Jacob 66–67, *67*

T4 130, 275
Tales from the Secret Annex (Het Achterhuis)
    55, 56, 97
Tas, Salomon 109
Theresienstadt 70, 87, 101, 135, 208, 211,
    262, 265–267
Trapp, Abraham *36*
Treblinka 130, 136
typhus 121, 139, 206, 219, 225, 242, 251,
    254–258, 264–266, 310, 313

Unger, Arthur 186, 288
United States 25, 29–31, 38, 254, 285
Upper Silesia 126, 137
Utrecht 116

Velsen 116
Verhoeven, Rian 117
Volkenrath, Elisabeth 200
Vorontsov, Aleksandr 191
Vorrink, Koos 113

Voskuijl, Bep 19, *20*, 31, 46
Voskuijl, Johannes 19, *20*

Wachsmann, Nikolaus 50, 129, 130, 142,
    179, 235
Wajnsztok, Diana Malka 213
Wannsee Conference 130, 132
Weinberg, Edgar 86, *86*
Wenck, Alexandra-Eileen 219
Westen (synagogue) 40
Westerbork 69–79, *71*, *74*, *77*, *78*, 84–92
    acquaintances in 92–99
    arrival at 79–84
    film 73, *86*, 105–106
Wiener, Ruth 231, *232*, 233, 244
Wincoop, Jaap van 296, 298
Wind, Eddy de 144–145, *145*, 160, 161,
    162–164, 188–189
Wineman-Silberberg, Freda 60
Winter, Judik de 95–96, 207, 211, 304
Winter-Levy, Rosa de 53, *53*, *54*, 95–97,
    108, 196, 197, 200–201, 203, 206–209,
    210–215, 217–318, 304–305, 312
Wirths, Eduard *153*, 154
Wirtschafts-Verwaltungshauptamt (WVHA)
    125
Wuppertal 119–120
Würzburg 39

Zaan region 116
Zentralstelle für jüdische Auswanderung 46,
    46, 63, 65, 80
Ziereis, Franz 274, *275*
Zwarte, Sientje de 213
Zwolle 69, 107
Zyklon B 128–129, 275, 292

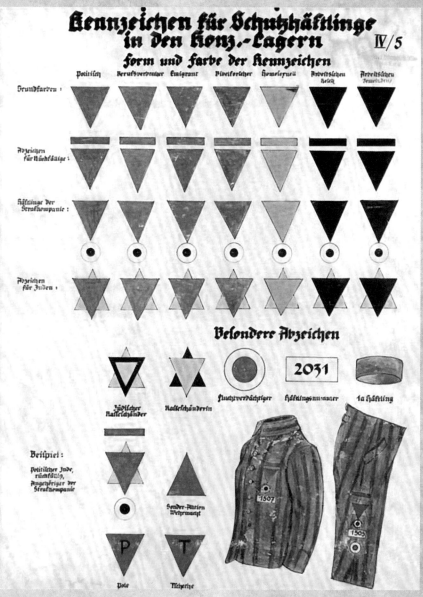

Badges used to identify groups of prisoners in concentration camps, 1936